New^THE
Relationship

THE
New
Relationship

Human Capital in the American Corporation

MARGARET M. BLAIR

THOMAS A. KOCHAN

Editors

BROOKINGS INSTITUTION PRESS
Washington, D.C.

#4264 3464

Copyright © 2000
THE BROOKINGS INSTITUTION
1775 Massachusetts Avenue, N.W., Washington, D.C. 20036
www.brookings.edu

Library of Congress Cataloging-in-Publication data
The new relationship: human capital in the American corporation /
Margaret M. Blair and Thomas A. Kochan, eds.
p. cm.
Includes bibliographical references and index.
ISBN 0-8157-0902-1 (cloth : alk. paper)—ISBN 0-8157-0901-3
(paper : alk. paper)
1. Personnel management. 2. Human capital. 3. Corporations.
I. Blair, Margaret M., 1950– II. Kochan, Thomas A.
HF5549 .N376 2000   99-050476
658.3'00973—dc21   CIP

9 8 7 6 5 4 3 2 1

The paper used in this publication meets minimum requirements of the
American National Standard for Information Sciences—Permanence of Paper
for Printed Library Materials: ANSI Z39.48-1984.

Typeset in Adobe Garamond

Composition by R. Lynn Rivenbark
Macon, Georgia

Printed by R. R. Donnelley & Sons
Harrisonburg, Virginia

The Brookings Institution is an independent organization devoted to nonpartisan research, education, and publication in economics, government, foreign policy, and the social sciences generally. Its principal purposes are to aid in the development of sound public policies and to promote public understanding of issues of national importance.

The Institution was founded on December 8, 1927, to merge the activities of the Institute for Government Research, founded in 1916, the Institute of Economics, founded in 1922, and the Robert Brookings Graduate School of Economics and Government, founded in 1924.

The general administration of the Institution is the responsibility of a Board of Trustees charged with safeguarding the independence of the staff and fostering the most favorable conditions for scientific research and publication. The immediate direction of the policies, program, and staff is vested in the president, assisted by an advisory committee of the officers and staff.

In publishing a study, the Institution presents it as a competent treatment of a subject worthy of public consideration. The interpretations or conclusions in such publications are those of the author or authors and do not necessarily reflect the views of the other staff members, officers, or trustees of the Brookings Institution.

Foreword

THE U.S. ECONOMY appears to be undergoing a massive transition from an industrial base to something called "information based." Large corporations are being transformed, merged, or acquired; new corporations in new lines of business are coming into existence at a rapid pace; and companies are outsourcing, reorganizing, or in some cases, simply eliminating traditional work. As a result, the largest corporations have dramatically reduced their work forces, even as small- and medium-sized companies in new sectors have grown fast enough to more than absorb the "downsized" workers. These changes, although not well understood, seem to be altering the nature and terms of traditional relationships between corporations and their employees.

In this book leading academics from several different disciplines document and assess the changes under way, analyze their causes and consequences, and consider the possible policy implications. Seven of the chapters were written for a conference on Corporations and Human Capital, jointly sponsored in January 1998 by Brookings and the MIT Program on the Organization of the Twenty-First Century. Chapter 2, by Brookings Senior Fellow Charles Schultze, was added later.

Theresa Walker edited the manuscript, and Jennifer Eichberger and Takako Tsuji verified the factual content. Carlotta Ribar proofread the book, and Julia Petrakis prepared the index. Amy Barrett, Karen Boyajian,

Charlene Mui, and Lisa Chavez helped to organize the conference and coordinate the efforts of all of the contributing authors. Gabriel Loeb and Hannah Zwiebel provided valuable research assistance.

The editors and the Brookings Institution are grateful to the Alfred P. Sloan Foundation, Springs Industries, Pfizer Inc., the Dorothy Perlow estate, Georgetown University Law Center, and the MIT Program on the Organization of the Twenty-First Century and its sponsors for providing financial support, directly and indirectly, for this project. Margaret Blair would also like to thank Carol Emmott, Thomas Green, Warren Hellman, and Nell Minow, who have served as an informal advisory board for the larger project of which this book is a part.

The views expressed in this book are those of the authors and editors and should not be attributed to any of the persons or organizations acknowledged above, or to the trustees, officers, or other staff members of the Brookings Institution, or to any organizations or employers with which the authors are associated.

MICHAEL H. ARMACOST
President

December 1999
Washington, D.C.

Contents

THE
New
Relationship

1

MARGARET M. BLAIR
THOMAS A. KOCHAN

Introduction

L ARGE PUBLICLY TRADED corporations have been the dominant organizational form in the U.S. economy throughout most of the twentieth century. But as we move into the twenty-first century, this organizational form appears to be undergoing substantial changes, and its
dominance in the economy is being challenged by a variety of alternative forms, including partnerships, closely held corporations, joint ventures, venture capital firms, and virtual organizations. Furthermore,
even within firms that retain the legal form of the publicly traded corporation, significant changes appear to be taking place in the way production is organized, and in the terms of the relationships between corporations and their employees.

The changes taking place, while poorly understood, seem to involve a
paradox: on the one hand, the economic value added by corporations and
other productive enterprises appears to be increasingly dependent on
inputs other than physical capital. By the end of 1998, the book value of
property, plant, and equipment in the publicly traded corporate sector represented only 31 percent of the total value of the long-term financial claims
on nonfinancial corporations (the sum of the book value of their long-
term debt, plus the market value of their equity). This compares with

83 percent just twenty years earlier, in 1978.[1] The excess of market value over book value is, as best we understand, driven by a massive increase in the importance of intangible assets, including things like patents, copyrights, and brand names, but also including many very poorly understood assets such as organizational capital, reputational capital, and importantly, human capital—the knowledge, skills, ideas, and commitment of the employees.

Even as human capital and organizational capital are growing in importance as a source of value in many firms, however, organizational forms and employment relationships appear to be changing in ways that tend to undermine loyalty and commitment and encourage mobility by employees. Financial market institutions have become more influential in the governance of corporations, and labor unions have become less influential. Prevailing ideology in academic and policy circles stresses that shareholders are the owners of corporations, that the economic purpose of corporations is to maximize value for shareholders, and that employees are employed at will. Temporary work and contract work are rising, and job security seems to be declining.

Are these trends consistent in ways that we do not understand, ways that contradict accepted theory and wisdom? Are the new employment relationships and organizational forms that are emerging able to harness the ideas and skills of the people who are actually doing the work as well as or better than the old forms? Or is the corporate sector eating its seed corn in some sense—getting a temporary boost in earnings by cutting payrolls and contracting out more work but failing to make the necessary new investments in training and building a committed and innovative work force?

As of early 1999, the slashing and downsizing that made headlines in the mid-1990s appeared, on the surface, at least, not to have hurt overall economic performance in the United States. Indeed, some observers have argued that the downsizing and restructuring of the 1980s and early 1990s were at least partly responsible for the strong economic performance of the late 1990s. Corporate equity values (as captured by, say, the Wilshire 5000, a very broad-based stock index) more than tripled in the nine years from 1989 to the end of 1998.[2] Although unemployment rose during the recession of the early 1990s, and declined only slowly throughout the subse-

---

1. Authors' calculations from Compustat data. Although book values, which measure historical costs, may understate the actual value of many hard assets, there is little reason to believe that the scale of such understatement is substantially larger today than it has been historically.

2. www.globalfindata.com/thcap.htm [November 15, 1999].

quent expansion, by the end of 1998 it had fallen to 4.3 percent, a thirty-year low.[3] Gross domestic product rose slowly but steadily in the 1990s, with growth averaging somewhat more than 2.5 percent a year in real terms from 1989 through 1998 (including the recession year of 1991).[4] Nonetheless, labor continues to be squeezed, with average hourly earnings for production workers (in inflation-adjusted terms) at the end of 1998 still below what they had been in 1968, and average weekly earnings (also in inflation-adjusted terms) still below what they had been in 1962.[5]

Unanswered Puzzles

Were the changes going on in employment relationships and in the corporate sector generally responsible for, or at least partially responsible for, the strong overall performance of the economy? Or is the economy performing well for other reasons, in spite of the changes in the terms of the relationship between companies and their employees? And how are these changes related, if at all, to the continuing pressure on low-income workers? The essays in this book will not definitively answer these questions, but they shed light on some aspects of the questions.

Job Stability

Charles Schultze begins the book by evaluating the extent to which job stability has been declining for American workers. Schultze finds a modest decrease in job attachment for the overall labor force since the late 1970s, but finds that some subgroups of the work force have experienced much greater loss in job stability than others. For women and young men, for example, average job tenure has not declined, while for mature male workers, average job tenure has declined by 25 to 30 percent. Moreover, Schultze notes a modest reduction in retention rates (the proportion of

3. *Economic Report of the President, 1999*, table B-42.
4. *Economic Report of the President, 1999*, table B-2.
5. *Economic Report of the President, 1999*, table B-47. This table reports average hourly earnings and average weekly earnings for production workers in the private nonagricultural sector, but the figures are based on wages only and do not include benefits. When benefits are included, data suggest that total hourly compensation has grown slowly in the past twenty years, though it was virtually stagnant from 1986 through 1996, and by the end of 1998 was only about 8.4 percent higher than in 1980. Authors' calculations from data in *Economic Report of the President, 1999*, table B-60, adjusted for inflation by the consumer price index.

workers with a given level of tenure who can expect to continue at their current jobs for some period of time longer, say, two more years (the two-year retention rate), or four more years (the four-year retention rate). If the decline in retention rates persists in the years ahead, Schultze notes, it will drag down average tenure further as the current cohort of workers ages. Schultze also found that the displacement rate (adjusted for cyclical fluctuations in the overall unemployment rate) for wage and salary workers in private nonfarm jobs drifted up from the early 1980s through 1993–94 but then fell back in 1995–96 to almost their original level (figure 2-1).

Schultze further found that the cost of displacement for long-tenured workers is large. He cited estimates from one well-known study of mass layoffs in the first half of the 1980s that the present value of the lifetime earnings loss for displaced workers with six or more years of tenure would average (after conversion to 1998 wage levels) about $115,000.[6] To evaluate the potential lifetime losses to workers with more substantial tenure, he used estimates generated by other researchers of how rapidly wages typically rise with tenure and labor market experience to simulate the path of future wages for laid-off workers over the remainder of their working lives. He then compares that path to the wage path that similar workers in other firms who were not laid off could expect over the same time span. He estimated that male workers with eleven to twenty years of tenure, who are laid off through no fault of their own, suffer a cumulative loss of earning power that on average has a present value of about $155,000. Just as the wage premium earned by workers with long tenure is rarely recognized as part of the wealth created by their corporate employers, the substantial losses in earning power experienced by laid-off workers is rarely counted against the gains that shareholders enjoy from corporate restructuring.

Workers who lose their jobs when productivity and wages are growing rapidly across the economy, and then find employment in new full-time jobs, can expect to experience wage increases that will enable most of them to recoup their absolute losses (even if not their relative losses) in no more than five to six years. But, according to Schultze, when wages are stagnant—as they were for twenty years prior to 1996—many laid-off workers with substantial tenure may still not have recovered their former absolute standard of living after ten or even fifteen years. Hence the downsizing and restructuring that occurred in the 1980s and early 1990s may have been especially devastating because it disproportionately affected

6. Jacobson, LaLonde and Sullivan (1993).

long-tenured male workers (who had been relatively well insulated from layoffs in previous eras), a group for whom the costs of job loss were especially large.

Historical Perspective

Peter Cappelli provides a sweeping review of the history of employment relationships, noting that the changes we are witnessing today, that appear to be moving work arrangements away from internal labor market systems toward more market-mediated systems, have their precedent in systems that were common in the nineteenth century and early twentieth century. In the 1800s, he notes, it was common in many industries for merchants to arrange for craftspeople working with their own equipment in their own homes to manufacture certain goods, especially textiles and shoes, according to orders placed by the merchants. The merchant would bring them the raw materials and come back later for the finished product. This system, referred to by economic historians as the putting-out system, bears a remarkable resemblance to the system used by some companies today who hire independent consultants (writers, programmers, graphic artists, and bookkeepers, for example) who work out of their own homes and provide services or deliver finished products to the firm. The advantages of the putting-out system for merchants were its flexibility and reduced fixed costs—exactly the same advantages cited today by companies who lay off their formerly permanent full-time employees and ask them to work as contractors. Of course, from the point of view of the employee, the fixed costs and the risks have not gone away. They have just been shifted from the company to the employee-contractor.

Similarly, just as merchants who used the putting-out system complained of quality control and reliability problems, critics of outsourcing arrangements today note exactly these same problems. The putting-out system eventually gave way to the inside-contracting system (precisely because of the quality-control and reliability problems, some historians say), in which the entrepreneur provided the factory, a power source, and raw materials, but hired contractors to come in, sometimes with their own equipment, hire their own workers, and take responsibility for some entire piece of the production process. Cappelli notes that the modern-day counterpart to these arrangements includes vendor-on-premises arrangements, such as Xerox operating an on-site copy center inside a larger organization. Cappelli cites data indicating that as many as 50 percent of manufacturing employees in the United States in the late 1800s were employed by inside contractors.

The inside-contractor system had problems too, however. Historians writing about manufacturing at the end of the nineteenth century noted frequent complaints by factory owners about the lack of control they had over workers and their difficulty in providing incentives for contractors to meet the quality standards of the factory owners. As a consequence, factory owners had to monitor their contractors closely, which proved costly. Factory owners also discovered that once the inside contractors had figured out how to organize the work flow, and had set up the equipment, the owners could readily duplicate this arrangement and hire foremen to supervise the workers at a much lower cost. In other words, once the knowledge about how to set up the work had been transferred to the factory owners, the factory owners discovered they did not have to continue paying the contractors for this specialized knowledge. Around the turn of the century, then, factory owners began rapidly replacing their inside contractors by foremen, and the contractor's employees by direct employees of the company. Nonetheless, for several decades after this transition, workers were still much more connected to their foremen than they were to their company, and turnover rates for industrial workers, especially unskilled workers, may have been as high as 150 percent a year in the early 1900s. This was partly a consequence of voluntary quits, but foremen were notorious for exploiting queues of workers at the factory gate in order to drive workers harder by threatening to fire them.

Scholars of the period have noted that where work was done by skilled craftspeople, rather than by unskilled workers on an assembly line, high turnover was not necessarily disruptive to organizations. In fact, it appears that turnover may have helped to speed up the spread of new knowledge. Similar observations are being made today about how the mobile culture of Silicon Valley has substantial economic benefits in speeding the transfer of knowledge from one firm to another.

It was the introduction of assembly-line–based mass production techniques, and the scientific management techniques that came along with it, that led companies to have an interest in long-term relationships with employees. Assembly lines required workers to learn skills that were very specific to their role in the production process, which in turn made on-the-job training much more important and thereby raised the economic returns to tenure. Companies began developing institutional arrangements, employment practices, and incentive systems to encourage employees to stay around, and the turnover rate in the industrial sector fell dramatically in the 1920s. Among the institutional arrangements that came out of this era was the managerial hierarchy—and the managerial class came to have the greatest job security. By the 1920s, most of the features of what we now recognize as internal labor market systems were in place. During the Great Depression, the huge surplus of unemployed workers caused some companies to shift back somewhat toward the drive system, but the labor shortages during World War II brought back internal labor markets as the dominant system. By 1970, labor market scholars estimate that 80 percent of workers in the United States had jobs with features characteristic of internal labor markets.

Since the 1980s, Cappelli argues, however, there has been a fairly dramatic shift back toward organizing production in ways that look much more like the old inside-contracting systems. Cappelli does not offer any data to quantify this shift, but he notes a variety of ways in which employment relationships are becoming more market mediated, in the sense that traditional bureaucratic employment structures are weakening, and employment is more likely to be based on a short-term, contractual relationship, and shaped by individualized incentives and pressures from outside labor markets. Cappelli does not tell us what percentage of workers now work under short-term or project-oriented contracts, rather than as permanent employees, but Schultze's evidence suggests that long-term relationships are still quite important, and, importantly, that the returns to tenure have not declined in the 1990s relative to the 1980s.

The key question of course is whether the internal labor market model adopted by most large corporations by the middle part of the twentieth century represented "progress," and hence that a shift back by the corporate sector in the direction of a market-mediated model would constitute a regression. Alternatively, internal labor markets and market-mediated relationships may simply represent alternative models, with each having its advantages and disadvantages in different environments. The internal labor market model may not, in fact, be a clearly superior model for all times and places, while the market-mediated model may have advantages for the information-based economy that we do not yet fully understand. He leaves for further research, however, the question of what developments, in technology or in the business environment, for example, might explain and justify a shift back toward more market-mediated relationships at the end of the century.

Discussant James Baron accepts Cappelli's premise that corporations are dividing up work in ways that entail greater organizational specialization, and more use of contractors, as firms focus on what have been called their core competencies.[7] But, he notes, "It is much less clear how these trends affect the nature of work and employment." While it is true that huge firms are emerging that specialize in contract work, or consulting work, or short-term project work, these firms do not themselves necessarily rely on temporary or contract workers. In fact, many such firms have prospered by relying on high-commitment, training-intensive approaches to human resource management. This view is supported by Schultze's observation that, while large, high-profile companies in manufacturing have gone through extensive downsizings in the past fifteen years, other firms in the nonmanufacturing sectors have grown fast enough to more than make up for the losses of manufacturing employment. Baron suggests that these trends complicate the problem of determining whether an employment relationship should be regarded as market-mediated or not. He suggests that the concept of "market mediation" in employment markets needs to be defined more precisely, in several different dimensions, and that, once this is done, more careful research is needed to evaluate the extent to which employment relationships today are in fact more or less market mediated than they have been in other eras.

Changes on the Shop Floor

Eileen Appelbaum and Peter Berg examine the changes that are taking place in shop floor organization, documenting, for example, the trend in some firms for supervisors to be eliminated and decisionmaking activities to be pushed down to front-line workers. The trend they document may provide one explanation for why the aggregate data show that job stability has declined for middle-aged men (who have traditionally filled many of the supervisor slots) but not so much for other kinds of workers.

Appelbaum and Berg undertake a detailed analysis of evolving approaches to shop floor organization, documenting in three industries many of the changes that business consultants and manufacturing experts have been talking about for the past decade. They note that new information technologies, combined with a growing emphasis on quality and on-time delivery as tools of competition, are making it much more attractive for firms to adopt workplace practices in which front-line workers are actively involved in information gathering and decisionmaking—tasks tra-

---

7. See, for example, Prahalad and Hamel (1990).

ditionally thought to be management tasks. These authors surveyed more than 4,000 employees in thirty-nine plants, in the steel, apparel, and medical electronic instruments and imaging industries to learn whether, and the extent to which, such changes are actually happening, and whether employees in more participatory settings are also more likely to have some portion of their pay tied to firm performance.

Although the Appelbaum and Berg sample is admittedly a biased one (drawn from firms that agreed to cooperate in the study), it covers significant portions of the firms in the three industries studied. A consistent finding, among all of the plants surveyed, was the recognition by plant managers of a need to adopt work organization and human resource practices that engage the capabilities of their employees in decisions about production and in quality improvements. Some of the plants surveyed are industry leaders in this regard, some are in a process of transition, and some recognize the need to change but are uncertain how to go about it or what specific workplace practices really pay off in their industries.

The authors found that in the plants they studied, horizontal information flows were often at least as important as, if not more important than, vertical flows between front-line workers and supervisors, that the tasks of monitoring and coordination were rapidly being shifted to front-line workers, that hierarchies were being flattened, and that the number of supervisors was being reduced. They also found that, where front-line workers have expanded responsibilities for problem solving and coordination of productive activities, they are also much more likely to have some portion of their pay (although generally only a very small portion) contingent on firm performance, through profit sharing and various kinds of group incentive pay, such as production or quality bonuses. These findings contradict the predictions of economic theorists who have stressed the free-rider problem with group incentives and the importance of vertical relationships between principals and agents, and who have argued that individual performance incentives would be much more effective than group incentives.

Appelbaum and Berg offer an intriguing interpretation of their finding about the importance of horizontal interactions and group incentives. They note that profit sharing and group incentives may be effective more because of their symbolic value than their intrinsic value. "It is the recognition of workers as stakeholders in the firm, and not the size of the incentive, that is significant and that provides incentives for workers to expend appropriate levels of discretionary effort," they suggest.

Discussant Kathryn Shaw notes that the Appelbaum and Berg results raise questions about what, exactly, is driving the changes that are taking place in workplace organization. Is it just that new information technology is available that makes flexible workplaces more possible, or could it also be true that workers in general have higher skills today than they did in the past, and employers are trying to make greater use of these skills? Or is it something else?

Role of Technological Change

Timothy Bresnahan, Eric Brynjolfsson, and Lorin Hitt provide some insight into these questions in their chapter. These authors examine the technological changes that are taking place in many workplaces, particularly those driven by or accompanying the spread of computer technologies. They argue that organizational changes that shift authority and decisionmaking activities downward and outward are complementary to the use of new information technologies, and they present data consistent with this analysis. Moreover, they argue that these organizational changes, together with increased use of computer technology, are jointly complementary with increased employee skill levels, measured in a number of dimensions.

Bresnahan and coauthors argue that information technology is transforming the workplace because employers who use information technology usually coinvent new approaches to workplace organization and new product and service offerings. Information technology and the organizational coinventions together change the mix of skills that employers demand. Specifically, employers may substitute computers for low-skill work while at the same time increasing their demand for workers with certain cognitive and social skills. They support their argument with firm-level data linking several indicators of information technology use, workplace organization, and the demand for skilled labor.

They find that information technology use is correlated with arrangements that call for broader job responsibilities for line workers, more decentralized decisionmaking, and more self-managed teams. In turn, they find that both information technology and these new organizational arrangements are correlated with worker skill, measured in a variety of ways. Significantly, they find that firms that attempt to implement only one of the three types of changes, without the other two, turn out to be less productive than firms that invest in all of the complements. And, in some cases, they turn out to be less productive even than firms that invest in none of the complements. The results highlight the importance of organizational changes accompanying advances in information technology in the changing demand for workers with different skill levels.

The evidence marshaled by these authors, then, provides evidence in support of one of the most prominent explanations that have been offered for the growing disparity in incomes. This is the theory that technological change in the past few decades has been "skill-biased," meaning that it has simultaneously increased the demand for skilled workers, even as it has reduced the demand for low-skilled workers.

Discussant Gary Burtless notes, however, that the results from Bresnahan and coauthors are based on data drawn almost exclusively from large corporations, and he questions whether they tell us much about trends in smaller and mid-sized companies. The latter account for a growing percentage of the nation's employment. Moreover, Burtless points out that firms that introduce new information technology might not only change the way that they produce goods and services within the firm, they may also change their decisions about whether to make or buy inputs, and in particular, they might, as Cappelli suggests they are doing, contract out more extensively to smaller producers. Hence a study that looks only at what is happening in 400 or so large companies may not be very revealing about the aggregate demand for skilled and unskilled workers. In fact, there is considerable evidence that employment has declined in the largest companies, and that those companies are now buying such services as office cleaning, cafeteria operations, photocopying services, and guard services rather than hiring their own employees to perform these functions. These changes would reduce the direct demand by these companies for low-skilled workers, but they would not necessarily reduce the aggregate demand for low-skilled workers. Rather, they would shift that demand from large corporations to smaller, specialized contractors.

Meanwhile, the contractors that do hire the low-skilled workers may tend to pay those workers less than the large firm would have paid, because the large firms have historically favored flat, paternalistic pay structures. Burtless then argues that, even if it is correct that technological change is encouraging a skill-biased reorganization in large corporations, this is not the whole story. We must still look toward factors such as the weakening of unions, the lowering of trade barriers, and the increased flow of immigrants for a complete explanation of why large

corporate employers could get away with the contracting-out strategies
that they are adopting.

Employee Sharing in Decisionmaking and Returns

Since at least the 1920s, theorists, policy analysts, and advocates have
argued that corporations should be restructured as employee-owned firms
in order to strengthen the voice of employees in the workplace and provide
greater protection for their interests. But other theorists and policy analysts
have argued, for a variety of reasons, that employee-owned firms would not
be efficient. Moreover, the latter group has argued that if employee-owned
firms were really more efficient, there would be gains for people who organize firms in that way, and we should therefore see more of them. Two of
the chapters in this volume look at empirical evidence about when and
why firms are organized in ways that give employees ownership-type claims
and responsibilities, and how such firms fare relative to firms organized as
standard, widely traded corporations.

Avner Ben-Ner, W. Allen Burns, Greg Dow, and Louis Putterman ask
why firms might choose ownership structures or management systems in
which employees participate directly in decisionmaking or in financial
returns. The authors have constructed a unique data set providing organizational detail about hundreds of private and publicly traded firms in
Minnesota. The data include information about whether those firms have
employee stock ownership plans (ESOPs) or profit-sharing plans, as well as
about human resource practices in the firm (especially those associated
with employee involvement in decisionmaking), and the nature of the
technology used by the firm (such as the degree of complexity of the tasks
that are performed by individual workers and how interdependent the
tasks are). The authors were also able to obtain employment information
for firms in their sample, such as the number of employees, and the average wages and tenure of their employees, as well as information about the
capital intensity and riskiness of the industries in which the firms operate.

The authors found evidence that greater task complexity leads to higher
levels of worker participation in decisionmaking. But task complexity is
not necessarily associated with worker participation in financial returns
(through profit sharing or share ownership). Worker participation in financial returns, by contrast, seemed to be most strongly associated with high
average worker tenure and high wages. Although it is not clear which is

cause and which is effect in the latter finding, the results suggest that the two different types of participation may serve different functions and may therefore be chosen in different circumstances. They also suggest that information and coordination problems may be at least as important in driving the choice of organizational form, if not more so, than the incentive problems that have been stressed in much of the theoretical literature.

The authors find little support for several widely repeated theories in the literature on worker-managed firms that purport to explain why worker-managed firms and other forms of worker participation in decisionmaking and in financial returns are not more common. In particular, theorists have speculated that workers would not want to share in financial returns because they are likely to be more risk averse than outside investors. Other theorists have argued that if a firm uses a high level of specialized assets in production, than the firm would have trouble getting outside debt financing. Hence it would have to rely more heavily on equity financing, and since workers would tend to be more wealth constrained, most of this financing would have to come from outside equity investors. Moreover, if the assets of the firm are highly specific, outsiders who financed those investments would want to be sure that workers are intensively monitored to be sure that they do not misuse or abuse those assets. All of these factors argue against worker participation in management or in financial returns in firms with substantial firm-specific physical assets. Ben-Ner and coauthors find, to the contrary, that, in their sample, firms with high levels of physical asset specificity were more likely to have ESOPs and more likely to use workplace practices that include employee involvement in decisionmaking than firms with lower levels of asset specificity. Like the result about task complexity, this result could be explained by appealing to information and coordination problems with specific assets: if employees who use highly idiosyncratic assets have better information than their managers do about how to use those assets optimally, then it might be more efficient for managers to delegate decisionmaking authority to them, despite the potential negative incentive effects of giving employees decision rights. The negative incentive effects of delegating decisions can then be counteracted to some extent by also giving employees a share in the financial returns.

Another theme in the literature on employee ownership and worker management is that the two forms of participation—in decisionmaking and in financial returns—are complements. (Appelbaum and Berg seemed to observe this phenomenon in their sample, for example.) Although

Ben-Ner and coauthors do not specifically refute this notion, they nonetheless find evidence that the two kinds of participation are driven by distinct causal forces.

Employee Share Ownership

Margaret Blair, Douglas Kruse, and Joseph Blasi look at companies that have adopted equity-based compensation systems, particularly those in which a substantial portion of the employer's stock is held by, or on behalf of, employees. They make no attempt to assess the direct impact of such compensation systems on employees, nor on productivity, but they inquire instead into the impact of employee ownership on the firm itself. Is it a viable, efficient, and stable organizational form for the equity of an enterprise to be substantially owned by employees? The authors consider this question by examining the track record of the twenty-seven publicly traded firms for which approximately 20 percent or more of their stock was held by or for employees in 1983, and comparing the experience of these firms over time (through the end of 1997) to that of a control sample of forty-five firms that were similar in size and in similar industries as of 1983.

The authors found no evidence that employee ownership on this scale was either an unstable arrangement or an ownership structure used primarily for transitions. Indeed, the ownership of a substantial block of shares by employees appears to be at least as stable a form as the ordinary widely traded corporation, and it may be an arrangement that stabilizes the firm itself, by making it less likely that the firm will be acquired, taken private, or thrust into bankruptcy. There is also evidence that the form is associated with more stable employment levels.

Blair and coauthors find that the employee-ownership firms in their study tended to be less capital intensive than publicly traded firms in general, but that this was largely a result of the fact that there were no employee-ownership firms in either mining or chemicals in 1983, two industries that are very capital intensive. Meanwhile a disproportionate share of the firms in their study (five out of the twenty-seven) were defense contractors. Since the authors had gone to considerable effort to identify every publicly traded firm that had at least 20 percent of its stock held by or for employees as of 1983, the uneven distribution of these firms was not a result of a sample-selection problem. The fact that some of the most capital-intensive industries did not include any employee-ownership firms is consistent with the theory that employee ownership is less likely to be feasible or attractive for a firm that must finance very large amounts of capital. But the prevalence of employee-ownership firms in the defense contracting sector was a surprise. They noted, however, that data on employee ownership in 1990 show a substantial increase—to at least 148 firms—in the number of publicly traded firms with at least 20 percent of their shares held by or for employees. Moreover, by 1991, employee ownership firms were pretty evenly distributed across industries.[8]

Finally, Blair and coauthors show that the greater apparent stability of the employee ownership firms in their study does not appear to have come at a cost in terms of productivity or financial performance, and it may in fact have enhanced performance. The employee-ownership firms had, on average, slightly higher rates of return on capital and slightly higher rates of productivity growth over the sample period, and hypothetical portfolios formed with the stocks of employee-ownership firms outperformed both the S&P 500 and comparable portfolios formed with the stocks of control firms, especially in the last four or five years of the sample period.

Both Derek Jones, who comments on the chapter by Ben-Ner and coauthors, and Stephen Smith, who comments on the chapter by Blair and coauthors, note weaknesses in the data used by these authors, calling attention to the general problems of getting good data on the aspects of firm performance that are most important for hypothesis testing, as well as on employee ownership itself. With the use of equity-based compensation systems growing in importance in the economy, any policy debate about those developments would be greatly enhanced by better data on employee share ownership.

Human Capital in High-Technology Sectors

Julia Porter Liebeskind examines new companies, organized in new ways, for insight into how corporations might best be organized when their primary asset is human capital. Using a sample of seventy-nine new biotechnology firms in California that went public from 1974 through 1995, her study examines their ownership structure, especially focusing on whether and to what degree employees of these companies hold their companies'

---

8. The list of publicly traded firms with substantial employee ownership in 1991 came from Blasi and Kruse (1991). No comprehensive data are available on the employee ownership levels of publicly traded firms since 1991.

stock. In biotechnology firms, she argues, the key assets of the firm are its scientists, since these employees are the source of all the intellectual property, such as patents and licenses, that ultimately give the firm a product to produce and sell.

Liebeskind notes that, to be successful, biotechnology firms must at a minimum solve three employment problems. They must attract highly skilled employees, often from academic settings, to the firm; they must induce these employees to develop human capital that has value to the firm; and they must induce these employees to stay around long enough that the firm can establish some intellectual property rights with respect to the ideas generated by these employees, or develop some commercial products based on their human capital. She looks at the systems of corporate control in her sample of firms for evidence concerning how they address these three problems.

Liebeskind argues that extant theories about how best to provide incentives for investment in human capital predict that new biotechnology firms, for which human capital may be the most important source of value, would tend to compensate employees heavily with stock or deferred stock ownership plans, or long-term stock options. She finds, however, that the biotechnology firms in her sample tend to have lower levels of stock ownership by insiders (managers and directors) than other researchers have found for other firms going public for the first time. Moreover, there was no evidence in her sample that firms were compensating nonmanagerial employees with stock at all. None of the firms had an ESOP or deferred stock ownership plan.

Liebeskind also found that shares were much more likely to be held in concentrated blocks by outsiders, especially by venture capital firms, than by insiders, both before and after the initial public stock offering. This also contradicts the theoretical predictions that employees would want to hold influential blocks in the firm in order to protect their human capital investments. She speculates that these findings might be explained by the fact that employees are risk averse, and these firms are even more risky than other types of IPOs. Hence, the incentive effects of share ownership by employees are not powerful enough to overcome the costs that would be imposed on employees who had to bear the risks of share ownership.

Liebeskind's data show, however, that employees in new biotechnology firms are very likely to be compensated with stock options. Stock options are less risky for employees than the stock itself since the downside risk is limited and since options can be repriced.[9] The data also indicate that options issued to employees tend to have very long vesting periods (ten years in the median sample firm) and are often restricted so that if the employee leaves the firm he or she may not exercise the option. Hence, if the options are "in the money," they provide a strong disincentive to employee mobility. Moreover, options tend to be distributed in fairly egalitarian ways, with nonsenior managers holding more than 70 percent of options in the median firm.

Liebeskind also found that nearly 40 percent of firms in her sample had antitakeover charter amendments in place, which could be interpreted as a mechanism for protecting human capital investments, and that, despite the high concentration of share ownership in the hands of venture capital firms, venture capital investors typically had only one board seat out of seven (whereas, managers typically held two board seats out of seven). And most boards had no representatives of corporate investors. Liebeskind interprets this to mean that, while the firms in her sample are not dominated by management, as the theory had predicted, they were also not dominated by the venture capitalists, nor by corporate investors, a fact, she notes, that may allow for impartial resolution of conflicts of interest between managers and outside investors that might otherwise impose considerable costs on the firm.

Discussant James Rebitzer cautions that biotechnology firms may not necessarily be significantly more human capital intensive than the other kinds of new ventures that form the comparison group. He also notes that the long lead times, high levels of risk, and the importance of factors over which researchers have little control (such as the FDA approval process) involved in biotechnology may make financial incentives less useful than they would be where financial results are more neatly and cleanly tied to the effort and intellectual contributions of the employees. He suggests that the extensive use of stock options in the compensation packages of employees of new biotechnology firms may be a mechanism by which firms screen potential employees, rather than primarily an incentive mechanism. Only the most entrepreneurial and the least risk-averse researchers would accept

---

9. Finance theorists might say that stock options are riskier than the underlying stock, because they have a higher variance of returns, and, in finance theory, risk is often measured in terms of the variance of returns rather than in terms of the downside potential. Stock options have less downside risk than the underlying stock, however.

significant amounts of stock options in lieu of higher cash compensation, he argues.

Rebitzer also notes that employees with those characteristics would probably not be the type to place a high value on job security. But, he suggests, it may be that in settings where innovation is important, the firms also do not place a high value on long-term relationships. There may be other, better mechanisms by which the firm can establish property rights over the ideas produced by their employees, mechanisms not yet identified in theoretical models. In Silicon Valley, he notes, long-term relationships do not seem to be the norm.

Measuring Human Capital Investments

The final chapter in this book takes on the difficult question of how to do a better job of identifying and measuring the human capital inputs that are becoming so important in most firms. Laurie Bassi, Baruch Lev, Jonathan Low, Daniel McMurrer, and G. Anthony Siesfeld provide evidence that corporate managers believe there would be significant benefits to their companies if they had better information about their investments in human capital, that financial investors also want such information, and that such investments are viewed favorably by financial markets. But they also demonstrate how weak and generally uninformative the current measurement systems are for measuring the value created by such investments. These authors note that most firms do not even know how much they spend on formal education and training programs, let alone on informal learning. More important, they have almost no systematic, high-quality information about the impact and value of the investments they are making in human capital.

The authors note that, although both firms and their investors would benefit by having better information, there is a substantial public good problem in attempting to develop such information. A measurement system that would be most useful would be broad based and generalizable, so that data from one firm would be comparable to data from another firm, or even so that data from one division in a firm would be comparable to data from another division in the firm. But of the few measurement systems that are out there being used in the private sector, most are competely idiosyncratic to the firm where they are being used. Moreover, although firms would benefit if other firms shared their information, no firm has an incentive to share its own information. Hence, the authors suggest that government organizations could play an important role in developing standardized information, and in encouraging the disclosure of such information.

Discussant Marleen O'Connor notes that the effort to identify and quantify investments in human capital and to track the implications of these investments for profitability and share value, are part of a larger movement under way in the accounting profession and in the international community to improve methods of measuring and reporting on intangible assets. This movement, she says, has the potential to be politically controversial if it is seen as a Trojan horse for the labor movement. The current focus on intangible assets is being driven primarily by individuals in the business community who are trying to improve their management of intangibles such as knowledge assets. However, the conclusions that these business leaders are coming to bear a striking similarity to ideas promoted by social activists in the 1970s who were interested in the social responsibilities of corporations toward their workers, as well as to issues being raised today by social activists concerned about diversity in the workplace and child labor practices. O'Connor points out that greater information about workplace practices might help to protect the interests of workers but also says that such clarity could have the opposite effect. Once it becomes known how much corporations are spending on training, for example, shareholders could pressure companies not to spend that much, especially if the link between training expenditures and profits is not clear.

Implications for Future Research

The chapters in this volume, then, do not resolve the paradox. While they lend some support for the idea that technological changes are an important factor driving organizational change, especially changes that give front-line workers much more decisionmaking authority and responsibility, they do not explain the decline in the stability of employment relations. In fact, several of the chapters suggest that technological changes should be having the opposite effect: the use of new information technologies, combined with workplace reorganizations that push decisionmaking downward, are associated with higher levels of human capital and more training, factors that should increase the returns to tenure and make employee commitment more important than ever to employees and employers.

An Interpretation

But there may be a story that can reconcile these seeming contradictions. Collectively, the chapters in this book are consistent with, and lend some support to, the following interpretation: the new computer-based technologies are encouraging the redesign of work by making it possible to push information analysis and decisionmaking down to teams of front-line workers. These workers are then held responsible for some substantial piece of output and empowered to solve the problems that arise in producing and delivering that output. But firms that restructure along these lines must often completely reorganize old hierarchical units, often eliminating large numbers of middle managers, as well as unskilled workers. To the extent that there was an old social contract with these mid-level employees, it had to be broken to accomplish the transition. That helps explain at least some of the downsizing activities of the late 1980s and early 1990s and may explain why measures of job stability have declined so much for older men (younger, unskilled workers have never had particularly stable employment).

By itself, increased use of information technologies and team-based production does not explain an increased eagerness of firms to contract out non-core activities. But if one adds in the fact that the new information-intensive, team-based production methods require higher levels of formal training and other investments in firm-specific skills, perhaps an explanation can be discerned: it may be more efficient for firms to specialize in the development and use of certain kinds or sets of skills. Teams are therefore built around what have been called "core competencies," and inputs that are not part of the core can often be purchased more efficiently, perhaps from another firm that specializes in the processes necessary to provide those inputs.

Most of the older men and unskilled workers displaced by the reorganizations of the late 1980s and early 1990s were eventually reemployed (as noted before, the unemployment rate had fallen to 4.3 percent by the end of 1998), though usually at substantially lower pay than they had been earning. Sometimes they were employed by the contractors that had become suppliers to the large firms. Occasionally, they themselves became the contractors, supplying services on a project-by-project basis to their old firm, but without benefits, and without any guarantee of a paycheck. A very few thrived under the new arrangements and came out ahead financially.

While overall performance and productivity have improved as a result of these changes, they have been costly to employees and to firms in terms of reduced employee loyalty. To win back employee loyalty and encourage workers—despite the shattering of the old "social contract"—to share information and to make deep commitments to their "teams," firms are increasingly turning to equity-based compensation schemes. Employee stock ownership may help to stabilize the firms by providing them with some protection from takeover, may help firms retain workers, and may even encourage greater commitment on the part of employees to cooperation, information sharing, and full participation in the teams. But employees may not always prefer stock ownership because of the financial risks it entails. Stock options, however, may provide many of the same benefits yet be less risky for employees. So, in the newest sectors of the economy, where human capital and intellectual capital are most important, but where employee loyalty is rare and there was never any old social contract to form a basis for expectations, we see stock options being used extensively to bind employees to their firms and, not incidentally, to share risks and rewards with them.

The above is just a story, built from anecdotes and snippets of facts. Even if it is true as far as it goes, it does not begin to capture the diversity of changes that are happening in the workplace, in employment relationships, and in organizational forms. Indeed, we may be able to say little with confidence except that the old internal labor market arrangements are in turmoil, that the market seems willing to pay a growing premium for the highest-skilled workers, and that firms appear to be experimenting with new arrangements to attract, keep, and organize those workers. Finally, it appears that the scholars and policy analysts are not the only ones having trouble figuring out what is going on. The firms themselves and their managers are for the most part feeling their way blindly in these efforts with only the most rudimentary information and crude hunches to guide them about what works, what investments in human resources pay off, or even in many cases, what they are already investing, and what they are getting for it.

Future Research Agenda

As a whole this volume provides a good starting point for understanding the implications of human capital becoming a more important input in corporate enterprises. But we need to continue the types of multidisciplinary research presented and stretch our thinking further if we are to understand and assess the full potential of this development. The following topics are important.

COMPLEMENTARITIES: HUMAN AND ORGANIZATIONAL CAPITAL. An important yet under-appreciated finding presented in this volume and elsewhere is that human and organizational capital are significant complements.[10] They add the most value when changes are made in an integrated way. By organizational capital we mean the structures, processes, and management systems used to organize work and utilize technologies. David Teece reminds us that real competitive advantage arises when firms or networks of firms organize themselves to translate individual knowledge and skills into assets that others have difficulty replicating.[11] The difficulty of replication lies in the fact that the value created arises out of the complex combination or interaction of human skills and organizational structures, routines, and processes.

The implication of this key point is that research on human capital needs to be embedded in the study of organizational processes. Yet too often these are treated as separate intellectual domains—economists view human capital as educational attainment; human resource specialists focus on discrete components of personnel policies, selection, training, job design, and compensation; and organizational theorists focus on incentive structures, transaction costs, setting organizational boundaries, and minimizing administrative costs within those boundaries. Only by examining these issues together are we likely to understand how different configurations of human and organizational capital within and across organizational boundaries might add value and enhance or destroy the competitive advantage.

Thus our first suggestion is to encourage more theoretical and empirical work that crosses the disciplinary boundaries needed to better understand and measure the effects of these complementarities. Doing so might provide better answers to questions such as why is it so difficult for organizations to transfer best-practice innovations (such as team-based work systems or integrated supply chains) to new settings. Is there, perhaps, too much focus on the observable features of these practices and not enough on the norms and social relationships that operate in them? Replication of these unobservable sources of value is more difficult. An understanding of this phenomenon would have significant implications for mergers and

10. See Ichniowski and others (1996); Milgrom and Roberts (1992).
11. Teece (1998).

acquisitions, as well as for research on learning and diffusion of innovations within and across organizational boundaries.

TURNING "EMPLOYABILITY" INTO A VIABLE CONCEPT. A puzzle alluded to in these chapters is why we would expect firms to invest heavily in human capital development of current employees when technologies and skill requirements are likely to change rapidly in uncertain ways in the future. Is the promise of employability (that is, "we cannot guarantee job security but we will ensure that you are employable if and when we have to lay you off") as vacuous as theory would predict? Yet if technological change is rapid and uncertain, and specialized human capital depreciates quickly, aggregate welfare (not to mention individual and family welfare) will depend on how our institutions—individual firms, or perhaps networks of firms, professional organizations, educational institutions, or other coordinating institutions—solve the employability problem. Perhaps leading firms understand this better than theorists, and we will observe reinvestment in education and skills at rates required to keep individuals employable, even though standard theory predicts it will not happen. If conventional theory is right, however, we need to study how different organizations and institutions that have a collective interest in ensuring that the average level of general, redeployable skill levels in the work force is high, but that lack the individual incentives to solve this problem, might do so by working together.

HUMAN CAPITAL AND CORPORATE GOVERNANCE. As human capital becomes a more important source of competitive advantage, employees are likely to begin challenging the social and political norms that have emphasized the primacy of other resources, such as finance capital. Some theorists argue that the big, integrated American corporation emerged as an important institution essentially in response to the need to pool large amounts of risk capital.[12] Moreover, conventional wisdom holds that executives are expected to be agents of shareholders. In most American corporations, finance is the most powerful functional group within the management structure, and investors and their institutional agents are the dominant external influence on the firm.

By contrast, human resources and, in unionized firms, labor relations, are either kept in positions of marginal influence or separated from the

12. Roe (1994).

centers of decisionmaking power (at least in the United States). As human capital grows in importance, however, we can expect its owners (the employees) and their individual and collective agents to seek greater influence and power in the key decisions that affect the organization.

Yet organizations and institutions seldom reallocate power and decisionmaking roles without resistance and conflict. Thus we would expect a great deal of resistance to granting employees greater voice in corporate governance processes. If this is so, existing corporations may lose ground to newer firms that from the outset are designed in ways needed to attract and retain the necessary human capital. Indeed, as the chapters in this book suggest, this is precisely why new human-capital–intensive firms tend to be structured as partnerships (for example, accounting firms, law firms, consulting firms, advertising agencies), or in ways that are similar to partnerships, and use various compensation, stock, and governance arrangements different from those found in most older, larger corporations founded in a different era. Thus an interesting question for future research is whether new firms that recognize and give greater prominence to human capital in both their compensation and governance structures gain a competitive advantage over existing firms that resist adapting in this way. Or will market signals overcome organizational resistance and lead to a gradual shift in corporate governance in old firms as well?

We might expect that both phenomena will be observed but in different settings. Some corporations will learn faster than others. What distinguishes these fast learners from others, and what changes in governance these firms implement will be worth studying? Real value can be added, and the private and social costs of conflict and resistance might be reduced, by having a body of research identifying ways this adaptation process can be negotiated and managed.

LEARNING TO PLAY NEW ROLES. If employees individually and collectively begin to assert a more active interest and role in corporate governance, they and their agents, and managers who interact with them, will need to learn a new set of technical and organizational skills. Effective shared governance requires substantive knowledge of the business, the ability to add value to decisionmaking and to manage processes in which multiple, diverse interests are present, and to negotiate solutions that maintain the commitment of the different parties over time. This is difficult, as case studies of efforts to bring employee and union representatives into various governance processes have shown.[13] Examining this shift in the roles and skill requirements of managers and employees and their representatives should be a high priority. Otherwise, the next generation of managers and employee representatives will carry over outdated processes, attitudes, and behaviors that may lead to the failure of human-capital–intensive organizations.

BEYOND SHAREHOLDER PRIMACY. As human capital asserts a more important and active role in firms, social and legal institutions within which firms function will also have to change. In particular, the shareholder primacy perspective that has dominated the investment community, business press, and national and international financial institutions and policymaking circles (as well as academic discussions) for most of the past two decades, must give way to a more nuanced perspective, that appreciates and supports the subtle balancing act required to keep both human capital and financial capital committed to firms.[14]

Considerable use of the term "stakeholders" and "stakeholder firms" can be found in different social science literatures, for example. Yet these terms often lack analytical precision. Moreover, they are only beginning to be translated into testable theories or propositions that would support empirical examination.[15] Developing more precise stakeholder models of the firm and testing these models in empirical research are essential tasks if there is to be a serious, analytically and empirically grounded debate over the goals of the corporation and its relationships to the multiple interests or stakeholders it is expected to serve.

But even with such careful theoretical work, the dominant paradigm will not give way quickly or easily because advocates of the old paradigm may perceive that their interests are at risk. Thus another important part of the research portfolio should address how the investment community in particular might adapt to the increasing role for human capital in the corporation of the future. Investors will need access to research documenting how the changes in human capital, organizational processes, and technologies affect firm performance, and they will need better information

---

13. Hammer, Currall, and Stern (1991); Hunter (1998); Gordon (1999).

14. See, for example, Blair and Stout (1999), for an argument that corporate law, properly understood, provides a solution to a team production problem, not a principal-agent problem.

15. See Kochan and Rubinstein (1999) for a new view of the stakeholder model.

about the nature and value of investments in these areas to develop new criteria for assessing firm performance.

Alternatively, the perceived conflicts of interest, whether real or not, will surely lead debates over the future of the corporation to spill over to political arenas in which solutions seldom are based on careful analysis of the realities of how organizations work in practice.

RESPONSES TO INEQUALITY. Finally, if returns to knowledge workers continue to increase or remain at their present levels, the inequality of incomes that has grown in recent years is likely to persist if not get worse. Elite knowledge workers will gain influence and command high levels of compensation, while less skilled workers will bear the brunt of pressures to control compensation costs or find their jobs outsourced to lower-cost and lower-wage firms. While tight labor markets in the late stages of the current economic expansion may ease some of the pressure on wages for low-skilled workers, they are unlikely to reverse the losses this group has suffered relative to high-skilled workers. Eventually, some institutional response will likely emerge to renegotiate these income differentials in the name of greater fairness and equity.

History tells us the default responses are unions and government regulations. While there may well be merit in rebuilding unions and strengthening government regulations, these institutions need not and probably should not take on the same features and approaches of their past models. How to structure these or other institutional responses in ways that reduce inequality and promote effective utilization of human capital and effective organizations are critical research and institution building tasks for the future.

Thus, we have just begun to explore the full dimensions of the issues raised as human capital grows in importance within firms and in the economy. We look forward to continuing to expand the frontier of work on this question and to engaging in what is sure to be a sustained and lively debate over its full implications and consequences.

References

Blair, Margaret, and Lynn A. Stout. 1999. "A Team Production Theory of Corporate Law." *Virginia Law Review* 85 (March): 247–328.
Blasi, Joseph Raphael, and Douglas Lynn Kruse. 1991. *The New Owners: The Mass Emergence of Employee Ownership in Public Companies and What It Means to American Business.* HarperBusiness.

Gordon, Jeffrey N. 1999. "Employee Stock Ownership in Economic Transitions: The Case of United and the Airline Industry." In *Employees and Corporate Governance,* edited by Margaret M. Blair and Mark J. Roe, 371–54. Brookings.

Hammer, Tove H., Steven C. Currall, and Robert N. Stern. 1991. "Worker Representation on Boards of Directors: A Study of Competing Roles." *Industrial and Labor Relations Review* 44 (July): 661–80.

Hunter, Larry W. 1998. "Can Strategic Participation Be Institutionalized? Union Representation on American Corporate Boards." *Industrial and Labor Relations Review* 51 (July): 557–78.

Ichniowski, Casey, and others. 1996. "What Works at Work?: Overview and Assessment." *Industrial Relations* 35 (July): 299–344.

Jacobson, Louis, S., Robert J. LaLonde, and Daniel G. Sullivan. 1993. *The Costs of Worker Dislocation.* Kalamazoo, Mich.: W.E. Upjohn Institute for Employment Research.

Kochan, Thomas A., and Saul Rubinstein. 1999. "Toward a Stakeholder Theory of the Firm: The Saturn Partnership." Working Paper. MIT Sloan School of Management.

Milgrom, Paul, and John Roberts. 1992. *Economics, Organizations, and Management.* Prentice Hall.

Prahalad, C. K., and Gary Hamel. 1990. "The Core Competence of the Corporation." *Harvard Business Review* 68 (May–June): 79–91.

Roe, Mark J. 1994. *Strong Managers, Weak Owners: The Political Roots of American Corporate Finance.* Princeton University Press.

Teece, David J. 1998. "Capturing Value from Knowledge Assets. The New Economy, Markets for Know-How, and Intangible Assets." *California Management Review* 40 (Spring): 55–78.

2

CHARLES L. SCHULTZE

Has Job Security Eroded for American Workers?

TWO DECADES AGO, workers entering upon new jobs in established firms could look about and observe that most of their older and more tenured fellow workers had climbed a fairly steep wage ladder and appeared to enjoy a relatively high—even if not absolute—degree of job security. During the past twenty years, however, a widespread perception has arisen that such expectations were increasingly being disappointed. Fueled in part by intense media attention and some dramatic examples among large companies, the belief has grown that an increased prevalence of corporate downsizing and layoffs among senior workers, at all skill levels, has seriously eroded the prospects for job security as a reward for long service.

This chapter deals with two major aspects of this issue. First it examines the empirical basis behind these developments and perceptions. Has job stability significantly decreased for the average American worker? Does the widespread public perception of lessened job security have a basis in reality? Has an increasing use of corporate downsizing as a business strategy eroded an earlier set of labor market norms in which firms placed a high

The research for this paper was supported by a grant from the Alfred P. Sloan Foundation. Barry Bosworth, Gary Burtless, and George Perry made helpful comments. Excellent research assistance was provided by Leah Brooks, Amanda Packel, and Shanna Rose. Robert McIntire and Steven Hipple of the BLS kindly allowed me to tap their extensive knowledge of the CPS Displaced Worker supplements.

value on preserving jobs for senior workers? Second, we look at the economic cost of layoffs to workers with substantial job tenure. Compared with their counterparts in European countries, American workers who are displaced from their jobs do not typically spend very lengthy periods in unemployment. But if they had acquired significant tenure in their old job, earning the higher wages that went with that tenure, they typically find that they have to take a large pay cut in the new job. In this chapter I review the literature and examine the data on the size of the wage losses suffered by such workers and make an effort to compare their current and prospective wages on the new job with the wage path they might have experienced had they been able to stay with the old firm. Finally I attempt, on the basis of relatively scanty data, to see whether for the typical displaced worker these costs of displacement have been rising or falling.

What's Been Happening to Job Security?

Much of the media reporting on the subject has consisted of anecdotes and dramatic examples, often involving large manufacturing corporations. Careful balancing of the evidence does suggest that the risk of job loss facing tenured workers did rise modestly from 1981–82 to 1993–94 but then declined in 1995–96. Eye-catching layoff announcements apart, the pattern of changes in job loss was not so pronounced as to be immediately evident from the statistical data—the pattern emerges only after close analysis. The various survey data about job tenure and layoffs suffer from response errors and are plagued by changes that have occurred over time in the wording of the questions asked of workers. Numerous researchers have spent much time and ingenuity in finding ways to correct or deal with these problems. But some temporal inconsistencies remain in the data. In the end, we will have to be satisfied with conclusions in which the terms "probably," "likely," and "on balance" feature prominently.

Why Media Reports Are Likely to Overstate the Downsizing Problem

For more than a decade the media have been full of announcements about major downsizing and permanent layoffs in large American corporations whose names are household legends—AT&T, GM, Boeing, and the like. Major newspapers have run special series featuring long gloomy articles heralding the demise of "lifetime" jobs and a sea change in the relationship of corporations and their long-service employees. Several major personnel firms compile and regularly publish monthly estimates of layoffs among large firms,which are in turn reported and commented upon in the media.[1] And yet, at the same time, the overall U.S. economy has been booming. Employment and output have been rising sharply, and unemployment has fallen to levels far lower than even the most optimistic predictions earlier in the decade. How can these two sets of phenomena coexist?

Several special characteristics of recent economic developments may explain some of the apparent paradox. First, even as overall employment has been growing rapidly, manufacturing employment has been falling. Second, within manufacturing the very large and prominent employers have typically contracted employment to a larger degree than others. Third, within nonmanufacturing industries, where employment on average has increased substantially, a not insignificant incidence of employment contractions has taken place among very large firms. And finally, the large firms that have experienced substantial layoffs, especially in manufacturing, often tend to have higher than average wages. Many of them are in industries that typically pay "above-scale wages"—that is, wages that are higher than those paid elsewhere in the economy for workers of comparable education and skills.[2] Furthermore, the wages paid in large manufacturing establishments are, on average, higher than those paid in small establishments.[3] And even though large firms typically own a number of establishments, the likelihood is that correlation between size and wage level is also applicable to firms. Many displaced workers from industries and firms with premium wages suffer greater than average wage losses even when reemployed, since they do not find a new job in another firm paying similar premium wages.[4] Much of the downsizing has been concentrated among such large premium-wage firms; not surprisingly, their downsizings have drawn media attention and public notice, even as employment has expanded strongly elsewhere in the economy.

In the ten years from 1987 to 1997 total payroll employment in U.S. nonfarm industries rose by 20 percent. Manufacturing employment fell

1. See, for example, the monthly layoff estimates published by Challenger, Gray, and Christmas, a large out-placement firm.

2. See, for example, Katz and Summers (1989) and Dickens and Lang (1993) for a discussion of industry wage premiums.

3. See Davis and Haltiwanger (1991) for evidence on the relationship between establishment size and wage level in manufacturing industries.

4. Workers from high wage industries do have a better than average chance of finding work in the same or another high wage industry, but the probability is still less than 50 percent. See Gibbons and Katz (1989, pp. 21–23).

by 2 percent. The decline in employment among very large manufacturing firms appears to have been far greater. Using data from the Fortune Industrial 500 (which are all in the manufacturing and mining sectors), I tabulated the employment change among the fifty firms that had
more than 50,000 employees in 1987 and remained in existence in
1997. Over these ten years their work forces were reduced by an average
of 20 percent—more than 1.2 million workers—whereas total employment apparently rose in the remainder of the manufacturing industry.
Thirty-five firms lost employment; fifteen gained. Average employment
per firm among these fifty large firms fell from 126,000 workers in 1987
to 102,000 in 1997.[5] Although the employment data refer to the firms'
worldwide employment, American multinationals in the manufacturing sector added to their overseas employment during this period, while
their domestic employment was falling. And so it is unlikely that the
employment data cited here for the Fortune 500 firms overstate the
decline that has occurred in their domestic work forces.

Many of these firms acquired new components or lost subunits through
mergers, acquisitions, and spinoffs. Their employment change is, therefore, not an accurate measure of changes among the individual units of the
firm that existed in 1987. Nevertheless, the size and widespread nature of
their reported loss of employment strongly support the hypothesis of a disproportionate concentration of job reductions among such firms.

Subject to the same caveats as noted above, very large firms outside of
manufacturing in the aggregate added employment over the period,
although only modestly. Total employment among the thirty-six nonmanufacturing firms with over 50,000 employees in 1987 (who could be
identified in 1997) grew from 4.4 to 5.0 million, and the average employment per firm increased from 122,000 to 139,000.[6] But even in this sector
a slightly larger number of firms lost employment than gained it. The bulk
of the 21 million gain in the number of nonmanufacturing workers
occurred among firms other than the giants, spread across a wide variety of
industries.

In short, the large overall expansion in job availability during the past
decade was accompanied by a much smaller number of job losses concentrated precisely where they would receive the maximum attention: sizable

    5. See Lazonick and O'Sullivan (1997) for a similar tabulation of employment in large industrial
corporations, 1954–95, and by individual firm, 1990–95.
    6. These data are derived from the Fortune 500 list of "service" firms, which covers a wide range
of industries outside of manufacturing and mining.

layoffs among a relatively small number of very large firms paying premium wages.

The fact that media reporting on and public perceptions about rising job insecurity and layoffs may have been exaggerated by some of the special characteristics of recent employment changes does not mean that the phenomenon does not exist. For a more balanced perspective one must examine the economywide data on what has been happening to average job tenure, employee retention rates at individual firms, and the incidence of permanent layoffs among senior employees.

Job Tenure

As a first measure of changes in job stability we turn to the Bureau of Labor Statistics (BLS) periodic survey on the job tenure of American workers. Changes in average job tenure among American workers do not themselves allow one to draw conclusions about job security. A decline in average tenure could reflect an increase in the frequency and extent to which workers voluntarily quit, either in search of better jobs or for other personal reasons. Nevertheless, observing what has happened to job tenure can be a useful first step in an inquiry about job security.

Periodically (recently every four or five years), as a supplement to its monthly Current Population Survey of American households (CPS), the Bureau of the Census asks a special set of questions about how long each currently employed worker in the household has been with the same employer. The first bank of table 2-1 (labeled "As published") summarizes the results in terms of median years of tenure among male workers by age groups. For several reasons, however, comparisons of average tenure over long periods cannot be taken directly from the survey data. First, starting in 1983 the bureau changed the wording of the question about job tenure. In years before 1983 people were asked how long they had held their present job. Thereafter they were asked how long they had worked for their present employer. Because of the ambiguity of the question in the earlier years, some workers who had shifted to a new job within the same firm presumably answered in terms of the number of years they had held the new job rather than how long they had been with the same employer. As a measure of job tenure with the same firm the earlier answers were biased downward relative to responses from later surveys. On the other hand, the responses in years after 1981 were tabulated in a different way than earlier responses, with the effect of lowering the subsequent published data on

Table 2-1. *Years of Job Tenure (Males)*

Year	Mean of group medians (1991 weights)	All ages	Median years				
			16–24	*25–34*	*35–44*	*45–54*	*55–64*
As published							
1963	6.8	5.7	0.8	3.5	7.6	11.4	14.7
1973	6.4	4.6	0.7	3.2	6.5	11.5	14.4
1978	6.3	4.5	0.7	2.7	6.9	11.0	14.6
1981	6.3	4.0	0.9	2.9	6.6	11.0	14.8
1983	7.0	4.1	1.3	3.2	7.3	12.8	15.3
1987	6.6	4.0	1.1	3.1	7.0	11.8	14.5
1991	6.3	4.1	1.2	3.1	6.5	11.2	13.4
1996	5.6	4.0	1.0	3.0	6.1	10.1	10.5
1998	5.3	3.8	1.0	2.8	5.5	9.4	11.2
Adjusted data							
1983	6.3	4.0	0.9	2.9	6.6	11.0	14.8
1987	5.9	3.9	0.7	2.8	6.3	10.0	14.0
1991	5.5	4.0	0.8	2.8	5.8	9.4	12.9
1996	4.9	3.9	0.6	2.7	5.4	8.3	10.0
1998	4.6	3.7	0.6	2.5	4.8	7.6	10.7

Source: See text.

median tenure.[7] While the two changes worked in opposite directions, there is no way of knowing the extent to which they offset each other.[8]

The second bank of table 2-1 represents an attempt to make a very crude correction for the major discontinuities in the data. It arbitrarily assumes that no significant change occurred in the tenure data in the

7. For purposes of tabulation, those workers who responded to the tenure question with a round number of years (for example, five years) were assigned a tenure halfway between that round number and the next highest integer (for example, 5.5 years). But beginning in 1996 a round number was taken to be the midpoint of a six-month period on each side (for example, between 4.5 and 5.5 years, so that a tenure of five years was assigned to the worker). This change in tabulation methods tended to lower the medians tabulated for later years relative to earlier years. The change in tabulation methodology was actually introduced for the 1996 survey, but the Bureau of Labor Statistics—for whom the Census Bureau conducts the survey—went back and retabulated the responses for 1983 through 1991 according to the new methodology so that the data *from 1983 on* are comparable in this regard.

8. See BLS Release "Employee Tenure in the Mid-1990s," January 30, 1997. The explanatory note discusses the changes outlined above, and table 1 provides median tenure data by age and sex on

two-year interval between 1981 and 1983, reports the 1983 median tenure as equal to 1981 tenure, and then extrapolates that year's estimates with the post-1983 changes reported in the CPS surveys. Notice that in the years before 1983 the annual rate of change in median job tenure for individual age groups tended to be quite small, so that this method of constructing a continuous time series is not likely to produce a misleading set of trends.

If age groups are disregarded, median job tenure for all male workers fell substantially in the years before 1981 and stabilized thereafter. However, for many purposes this is a misleading piece of data. Much of the decline during those years was owed not to reductions in tenure among each age group but to the entry into the labor force of the baby boomers. The fraction of young workers—who change jobs much more frequently than older workers—grew very sharply, pushing downward the median tenure for the work force as a whole. The first column in table 2-1 calculates an average of the median tenures within each age group, using *constant* (1991) employment weights. When the influence of demographic changes is thereby removed, the "average" tenure is seen not to have declined very much. Between 1963 and 1981, median tenure fell moderately for 25- to 44-year-olds and was roughly stable for other age groups. (The median tenure for the total male labor force includes workers over 65, but the fixed-weight average in column 1 excludes those older workers; much of the sharp decline in their median tenure over the period was the result of a trend to earlier retirement, and for the purpose at hand their inclusion in the average would have given a misleading impression.)

As shown in table 2-1, the modest rate of decline in male tenure before 1981 accelerated after 1983. From 1963 to 1981 the constant-weighted average of group tenures fell by 0.4 percent a year; since 1983 it has fallen by a far larger 1.8 percent a year. The median tenure of all but the two youngest age groups fell substantially. While some of the decline in the 55–64 group undoubtedly reflects the continuing trend to earlier retirement, the reduction in average tenure among 35- to 54-year-olds—which is not affected by retirement trends—is quite large. In a reversal of the situation during the pre-1981 period, the widespread decline in average tenure since then is masked in the overall median tenure calculation by the

a consistent basis from 1983 through 1996. Earlier data are taken from various issues of the *Monthly Labor Review*, 1963–1982, and the 1998 data from the BLS release "Employee Tenure in 1998," September 23, 1998.

Table 2-2. *Median Years of Tenure, Employed Wage and Salary Workers,*
Age 25 and Over

	Median tenure			With constant (1991) employment weights		
Year	Total	Male	Female	Total	Male	Female
1983	5.0	5.9	4.2	6.0	7.8	4.7
1987	5.0	5.7	4.3	5.9	7.3	4.8
1991	4.8	5.4	4.3	5.8	6.9	4.9
1996	5.0	5.3	4.7	5.5	6.2	5.1
1998	4.7	4.9	4.4	5.3	5.9	4.9

Source: See text. The constant weighted data exclude workers 65 and over.

aging of the baby boomers, which decreased the relative importance of
younger and low-tenured age groups. The constant-weighted mean of the
group medians shows a substantial drop since 1983.

The long-term growth in the participation of women in the labor force,
and their rising average job attachment, operated to increase their average
job tenure relative to that of men over the past thirty-five years. Adjusted
for changes in the age composition of the work force, the average tenure of
women 25 to 64 years old rose from a little under 55 percent of male
tenure in 1963, to about 60 percent in 1981 and, more sharply, to over
80 percent by 1998.[9] From 1963 to 1981 the increased ratio reflected a
modest decline in average male tenure accompanied by virtual stability in
female tenure. The main change in the ratio of male to female tenure came
after 1983 (table 2-2). Since that time the fixed-weight male tenure fell
rather sharply while the female average again was almost constant.

Job Retention Rates

The job tenure characteristics of a population are determined by the mean
retention rates that have characterized various age groups at each point in
their working history. Retention rates simply measure what fraction of a

9. The age-adjusted average tenure estimates for females are based on the same calculations as
those used to construct the first column in table 2-1 for men: they are a fixed-weight (1991 employment by age cohort) average of median tenure by age cohorts, covering workers from 25 to 64 years old.
While the change in the tenure question after 1981 (see p. 33) affected the level of reported tenure, it
probably had only a small effect on the male-female ratio.

given age group remains with the same employer after the passage of some specified time—one can thus speak of "four-year" retention rates, "eight-year" retention rates, and so on. Various kinds of changes in labor market behavior or industrial structure can produce reductions in retention rates—for example, a greater propensity of workers to quit, a higher frequency of layoffs, or a shift of output among industries that differ in employment stability. Changes in behavior or structure that lower retention rates for most or all age groups will gradually produce a reduction in the average tenure of jobs in the labor force, as each cohort of workers ages, from entry into the labor force through retirement, with a smaller fraction continuing with the same employer at each stage of his or her career. Because the effect on average tenure of reduced retention rates is compounded as cohorts of workers age, relatively small changes in retention rates for short periods can, if sustained over time, have large consequences for overall employment stability.

In a recent paper David Neumark, Daniel Polsky, and Daniel Hansen (1997, hereafter cited as NPH), have used the data from the Census tenure surveys to estimate average four-year retention rates for workers over several four-year periods in the past fifteen years. After making a painstaking series of adjustments and corrections to the data, trying to make them as nearly comparable over time as possible, NPH calculated separate retention rates for workers grouped according to their tenure in the initial year of each of three four-year periods, 1983–87, 1987–91, and 1991–95.[10] For illustration, take the group of workers who reported in 1983 that their tenure with their current employer fell within the range of two to just under nine years. Compare that with the number of workers who, in the

10. NPH had to make a number of painstaking adjustments to the raw survey data to make them usable for estimating retention rates. For example: at longer job tenures many survey respondents give answers rounded to the nearest five-year intervals; NPH had to estimate a "smoothed" distribution by individual years. The regular tenure survey for 1995 was delayed a year, which created a five- rather than a four-year interval from the prior survey in 1991. NPH were able to substitute the responses from a special 1995 survey of the contingent work force which collected tenure data. But in that survey the wording of the tenure question was changed. In the earlier regular tenure surveys respondents were asked about "continuous" work for the same employer, but that word was dropped in 1995, a change which could affect the comparability of the data over time (since some job separations are temporary). NPH used data from the 1996 survey (in which respondents has been asked the tenure question in both forms) to adjust the 1995 results. The authors also made an estimate of the effects on retention rates of cyclical fluctuations in overall employment, and adjusted their data to eliminate those effects. The changes in retention rates they report, therefore, more nearly represent the consequence of longer-term and structural changes. They describe how they handled these problems and adjustments on pp. 12–20 of their 1997 article.

Table 2-3. *Four-Year Retention Rates*

Gender and tenure (years)	Rates		Change	
	1983–87	*1991–95*	*Absolute*	*Percent*
Both sexes, all tenures	.54	.54	0	0
Male 0 to <2	.35	.39	.04	11.4
2 to <9	.64	.58	−.05	−8.3
9 to <15	.86	.79	−.08	−8.7
15+	.66	.63	−.03	−4.1
Female 0 to <2	.31	.39	.08	27.2
2 to <9	.53	.54	.01	1.9
9 to <15	.78	.71	−.08	−9.8
15+	.56	.63	.08	13.6

Source: Neumark, Polsky, and Hansen (1997).

survey four years later, reported that they had been with their current employer between six and thirteen years. The latter group are those who had retained their jobs for an additional four years. The ratio of the number of survivors to the number in the initial group is the four-year retention rate for that group over the 1983–87 period.

Table 2-3 shows the resulting four-year retention rates for the periods 1983–87 and 1991–95, and the change in rates between the two periods as reported by NPH.[11] For men, worker retention rates fell at all levels of initial tenure, except for workers with less than two years of tenure. For men with initial tenures of two to fifteen years the reductions in retention rates amounted to about 9 percent. Conversely, women showed increased retention rates, except puzzlingly for those with initial tenure of nine to fifteen years.[12] As was pointed out earlier, the average tenure of a working population is determined by the compounding of retention rates as workers accumulate labor market experience over their working lives. A once-and-for-all change in labor market behavior and industrial structure that reduced retention rates for *all* tenure groups would slowly lead to a lower average tenure for the overall work force, as entering cohorts of workers

11. NPH (1997, table 4).

12. The absolute and percentage changes shown in the table were calculated from unrounded retention rates.

gradually felt the full effects of the lower rates as they accumulated labor market experience. Because of the compounding effects of a sequence of four-year retention rates, the ultimate decline in tenure would be proportionately much larger than the decline in the individual retention rates that produced it.[13]

During the period covered by the NPH study, 1983–87 to 1991–95, the increase in retention rates at low levels of tenure significantly attenuates the long-term effect of the reduction in retention rates that occurred (for males) in all higher tenure groups. Once workers have gained even a modest amount of tenure, there is a large rise in the probability that they will remain with the same firm for another four years (table 2-3). The increase between the early 1980s and the early 1990s in the retention rate for the lowest tenure group of males (0 to <2 years) had the effect of raising the proportion of workers moving into the next higher tenure group with its larger retention rate for the subsequent four years. Thus, the rise in retention rates for the low tenure group significantly attenuated the effect on average tenure of the reduction in the retention rates for the higher tenure groups.

Table 2-4 provides an illustration of this phenomenon with a rough and ready simulation of the "steady state" consequences of the change in the NPH four-year retention rates for men. In the left-hand panel the simulation starts with an incoming cohort of 100 workers into the zero to less than two-year tenure group. It then shows the probability of a member of that cohort achieving tenures of various lengths, assuming that the retention rates of the particular period persisted over the next twenty years. (To carry out the simulation I interpolated the retention rates estimated by NPH to yield rates for a sequence of tenure groupings at four-year intervals over a twenty-year range, and then compounded those rates to produce the results shown in table 2-4.)[14] Even though the retention rates for all male cohorts above the zero to less than two-year interval fell between 1983–87

---

13. As an illustration, suppose that the average retention (or "survival") rates for the next three four-year periods for a cohort of workers just entering the labor force are 0.40, 0.65, and 0.80 respectively. At the end of twelve years, 21 percent of those workers will have achieved twelve-year tenure with the same firm (0.40 × 0.65 × 0.80). If a 10 percent reduction occurs in each of these four-year retention rates, and the passage of time allows the new rates to compound their individual effects fully, only 15 percent of a new entering cohort will have achieved twelve years of tenure, a reduction of 29 percent.

14. Thus, for example, I estimated the retention rate for workers with six to thirteen years of tenure as follows: I assigned the NPH retention rates to their midpoint. The retention rate for the six- to thirteen-year tenure group (with a midpoint of 9.5 years) is estimated from a linear interpolation based on the midpoints of the NPH groups. The same approach was used to estimate retention rates for other

Table 2-4. *Simulated Distribution of Male Workers*
by Tenure Given Steady State Retention Rates

Midpoint of tenure interval (years)	Cohorts with 0 to <2 yrs.tenure, retention rates of period:		Cohorts with 2 to <9 yrs.tenure, retention rates of period:	
	1983–87	1991–95	1983–87	1991–95
1	100.0	100.0	. . .	. . .
5.5	32.7	36.3	100.0	100.0
9.5	20.8	21.2	63.7	58.1
13.5	16.2	15.0	49.6	41.3
17.5	13.4	11.4	40.8	31.3
21.5	9.7	7.7	29.5	21.3

Source: Based on author's interpolation of 4-year retention rates in Neumark, Polsky, and Hansen (1997). See text.

and 1991–95, the probability of achieving a nine-to-ten-year tenure was roughly unchanged. And the probability of reaching a tenure of seventeen to eighteen years declined only a little. However, if we confine our attention to workers who had already achieved significant tenure, we find that their probability of achieving really long tenure fell substantially, as illustrated in the right-hand panel of the table.

In sum, *if the changes in retention rates among men that have occurred in recent years do not reverse themselves*, three consequences will occur: first, after a year or so on a new job, workers will initially have an increased probability of remaining with the same employer for four to eight more years. But, second, having achieved that moderate tenure their chances of remaining with the same firm for an extended number of years thereafter will be reduced. And third, a simple extension of the calculations underlying the simulations in table 2-4 shows that the effect of the second consequence outweighs the effect of the first, so that average tenure for the male work force as a whole should continue to inch down for some time to come.[15]

---

tenure groups at four-year intervals, up to an interval of eighteen to twenty-five years. I assumed that the NPH retention rate for the open-ended fifteen plus years approximated the retention rate for individuals with twenty years of tenure.

15. The average refers to the mean of a truncated distribution that does not cover workers beyond the eighteen- to twenty-five-year tenure group.

The reduction in job attachment that has occurred among senior workers is not massive, but neither is it trivial—for example, if retention rates do
not change, workers who have already moved into the two-to-nine-year
tenure group, face a reduction of almost one-fourth in the probability of
eventually achieving tenure in the fourteen-to-twenty-one-year range (that
is, a decline from 40.8 to 31.3 percent).

The reduction in job attachment for men evidenced by the tenure data
is not itself evidence of greater job insecurity. To the extent the reduction in
retention rates and tenure averages reflected a rise in the frequency of voluntary quits, or among older workers, by a shift in preferences toward earlier retirement, they would not imply a loss of job security. However, if the
changes in average tenure over the past several decades were driven by a rising incidence of permanent and involuntary layoffs among workers with
significant job tenure, then they do give evidence of a decline in job security. An examination of trends in the BLS published data on displaced workers (from periodic supplements to the CPS), and some recent published
research based on other data sources will shed some light on this matter.

Worker Displacement Rates

Based on the responses collected in a special supplement to the CPS, the
Bureau of Labor Statistics periodically publishes data on the number of
"displaced workers." These are workers who have been involuntarily and
permanently laid off from their jobs because of plant closings, downsizing,
or insufficient work.[16] The data, usually collected in January or February of
every other year, are based on responses to a question that asks if workers
have been permanently laid off at any time over the prior three years for
one of the reasons listed above.[17]

16. I have used the term "downsizing" for the job loss category the BLS calls "position or shift abolished." In its displaced worker survey the BLS collects and makes available to researchers but does not
itself publish summary tabulations of data on the number of workers who are permanently displaced
for an additional set of reasons: the ending of a self-employment job, the completion of a seasonal job,
or "other" reasons. I employ the more restrictive definition of displaced workers that the BLS uses in
its publications, but will, at a later point, refer to other research that uses the broader definition.

17. In surveys before the one conducted in 1994 workers were asked whether they had been laid
off at any time over the prior *five* years. Since workers are asked to specify the year in which they were
laid off, the BLS was able to go back and retabulate the earlier data to include only layoffs during the
prior three years. But, as noted later, the pre-1994 tabulations are still not fully comparable with those
of subsequent years.

Since our interest is to examine the problem of job losses among senior workers I use the BLS tabulations of displacement among private nonfarm wage and salary workers who had three or more years of tenure. And since there is evidence that some workers who report they have been displaced in the year immediately before the survey are subsequently rehired by the same firm, the count of displaced workers is restricted to those who report they were displaced in the second and third years before the survey. Thus from the 1994 survey workers who were displaced sometime between January 1991 and December 1992 are counted. The *rate* of worker displacement for a time period (for example, 1991–92), is the ratio of the total number displaced during those two years to the average employment for the relevant age and tenure group for those years. It thus refers to the fraction of the employed labor force who are displaced in a given two-year period—it is not an annual rate of displacement (which the reader can calculate by dividing the numbers we give by 2).

Even though the displacement data do not include temporary layoffs, the incidence of plant closings and downsizing rises and falls with the business cycle. The displacement rate for wage and salary workers in the private nonfarm economy peaked in the recessions of 1981–82 and 1991, fell sharply in the two recoveries that followed, and by 1995–96 ended up below any of the earlier periods except 1987–88 (see the line labeled *actual* in figure 2-1). To determine if there has been any longer-term change in the displacement rate, however, we have to try to remove from the data the effects of the business cycle. Because of the recent changes in the behavior of the labor market, and in the absence of a full model of the relationship between permanent layoffs and the macro economy, it is not straightforward to choose what adjustment measure to use. Figure 2-1 is based on what I consider the preferred approach. I regressed the displacement rate on the current and one-year lagged unemployment rate and used that relationship to calculate what the displacement rate would have been in each period at a constant (6 percent) unemployment rate. The result is shown in the figure as the line labeled "adjusted."[18] It indicates that the cyclically adjusted displacement rate drifted slowly up from 3.9 percent in 1981–82 to 4.4 in 1993–94 and then in 1995–96 fell back to almost its original

18. The coefficients (and t-statistics) on current and lagged unemployment rates were, respectively, 0.81 (5.7) and –0.54 (4.0), with an adjusted R^2 of 0.82. The unemployment rate coefficients indicate that some of the cyclical effect came from the change (rather than the level) of unemployment.

Figure 2-1. *Worker Displacement Rate, 1981–82—1995–96*

Actual and adjusted to 6 percent unemployment

Percent

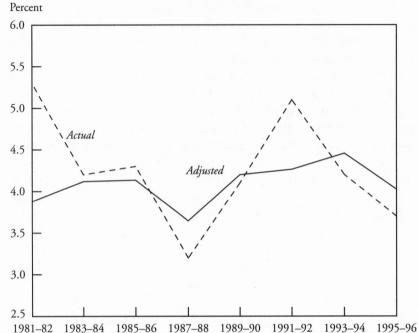

Source: Hipple (1997); unpublished BLS tabulations; and author's estimates. Data are for private nonfarm wage and salary workers.

level.[19] The rise in the overall adjusted displacement rate prior to 1995 means that for any given level of unemployment the *annual* rate of displacement rose by 0.25 percentage point over the period, that is, from 1.95 to 2.2 percent. While this was a nontrivial relative increase, its absolute

19. An alternative adjustment relates the displacement rate to the gap between the actual and the "full-employment" rate of unemployment or the "non-accelerating-inflation rate of unemployment" (NAIRU). A cyclical adjustment, based on a recent estimate of the NAIRU by Gordon (1998) in which it falls from 6.4 percent in 1989 to 5.3 percent in 1998, produces a slightly smaller updrift in the rate to 1993–94 (0.3 versus 0.5 percentage point) and a slightly higher R^2 (.87 versus .82). But the NAIRU is measured with much uncertainty. Moreover, this method of adjustment implies that the improving macroeconomic conditions that accompany a falling NAIRU have no effect on worker displacement, which is an unlikely outcome. Conceptually, the adjustment method used above seems the preferable one.

magnitude was a good bit less than one would infer from the media treatment of the "downsizing" problem.

With only eight observations the rise until 1993–94 in the cyclically corrected displacement rate is obviously not precisely measured. And it is too soon to judge if the recent decline in the rate is a "permanent" change.

In a 1997 article, Henry Farber intensively analyzed the results of the displaced workers survey from its inception. He found an increase of 14 percent in the three-year displacement rate between 1981–83 and 1993–95.[20] On a cyclically adjusted basis the rise would have been a good bit larger, since unemployment in 1993–95 was much lower than in 1981–83. Farber, however, covered a broader set of data than that which underlies the analysis presented above. Most important Farber includes as displaced workers not only those who reported being laid off for the three reasons recognized by the BLS in its definition of displaced workers (see "Worker Displacement Rates" and note 16) but also workers who cited "other" reasons as the cause of their layoff. Layoffs owing to this "other" category account for more than all of the rise in Farber's overall displacement rate—that is, unadjusted for cyclical variation, the rate of layoff confined to those displaced for the three reasons used in the BLS definition actually falls.[21] Farber notes that the "other" category may include misreported quits and possibly workers who accepted buyouts or other early retirement incentives. In analyzing involuntary separations we ought not to include the former group, while the appropriate treatment of the latter would depend on the circumstances of each case. The "other" category may also include individuals laid off for disciplinary or related reasons, whom we would presumably want to exclude from an analysis of job security. A more recent assessment of the displaced worker survey within the BLS suggests that "a fifth of the 'some other reason' responses *might* be interpreted as indicating a job displacement."[22] On balance, confining the data to workers laid off for the three reasons used in the BLS criteria seems the best choice.

Because this chapter concentrates on the job security of senior workers, the displacement rates examined are confined to workers who had three or more years of tenure in their prior job, for whom the costs of job loss tend

---

20. See Farber (1997, figure 1, table A-1).
21. See Farber (1997, figure 1, table A-1).
22. Esposito and Fisher (1998, executive summary).

to be substantial, whereas Farber includes all workers regardless of tenure.[23] And for the reasons cited earlier, I restrict the data to workers who reported a job loss in the second and third year preceding the survey; Farber includes job losses in all three years.

Both Farber's study and the analysis presented here conclude that the displacement rate increased between the early 1980s and the mid-1990s. Farber's data show that the "other" category of displacement—whose significance is unknown—essentially accounted for all of the rise. The overall rate of displacement arising from the combination of slack work, downsizing, and plant closings remained stable or declined. Our analysis indicates that once allowance is made for swings in the overall economy, the "core" displacement rate probably rose until 1993–94—at any given level of unemployment the rate of displacement was higher than it had been a decade or so earlier. By the time of the latest survey, however, the cyclically adjusted rate had fallen back, and the continuing decline in the unemployment rate had pushed the actual, unadjusted displacement rate down to a level still above 1987–88 but the second lowest since the surveys began.

Some people have suggested that increased worker fears about job insecurity played an important role in holding down wage growth and inflation in the 1990s. But the magnitude of the rise in the adjusted annual rate of displacement between the 1980s and 1993–94 seems much too small to have had a major impact on wage behavior, and since then the rate has fallen.

The Duration of Post-Layoff Unemployment

Figure 2-2 traces changes over time in the fraction of workers displaced from full-time jobs who were re-employed at the time the displaced worker

23. Farber has to make corrections to the survey results for a discontinuity in survey methods. As noted earlier, the surveys before 1994 asked workers about permanent displacements during the prior five years, leading to substantial recall errors for the earlier years. In 1994 and subsequent surveys the question was changed to refer to displacements during the prior three years. The BLS published retabulations of the earlier survey responses to exclude displacements in the fourth and fifth prior year. But, as Farber notes, the surveys ask workers to report only one displacement (the one from their longest job). Workers who lost their jobs in the fourth or fifth prior year, found new jobs, and were then displaced again before the survey—and Farber presents evidence from another source that such events were not uncommon—would not be counted as displaced in the BLS retabulation of the earlier survey responses. But such displacements would be recorded in the 1994 and later surveys, biasing up their average displacement rates relative to the earlier ones. (See Farber, 1997, pp. 62–66). Excluding work-

Figure 2-2. *Re-Employment of Displaced Workers*[a]

Fraction re-employed at survey date

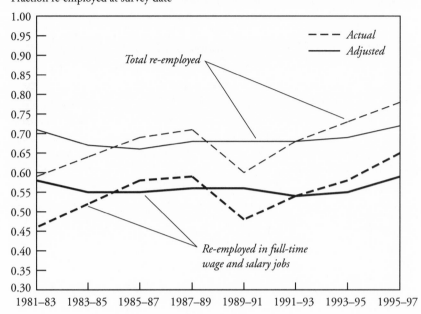

Source: Based on BLS tabulations from displaced worker surveys and author's estimates.

a. Workers displaced from full-time jobs (all tenure levels). Dashed lines are actual re-employment ratios. Solid lines are ratios adjusted to a constant 6 percent unemployment level.

survey was undertaken. Thus the first observation in figure 2-2, 1981–83, gives the percentage of workers laid off in those years who were re-employed by January 1984. The total re-employment number includes those with part-time jobs, the self-employed, and unpaid family workers. The data are limited to workers who had three years or more tenure in their pre-displacement jobs and unlike the data used earlier include layoffs in all three years covered by the survey.

The data are shown as originally reported and as adjusted to remove the estimated effect of fluctuations in the overall unemployment rate. The unadjusted re-employment rates showed a strong cyclical component and drifted up over time. But most of the upward drift simply reflected the

ers with less than three years of tenure on the prior job and excluding layoffs reported in the immediately prior year, however, substantially reduces, although it does not eliminate, this problem.

long-run improvement in the overall strength of the economy. Once adjusted for unemployment, the rates are essentially flat, with perhaps some sign of a little improvement in the final period.[24]

The re-employment rate (or better, its complement) is an imperfect measure of the extent to which displaced workers go without jobs, either unemployed or "out of the labor force." Individual workers shown as reemployed in the survey may have spent anywhere from one month to three years without a job. Some of them may have held a succession of temporary jobs in the period after displacement. Moreover, the BLS tabulation from which figure 2-2 was constructed includes workers laid off in the year immediately before the survey, some of whom—as we noted earlier—may have mistakenly reported temporary layoffs as permanent ones. Nevertheless, the survey data strongly suggest that the length of time between jobs for displaced workers has not significantly changed over the past fifteen years, except perhaps for a small improvement in the most recent period.

White-Collar versus Blue-Collar Displacement Rates

While the overall displacement rate has changed only moderately since the early 1980s there has been a shift in its occupational composition. As shown in table 2-5 the cyclically adjusted displacement rate for white-collar workers has risen fairly substantially relative to the blue-collar rate. These rates are based on data for all employed persons, not just the private nonfarm wage and salary workers whose displacement rates are shown in figure 2-1.[25] To assess how the relationship of the two rates has changed over time it was necessary to make a separate cyclical adjustment for the two rates, since recessions have a much larger effect on blue-collar than on white-collar rates. The two rates were regressed against the overall unemployment rate for the current period and with a year's lag, as well as a

24. The two reemployment fractions were regressed against the overall unemployment rate in the first and second years before the survey. Thus for the 1981–83 period, the dependent variables were the unemployment rates in 1983 and 1982

25. In the BLS tabulations displaced government and farm workers are included in the blue- and white-collar totals, and the employment denominator includes self-employed persons. If blue-collar workers are combined with service and agricultural workers, the basic story remains essentially the same—the white-collar displacement rate rises sharply relative to that for other workers. The paucity of the data limits the precision of the cyclical adjustments (but the t-statistic on the time trend in the white-collar equation was 4.3).

Table 2-5. *Ratio of White-Collar to Blue-Collar Displacement Rate*
Workers with 3 or more years tenure; cyclically adjusted

Period	White-collar rate	Blue-collar rate	Ratio
1981–82	1.6	4.4	.36
1983–84	1.9	4.4	.44
1985–86	2.4	4.0	.61
1987–88	2.4	3.9	.62
1989–90	2.8	4.9	.57
1991–92	3.1	3.8	.82
1993–94	3.3	4.2	.79
1995–96	3.1	4.0	.78

Source: BLS tabulations from displaced worker supplements and author's cyclical adjustments.

time trend for white-collar workers, and the results used to estimate what the rates would be with a constant 6 percent unemployment rate. At the beginning of the period permanent layoffs among white-collar workers were one-third as large as layoffs among blue-collar workers. Since then the white-collar rate has risen substantially, while the blue-collar rate has irregularly edged downward, until in the early 1990s the white-collar rate reached and then remained at four-fifths of the blue-collar rate. Some modest part of the rise in the white-collar rate appears to have come from an increase in layoffs among government workers.

Although the data do not reach far back into the past, a relatively high frequency of layoffs among blue-collar workers has most probably always existed. But layoffs of this magnitude are a new thing for white-collar workers, which may help explain the vivid public perceptions and media publicity about layoffs in recent years.

How Serious Are the Problems with the Tenure and Displacement Data?

The reliability of the tenure and displacement data depends on how accurately survey respondents to the CPS—those who are at home when the survey is taken and often not the worker whose tenure or layoff is being measured—recall events of some years ago. It is unlikely, however, that for the purposes we have used the data, the recall errors seriously bias the results.[26] But a good assessment of whether and to what extent job insecurity has been increasing is made more difficult by the fact that some parts of the relevant data are either not available over long enough periods or not fully comparable over the time they are available owing to changes in the wording of certain survey questions or in the procedures for tabulating and summarizing the results.

The text and the footnotes in the previous pages have identified some of the major problems. The survey question about workers' tenure with a firm was reworded starting in 1983, making comparison with the prior period difficult; the special survey on contingent work in 1995—whose responses about job tenure were needed by NPH to derive a series of four-year retention rates—asked a tenure question worded a little differently from the regular tenure surveys. From 1983 on, the reductions in median tenure for men 25 years of age and over shown in table 2-1 and the male-female comparisons in table 2-2 are not afflicted with the data incomparabilities discussed above. The comparability of the NPH four-year retention rates shown in table 2-3 and the longer-term survival probabilities estimated in table 2-4 depend on the accuracy of the corrections that NPH have to apply to the raw data from the 1995 special survey. The methodology for making the corrections appears reasonable, and the data on which the corrections are based seem appropriate to the task. Nevertheless, the corrections introduce an element of uncertainty into the retention rate estimates.

The displaced worker surveys in 1994 and later years asked workers to recall layoffs over the prior three years, whereas earlier surveys had asked for recollections of five years. For workers with less than three years of tenure, simply dropping the recollections for the fourth and fifth prior years in the earlier surveys introduces a potential downward bias in the results.[27] This problem is substantially lessened but not eliminated when the analysis is confined to workers with tenure of three years or more. In the 1996 survey there was a marked increase in nonresponse rates on the supplement questions. Special weights were therefore calculated for the 1996 and the 1998 supplements (and retroactively for 1994) to adjust for that nonresponse,

---

26. Many of the errors arise when respondents liberally round their answers about tenure to the nearest five- or even ten-year intervals. This is not so much of a problem when the average level of tenure for large demographic groups is measured, as we have done. However when researchers need information about *changes* in tenure, as NPH require to estimate their retention rates, then such errors can become a problem. While NPH made various smoothing adjustments to the raw data in order to correct for rounding and related problems, the resulting estimates are not error free.

27. See note 24.

but of course the introduction of the special weights may not have perfectly adjusted for the effects of the change in response rates. Other, apparently smaller, alterations were made in the survey and tabulation methodology in the 1994 and later surveys.

Some of the various changes discussed above in survey design and tabulation methodology for the displaced worker supplements would tend to raise and some to lower the more recent results compared with the earlier ones. Undoubtedly some net noncomparabilities remain. While I would judge it unlikely that their elimination would cause the pre-1995 updrift in the cyclically adjusted displacement rates depicted in figure 2-1 to disappear, the existence of such noncomparabilities attaches substantial uncertainty to any quantitative conclusions.

How Large Are the Earnings Losses from Layoffs?

To the extent that workers gradually acquire *general* skills that are widely applicable throughout many firms and industries, their productivity and their wages will tend to rise as they gain labor market experience, whether in one firm or in a succession of different firms. If laid off, they will be able to transfer to other employers their acquired human capital and command commensurate wages (as long as the layoff is not seen to be caused by their own failings). Thus wage premiums attributable to generally applicable skills are not *"at risk"* from layoffs. But there are also components of the wage premiums earned by workers that cannot be transferred to other firms and are therefore "at risk"—when laid-off workers are re-employed at a new firm, they will suffer a wage loss compared with what they earned in prior employment.[28] It is the magnitude of these at-risk wage premiums and the corresponding wage losses associated with layoffs that we want to estimate—their level and, if possible, their change over time.[29]

There are three potential sources of such at-risk wage premiums. First, workers may, and in most jobs generally do, acquire *firm-specific skills*—skills and competencies that are only applicable in the particular firm. These need not represent only a familiarity with the technological characteristics of the firm but can also reflect a wide range of acquired competencies—familiarity

28. See Becker (1964) for the seminal discussion of the forms of human capital and their effect on wage patterns.

29. For a recent review of the literature on the causes and magnitude of wage losses after job displacement see Kletzer (1998).

with firm procedures; knowing whom to call upon—and whom not—when the unexpected happens; an appreciation of the strengths and weaknesses of close associates in the firm; gradually acquired knowledge about the idiosyncrasies of firm customers; and so on down the line. As employees gradually develop these skills within a firm, their resultant rising productivity will tend to be reflected in an increasing wage premium.[30]

Second, given the necessarily limited information they possess, workers and firms initially know only a limited amount about their suitability for each other. The degree of a "good" match varies from case to case, and only over time do workers and firms learn the extent of the suitability of the match. Good matches typically lead to promotions, which in turn inaugurate a new period of learning about match suitability (remember the "Peter principle"). The gradual unfolding of knowledge about the goodness of the match thus leads to rising wages, as firms discover the latent productivity potential of an employee, and employees decide to stay with a good match. Poor matches lead to job separations and a new try by both parties. And, of course there is a wide spectrum of specific outcomes, ranging from highly successful to quite unsuccessful matches. Thus, increasing tenure with a firm will tend to be associated with increasing but differentiated wage premiums not just because of the development of firm-specific skills but through the process of learning by which the existence of a good match is confirmed, tested with promotion, and reconfirmed. Central to this whole process is the inherent inability of firms and workers, but especially the former, to make a full evaluation of each other except over time, through observing actual performance. Upon layoff, the typical employee with substantial tenure, who has passed the test of time and is paid accordingly, has to start all over again in a new firm, at a lower entering salary.[31]

A third possible source of at-risk wage premiums cited in the literature is the payment of antishirking bonuses. Because it is difficult to monitor closely the performance of individual workers there would be a natural tendency for employees to shirk on the job and put in less than expected effort if shirking were costless—that is, if upon being caught shirking and fired they could find another job at the same wage. By underpaying new employees, but promising a rising wage in the future, the firm can provide

---

30. See Becker (1964); Mincer (1986, 1988); Topel (1991).

31. For analyses of the labor market process by which workers are matched with jobs with higher wages, productivity, and durability see Jovanovic (1979); Hall (1982); Topel and Ward (1992).

incentives against shirking—employees with any length of service at the firm who are caught shirking and fired will have to start all over again at a lower rate of pay in another firm.[32]

Much ink has been spilled in the economic literature in controversies about the relative importance of these three phenomena described above— firm-specific human capital, good job matches, or antishirking bonuses— for the existence of at-risk wage premiums that are lost when layoffs occur.[33] In addition, Robert Gibbons and Lawrence Katz have argued that in situations other than plant closings, when employers have some discretion about whom they could lay off, they tend to dismiss workers with low ability.[34] Potential employers recognize this phenomenon, and it is reflected in their wage offers to such workers, thereby explaining a modest part of the observed wage losses suffered after displacement.

It is not our task here to assign responsibility to the various factors that cause earnings losses for diplaced workers. Our interest is in trying to estimate the size of those losses and whether their magnitude has changed in recent years.

The Magnitude of Earnings Losses for Tenured Employees after Permanent Layoff

Lori Kletzer, in her comprehensive 1998 survey of the literature about job displacement, summarizes the empirical evidence about the size of earnings losses suffered by workers after displacement. She cites, as one of the most important studies of earnings losses, the work of Louis Jacobson, Robert LaLonde, and Daniel Sullivan.[35] They used quarterly earnings histories from 1974 through 1986 of a 5 percent sample of Pennsylvania workers drawn from state administrative records. They estimated the earnings loss suffered by workers with six or more years of service with their employers

---

32. Lazear (1979, 1981).

33. For an overview of the controversy and evidence that the wage-tenure relationship stems primarily from the accumulation of firm-specific capital, see Topel (1991) and Kletzer (1989). For the view that a major part of the tenure wage-relationship stems from a sorting process involving the making of good matches and from the propensity of able employees to change jobs less often, see Altonji and Shakotko (1987) and Abraham and Farber (1987). (Any component of tenure-associated wage premiums that arise because more able and productive workers tend to change jobs less often would not be at risk upon layoffs—superior ability and productivity would earn commensurate pay in the new job.)

34. Gibbons and Katz (1991).

35. See Kletzer (1998, pp. 122–30); Jacobson, LaLonde, and Sullivan (1993a, 1993b).

who separated from their jobs between 1980 and 1986. Because they lacked data allowing them to distinguish permanent job loss from quits and other separations, they drew a subsample of workers whose firms' employment in the year following their departure was at least 30 percent below their maximum levels in the late 1970s, in the belief that the vast majority of such workers were separated involuntarily. In comparison with similar workers in the state who stayed with their jobs during the period, earnings of separated workers began to decline three to four years before separation. The authors attribute some of this pre-separation earnings decline to the incidence of temporary layoffs. Firms engaging in substantial permanent layoffs were apparently "in trouble" well before such layoffs began. Earnings in the year after separation fell still further. In the next several years earnings of displaced workers partially caught up with those of other workers, but even five years after separation a substantial gap remained, equal to about 25 percent of former earnings.[36]

These data have some shortcomings as measures of the likely magnitude of the at-risk component of wages. The worker-separations include a probably small but still unknowable number of workers who voluntarily quit, in many cases for a job paying higher wages. The data also include workers who reported earnings in any year even though they may have been unemployed for part of the year. As a consequence the average earnings loss includes not only the effect of lower wages in postseparation jobs but also, for some workers, the effect of zero wages during later periods of unemployment. The study, nevertheless, is especially valuable for two reasons. First, it points to the fact that firms whose work forces are greatly reduced have typically been through a period of substantial troubles and reduced labor demand well before the mass layoffs occur. And second, it shows that the earnings losses of displaced workers with substantial job tenure tend to persist long after they are re-employed.

Evidence from the Displaced Worker Survey

To look closely at more recent evidence about the extent to which the wage premiums earned by senior workers[37] are at risk in case of layoff and are more than a payoff to general labor market experience or an artifact of the

36. Jacobson, LaLonde, and Sullivan (1993a, p.137).
37. For convenience the term "senior" workers refers to workers who have stayed with a firm long enough to have a significant at-risk wage component included in their compensation.

Table 2-6. *Earnings Changes among Displaced Workers by Years of Tenure on Old Job, 1993–96*

	Years of tenure on old job				Average	
					All	6 years
Item	0–5	6–10	11–15	16+	tenures	or more
All re-employed workers						
Percent wage loss in new job	8	18	29	39	14	27
(Standard error)	(1)	(3)	(5)	(5)	(1)	(2)
Percent of displaced workers	71	15	6	8	100	29
Percent owing to plant closing	39	46	49	51	42	48
Re-employed in full-time wage and salary jobs						
Percent wage loss in new job	2	8	21	28	6	17

Source: See text.

greater staying power of more able employees, we examined the data from the 1996 and 1998 Displaced Worker Surveys, whose evidence about the frequency of layoffs was summarized above. Besides asking about the occurrence of layoffs, the survey also asks for other information, including the earnings of the laid-off employee in the old job and, if re-employed at the time of the survey, the wage in the new job.

As noted earlier, there is evidence that a significant number of layoffs reported in the year immediately before the survey turn out not to be permanent. Workers are subsequently recalled. To deal with this problem I included only the data for layoffs reported for the first two years covered by each survey, 1993–94 and 1995–96. These years were in the early and middle years of an economic recovery, with an unemployment rate averaging 6.5 and 5.5 percent respectively. The data include displaced full-time wage and salary employees of both sexes, age 20 to 64, who were laid off from the private nonfarm sector and were re-employed in wage and salary jobs at the time of the survey.[38] Table 2-6 shows the wage loss suffered by workers who had found new jobs by the time of the survey. For comparability, all earnings levels were adjusted to the date of the 1998 survey (February 1998) with changes in the employment cost index (ECI) for wages and salaries in private industry. Thus, the reported lost wages,

38. Workers reporting weekly earnings of less than sixty dollars on either old or new jobs were excluded.

which reflected the situation one or more years prior to the survey, are increased to reflect the economywide wage increases between then and the time of the survey.[39]

The restriction of reported displacements to those that occurred in the second and third year before the surveys improves the quality of the data. I made separate estimates of wage losses for workers displaced in 1995 and 1997, the years immediately before the 1996 and 1998 surveys. The average wage losses for re-employed workers who reported layoffs in those years were lower than the losses shown in table 2-6 from displacements in the other years covered by the surveys. The results appear to confirm the suspicion that some workers who reported displacement in those years and were re-employed by the time of the survey had been recalled to their old jobs. However, the gain in data quality comes at a cost—about 36 percent of the survey sample is lost. With 2,049 total observations, the size of the remaining sample becomes rather small for the highest tenure groupings. But while the magnitude of the average wage loss at high levels of tenure is therefore measured with some imprecision, the broad pattern of wage losses that escalate with the length of tenure is similar to the findings of studies using earlier data from displaced worker surveys and with what we know about the shape of the wage-tenure profile.[40] Since the study by Jacobson, LaLonde, and Sullivan finds that the earnings of workers in establishments that experience large-scale layoffs often do not keep pace with wages elsewhere in the economy, the losses shown in table 2-6 should be seen as those suffered by displaced workers relative to the wage path experienced by similar workers at other firms elsewhere in the economy.[41] Alternatively, the wage data could be adjusted by the consumer price index, which would in effect give estimates of the absolute (rather than relative) real wage loss suffered by the displaced workers.Substituting this adjustment would lower the wage losses reported in table 2-6 by about one and a half percentage points.

Clearly, for workers with substantial tenure on the old job the immediate earnings losses from displacement are very large. The re-employed displaced workers can typically expect their earnings to begin rising with seniority increments and for some of them with promotions. But as we dis-

39. The wage losses for each tenure group are the means of individual changes in log wages, which were then converted to the equivalent percentage loss.

40. See Topel (1991); Kletzer (1991).

41. This measure of the loss does not include any seniority increments that the displaced workers may have forgone because of layoff.

cuss below, many of them continue to remain permanently well below the earnings path of similar workers who do not suffer displacement.

All of the displaced workers whose wage losses are measured in table 2-6 had previously been working full time in wage and salary jobs. But some 11 percent of them (17 percent in the highest tenure category) were re-employed in part-time jobs at the time of the survey, and their earnings losses were very much larger than those who found full-time jobs. To a lesser extent this was also true of displaced workers who turned to self-employment.[42] When we exclude those re-employed in part-time and self-employment jobs, the average earnings losses become much smaller, as shown in the bottom line of the table. It is likely that many of the part-time and self-employed workers eventually find full-time wage and salary jobs. But it is also likely that a number of older workers take part-time jobs as a transition to retirement.

So far the analysis has been restricted to employees who worked full time at their old jobs (thirty-five hours or more a week). A separate tabulation of re-employed workers displaced from part-time jobs, most of whom had accumulated only a little tenure, reveals that more than half of them had found full-time jobs. On average their weekly earnings were substantially higher than they had been. Even though such workers accounted for only 10 percent of all re-employed displaced workers, their inclusion in the esti-mates would have significantly lowered the average size of the wage loss. The estimates of wage losses among workers displaced from full-time jobs, which are used throughout this chapter, are thus somewhat higher than estimates based on displacement from both full- and part-time jobs.

The percentage of displaced workers with long tenure is much less than proportional to their representation in the work force. Thus, employees with eleven or more years of tenure made up 24 percent of the work force but only 15 percent of displaced workers.[43] Moreover, half of the displace-ments among longer-tenured workers arise from plant closings (rather than from reasons of "insufficient work" or "position or shift abolished"), whereas only 39 percent of displacements among the shortest-tenured

42. Beginning with the last several surveys, earnings data were collected for the relatively small number of workers, previously in wage and salary jobs, who turned to self-employment after displace-ment. They are included in table 2-6. Had they been omitted, the average earnings loss for all workers shown in table 2-6 would have been about 1 percentage point lower. I increased the supplement weights for this group for the 1996 survey to compensate for the fact that in this survey the earnings of the self-employed were not collected for the two outgoing rotation groups in the sample.

43. These tenure data are taken from BLS tabulations from the January 1996 tenure supplement to the CPS.

workers were so caused. The accumulation of substantial tenure with a firm still appears to carry with it some degree of job security, at least relative to more junior workers.

Additional Factors Affecting the Size of At-Risk Wage Premiums

The age of workers has an important effect on the earnings loss they are likely to suffer upon displacement. The fewer the years left to retirement, the shorter the time period over which potential employers can recoup any direct and indirect investments they might make in a new employee's human capital development. Employers may also believe that for some types of jobs older workers are likely to be less capable of quick learning and adaptation. For the former, and possibly the latter, of these reasons a wide range of jobs may be foreclosed to older displaced job seekers, and other jobs may be available only at an extra wage discount. We can indirectly observe the effects of age on earnings losses in figure 2-3, which compares the wages of displaced workers with various amounts of tenure on their old job with what those same workers earned in their new jobs.[44] At the time of the survey, the average age of workers with tenure of five years or less was 36 years; among workers with more than sixteen years of tenure at the same firm the average age was 49. After displacement, workers with substantial tenure not only took much larger earnings losses than their less-tenured colleagues, their earnings were little higher than those of much younger re-employed workers with a good bit less experience and lower than workers with six to ten years of tenure in their old jobs. The low re-employment earnings of the highest tenure category (sixteen+ years) stems in part from the fact that a larger-than-average fraction of such workers (27 percent versus 17 percent) found work in part-time or self-employment jobs.

The Long-Term Cost of Job Loss

So far we have concentrated on the immediate loss in annual wages suffered by re-employed displaced workers, as measured by the difference between their wage in the first year or so on the new job versus their pre-displacement wage. But under normal circumstances workers can expect

---

44. In figure 2-3 the earnings plotted for each tenure category on both lost and new jobs is the mean weekly earnings for that category.

Figure 2-3. *Weekly Earnings of Re-Employed Displaced Workers*

Weekly wage (dollars)

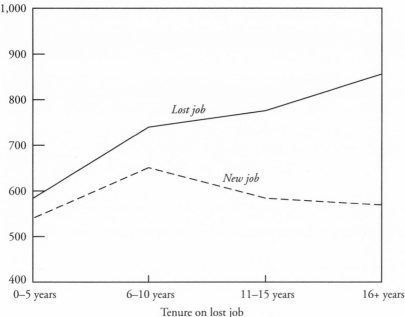

Tenure on lost job

Source: Data from displaced worker surveys of February 1996 and February 1998. See text for details.

their wage with the new firm to grow over time as they accumulate additional labor market experience and their tenure at the new firm begins to rise. Of course, workers with the same characteristics elsewhere in the economy, who were not laid off, will also receive wage increments as their seniority and work experience accumulate. But almost all studies of the effect of tenure on wages find that the wage gains are larger in the early years of tenure and then tend to become less steep and eventually flatten out. And so, if we measure the annual wage loss as the difference between the expected wage path of the worker had she stayed at the old firm and her wage path at the new firm, the size of that loss will shrink over time. However, displaced older workers with large wage losses may be too close to retirement to have a chance for substantial catch-up.

As I noted earlier, Jacobson, LaLonde, and Sullivan followed workers with six or more years of tenure for several years after displacement. They found that the difference between their postdisplacement earnings and those of other workers with similar characteristics who had not been displaced, while narrowing initially, still averaged, five years after displacement, about 25 percent of former earnings. When I converted their estimates to the economywide wage levels prevailing in early 1998, this figure amounted to an annual earnings loss of $9,400. On the assumption that annual losses remained at about $8,600 in the time remaining to retirement at age 65, the authors estimated a cumulative present value for losses which (when converted to early 1998 wage levels) amounted to $115,000. These losses include not only those occurring after displacement but the reduction in earnings that according to Jacobson, LaLonde, and Sullivan, typically began several years before displacement.[45]

As an alternative rough estimate of lifetime earnings losses, for workers with very long seniority on the job, I combined the average initial earnings losses from the 1996 and 1998 displaced workers surveys with Robert Topel's equations for tenure and experience premiums to simulate and compare two average earnings paths for workers with eleven to twenty years of tenure: an economywide "baseline" path for those who did not suffer displacement; and a "new" path for re-employed displaced workers of similar age and tenure on the lost job.[46] Since the Topel equations for tenure and experience profiles relate to hourly wages rather than weekly earnings, and were derived from data for white males, I restricted the simulation to white males employed in full-time wage and salary jobs. For such workers with eleven to twenty years of tenure in the old job, who on average had nineteen years to go before retirement (assumed to be age 63) the cumulative present value of losses, measured as the difference between the two paths and converted to early 1998 economywide wage levels, was about $155,000, equal to 22 percent of the cumulative earnings of the nondisplaced workers. (The details of the simulation are given in the Appendix to this chapter).

Use of the Topel experience and tenure equations to project future earning of both sets of workers—those who were not displaced and those displaced and re-employed at the survey date—implies that both remain with their current employer until retirement, or that any subsequent job changes are such as to preserve, on average, the difference in present values resulting from the simulation. It also incorporates the arguable and uncertain assumption that re-employed displaced workers begin to accumulate

---

45. Jacobson, LaLonde, and Sullivan (1993a, 1993b).
46. Topel (1991).

seniority premiums at the same rate as other newly hired workers. In a 1989 article Lori Kletzer analyzed the early (1984 and 1986) displaced worker surveys, which covered displacements during the five preceding years.[47] Displaced workers with jobs at the survey date had been employed for various lengths of time, up to something a little less than five years, prior to that date. Kletzer found that the survey-date earnings of otherwise similar workers were positively related to the length of time they had been at work since their displacement, with a coefficient that implied a substantially faster catch-up in the earlier years than reflected in the Topel tenure and experience equations. However, Jacobson, LaLonde, and Sullivan found that rapid catch-up ceased rather quickly. And given the nature of their data an important part of that early rapid catch-up reflected workers moving from immediate postdisplacement quarters of unemployment and zero earnings into employment status.

I cannot resolve this question. On the one hand, it is possible that the $155,000 lifetime earnings loss cited above is too high because it understates the extent of catch-up for re-employed workers. On the other hand, it understates losses for three reasons: it measures earnings losses from those at the date of displacement rather than from the higher amounts of several years earlier. It is based only on workers who found full-time re-employment and ignores the substantially larger losses of a significant minority of workers who took part-time and self-employment jobs. The part-time jobs may be only a temporary state for most workers but a permanent condition for some older ones. And finally it excludes any losses during periods of unemployment between displacement and the survey date. On balance, the simulation lends weight to the conclusion that for workers with substantial tenure, job loss leads to very large and long-lasting earnings losses.

Have Wage Losses from Layoffs Increased during the Past Two Decades?

From the displaced worker surveys between 1984 and 1996, Henry Farber tabulated the mean percentage loss in weekly earnings for displaced workers at the time of the survey during seven overlapping three-year periods—1981–83, 1983–85, and so on through 1993–95. The average wage loss over the entire period for all workers—including both full and part time—

47. Kletzer (1989).

was 13 percent.[48] The magnitude of the losses is clearly cyclical. The losses were about 15 percent in the three periods that included part or all of the recessions of 1982 and 1990–91. The mean losses then dropped into the 10 to 13 percent range in the other periods.

There was no discernible time trend in the size of the earnings losses as tabulated by Farber. But in a pooled time series and cross-section regression, which related earnings losses to age, education, gender, reason for job loss, and several other variables, Farber finds evidence that the 1993–95 period had significantly and substantially lower average losses than did other periods.

Using the 1984 and 1986 displaced workers supplements, Robert Topel tabulated the initial earnings losses at various tenure levels suffered by re-employed displaced workers who reported job losses in the years 1979 through 1985.[49] For a number of reasons, it is difficult to compare his results with the 1993–96 tabulations in table 2-6. Unemployment was much higher in the earlier period. Topel used the survey responses of displacements over the prior five years rather than the responses from the second and third prior years that underlie table 2-6, and this difference in time spans could affect the results. He covered only male workers and used a price not a wage deflator. Most important, his text does not indicate whether he included workers losing part-time jobs and those finding re-employment in such jobs. On the assumption that, in the absence of any statement to the contrary, Topel included all types of transitions (and there is some indirect evidence that he may in fact have done so),[50] I re-tabulated the 1993–96 survey responses to include displacements of part-time workers and made other changes to come as close as possible to Topel's universe of workers and his methodology. Averaged across *all* tenure classes the 1979–85 earnings losses were much larger than the retabulated 1993–96 losses, 13 percent versus 3 percent. But all of the difference was accounted for by workers with less than eleven years of tenure. Among very long

48. Farber (1997, p.101, table 9). Farber includes workers displaced for "other" reasons from surveys before 1994, but earnings data on the old job were not collected for such workers in subsequent surveys. Wage losses within each period were deflated by the CPI.

49. Topel (1991).

50. In their 1991 article cited earlier, Gibbons and Katz examine layoffs among male workers from the same 1984 and 1986 displaced workers surveys that Topel used. But they explicitly restrict their analysis to workers displaced from full-time jobs and report a sample size that is only 78 percent as large as Topel's. There are some other, smaller, differences in their coverage of workers, but they cannot explain anything like this large a discrepancy in sample size, suggesting that Topel did indeed include workers displaced from part-time jobs.

tenured workers, those with eleven or more years of tenure, the losses are virtually the same in the two periods (slightly under 30 percent) despite lower unemployment during the latter period.[51]

Part of this result might conceivably reflect a much lower cyclical sensitivity of earnings losses among long-tenured than among short-tenured workers. Some of it may arise from other irreconcilable differences between the two sets of data. But the difference in the two sets of tabulations may also signal the possibility that, for any given level of unemployment, the costs of job loss for workers with very long tenure have worsened relative to those with shorter tenures, or even absolutely.

Although it is difficult to assess the extent to which the wage losses experienced by re-employed displaced workers have been changing during the past fifteen years by more than can be explained by changes in the level of unemployment, I can assert with some confidence that the slowdown in aggregate productivity and real wage growth that occurred after 1973 had the effect of worsening the absolute economic losses from permanent layoffs.

As discussed earlier, re-employed displaced workers start to accumulate further general labor market experience as well as tenure with the new firm. As a consequence their wages rise and the *absolute* size of their loss in living standards begins to fall. If economywide real wage gains are also occurring, their wages will rise still more rapidly. Since workers throughout the economy would also be receiving these gains, the *relative* wage position of the former displaced workers would not be helped by the macroproductivity growth, but the absolute size of the loss in their living standards would steadily shrink. Before 1973, economywide productivity and real wage gains averaged around 2.5 percent a year. A wage loss of, say, 20 percent could be recouped in about nine years from this source alone. But after 1973, productivity growth fell to an average of 1.1 percent a year. And real wages measured in terms of purchasing power over consumer goods, increased very little between 1973 and 1996. Re-employed workers could still benefit from their accumulation of general and firm-specific human capital in their new jobs, but they experienced a far slower overall recoupment of their

51. Topel reports losses for two long-tenure categories, eleven to twenty years, and twenty-one years and over. Retabulated 1993–96 results for each of those two categories were virtually the same as his, and the 30 percent loss given in the text was derived as a weighted average of the two, using 1993–96 relative weights in both cases—Topel gives no weights. It is worth noting that for workers with less than five years of tenure, the retabulated 1993–96 data show a small earnings gain, in part reflecting the fact that the large bulk of workers displaced from part-time jobs are in the lowest tenure category, and more than half of those are re-employed in full-time jobs.

wage losses than was earlier possible. If the Topel equations measuring wage premiums from tenure and experience are a reasonable measure of the wage path for re-employed displaced workers, many of them with substantial tenure would not recover their prior living standards after ten or fifteen years in a world of zero real wage growth. The effects of the post-1973 slow-down in productivity and real wage growth on the ability of displaced workers to recover their old living standards almost surely helps explain increased worker concern about the problem of job insecurity during the past several decades.

Conclusion

In combination, the results of the CPS tenure and displaced worker surveys and an analysis of the retention rates calculated by NPH suggest two conclusions. One, a modest decrease in job attachment has occurred for the overall labor force since the early 1980s. For women and young men average job tenure has remained about constant, while it has fallen substantially—25 to 30 percent—for mature male workers. If job retention rates for those workers remain at current levels, the average length of association between workers and their employers will continue to inch downward, as the current cohort of workers ages to retirement. Two, there is evidence, subject to some uncertainty, that during the 1980s and early 1990s the decrease in job attachment was accompanied by a modestly higher rate of permanent layoffs among senior workers. Adjusted to remove the effect of cyclical fluctuations, the displacement rate drifted slowly upward from the early 1980s until 1993–94, but then it fell back. On balance, changes in the overall displacement rate are unlikely to have played a large role in creating the surprising recent moderation in wage demands.

The sometimes apocalyptic tone of media coverage about the issue of downsizing and the depth of public concern may be explainable by several features of the layoffs that have been occurring over the past fifteen years or so. As employment was rising generally it was falling within the manufacturing sector. And within that sector, a large number of the country's largest and most visible firms, typically paying above-scale wages, cut their employment by disproportionate amounts. And even outside of manufacturing, layoffs occurred among more than half of the very large firms (employing 50,000 or more), even as employment was expanding rapidly elsewhere in the nonmanufacturing sectors. Although some of the reported employment losses may have represented spinoffs of units to other firms, the magnitude of layoffs among large-size, high-paying firms was substantial, eye-catching, and atypical of what was going on elsewhere in the economy. Moreover, during the 1980s and early 1990s the previously low rate of displacement among white-collar workers began to approach that among blue-collar workers. Small wonder that downsizing and job insecurity began to be perceived as a major economic threat.

The magnitude of the earnings losses suffered after permanent job separation by workers with substantial tenure at their firm is very large. Among workers laid off in 1993 through 1996 and subsequently re-employed, the initial wage loss ranged from an average of 18 percent for those with six to ten years of tenure to 39 percent for those with more than fifteen years of tenure. Losses were especially large among older workers with long prior job attachments earning substantial seniority premiums, whose age and closeness to retirement discouraged potential employers from hiring them for promising jobs that required substantial learning and training. For displaced workers with relatively long tenure on the old job, a substantial shortfall of wages relative to similar workers who were not displaced tends to persist for many years and for many is never made up before retirement.

While relatively sparse, the available evidence does not suggest that the size of earnings losses for the average displaced worker has increased since the early 1980s. We do know, however, that for most of the past twenty-five years the *absolute* value of the loss in living standards among displaced senior workers has been larger than it was for the prior postwar generation, owing to the post-1973 slowdown in the growth of productivity and real wages. The slowdown in real wage growth after 1973 has greatly lowered the extent to which re-employed displaced workers with substantial wage losses are able in subsequent years to climb back to the absolute living standards they had earlier enjoyed. This sluggishness of economywide real wage growth in recent decades has thus worsened the consequences of layoffs and downsizing and almost surely contributed to the heightened public concern about job security.

Appendix: A Simulation of Long-Term Earnings Losses

The estimate of lifetime earnings losses for displaced workers with eleven to twenty years of tenure combines the displaced workers survey data on initial losses with Topel's 1991 estimates of the slope of the wage profile as a function of tenure and experience. For workers with eleven to twenty years of tenure prior to time of displacement, I calculated two hypothetical wage paths. The first, a "baseline" path, was simulated by assuming there had been no worker displacement and then using Topel's estimates of the slope of the tenure and experience premium to increment the mean predisplacement average wage of workers in that group until retirement, assumed to occur at age 63. The second simulation, a "new" path, started from the lower mean earnings in the new job and followed the Topel tenure and experience track upward, beginning at zero tenure in the first year and also continuing until retirement. As noted in the text, the baseline earnings path does not represent what displaced workers might have earned had they stayed with the same firm (in many cases a troubled one), but the earnings path of other similar workers elsewhere in the economy.

The average worker was assumed to have been employed for a year before the survey date, and the survey wage to have reflected one year's wage and experience premium. A number of auxiliary assumptions had to be made. Economywide wage gains were assumed to occur equally in old and new jobs. As was done for the data in table 2-6 all earnings values were "inflated" to the date of the 1998 survey using the ECI index for wages and salaries in private industry. Averaged over the remaining years of their working lives, workers on old and new jobs were assumed to work 94 percent of full time—that is, future unemployment or slack work is assumed to reduce their full-time employment by 6 percent. The simulated future stream of real earnings was discounted to present value at a 4 percent discount rate.

References

Abraham, Katherine G., and Henry S. Farber. 1987. "Job Duration, Seniority, and Earnings." *American Economic Review* 77 (June): 278–97.

Altonji, Joseph C., and Robert A. Shakotko. 1987. "Do Wages Rise with Job Seniority?" *Review of Economic Studies* 54 (July): 437–59.

Becker, Gary S. 1964. *Human Capital: A Theoretical and Empirical Analysis, with Special Reference to Education*. Columbia University Press (for NBER).

Davis, Steve J., and John Haltiwanger. 1991. "Wage Dispersion between and within U.S. Manufacturing Plants, 1963–86." *Brookings Papers on Economic Activity, Microeconomics*: 115–80.

Dickens, William T., and Kevin Lang. 1993. "Labor Market Segmentation Theory: Reconsidering the Evidence." In *Labor Economics: Problems in Analyzing Labor Markets*, edited by William Darity, Jr., 141–80. Kluwer Academic.

Esposito, James L., and Sylvia Fisher. 1998. *A Summary of Quality Assessment Research Conducted on the 1996 Displaced-Worker Job-Tenure Occupational Mobility Supplement*. BLS Statistical Notes Number 43. Washington: Bureau of Labor Statistics.

Farber, Henry S. 1997. "The Changing Face of Job Loss in the United States." *Brookings Papers on Economic Activity, Microeconomics:* 55–128.

Gibbons, Robert, and Lawrence Katz. 1989. "Does Unmeasured Ability Explain Inter-Industry Wage Differences?" Working Paper 3182. Cambridge, Mass.: National Bureau of Economic Research.

———. 1991. "Layoffs and Lemons." *Journal of Labor Economics* 9 (October): 351–80.

Gordon, Robert J. 1998. "Foundation of the Goldilocks Economy: Supply Shocks and the Time-Varying NAIRU." *Brookings Papers on Economic Activity* 2: 297–333.

Hall, Robert E. 1982. "The Importance of Lifetime Jobs in the U.S. Economy." *American Economic Review* 72 (September): 716–24.

Hipple, Steven. 1997. "Worker Displacement in an Expanding Economy." *Monthly Labor Review* 120 (December): 26–39.

Jacobson, Louis S., Robert J. LaLonde, and Daniel G. Sullivan. 1993a. *The Costs of Worker Dislocation.* Kalamzoo, Mich.: W. E. Upjohn Institute for Employment Research.

———. 1993b. "Earnings Losses of Displaced Workers." *American Economic Review* 83 (September): 685–709.

Jovanovic, Boyan. 1979. "Job Matching and the Theory of Turnover." *Journal of Political Economy* 87 (October): 972–90.

Katz, Lawrence F., and Laurence H. Summers. 1989. "Industry Rents: Evidence and Implications." *Brookings Papers on Economic Activity* Special Issue: 209–75.

Kletzer, Lori G. 1989. "Returns to Seniority after Permanent Job Loss." *American Economic Review* 79 (June): 536–43.

———. 1998. "Job Displacement." *Journal of Economic Perspectives* 12 (Winter): 115–36.

Lazear, Edward P. 1979. "Why Is There Mandatory Retirement?" *Journal of Political Economy* 87 (December): 1261–84.

———.1981. "Agency, Earnings Profiles, Productivity, and Hours Restrictions." *American Economic Review* 71 (September): 606–20.

Lazonick, William, and Mary O'Sullivan. 1997. *Investment in Innovation.* 37 ed. Jerome Levy Economics Institute.

Mincer, Jacob. 1986. "Wage Changes in Job Changes." *Research in Labor Economics,* vol. 8, edited by Ronald G. Ehrenberg, 171–97. JAI Press.

———. 1988. "Job Training, Wage Growth and Labor Turnover." Working Paper 2690. Cambridge, Mass.: National Bureau of Economic Research.

Neumark, David, Daniel Polsky, and Daniel Hansen. 1997. "Has Job Stability Declined Yet? New Evidence for the 1990's." Working Paper 6330. Cambridge, Mass.: National Bureau of Economic Research.

Topel, Robert. 1991. "Specific Capital, Mobility, and Wages: Wages Rise with Job Seniority." *Journal of Political Economy* 99 (February): 145–77.

Topel, Robert, and Michael Ward. 1992. "Job Mobility and the Careers of Young Men." *Quarterly Journal of Economics* 107 (May): 439–79.

U.S. Bureau of Labor Statistics. 1963–98. Articles on "Employee Tenure" (and unpublished tabulations). *Monthly Labor Review,* various issues.

———. 1984–1998. Articles on "Worker Displacement" (and unpublished BLS tabulations). *Monthly Labor Review,* various issues.

3

PETER CAPPELLI

Market-Mediated Employment: The Historical Context

Reports of corporate life over the past decade suggest a historic break in the social contract between employers and employees. One cover story after another described how the traditional relationship in the workplace has been overthrown, especially in large corporations.[1]

—Entire functions and departments are routinely outsourced to contractors as businesses focus their operations on a few aspects that they do well. In many cases, contractors come inside the organization's facilities, working alongside the company's direct employees. The contractors hire and manage their own work teams, sometimes negotiating pay and employment terms independently for each worker. Operating departments are given tremendous autonomy and are increasingly treated like separate businesses.

—The prospect of a lifetime career with the same company is in decline, especially for managerial employees, and job security has become much more contingent on the short-term needs of the employer. Middle management has shrunk as employers thin their bureaucratic structures. Employers routinely tell workers that the only real job security is "employ-

1. *Fortune* and *Business Week* ran prominent cover stories on this topic. See William Bridges, "The End of the Job," September 19, 1994, pp. 62–74; and "Rethinking Work," *Business Week,* October 17, 1994, p. 74.

ability," the ability to find a job elsewhere, and the fear of layoffs has kept employee performance high even in the face of massive restructurings.

—Companies increasingly rely on hiring from the outside market to meet their skill needs. Silicon Valley is presented as the model for a competitive economy with its rapid mobility of employees across companies and "learning by doing" as opposed to formal training programs. Employers make much greater use of temporary workers with no real attachment to the firm.

—Top executives see their compensation tied to the market value of their firm, pressing them to act more like shareholders than traditional managers, and the gap between their compensation and that of lower-level workers has grown to enormous proportions. Pay for most employees is increasingly contingent on individual performance as well as on the performance of the organization. Seniority in the job plays much less of a role in determining pay, and efforts to maintain a wage structure where the rates of pay are adjusted to maintain the perception of equity are virtually dead.

—Centralized human resource functions that designed elaborate internal employment practices and developed long-term human resource plans are pared down. Personnel decisions are increasingly shifted to line management, and the human resource function is encouraged simply to support line management. In some establishments, autonomous work groups of skilled employees decide by themselves who gets hired, how work should be allocated, how to train new workers, and in some cases how pay increases should be distributed among members of the group.

The common thread in these developments is that they represent a weakening of the traditional bureaucratic employment relationship, with its long-term commitments and internal labor market practices, that buffered employment from outside markets. In its place, more immediate market forces increasingly govern the internal operations of firms and, in turn, the employment relationship. The phrase "market-mediated employment relationships" might describe the new practices that are based around more short-term, contractual relationships shaped by pressures from the outside labor market and individualized incentives.

These developments are often presented as revolutionary, as breaking down best practice principles about how employees should be managed and companies run. Many thoughtful observers of the workplace are deeply disturbed by these developments because they see them as violating fundamental and long-standing social conventions.

In fact, all of these "new" developments just described were widespread in American industry one hundred years ago, where they constituted the dominant model for managing firms and employees. What we now refer to as the "traditional" system of long-term employment relationships and employment practices associated with internal labor markets is a relatively recent invention, in existence for much of the economy only since the 1930s. The recent accounts of virtual companies run by venture capitalists who outsource operations, hire contractors to work inside, and rely on short-term employees and contingent compensation may in fact be a better description of the business world at the beginning of the twentieth century than at its end.

We've Already Been Here

A look at why arm's-length, market-mediated employment practices were prevalent in earlier periods helps illustrate several general points. First and most obviously, it suggests that even basic characteristics of the employment relationship are not permanent features but change and adapt to new environments. The second and more important is the nature of changes in employment relationships. Sometimes an implicit assumption is made that the "traditional" model of corporate employment based on internal labor markets is innately superior as a method for managing employees. It replaced older methods, one might argue, because it was better, much as the internal combustion engine replaced the horse. One implication of this view is that employers who abandon it now are making a fundamental mistake that will come back to haunt them.

A closer look at the arm's-length, market-mediated practices from the period before internal labor markets suggests that, at least from the employer's perspective, they may well have been adapted to the prevailing circumstances. Their decline and the subsequent rise of internalized employment practices were not necessarily driven by inherent problems with the older system but by changes in the governance structure of firms and, most important, in production techniques that created a new set of demands on the employment relationship.

The environment for business has been changing in the United States over the past decade or two—by some accounts dramatically so. Some of the developments in the governance and organizational structure of firms look remarkably like the systems that were in place around the turn of the century. That we are seeing a return of arm's-length, market-based employment practices at the same time may be more than a coincidence. It may suggest that older, more market-based systems are better adapted to this new environment. More fundamentally, the developments suggest that employment systems are contingent on other aspects of the business environment. Trying to assess which ones are better or worse independent of their operating context is probably a mistake.

In a more speculative mode, the resurgence of arm's-length, market-mediated employment relationships may suggest that the model of life-time employment relationships based on internal labor markets was the aberration and not the present developments. We may in the future look back on the lifetime employment relationships that operated in large corporations from roughly the 1930s through the 1980s as a temporary departure from the more robust forms of market-mediated relationships.

Back to the Future?

The historian Alfred Chandler Jr. describes the typical firm of the 1800s as a single-unit operation that carried out only one function. These firms were masters of the 1990s advice that companies should pare themselves down to their core competencies—those few tasks that they truly performed well—and either outsource or get rid of everything else.[2]

To illustrate, before William Durant brought General Motors together as a giant corporation with an enormous management bureaucracy tailored to complex, integrated operations, he headed one of the largest carriage companies in the country. His original operation, the Durant-Dort Carriage Company, was strictly a marketing company, much like the modern Subaru automobile company in the United States. Just as Subaru has its cars built for it by Fuji Heavy Industries, Durant-Dort contracted with a local builder to produce the carriages that Durant-Dort branded, distributed, and sold. When its business expanded beyond the capacity that its builder could meet, Durant-Dort itself took on the problem of building carriages. Here again, it tried to keep its tasks as simple as possible. The company only assembled carriages, contracting with local suppliers to provide all of the components.[3]

2. Chandler (1977).
3. This example is described in Chandler (1962, p. 116).

The governance and organizational structure of early streamlined companies like Durant-Dort was equally simple. At the top were executives who were partners or major stockholders. In other words, the executives were the venture capitalists of their day who were compensated (in some cases enormously so) based on the value of their shares. They handled finances and managed the distribution and sale of goods. There were no managers beneath them. "As late as 1840," Chandler notes, "there were no middle managers in the United States."[4] The authority for producing goods was pushed down to the foremen and workers who did the work. The organizational chart of these early firms, as a result, was almost completely flat.

What seems most striking about these firms from a contemporary perspective is how little they did inside the organization itself and how many of their operations were handled by the market. Instead of administrative principles, Chandler observes that "the activities of these small, personally-owned and managed enterprises were coordinated and monitored by market and price mechanisms."[5] Many of their functions were pushed onto outside suppliers and contractors. And the list of outsourced activities went well beyond acquiring parts and supplies. For example, few, if any, large companies sold their products directly to individual consumers. They supplied independent merchants who sold the products for them. And their relationships with these merchant-customers were typically managed not by their own employees but by independent agents. In the late 1800s, a company like DuPont had 215 independent agents who managed the relationships for the company with merchants across the country. These agents were paid on the basis of commissions and in many cases represented more than one company.[6] Some agents, like those working for the McCormick agricultural implement company, had enough business that they hired their own salesmen to work for them (indirectly for the client companies).[7] Arrangements like these persist in some industries, especially in insurance where independent agents and brokers represent many insurance companies to clients. In industries like pharmaceuticals, they are making a comeback in the 1990s with sophisticated independent companies that supply hospitals and pharmacies, mediating the relationship between customers and manufacturers.

4. Chandler (1977, p. 3).
5. Chandler (1977, p. 3).
6. See Zunz (1990, p. 17). A description of agents having multiple clients, including DuPont, is provided in Yates (1989, p. 205).
7. Yates (1989, p. 157).

It is no surprise to find companies in the late 1800s taking a similar approach to issues associated with production. The earliest and perhaps the most extreme examples of arm's-length, market-mediated relationships were the "purchase" system, where merchants bought finished products from home workers who provided their own tools and materials, and the more common "putting-out" system, where the merchant played the role of coordinator—providing materials to the workers and paying them based on finished product (minus material costs). In both cases, the relationships with the home workers were like those of independent contractors.

The putting-out system was important in the United States mainly in clothing and shoemaking and dominant in England across many industries. The introduction of more productive and expensive manufacturing equipment helped bring about its demise as jobs moved inside factories.[8] It persisted for some time in England even after the rise of factories in part because it was more flexible and easier to adjust output to changing market demand—the overhead costs were lower, and what fixed costs existed were pushed off onto the workers. Putting out also allowed the employer to reach out to a larger labor force that lived beyond commuting distance to its operation, essentially increasing the employer's bargaining power with labor by increasing labor supply.[9] The flexibility and reduced fixed costs of the purchase and putting-out systems (especially real estate and facilities costs) are the same advantages put forward by companies today who ask their permanent employees to become independent contractors and work under contract to the company. Employers pursue similar strategies when they ask employees to give up their offices and operate from home with the employer covering the costs of their materials and home office. These employees are managed with compensation heavily contingent on individual performance.[10]

Whether or not the putting-out system was inherently inefficient is a topic of considerable debate. There is agreement that embezzlement was a serious problem. Because the relationship between raw material inputs and cloth outputs was variable, the contractors had some scope to divert materials to their own purposes, especially the better-quality materials. Battles between owners and workers over rights to scrap material—and how much

---

8. See Landes (1969).

9. See Jones (1982).

10. These arrangements are most common for sales representatives whose individual performance can easily be monitored. The concept of "hoteling," providing only temporary office space on a reservation basis to employees who operate from the road, is a related development.

was scrap—were commonplace. The other problem was the variability of effort and production generated by the home workers. If other opportunities came up, such as the periodic demands of farm labor, these workers could well stop their contracting work altogether. Although the owner did not have to pay them, his capital in the form of material costs was tied up, and his production and business also ground to a halt. These classic agency problems make clear that an arm's-length contracting relationship based on payment per unit of output did not eliminate management problems for the owners.[11] Contemporary critics of outsourcing arrangements point to exactly the same problems of monitoring quality and performance and ensuring reliability when work moves outside the firm. (Advocates of agency theory are inclined to see these problems as manageable through properly designed contracts and incentive systems.)

Relationships similar to the putting-out system also existed for products that were produced on site. In the mining industry, for example, it was typical well into the twentieth century for coal miners to contract separately for the mining of each rock face. The lead worker or hewer would negotiate a rate of pay on behalf of the group and contract again when moving onto a different rock face.[12] These arrangements persist into the present, in uranium mines in the United States, for example.[13]

The development of more complicated production systems and factory production that brought production inside a company's facility did not eliminate arm's-length employment relationships and market-based contracting. In the steel industry, for example, skilled workers before 1890 were paid like contractors, a given rate per ton of steel produced, with the added twist that the rate varied with the price of steel, an early form of gainsharing (that is, when increases in company performance are shared with employees). These skilled workers, in turn, hired their own less skilled "helpers" and paid them out of their own pocket.[14] At some iron works, the organization of work was like a modern "autonomous work team," where the skilled workers had complete autonomy to make all the employment decisions such as hiring, wage setting, and training.[15] In the textile industry, senior workers engaged in spinning and weaving were paid piece rates

11. A good description of the problems of the putting-out system is in Clawson (1980, pp. 44–49).
12. Trist and Bamforth (1951, p. 6).
13. I am indebted to Sid Winter for this observation.
14. See Stone (1974).
15. See Montgomery (1976, p. 488).

that they negotiated with the owners. Then they hired their own assistants to whom they paid straight wages.[16]

Even in the most complex manufacturing facilities, elaborate contracting relationships were common, and they bear more than a passing resemblance to contemporary practices. The "inside contracting system" saw contractors taking the entire responsibility for some aspect of the production process and doing the work inside the owner's premises, just as today vendors like Xerox operate on-site reprographic centers for client companies or as EDS runs its data processing activities (the "vendor-on-premises" concept). In a sense, the inside contracting system was a logical extension of the putting-out system, bringing that arm's-length relationship inside a firm's facilities. Contractors received payments from the firm for each unit they produced and in turn had nearly complete autonomy over how production occurred, including all aspects of employee management. Arrangements with employees differed across contractors even though they all worked in the same facility. Contractors hired their own workers, paying them piece rates and managing them however they saw fit.[17]

To deal with the problem of employees wasting materials in the putting-out system, each employee was in turn treated as if the employee were a contractor. At the Springfield Armory, which many consider the prototype of the modern American factory, separate accounts were kept on each worker that detailed the worker's scrap and wastage rates, tools, units of product in process, and materials used. Workers had to pay for any excess materials used, and they also had to place their personal stamp on each piece they completed so that parts found defective could be deducted from their earnings.[18] Compensation contingent on individual performance and associated monitoring of workers has made a comeback in the contemporary workplace as information technology has made it possible to produce detailed reports on the performance of workers in jobs as diverse as call center operators and nurses.

The inside contractor system operated extensively in the manufacturing sector. Some estimates suggest that as many as 50 percent of the manufacturing employees in the United States in the late 1800s were employed by inside contractors.[19] The Pope Manufacturing Company, for example, was

16. See, for example, Tilly and Tilly (1998, p. 42).
17. See Wiebe (1967), for evidence about the considerable autonomy that contractors had in their operations.
18. See Buttrick (1952, p. 205).
19. Clawson (1980, pp. 72–80).

fairly typical in having twenty departments all run by inside contractors in the manufacture of the Columbia bicycle.[20]

The advantages of these arrangements for the owners and operators of the firm were many, and the list sounds much like the contemporary attributes offered for outsourcing operations. Perhaps the most important was that the owners did not have to involve themselves in the details of production. They did not have to be experts themselves in the production process nor worry about personnel matters associated with getting the work done. They could concentrate on their own competencies, which concerned finance, and not have to worry about monitoring production for performance, quality, and costs. In short, the internal control function was unnecessary.

Further, many of the risks of doing business were pushed off from the firm and onto its contractors and in turn onto their employees. For example, if sales eroded, the firm did not have to keep paying their contractors. The practices described in the steel industry went even further toward arrangements that parallel modern gainsharing. Here, if production was steady but prices declined, the firm was protected because the payments to skilled workers also declined, limiting substantially the firm's liability. Particularly with the inside contracting model, capital costs are significantly lower for the firm because at least some of the equipment is owned and financed by the contractors and their workers, not by the firm.

These attributes contributed to significantly lower costs for using contractors. A representative example comes from the early years of the Pratt and Whitney machining company. Like most manufacturers, Pratt and Whitney had its own employees who worked side by side with the internal contractors. If a contractor was too busy to take on a new order, it went to Pratt and Whitney's own employees where the total costs of completing the order would be about 70 percent higher than if the contractor had done it. The higher quality and wages of Pratt and Whitney's own employees were only part of the explanation. The rest was related to the greater managerial expertise of the contractor, motivated by his more direct interest in the outcome. An illustrative story comes from the Baldwin Locomotive Works in Philadelphia, where a contractor's operation relied on using one of Baldwin's elevators. When the elevator broke, it usually took the company about two weeks to fix it; when a contractor was relying on that elevator

20. Hounshell (1984, p. 205).

and had responsibility for maintaining it, he managed to get it repaired in two days.[21]

The contractor relationship was negotiated, influenced by the possibility of competition from other contractors, and forced the contractors to share at least some of the gains of their innovations with the owners. When contracts were renegotiated—generally once a year—the owners were typically able to cut the prices paid to the contractors and gain some share of the benefit from the contractors' cost-cutting innovations. A dramatic example of the declining costs to owners comes from the Winchester Repeating Arms Company, where the prices received by its contractors fell by half over twenty years.[22]

A cottage industry has developed around debating what caused the downfall of the inside contractor system, but something of a consensus has developed around the following factors. The economist Oliver Williamson has been eloquent and exhaustive in arguing that these arm's-length, market-based transactions had inherent inefficiencies. For example, when William Durant's carriage business expanded rapidly, he found that his suppliers were not always reliable—they often had other customers whose needs had to be met as well. And so the Durant-Dort Carriage Company eventually got into the business of making its own components to ensure their supply. The owner was very vulnerable to mistakes that the contractors might make, such as defective parts or poor delivery. Trying to create incentives for the contractors to meet the interests of the owners was a very difficult exercise that eventually required the owners to monitor their contractors more carefully on matters of quality, a burdensome exercise. As technology advanced and became more integrated, it became more difficult to identify discrete products that could easily be turned over to contractors and more difficult to coordinate them.

Other issues concerned labor and the need to improve its efficiency. In steel, the skilled workers who had something like contractor status resisted productivity improvements that made them work harder or took some of their control away. In manufacturing, the contractors were forced to innovate and improve productivity by cutting their payments, but other problems remained. The historian John Buttrick observed that "difficulty with the labor force was almost the sole reason for the abandonment of the

21. These examples come from Clawson (1980, pp. 81–89).
22. See Clawson (1980, p. 81).

(inside contracting) system."[23] Among the labor problems were high turn-over and difficulty in securing adequate supplies of skilled labor. Whether employees' concerns about inequitable treatment across contractors in the same facility contributed to these problems is a topic for speculation. In the 1990s, an extensive literature has grown up around similar issues, the conflicts, real or imagined, between "permanent" and contract employees working side by side in the same organization.[24] Petty rivalries among contractors may have been more pertinent. The production manager at the Singer Sewing Machine Company, for example, describes how one contractor was guilty of "much fault finding with the work received from (another contractor), much of which fault is merely theoretical and having no practical value."[25]

The most immediate issue for the owners, however, and the one that led to change was simply the owner's sense that the contractors were making too much money. Because contractors were working inside the owner's facility, it was very easy for the owners to learn what the contractors did. The set-up of machines and equipment, the work flow, the management of employees, and other functions could easily be duplicated, especially if the workers remained in place. It did not take long for the owners to ask themselves why they could not get rid of the contractor and replace him with a much cheaper foreman. Once the design and set-up work had been done, all the foreman had to do was manage the employees, and a foreman cost only about one-third what a contractor earned.[26]

The experience at the Singer Sewing Machine Company illustrates the pattern. When the company's own employees could not master assembly operations using interchangeable parts, the owners brought in contractors who took over the operations and got the process to work. Once the company learned how to duplicate what the contractors had done, it became unhappy with the level of profits the contractors were receiving and replaced them with much cheaper foremen who were paid salaries.[27]

23. Buttrick (1952, p. 217).
24. Among the surprising results from this research is that the more contingent workers do not nec-essarily have worse attitudes—or even lower commitment—than the permanent ones. See, for ex-ample, Smith (1994, pp. 284–307); Pearce (1993, pp. 1082–96).
25. Hounshell (1984, p. 110).
26. Clawson (1980, pp. 119–21) calculates that "the average contractor made more than three times as much as the average employee," so a foreman could receive some premium over the average worker and still cost about one-third of the contractor's earnings.
27. Nelson (1975, p. 37).

Owners across the country moved rather quickly to replace inside contractors with foremen. Buttrick reports that efforts to convert individual contractors to foremen were not always successful, and about half quit rather than suffer the decline in income and status.[28] This is a contrast with outsourcing efforts in contemporary companies, where direct employees are sometimes forced to become contractors or work for contractors of the company, performing the same tasks they had as direct employees. In the contemporary examples, the move from employee to contractor is generally seen as a step down even though in many cases total compensation may increase.

With the new arrangement, when the foreman-as-employee replaced the contractor, the contractor's work force also became direct employees of the company. Internal contracting soon went from being a central feature of American industry to an artifact as the companies converted the contractor's role to a management function. But in many ways, the actual practice of managing employees and the underlying principles of managing employees changed relatively little. It does not seem that the owners objected to the principles of inside contracting, just to the amount that they had to pay the contractors. Several examples suggest that they tried to preserve the basic arm's-length relationship and incentive structure that inside contracting offered. Henry Towne, the industrial engineer, developed a widely used payment plan for direct employees involving incentives to cut costs that was the same plan that had previously been in place for inside contractors. Frederick Taylor adapted Towne's plan for his own gain-sharing ideas.[29] It was typical for the new foreman position to be paid piece rates based on his group or department performance, creating incentives and a governance arrangement that were identical to those operating for the inside contractors. Other foremen received bonuses based on cost-cutting incentives. In the contemporary world, the rise of incentive compensation for middle management based on work group performance is similar in design, although not in magnitude, to the incentives that faced inside contractors and foremen.

For the individual employee, even less changed. They were for all intents and purposes working for the foreman, not the company, just as they were the employees of the contractor before. The foremen retained virtually all of the powers that the contractors had (retaining less of the gains from cost

28. Buttrick (1958, p. 220).
29. Chandler (1977, p. 275).

reductions, however), such as unilateral control over hiring, firing, management of employees, and control over operations in their area, at least through World War I.[30] The threat of unemployment provided the incentive for employees to go along with the cost-cutting incentives that motivated the foremen.[31] The compensation for individual workers was based on piece rates, much as before. Given these powers, the individual employee could be forgiven for failing to notice much difference between being managed by an inside contractor or a foreman.

Piecework proved an imperfect mechanism for managing workers. Besides requiring monitoring of output and quality, it left the pace of work to the individual workers. Some worked faster, some slower, and slow performance meant that capital was sitting idle. Because workers had the very real belief that the piece work rates would be cut if they worked fast and earned lots of money—just as the contractor's rates were cut—they typically held back effort. The main task of foremen as a result was to get that effort up.

And the technique they used became known as the "drive" system. One might think of this in contemporary terms as motivating through stress. Speaking before a congressional committee in 1912, a steel industry expert explained the role of foreman in that industry where they were known as "pushers."

Q: Who does he push?

A: He pushes the gang.

Q: Explain how he does this.

A: It is done in various ways, through motions and profanity.[32]

In other words, the foreman yelled at the workers, threatened them, and sometimes hit them to make them work faster and harder. Harvard Professor Sumner Slichter's investigation of factory work in 1919 concluded, "The dominant note of the 'drive' system is to inspire the workmen with awe and fear of management, and having developed that fear among them to take advantage of it."[33]

Despite its unpleasantness, the drive system worked for the company. What made it work was the fear of getting fired at a time when jobs were scarce, worker savings minimal, and unemployment insurance was nonexistent. The manager of a Philadelphia manufacturing plant explained its

30. Clawson (1980, p. 127).
31. Jacoby (1985, p. 20).
32. Nelson (1975, p. 43).
33. Slichter cited in Nelson (1975).

simple strategy for managing people. "We are not interested in problems of personnel. We have a lot of work; but there are always more people to do it than there is work."[34] Sanford M. Jacoby reports how this fear was manipulated in a typical plant. The assistant superintendent asked, "Has anyone been fired from this shop today?" When told no, he replied, "Well, then, fire a couple of 'em. It'll put the fear of God in their hearts."[35] Boyd Fisher, vice president of the Detroit Executives' Club in 1917, described what he saw as the enlightened view of personnel management. "I believe in firing men as a final means of keeping men," using the threat of dismissal to maintain discipline.[36]

The only real relationship between the company and its workers in this period was between workers and their foreman, and that relationship was typically transient. Turnover rates averaging 150 percent a year in the early 1900s were common for industrial employees.[37] A representative from ARMCO steel described how its typical foremen addressed the staffing problem raised by so many workers leaving. "He went to the gate, looked over the crowd, picked out the man he wanted, and hired him."[38] The foreman would set a rate of pay on the spot, one that might well vary from what workers hired the day before were paid or what those hired by a different foreman received.

Eventually, employee turnover would become a major problem for employers and a spur for changing employee relationships when production arrangements changed. But it is not obvious how much of a problem it was for most industrial firms, or in some cases even for their employees, in the early years of the twentieth century. An inordinate amount of the high turnover was accounted for by very short service employees: 64 percent of the total turnover in a survey of Philadelphia area firms, for example, was among employees with less than three months of tenure. Turnover was also disproportionately high among unskilled workers, in some cases 300 percent a year, roughly ten times the level for clerical workers (which included lower administrative functions) in the same plants.[39] Some large part of the overall high turnover might therefore be seen as relatively costless screening of employees, with the ones who did not fit leaving relatively quickly: The

34. Willits (1917, p. 3).
35. Jacoby (1985, p. 21).
36. Fisher (1917, p. 16).
37. See Brissenden and Frankel (1922).
38. Nelson (1975, p. 79).
39. Bezanson and others (1925, p. 5).

cost of replacing unskilled workers who accounted for most of the turnover was reasonably low since their work required few firm-specific skills. The fixed costs of employment, such as unemployment insurance liabilities, had yet to develop in this period, making the costs of all turnover less expensive. The turnover of more experienced workers was often relatively modest.

More important, turnover was actually functional in several ways, not only for the employees but even for the employers. Virtually all of the turnover of experienced employees (the ones whose departure was potentially costly) reported in studies like Slichter's or the Philadelphia studies noted above was for jobs elsewhere, generally in the same industry. Even where the nature of the work varied considerably across companies, situations suggesting firm-specific knowledge and potentially costly turnover, mobility across firms was essential for the employees in order to secure a broad base of experience. The researchers in the Philadelphia study found in their interviews with employees the "consistent reiteration of the belief that such changes were essential in developing the highest degree of skill." A toolmaker in their study offered the following career advice to new workers. "Move around not so much for the sake of changing, but with a desire to add some special experience along new lines and when [you have] found a good position settle down and go after the best position in the shop."[40] This is, of course, the same advice that employers in the 1990s were giving their employees in the form of the "employability" doctrine—that changing jobs and employers was essential in order to keep learning and maintain employment prospects.

Mobility of this kind across employers also facilitated organizational learning. Other toolmakers in the Philadelphia study observed that in shops where men stayed put, they were protective of their jobs and their knowledge and resisted new ideas, "but in a shop where men have changed a lot, you will find the men cannot do enough for each other in helping a new man make good."[41]

Perhaps the best illustration of the functional nature of more casual employment relationships is provided by Anne Bezanson's study of the tapestry industry in the decades before the Great Depression. Her description of the arrangements in that industry sound remarkably like contemporary descriptions of the high-tech industries in Silicon Valley: the twenty-five tapestry mills concentrated in Philadelphia accounted for

40. Bezanson and others (1925, p. 71).
41. Bezanson and others (1925, p. 72).

94 percent of the U.S. output, creating a dense network of employers. Most of them were small and offered little formal training to their employees. Workers generally began working in related industries before moving into the tapestry companies. And the movement of employees across firms was regular, taking skills and information about production methods with them. As she concludes, "Both the employer and the workman gain from the informal passing of technical knowledge from shop-to-shop. Only in this way is trade lore passed from mill to mill."[42] This flow of skills and information across firms not only helped keep the existing firms competitive but also helped attract firms to locate in that area as they could easily acquire a work force skilled in the latest industry techniques. The accounts of Silicon Valley's distinctive competencies point in particular to the movement of employees across firms that facilitates their own learning and that of their firms as well, allowing them to restructure and innovate quickly.[43]

Others observed that industries that developed their own employees internally through apprenticeships and retained them often lacked breadth in employee skills, while more craft-based industries saw a regular pattern of hiring across employers to meet skill needs.[44] Researchers in this earlier period noted that especially where jobs were organized along something like craft models, turnover was not necessarily disruptive to organizations. One studying health care noted, "An efficient hospital may depend on having a resident-medical staff which is continually being recruited, with a relatively high turnover rate, rather than on having a staff of physicians who are afraid to cut loose and practice for themselves, and who by lingering on the staff for many years markedly reduce the turnover rate."[45]

Of course, for the employees, voluntary turnover is almost by definition functional given that workers only move if they see an advantage in doing so. The turnover studies noted above uniformly observe that differences in potential earnings drive interplant mobility and are useful in that sense in forcing management to adjust their wages and keep them up to market levels. A follow-up to the Philadelphia turnover studies some forty years later concluded that the key to upward mobility for production workers continued to be changing employers, despite the rise of internal labor markets. "Upward movement between broad levels of skill for most members of a

42. Bezanson (1928, pp. 463–64).
43. See, for example, Saxenian (1994).
44. Nelson (1975, pp. 90–105).
45. Industrial Relations Department of the Wharton School (1922).

labor force is likely to result from changing employers, not from staying with one employer."[46]

The Need for a Different System

Reformers argued long and hard about the inequities and problems associated with the drive system, generally with little effect.[47] The real challenge to the drive system and to arm's-length, transactional employment systems more generally came not from their internal problems but indirectly from innovations in industrial engineering that altered the production process. The lack of coordination across work groups was a problem common to the drive system and internal contracting that made it challenging to manage the flow of work within an organization.

Other aspects of the problem were more fundamental. The simple problem of finding where a breakdown in the flow of production was occurring was beyond the capabilities of most companies because they lacked any basic cost accounting. Alfred Chandler describes how early leaders of the Society of Mechanical Engineers wrestled with this problem by developing basic systems for tracking components and products as they moved through the work process. Even these primitive internal control systems were able to reveal bottlenecks, suggesting where efficiencies could be achieved, and in the process challenging the control and power of the foremen over the production process.[48]

Frederick W. Taylor was perhaps the most creative of the early engineers working on internal control systems, and the famous system he proposed created a separate planning department in each company to determine scientifically the optimal flow of work through the system.[49] But the implica-

46. Palmer (1962, p. 4).

47. Not everyone saw the bureaucratic management practices associated with internal labor markets as better for employees than systems like internal contracting or even the putting-out system. Specifically, workers had more autonomy in the latter. See, for example, Marglin (1974, pp. 60–112).

48. See Chandler (1977, pp. 272–77) for a description.

49. The best-known aspects of "Taylorism" are the changes in the way tasks are performed—how they are broken down into simple components based on time and motion studies. At the Ford Motor Company, for example, about two-thirds of the work force were skilled mechanics in 1910. Four years later, after Ford had adopted assembly line techniques with single-purpose tools and standardized production, the skill level of the work force had declined dramatically. Half of the work force were now recent immigrants with little or no previous industrial work experience. For an account, see Meyer (1981).

tions for management were equally important. Under systems like Taylor's, the task of supervision became much more complicated, too complicated for a single foreman, Taylor thought. So instead of a single foreman, workers now had several bosses responsible for different aspects of the work such as inspection and quality, the flow of product on the shop floor, and the pace of work. The phrase "scientific management" was introduced by Louis Brandeis to describe these new practices, particularly Taylor's system, for which Brandeis became a powerful advocate. He saw in these new approaches a more objective set of rules for running business and a counter to the personal power and often arbitrary business decisions made by company owners.[50]

Several fundamental outcomes affecting employment were associated with these new internal control systems and, in particular, with the arrangements suggested by Taylor and his followers. First, companies had to take control over work decisions away from the foremen, reducing in the process the power of unemployment and the market in employee management. Authority over individual workers in the new systems was dispersed across supervisors, and managers were put in place above the foremen to control and coordinate the decisions of these foremen, thus coordinating employee management within the firm.[51] Consequently, companies were creating a cadre of professional middle managers who stood between the executives and the workers. Historian Hugh Aitken quotes a supporter of Taylor's principles, who nevertheless warned other employers that a consequence of these techniques was to create "an astonishing number of 'nonproducers' " in the form of these new managers.[52]

The techniques of assembly line-based mass production in particular appeared to change the interest of employers in retaining their production employees. It is no coincidence that studies of "the problem" of employee turnover mushroomed soon after mass production techniques gained hold. Thinking of assembly line jobs as skilled is a bit of a stretch, but these jobs did seem to require some minimal knowledge specific to each production layout. Some evidence suggests that internal promotion systems, which facilitate on-the-job training, were driven by the firm-specific demands of these new production systems.[53] Other arguments suggest that these

50. Brandeis (1967).

51. A description of how scientific management changed the jobs of foremen is provided by Hathaway (1914).

52. Aitken (1960, p. 88).

53. See Sundstrom (1988).

demands more generally encouraged employers to secure a stable work force, helping to account for the sharp declines in industrial turnover during the 1920s. Historian Laura Owen quotes a representative of the Sargent hardware manufacturing company who describes how the company had been organized around departments, each operating like little factories with independent foremen under contract to the company managing production and employee relations. As the company mechanized and coordinated its operations, it had to eliminate the independent foremen model, but then it also had to search for a new method of managing employees and securing their effort.[54]

Perhaps the best known of the pioneers in the effort to transform the employment relationship and bring it more within the control of the company was Henry Ford. In 1913 Ford Motor Company had a turnover rate among its employees of 370 percent with daily absentee rates as high as 10 percent. A company study of employee concerns led to some significant reforms. The foreman's ability to hire and fire was eliminated and transferred to a central employment department. A new pay scheme was introduced based on seniority and objective performance measures, taking away the foreman's control over pay as well. And wages were essentially doubled—the famous $5.00 a day plan—for eligible workers: married men with at least six months of seniority whose home life had passed the scrutiny of the company's sociological department to ensure that the new wage bonanza would not be squandered on drink or other wasteful habits. Turnover dropped to about 54 percent, and overall productivity rose by around 50 percent, driven in large part by greater worker discipline.[55]

The move toward bringing the management of employees inside the firm and away from independent foremen was not universal, however. The power foremen retained varied considerably across industrial settings. They lost the most power and control (put differently, the reforms were greatest) in mass production precisely because its operating technology was especially vulnerable to turnover.[56] Despite the success of these reforms at reducing turnover, the superintendents in the plants where the reforms occurred worried about how discipline would be maintained after the power of the foremen had been eroded.[57] Other evidence suggests that companies did not modify the informal method of recruiting that relied on

54. Owen (1991, p. 117).
55. See Raff and Summers (1987).
56. Nelson (1975, p. 35).
57. Willits (1917, p. 55).

the foreman's discretion across the board but only when there were labor shortages.[58]

Besides changes in production technology, the other factors driving a change in the employment relationship were changes in the organizational structure of business enterprises, from the small, single-unit operation to the large, multiunit enterprise. Alfred Chandler describes the development of the modern business enterprise in the United States as having two important characteristics.[59] The first is that it internalized the business transactions that previously had been performed by the market. Whereas the Durant-Dort Carriage Company bought carriages in market transactions and then sold them, the General Motors Corporation that Durant later ran produced components, assembled them into cars, and distributed them to the market all within the same corporate umbrella.

Chandler's second characteristic of the modern enterprise is that it was run by a hierarchy of middle and executive managers. Their function was to coordinate the transactions that had previously taken place in the market. Rather than going to the market to buy some component like steering wheels, and being subject to whatever combinations of price and quality were available, the managers in the modern enterprise had to design and produce the components inside the company to meet cost and quality targets that contributed to the overall design of the final product. Then they had to produce just enough of the components by the appropriate deadline to fit them into the production schedule for the cars the company produced.

As it became more efficient to internalize the business transactions that had in the past been performed by the market, it also became more efficient to transform the employment relationship, moving from an arm's-length relationship that relied on the labor market for governance to one that was internalized in the firm. Meeting these tightly defined production and cost targets required a reasonably predictable supply of skills and human resources, and that was difficult to obtain by relying on the labor market where both the price and quantity of available skills could be highly variable. Companies internalized employment, moving away from the market, in order to make the supply of skills and labor more predictable.[60]

---

58. Nelson (1975, p. 88).

59. Chandler (1980, pp. 9–40).

60. The story of the internalization of employment practices and of the associated ebb and flow of the personnel function has been described at length elsewhere. See Kochan and Cappelli (1984) and Baron, Dobbin, and Jennings (1986, pp. 350–83). Jacoby (1985) provides the definitive exploration of the topic.

These developments also created a larger cadre of managerial jobs with even more permanent relationships to the employer. While the shock troops of the new production techniques were consultants like Taylor, who moved from company to company, the ranks of engineers, clerks, supervisors, and other 'nonproducers' began to grow as soon as the new accounting and work organization practices were introduced. In addition, the demands of multiunit enterprises created an additional cadre of managers. The employment relationship for management positions always relied less on the outside market than for production workers. As Jacoby observes, even from the earliest days of manufacturing, "The employer had a gentlemen's agreement with his top salaried employees that they would not be dismissed except for disloyalty or (under extraordinary circumstances) poor performance."[61] When managerial and white-collar employment expanded, that gentlemen's agreement expanded to cover them as well.

The efforts to internalize the employment relationship for production workers accelerated as the United States became involved in World War I. The drive system was based on the fear of job loss, and its logic eroded quickly when jobs were abundant. With the labor shortage created by wartime production, employers soon reported that worker discipline on the shop floor eroded—in some cases to the point of collapse—employee effort declined, and quit rates rose.[62] With the fear of unemployment as a motivator declining, all employers, not just those involved in mass production, had to be creative to address the problem of declining shop floor discipline. They responded much as Ford and other assembly line companies had done earlier by creating separate personnel departments that took over many of the tasks of supervisors. Roughly 40 percent of larger employers had personnel departments by the end of the 1920s, although some may have existed largely on paper.[63] The welfare capitalism movement that coincided with these innovations had union avoidance as its primary goal, although dealing with turnover and motivation were important objectives as well.[64]

Leading companies developed many of the personnel practices that are still common among progressive employers today and that help define the characteristics of internal labor markets. For example, their employees were evaluated for promotion not only based on their current performance but

61. Jacoby (1985, p. 279).
62. Jacoby provides evidence of the employee response to tighter labor markets.
63. Jacoby (1997, p. 29).
64. See, for example, Brandes (1976).

also on a range of attributes such as interpersonal skills. Many paid atten-
dance bonuses and had a range of pay for performance plans. Following the
military's introduction of standardized tests for placement, employers
began using systematic selection tests for recruiting new workers. Under
pressure from wartime manpower agencies and from trade unions, they
worked to reduce wage inequities within and across organizations by introducing job analyses and other systems to classify jobs and set wage rates systematically. Perhaps the most important innovations were policies to
develop systems of promotion from within. These efforts began with job
classification systems that were used to arrange jobs into "promotion lad-
ders" based on similarity of skills. The idea was that workers could learn the
skills they needed for promotion to the next position by mastering their
current job. These systems, it was argued, would increase skills and reduce
the manpower shortage. They would also reduce turnover and make workers more loyal by giving them some longer-term incentive to stay with the
company.

As Jacoby documents, however, these programs came under attack as
soon as the wartime labor shortages subsided. The foremen resisted these
innovations from the beginning because they took away their control and
power. And as the example at Ford Motor Company suggested, in many
cases the innovations were designed precisely to do that. Line management
generally aligned itself with the foremen and saw these personnel innovations as interfering with getting production out. The recession in 1920 saw
deep cuts in personnel departments. Some companies, like International
Harvester, took personnel out of the central office and made it a line function that reported to the production department. Labor discipline and productivity improved as unemployment rose, and the drive system made
something of a comeback that accelerated during the Great Depression.[65]

Pressure from industrial unions and, once again, wartime labor shortages during World War II finally cemented the new employment practices
in place. By 1947 Sumner Slichter examined how the employment relationship had changed and concluded that "millions of jobs which previously had been held on a day-to-day basis [were converted] into lasting

---

65. See Jacoby (1985, pp. 162–79). Some companies resisted this apparent recidivism, however,
and invested substantial resources to stabilize and buffer employment relationships from market forces
even during the Great Depression. The reasons for doing so were not entirely grounded in the efficiency gains associated with such systems, however, and included factors such as deep ideological objec-
tions to unionization, a philosophy of rent sharing with employees, and reasonably protected product
markets that supported high profits. These arguments are developed in detail in Jacoby (1997).

connections."[66] By 1970 Peter B. Doeringer and Michael J. Piore calculated that the vast majority of the U.S. work force, perhaps as much as 80 percent, had jobs inside internal labor markets.[67]

Lessons for the Present

One of the most important trends at the end of the 1990s is the return of arm's-length, market-mediated employment relationships. Developments in financial markets, especially for publicly traded companies, seek to make executives operate much more like stockholders, like the executives of the 1880s. Companies continue to shed operations that are not their core competence, turning to outsourcers to supply components or provide functions that had previously been handled inside. Rather than internalizing aspects of production, sourcing decisions that make better use of external supply chains are seen as the key source of competitive advantage.[68] The most closely watched innovation in manufacturing is the return of the inside contractor model to automobile assembly. New production techniques like just-in-time inventory processing have made it possible to coordinate complex assembly operations with independent suppliers, and the inside contractor model simply takes that a step further. Volkswagen, Chrysler, and General Motors have new facilities in Brazil that are essentially operated by suppliers who not only produce components but assemble the vehicles inside the facility of the "host" company. Only 200 of the 1,000 employees at Volkswagen's plant in Resende, Brazil, are employed by Volkswagen, for example, and virtually none of them is involved in assembling the vehicles. The lessons from these plants are to be transferred to facilities around the world.[69]

Inside what remains of the "core" company, the move to decentralize operations down to the line level and make even production employees feel as though they are responsive to the market is typified by creating profit-and-loss centers for subunits of the organization. A company like ABB, for example, has its 250,000 employees organized around 5,000 profit-and-loss centers, roughly 1 for every 50 employees. Such arrange-

---

66. Slichter (1947, p. 35).

67. Doeringer and Piore (1971).

68. See, for example, Fisher (1997).

69. See, for example, Sedgwick (1997); Diana Jean Schemo, "Is VW's New Plant Lean, or Just Mean?" *New York Times*, November 19, 1996, p. D1.

ments create incentives that are similar to the inside contracting or independent foremen models of the 1800s where each department had financial and operating autonomy. Contingent work and contingent compensation continue to increase in importance, and companies increasingly rely on the external market to meet their staffing needs with roughly 30 percent of firms in 1996 reporting that they were laying off and hiring at the same time.[70]

The extent to which these developments describe the U.S. economy at the end of the twentieth century is a question that extends well beyond the bounds of this chapter, but there seems little doubt that, at least for larger corporations, the trend is toward unbundling firms and market-mediated employment relationships. There is certainly no evidence of greater internalization of operations or employment.

The contemporary movement toward employment models that were dominant a century ago raises some interesting questions about how to understand the development of employee management over time. It is tempting to think of that development in structural-functional terms akin to natural evolution, where superior techniques beat out older, inferior ones. The issue is what is implied by superior. The fact that market-mediated, arm's-length employment relationships were dominant, declined in the face of internalized practices, and are now undergoing a resurgence against the internalized model suggests rather powerfully that one system is not universally better than another—that context matters.

The market-mediated employment system worked reasonably well for employers until their operating environment changed. Developments in production systems and in the governance and organizational structure of firms changed the priority of goals that employment systems might serve, increasing the importance of stability and predictability to improve coordination while reducing the importance of flexibility and individual or group initiative. The change in goals accounts in large part for the superiority of internalized arrangements for managing employees in the early years of the twentieth century. The internal model succeeded not because it was innately superior but because it was a better match with the changing environment.

---

70. Perhaps the first acknowledgement that employers were shifting internalized employment relationships to the market outside the firm was Pfeffer and Baron (1988). A description of the move toward more market-oriented employment relationships as well as detailed documentation on these trends is provided in Cappelli and others (1997).

One of the reasons why it is difficult to rate employment systems as good or bad is that systems of managing employees are not like a technology aimed at solving a single, clearly defined problem that remains constant over time. Instead, they are designed to address a set of sometimes conflicting goals whose importance may change over time. Certainly there are examples of technologies in employee management that one might be able to rank by objective performance criteria, such as the design of selection tests to improve the success rate of hiring decisions. But broad systems of employee management, such as the make-or-buy decision associated with internal versus market-mediated employment practices, serve multiple goals. Their relative importance changes over time. Assessing the merits of a system of employment practices must therefore be done in the context of the environment in which it operates. In that sense, employment relationships are more like a choice variable or a strategy.

Finally, if the decline of market-mediated employment relationships and the rise of internalized ones in the early twentieth century seem explained by changes in production systems and governance structures, then perhaps the explanation for their return at the end of the century should also be traced to changes in these systems and structures. The return of these market-mediated employee management models seems to suggest something about their robustness. Although it is difficult to do more than speculate about the answer, their return raises the question of whether they are a more fundamental method for managing employees than the internal labor market models. Perhaps we may eventually come to see the period of internal labor markets as the exception to a history of market-mediated employment relationships.

COMMENT BY

James N. Baron

In this literate and provocative paper, Peter Cappelli suggests in the words of the immortal Yogi Berra—"it's like *déjà vu* all over again." Many of the organizational and human resource transformations we are observing involve a resurgence of what Cappelli calls "arm's-length, market-

These comments were drafted while the author was a Marvin Bower Fellow at Harvard University Business School.

mediated" employment relations. Indeed, one could argue that the historical parallels are even more extensive than those his chapter discusses. Cappelli makes only passing reference to the fact that new technologies and information systems have enabled many organizations to develop modern-day counterparts to the scientific management techniques widely employed earlier in this century.

His chapter stimulates a number of questions that suggest fruitful lines of empirical research on corporations and human capital. Although Cappelli raises a host of interesting questions about organizational forms, governance arrangements, financial control, and other topics, in this comment I concentrate on issues relating to human capital and the employment relationship.

First, Cappelli's chapter raises a fundamental issue: how should we conceptualize and measure the extent to which a particular relationship is *mediated by* the market versus *insulated from* the market? For instance, consider a contract employee who is an information technology specialist for EDS, working, say, inside Coca-Cola or General Motors. Is that person truly in a more market-mediated employment relationship than she would be if she were performing a similar job as an employee of Coca-Cola or GM? It is not obvious to me that the answer is yes. Outsourcing companies like ServiceMaster, for instance, have prospered by relying on "high-commitment," training-intensive approaches to human resource management, which emphasize career development for their employees (who provide outsourcing services—including such mundane tasks as pest control and facilities maintenance—to client companies). In fact, opportunities for training, advancement, and employment security conceivably might be greater at a specialized provider such as EDS or ServiceMaster—and their employees might also reap distinctive psychological benefits from being around others doing the same kinds of jobs—compared with employees who are banished to information technology jobs or maintenance positions at Coca-Cola or GM. Clearly, the trends that Cappelli describes entail increasing organizational specialization and division of labor as firms focus on their core competencies. But it is less clear how these trends affect the nature of work and employment or the aggregate distribution of monetary and nonmonetary outcomes that individuals reap from their labors. This is a promising area for research, with vital implications for public policy.

In studying the consequences for employees' careers, I suspect we would benefit from differentiating among the various forms that nonstandard employment relations can take and identifying the crucial dimensions along which they vary. Some time ago, Jeff Pfeffer and I suggested that employment relations are evolving away from the conventional hierarchical form on at least three dimensions: duration (shorter-term engagements versus long-term relationships); delegation of responsibility for administering the employment relationship to third parties (outsourcing firms, temporary agencies, employee leasing companies, and so on); and a weakening of the locational attachment between employees and firms (for example, home work and telecommuting).[71] I suspect other dimensions could profitably be identified as well. Different types of nonstandard employment relations that Cappelli discusses—independent contractors, outsourced employees, temps, and so on—vary along these dimensions. Indeed, big variations exist *within* any particular category. For example, some independent contractors undertake very short-term engagements and work off site under the control of third parties. Others, for all intents and purposes, are just regular employees for whom the employer is trying to avoid tax and legal liability. Even among truly "contingent" employees (those with no explicit or implicit contract for continuing employment), recent Bureau of Labor Statistics data reveal marked differences in wages and benefits depending on whether the labor is provided by independent contractors, on-call employees, individuals working for temporary help agencies, workers who are what Cappelli calls "internal contractors" (for example, copier technicians employed by a contracting company who regularly carry out their work at a particular client's premises), and so on.[72]

In considering how market-mediated all this activity is, I was left wondering whether evidence exists to support a key implication of Cappelli's argument, namely, that increased reliance on outsourcing, independent contractors, temporary workers, and the like has strengthened the operation of market forces. For instance, are labor supply and demand adjusting to each other, or are interfirm wage differentials narrowing more over time in those industries and labor markets where so-called market-mediated employment relations are used most extensively? Again, this subject strikes

71. Pfeffer and Baron (1988).
72. See the tabulations provided by the Bureau of Labor Statistics, based on the February 1997 Current Population Survey (http://stats.bls.gov/news.release/conemp.toc.htm [September 21, 1999]) (particularly table 13). That web site also contains tables describing how workers vary across different types of employment arrangements by age, education, type of work, industry, and the like.

me as empirically researchable. My guess is that the answer may well turn out to be no, for several reasons.

First, how truly "arm's length" and "market mediated" are these forms of employment that Cappelli discusses? My impression is that outsourcing, reliance on temporary help agencies, and use of independent contractors all can—and often do—have a strong relational contracting flavor.[73] In some cases (usually involving lower-skilled personnel), the individuals who last week were regular employees of firm X find themselves out of a job, but they are referred for possible employment to the outside contractor or temp agency to whom firm X has delegated the activity (though under worse terms of employment than they previously enjoyed at X). In other cases, especially when the workers are highly skilled professionals, they are out of a job and then hired back by their previous employer as independent contractors or consultants, possibly on better terms than before. In a 1996 article, "More Downsized Workers Are Returning as Rentals," the *New York Times* reported on a government study, which found in 1995 that 17 percent of contingent workers had had a "previous different relationship" with the company that now retained their services. The share exceeded 22 percent for individuals currently working as self-employed independent contractors.[74] These do not sound like the arm's-length, short-lived exchanges described in economists' models of spot contracting.

And even when the relationship between an organization and the specific *individual* performing a task (for example, an independent contractor or temp) is brief and conducted at arm's length, the relationship between the client and the *firm* supplying the labor services is often an intimate and long-standing one. Relatively enduring relationships between client organizations and their labor suppliers may reflect purely personal ties among the actors involved, but frequently a lot of relationship-specific capital is also involved in placing contingent workers in a given firm. Indeed, given the enduring and frequent relations that these labor market intermediary organizations often have with their clients, both parties to the transaction may develop strong reputational interests that promote long-term cooperation, more so than might be present in the dealings between that same client firm and its individual employees. Viewed this way, labor market

73. For a similar point of view, see Bradach (1997).
74. Louis Uchitelle, "More Downsized Workers Are Returning as Rentals," *New York Times*, December 8, 1996, pp. 1, 34.

intermediaries may have the potential to improve employment relationships, through a process of reputation-based cooperation with employers
that is similar to the role that labor unions are sometimes said to play in
promoting reputation-based cooperation with employers.[75] Consider that
most outsourcing and temporary help organizations, in order to preserve
their enduring relationship with a client, will provide quality guarantees
(and sometimes price guarantees). Certainly a company cannot achieve
such a guarantee when it hires an individual employee. In short, a number
of the so-called arm's-length, market-mediated arrangements that Cappelli
describes may essentially involve replacing relational contracts between
firms and *employees* with relational contracts between firms and their labor
contractors.

Furthermore, the temporary help industry and many sectors of outsourcing tend to be dominated by a few very large players (for example, think of the
large information technology outsourcing firms or the share of their respective
temporary markets captured by Kelly Services, Manpower, Robert Half,
Adecco, and others). According to the 1992 *Census of Service Industries*, the
top four firms within the personnel supply industry (SIC 736) were responsible for 70 percent of the payroll in that industry.[76] Given the tremendous
consolidation that has taken place within that industry, the concentration
may be even greater today. On the buyer side of the market, studies have also
documented that reliance on at least some types of market-mediated employment relations—such as temporary help, call-in help, and limited-duration
hires—tends to be concentrated in larger organizations.[77] Thus, the possibility of something akin to bilateral monopoly certainly seems to exist. If this suspicion is correct, then it may not be very appropriate to think of these new
forms of labor contracting as market mediated or arm's length.

Indeed, Cappelli's exposition provides one piece of indirect evidence to
suggest that use of these employment techniques does not necessarily
strengthen market influence. He recalls that when outside contractors were
first used to coordinate and oversee production, owners replaced them with

75. See Baron and Kreps (1999, chap. 6).

76. In comparison, 79 percent of the value of shipments produced by aircraft companies in 1992
came from that industry's top four firms; the corresponding figures were 84 percent for motor vehicles,
45 percent for computers, and 41 percent for semiconductors. (I have characterized concentration in
the personnel industry based on the value of payrolls, because this seems most analogous to the value
of shipments in a manufacturing context.)

77. Mangum, Mayall, and Nelson (1985). However, the propensity to outsource at least some
types of services appears to *decline* with establishment size. See Abraham and Taylor (1996).

foremen, who cost only one-third of what a contractor earned. But if use of contractors supposedly invokes market forces and helps firms undo the distorting effect of organizational custom and politics on wages, then how could it be that firms previously using contractors in lieu of foremen were suddenly able to reduce their labor costs by two-thirds by shifting to foremen? And this observation raises a related question: why were so-called insiders so much cheaper than nonemployees in an earlier era, when most observers today seem to believe the opposite is true (that is, that "insiders" cost more)?

Another topic warranting more systematic research concerns variation across firms and industries in the prevalence of different forms of market-mediated employment relations. For instance, in the information technology arena, outsourcing has lately been getting a lot of negative press in trade publications aimed at professionals in the field. A close look at who is using these different types of flexible employment arrangements is likely to reveal a lot about their determinants and consequences. It would be particularly instructive to examine their relative intensity of use in enduring organizations versus new enterprises. Cappelli's arguments about an enhanced need for flexibility and for resetting wages to competitive levels suggest that one would expect to see these arrangements most often in the longest-lived organizations, which are subject to strongest inertial forces (for example, unionized companies). Perhaps those same inertial forces, however, have deterred the use of such arrangements.

A recent longitudinal look at the domestic motor vehicle tire market by Donald Sull speaks to this issue. Sull documented how the tendency for Firestone Corporation to groom its top executives from within deterred them from taking the bold steps needed (namely, to close down plants) once demand for older "bias" tires declined sharply owing to the introduction of products incorporating the new "radial" technology. Sull shows that Firestone chief executives groomed from within were much less likely than those brought in from the outside during this period to implement the major restructuring required by changing market conditions. When insider executives did reallocate resources, they were least likely to divert resources away from the plants and divisions where they had previously been employed within Firestone.[78] If adoption of these new, market-mediated employment relations reflects a need for enhanced

78. Sull (1996).

flexibility, as Cappelli argues, does it take revolutionary upheavals in organizations to do this kind of resetting (and, if so, what are the triggers)? Is there evidence in the contracting choices of new enterprises suggesting that these practices are becoming institutionalized (that is, today's start-ups rely more extensively on outsourcing and contingent work than start-up firms did previously)?

A somewhat different explanation for increased use of market-mediated employment relations emphasizes the learning opportunities they provide for firms. Even when an organization has its own employees carrying out a particular activity, there may be incentives to contract with various external providers of the same service in order to gain access to new knowledge and technology, to benchmark performance of the "insiders," and so on. We presumably could differentiate among firms and industries in terms of the need for such learning (for example, as a function of the rate of technological change in their industry, the tenure distribution of their labor force, and so on). It would be useful to examine whether the value of exploiting learning opportunities helps explain the extent and forms of outsourcing and contingent employment.

Of particular interest, it seems to me, is the prevalence of hybrid arrangements. Consider Hewlett-Packard (HP). They have some engineering operations conducted by long-standing HP employees and some tasks done by former HP employees who now work as free-lance independent contractors. Other activities are carried out by individuals working for firms like Tata Consulting Services and Blue Star, which hire and train technical personnel in India and Russia and elsewhere and then post them to do projects for firms like HP at the client's facilities. Still other technical work is being done offsite for HP by contractor firms in places like Bangalore, India. On first blush, explanations for these variations simply based on differences in the tasks being carried out is inadequate, though the kind of task is certainly relevant. Perhaps one reason why HP uses so many contracting forms is that given the strains of inflexibility and high cost associated with its main-line, high-commitment employment system—involving fairly stable, enduring, high-wage employment—it has more to gain by experimenting with various forms of labor contracting that give it access to knowledge and best practice that can then be transferred to its regular work force.

If the goal in availing oneself of these market-oriented employment relations is to transfer to the main-line work force knowledge gained from the outside, the amount of knowledge transfer is likely to depend on the similarity between the "contingent" and "regular" work force, so that the main-line work force does not resent the contingent work force, reject it as incompetent, and so on. This reality may help explain why some companies that rely extensively on contract help, such as 3COM, insist that their personnel contractors supplying people to work on site at 3COM offer benefits comparable to what 3COM employees receive.[79] Yet the more that the contingent and regular work force start to become comparable in skills, education, pay, and the like, the less compelling many of these "market-mediated" rationales are for why firms are doing this. Something else must be going on. In short, there is much to learn from examining hybrid forms—who uses them, where, why, and how.

We also know remarkably little about the ultimate consequences of different labor contracting arrangements. Of course, numerous obvious and important questions arise about what these changes in employment relations mean for workers, individually and collectively: their pay, training, careers, job satisfaction, union clout, and the like. I have already suggested that I suspect the answer will vary a lot across different kinds of employment contracting forms and organizational settings.

Many equally obvious and important questions could also be asked about how these trends are affecting the structure and performance of organizations. An especially intriguing topic concerns the effects that layoffs and other efforts to shift to more market-mediated employment relations have on a firm's reputation. The list of organizations announcing large layoffs in recent years includes such venerable enterprises as IBM, Apple, Levi Strauss, Eastman Kodak, Citibank, and the Pentagon, all known in the past as exemplars of internal labor markets. The current obsession with "employability" and the new doctrine of workers "owning their own careers" that one encounters so often—especially in Silicon Valley, where I live—is somewhat surprising, given that the other thing one hears about constantly, especially in the valley, is how hard it is to find, hire, and retain really good people (especially engineers). Unemployment is now lower than it has been in a quarter century, so these trends are being played out in a very different labor market context than existed during the historical period that Cappelli chronicles. If companies continue to encounter intense competition for talented employees, employers will probably begin

---

79. Debra Engel, former senior vice president of Corporate Services, 3COM Corporation, personal communication.

experimenting with ways of strengthening their position within the labor market, including perhaps a migration back to internal labor markets.[80] It would be interesting to examine the enduring reputational consequences of prior actions by employers pursuing more market-mediated arrangements (layoffs, outsourcing, and so on), and whether those prior actions constrain firms' ability in the future to pursue certain human resource strategies in response to labor market competition.

Finally, three broader implications of the trend that Cappelli describes toward more contingent employment relationships intrigue me. First, what are the implications, if any, of a resurgence of marketlike employment relations for patterns of labor market inequality by gender, race, ethnicity, and the like? It is not hard to find examples of occupations and work settings in which inequalities along these dimensions have begun to appear. (Indeed, consider within academia the demography of tenure-line versus "gypsy" faculty.) And, of course, it is well known that the long-term employment relations of the first-tier Japanese firms, so admired in the 1970s and 1980s, were achieved in large measure by relying on contingent employment for women, school-leavers, and other lower-status categories of workers.

Second, what are the implications for unionization and labor relations? Earlier in this century, those firms and industries in which employers embraced scientific management and the "drive system" were the ones that experienced the fastest growth of industrial unionism in the late 1930s following passage of the Wagner Act.[81] Will labor historians fifty or one hundred years hence chronicle how the present-day trends in employment relations that Cappelli describes eventually triggered a resurgence of labor organization and governmental intervention in labor markets?

Third, the business school professor in me cannot resist asking: if the trend Cappelli discusses is real and enduring, what are its implications for managers and management? He notes that during the first wave of independent contracting, one of the strong arguments for contracting out the internal control and supervision function was that it permitted owners to

---

80. I know of a prominent high-tech firm, for instance, which has in many ways been the epitome of Silicon Valley's culture of leanness, meanness, and flexibility. Having recently commissioned a large-scale study of what differentiates this firm in the minds of past, current, and prospective employees, the head of HR at this company discovered that the answer was: *absolutely nothing*. Consequently, he has persuaded the firm's top management to endorse an HR initiative aimed at redefining this firm as a place that, in contrast to competitors, offers *careers*.

81. See Baron, Dobbin, and Devereaux (1986).

exploit their core competencies, which were financial. By using independent contractors, owners, says Cappelli, "did not have to be experts themselves in the production process nor worry about personnel matters associated with getting the work done. They could concentrate on their own competencies, which concerned finance, and not have to worry about monitoring production for performance, quality, and costs." A big difference between then and now is that in the interim, hundreds of institutions have gone into the business of producing people who are supposedly experts in production and the management of people, and who have the letters MBA after their name to prove it. So if those things are no longer part of the core competence of a firm's management, then what is? Now liberated from pedestrian concerns about how to produce things and manage people, just what is it exactly that managers are supposed to do with their time? Research examining how shifts toward more market-oriented employment relations are affecting the amount and kinds of managerial and administrative expertise that firms seek would be very illuminating.

References

Abraham, Katharine G., and Susan K. Taylor. 1996. "Firms' Use of Outside Contractors: Theory and Evidence." *Journal of Labor Economics* 14 (July): 394–424.

Aitken, Hugh G. J. 1960. "Taylorism at Watertown Arsenal: Scientific Management in Action 1908–1915." Harvard University Press.

Baron, James N., and David M. Kreps. 1999. *Strategic Human Resources: Framework for General Managers.* John Wiley.

Baron, James N., Frank R. Dobbin, and P. Devereaux Jennings. 1986. "War and Peace: The Evolution of Modern Personnel Administration in U.S. Industry." *American Journal of Sociology* 92 (September): 350–83.

Bezanson, Anne. 1928. "The Advantages of Labor Turnover: An Illustrative Case." *Quarterly Journal of Economics* 42 (May): 450–64.

Bezanson, Anne, and others. 1925. "Four Years of Labor Mobility: A Study of Labor Turnover in a Group of Selected Plants in Philadelphia." *The Annals of the American Academy of Political and Social Science* 119 (May). Wharton School of Finance and Commerce. University of Pennsylvania.

Bradach, Jeffrey. 1997. "Flexibility: The New Social Contract between Individuals and Firms?" Working Paper 97-088. Harvard University, Graduate School of Business Administration.

Brandeis, Louis D. 1967. *Other People's Money, and How Bankers Use It.* Harper and Row.

Brandes, Stuart D. 1976. *American Welfare Capitalism, 1880–1940.* University of Chicago Press.

Brissenden, Paul F., and Emil Frankel. 1922. *Labor Turnover in Industry: A Statistical Analysis.* Macmillan Company.

Buttrick, John. 1952. "The Inside Contract System." *Journal of Economic History* 12 (Summer): 205–21.

Cappelli, Peter, and others. 1997. *Change at Work*. Oxford University Press.

Chandler, Alfred D., Jr. 1962. *Strategy and Structure: Chapters in the History of the Industrial Enterprise*. MIT Press.

———. 1977. *The Visible Hand: Managerial Revolution in American Business*. Belknap Press.

———. 1980. "The United States: Seedbed of Managerial Capitalism." In *Managerial Hierarchies: Comparative Perspectives on the Rise of the Modern Industrial Enterprise*, edited by Alfred D. Chandler Jr. and Herman Daems. Harvard University Press.

Clawson, Daniel. 1980. *Bureaucracy and the Labor Process: The Transformation of U.S. Industry, 1860–1920*. Monthly Review Press.

Doeringer, Peter B., and Michael J. Piore. 1971. *Internal Labor Markets and Manpower Analysis*. Lexington, Mass.: Heath.

Fisher, Boyd. 1917. "How to Reduce Labor Turnover." *The Annals of the American Academy of Political and Social Science* 71 (May).

Fisher, Marshall. 1997. "What Is the Right Supply Chain for Your Product?" *Harvard Business Review* 75 (March): 105–16.

Hathaway, H. K. 1914. "The Planning Department: Its Origin and Function." In *Scientific Management: A Collection of the Most Significant Articles Describing the Taylor System of Management*, edited by Clarence Bertrand Thompson. Harvard University Press.

Hounshell, David A. 1984. *From the American System to Mass Production, 1800–1932: The Development of Manufacturing Technology in the United States*. Johns Hopkins University Press.

Industrial Research Department of the Wharton School. 1922. "A Study in Labor Mobility." *Annals of the American Academy of Political and Social Science* (September).

Jacoby, Sanford M. 1985. *Employing Bureaucracy: Managers, Unions, and the Transformation of Work in American Industry, 1900–1945*. Columbia University Press.

———. 1997. *Modern Manors: Welfare Capitalism since the New Deal*. Princeton University Press.

Jones, S. H. R. 1982. "The Organization of Work: A Historical Dimension." *Journal of Economic Behavior and Organization* 3 (June–September):117–37.

Kochan, Thomas A., and Peter Cappelli. 1984. "The Transformation of the Industrial Relations and Personnel Functions." In *Internal Labor Markets,* edited by Paul Osterman, 133–61. MIT Press.

Landes, David. 1969. *The Unbound Prometheus: Technological Change and Industrial Development in Western Europe from 1750 to the Present*. London: Cambridge University Press.

Mangum, Garth, Donald Mayall, and Kristin Nelson. 1985. "The Temporary Help Industry: A Response to the Dual Internal Labor Market." *Industrial and Labor Relations Review* 38 (July): 599–611.

Marglin, Stephen A. 1974. "What Do Bosses Do? The Origins and Functions in Hierarchy in Capitalist Production." *Review of Radical Political Economics* 6 (Summer): 60–112.

Meyer, Stephen III. 1981. *The Five Dollar Day: Labor Management and Social Control in the Ford Motor Company, 1908–1921*. State University of New York Press.

Montgomery, David. 1976. "Workers' Control of Machine Production in the Nineteenth Century." *Labor History* 17 (Fall): 485–509.

Nelson, Daniel. 1975. *Managers and Workers: Origins of the New Factory System in the United States, 1880–1920.* University of Wisconsin Press.

Owen, Laura Jane. 1991. "The Decline in Turnover of Manufacturing Workers: Case Study Evidence from the 1920s." Ph.D. dissertation. Yale University.

Palmer, Gladys L. 1962. *The Reluctant Job Changer: Studies in Work Attachments and Aspirations.* University of Pennsylvania Press.

Pearce, Jone L. 1993. "Toward an Organizational Behavior of Contract Laborers: Their Psychological Involvement and Effects on Employee Co-Workers." *Academy of Management Journal* 36 (October): 1082–96.

Pfeffer, Jeffrey, and James N. Baron. 1988. "Taking the Workers Back Out: Recent Trends in the Structuring of Employment." In *Research in Organizational Behavior,* vol. 10, edited by Barry M. Staw and L. L. Cummings, 257–303. JAI Press.

Raff, Daniel M. G., and Lawrence H. Summers. 1987. "Did Henry Ford Pay Efficiency Wages?" *Journal of Labor Economics* 5 (October): pt. 2, S57–S86.

Saxenian, AnnaLee. 1994. *Regional Advantage: Culture and Competition in Silicon Valley and Route 128.* Harvard University Press.

Sedgwick, David. 1997. "Proving Ground: Brazil Offers Makers and Suppliers a Place for Beta Testing Manufacturing Ideas." *Automotive News.* August 4.

Slichter, Sumner H. 1947. *The Challenge of Industrial Relations: Trade Unions, Management, and the Public Interest.* Cornell University Press.

Smith, Vicki. 1994. "Institutionalizing Flexibility in a Service Firm: Multiple Contingencies and Hidden Hierarchies." *Work and Occupations* 21 (August): 284–307.

Stone, Katherine. 1974. "The Origins of Job Structures in the Steel Industry." *Review of Radical Political Economics* 6 (Summer): 113–73.

Sull, Donald. 1996. "Organizational Inertia and Adaptation in a Declining Market: A Study of the U.S. Tire Industry." Ph.D. dissertation. Harvard University, Graduate School of Business Administration.

Sundstrom, William A. 1988. "Internal Markets before World War I: On-the-Job Training and Employee Promotion." *Explorations in Economic History* 25 (October): 424–45.

Tilly, Chris, and Charles Tilly. 1998. *Work under Capitalism.* Westview Press.

Trist, E. L., and K. W. Bamforth. 1951. "Some Social and Psychological Consequences of the Long Wall Method of Coal-Getting." *Human Relations* 4 (February): 3–38.

Wiebe, Robert H. 1967. *The Search for Order, 1877–1920.* Hill and Wang.

Willits, Joseph, ed. 1917. "Stabilizing Industrial Employment." *The Annals of the American Academy of Political and Social Science* 71 (May).

Yates, JoAnne. 1989. *Control through Communication.* Johns Hopkins University Press.

Zunz, Oliver. 1990. *Making America Corporate.* University of Chicago Press.

4

EILEEN APPELBAUM
PETER BERG

High-Performance Work Systems: Giving Workers a Stake

M ODERN MANUFACTURING PRACTICES and new forms of work organization are influencing the structure of firms and the use of human capital. The development of microprocessor-based information and computer technologies and increased competition on the basis of quality and on-time delivery have encouraged firms to adopt new workplace practices. These forms rely on the participation of front-line workers in decisions and increased horizontal and vertical flows of information within the firm. They have implications for the structure of firms, for investments by these workers in firm-specific human capital, and for the extent to which compensation is contingent on the performance of the firm.

The theoretical arguments developed in this chapter assume that workers in more participatory firms are responsible for the monitoring and decisionmaking tasks that supervisors and managers carry out in traditional, vertically coordinated organizations. We use a unique data set of more than 4,000 employees across 39 plants in the steel, apparel, and medical electronic instruments and imaging industries to examine this assumption and to describe the nature and extent of horizontal coordination and decisionmaking among nonsupervisory employees (table 4-1). If workers in these

We thank the Alfred P. Sloan Foundation for generous financial support.

Table 4-1. *Number of Blue-Collar Workers, White-Collar Workers, and Supervisors, by Industry*

Industry	Total	Blue collar	White collar	Supervisors
Steel	2,082	1,886	0	196
Apparel	995	970	0	25
Medical	1,004	394	610	0
All industries	4,081	3,250	610	221

plants have assumed some of the major responsibilities of monitors and managers, we would expect their compensation to resemble that of supervisory and managerial employees, whose pay is usually based in part on claims on the firm's residual income. Thus we also examine firms' use of contingent pay for workers in more participatory settings and whether these workers are more likely to share the firm's rents and risks.

This chapter examines modern manufacturing practices in the three industries from which we have drawn our employee samples. We contrast vertical and horizontal coordination of the production process and draw the implications of horizontal coordination for the responsibilities, human capital investments, compensation, and stakeholder interests of front-line workers. Next, we use our data to analyze the extent of participation of front-line workers in self-directed and offline quality improvement or problem-solving teams and the relationships between contingent pay and participation and communication. We find compelling evidence that companies that strive to meet world class standards for quality, reliability, and on-time delivery have given front-line workers major responsibility for horizontal coordination of the production process previously carried out by supervisors and lower-level managers.

These firms have also changed their compensation systems to reflect participation by front-line workers in management decisionmaking.

Modern Manufacturing Practices

Practices associated with high-performance work systems make use of horizontal coordination and communication within and among functional units in a firm and rely less on coordination of these units through vertical layers of hierarchy. These practices have emerged as critical to firms in industries in which information technologies have altered the standards of competition. For example, Paul Milgrom and John Roberts argue that the rapidly falling cost of information technology has reduced the cost of flexible equipment, which facilitates the achievement of economies of scope in manufacturing as companies vary product features and produce smaller lot sizes of various models and styles.[1] It does this by reducing the time and cost involved in changeovers from producing one product to another on the same assembly line, thus increasing the number of new or existing products that can be produced per period and increasing the advantages accruing to work organization and human resource practices that reduce inventories and increase the skills and problem-solving capabilities of the work force.

The identification of modern manufacturing with flexible machinery and product variety owes much to the widely studied experiences of assembly-line operations in the auto industry.[2] But information and computation-intensive technologies also affect industries that do not make use of flexible, highly computerized, and sophisticated machinery. There is nothing technologically sophisticated about sewing operations in apparel manufacturing, for example, which remain almost impossible to automate. Nevertheless, the falling cost of computerized inventory management and control systems adopted by retailers in order to reduce their stocks of inventory is an important factor in the diffusion of modern manufacturing practices in this industry. Tight inventory controls by retailers who use point-of-sale inventory systems and electronic data interchange (EDI) with manufacturers to place orders have increased the payoff to some apparel manufacturers from team sewing.[3] Self-directed teams balance the work load among operators and reduce the need for buffers of work-in-process inventory. Team sewing factories can readily meet retailers' demand for quick response.

There are higher capital and training costs associated with team sewing than with traditional work organization, however, and operators engaged in problem solving or other team activities may spend less time actually sewing. These costs are offset to some extent by reductions in the cost of work-in-process inventory, by the fact that production requires less floor space as a result of elimination of the bundles, and by the elimination of some service, warehouse, and supervisor positions as these functions are absorbed by the sewing teams.[4] The real payoff to changes in work organization, however,

1. Milgrom and Roberts (1990).
2. See Berggren (1992); MacDuffie (1995); MacDuffie and Krafick (1992).
3. Batt and Appelbaum (1995); Berg, Appelbaum, and others (1996); Dunlop and Weil (1996).
4. Berg and others (1996).

comes not from a reduction in production costs but from the resulting increase in revenues as apparel manufacturers with a quick-response capability develop long-term relationships with major retailers.

In steel the introduction of information technologies, though not flexible equipment, has increased the payoff to the adoption of modern work organization.[5] In steel, information and computation technologies enable customers to inspect for, and steel mills to achieve, tight conformance to specifications for gauge, shape, flatness, strength, or surface quality. Computerized process controls monitor and adjust temperature and speed for uniform heating, rolling, shaping, or finishing of steel. Computerized inspection equipment records weight, gauge, flatness, and surface quality of sheet products, and gauge, dimensions, and strength of bar products. In addition, sheet and bar producers who supply the auto industry and other high-end original equipment manufacturers have been affected by the just-in-time inventory practices of their customers. These practices place a premium on the on-time delivery of perfect quality steel. Since manufacturers hold minimal inventories, late delivery or delivery of steel that does not meet customer specifications can bring production by the manufacturer grinding to a halt. Any steel company that cannot meet stringent standards for quality and on-time delivery cannot compete in this segment of the steel market.[6]

On-time delivery of steel that meets customer specifications requires that mills adhere strictly to production schedules and that the steel they produce has the intended chemical, shape, and surface qualities. Problems, such as cobbles that cause the equipment to be shut down or marred surfaces or failure to meet strength requirements that make the steel unusable by its intended customer, can arise at various points in the production process. Some mills have found offline problem-solving or quality improvement teams, made up of production and maintenance workers drawn from different work groups, effective in reducing such problems. Moreover, coordination among stages of the production process, which in an integrated steel mill may be spread over large distances, adds to the need for communication among front-line workers.[7]

5. Ichniowski, Shaw, and Prennushi (1997).

6. Berg (1997).

7. An integrated mill makes its own steel by reducing iron ore to pig iron in a blast furnace and then converting pig iron to steel in a basic oxygen furnace. To support this operation, an integrated mill must sell large volumes of steel, and generally does so by producing a wide variety of products. A minimill makes the steel it uses by melting steel scrap in an electric arc furnace. The lower costs associated with this process mean that a minimill can be profitable producing a much lower volume of steel.

Modern minimills first started operating in the 1960s, producing commodity steel (reinforcing bars for concrete, or "rebar") for the construction industry. Imported steel had already made large inroads into the U.S. market for rebar, taking market share away from the integrateds, and the new minimills competed directly with these foreign imports. A low-wage strategy was not an option, since the mills had to match the prevailing wage in the industry either because they were unionized or because they wanted to avoid unionization. The mills turned, instead, to a more flexible deployment of labor to reduce manhours per ton and unit labor costs. The small physical size of the minimills, the close proximity of departments within the mill, and the absence of finishing lines facilitated less rigid job definitions and greater communication among workers and managers.

The situation is somewhat different in the medical electronic instruments and imaging industry. Mass production has never been widely introduced in this industry. Many firms began as small ventures by single entrepreneurs, and even for the somewhat larger plants in our sample, this legacy remains. Workers have traditionally enjoyed a certain degree of participation in production decisions. There is little automation of the production process. Manufacture of technologically sophisticated components is organized on a craft basis, while assembly of final products is done to order in small batches. Internal firm hierarchy has traditionally been flat, and there are few first-line supervisors, even in traditional work systems. As a result, the differences between new and old work systems are less distinct in this industry.

This is true in the case of ultrasound equipment, for example. A craft production process is used to make transducers for the ultrasound probe. Crystals are cut to size by automated saws, but all of the other operations— lapping, matching, layering, and testing—are done by hand to meet precise specifications for the velocity of sound waves through the materials. The back end of an ultrasound machine is a personal computer and monitor that processes and stores information collected by the probe. Subassemblies of probes, PC boards, and monitors, as well as cables, frames, and wheels are assembled and tested by workers. Traditionally, this was done in various assembly areas (for example, mechanical, electrical, monitor, and PC board assembly). Many large firms, however, have introduced team or cell production in their assembly processes to facilitate multitasking by blue-collar workers. Operators in cell production do more testing and other technical tasks and are more likely to be formally involved in production decisions.

Because the product life cycle of ultrasound equipment is relatively short, companies are under competitive pressure to develop and bring to market new generations of equipment that take advantage of the continuing declines in the cost and increases in the computing capabilities of the computers on which they are based. Computer-aided design software has increased the capacity of firms to design products quickly. But the link from design to manufacturing in this industry has traditionally been weak. The challenge has been to build machines that incorporate the latest generation of technology and that can be built to work reliably. Organizational innovation for both blue- and white-collar employees has proved critical to reducing the time required to bring more powerful machines with customized design features to market.

As these examples illustrate, computer and information technologies have made it possible for firms to manage inventories more tightly than before and have increased the payoff to practices that are complementary to this reduction in buffers of work-in-progress or finished product inventories. For companies that now hold very little inventory, and for the firms that supply them, the importance of on-time delivery of perfect quality goods has increased dramatically. As a result, the payoff to these firms of introducing complementary sets of work organization and quality practices is far greater than what can be achieved by the piecemeal introduction of either alone. In addition, coordination and communication among workers to solve problems and regulate production assume a key role. Firms tend to foster communication and coordination by adopting human resources and industrial relations practices that encourage and reward these coordination and problem-solving activities by front-line workers, and that discourage turnover and absenteeism, which are more disruptive in new work systems than in more traditional settings.

Implications for the Theory of the Firm

Standard microeconomic theory views the firm as the economic unit in which purchased inputs are transformed into outputs according to exogenously given technical rules specified by a production function. These products are then sold in the market to households and other firms with the goal of maximizing the firm's profits. The price system, or market, coordinates the allocation of resources to the uses in which their value is greatest.

Coase challenged this view of the firm-as-production-function. He noted that if production is regulated by price movements, then production could be carried on without any organization at all.[8] The question he addressed is why firms exist—that is, why there are organizations within which market transactions and the price mechanism are superseded by the entrepreneur who coordinates and directs the various factors of production.

Coase's ideas have given rise to a rich economics literature that has begun to provide explanations for the existence of production organizations "with such characteristic features as long-term contracts, risk bearing by owners, and hierarchical or centralized coordination of those engaged in the production process."[9] Three types of problems have been considered—"team production" and the "free rider" problem that arises when the joint output produced by individual resources is not separable; "principal-agent" problems that arise when one economic actor (the principal) hires another (the agent) to act on his or her behalf in situations in which the principal has difficulty monitoring the agent; and "incomplete contracting" problems that arise in situations in which it is impossible or too costly to write and enforce complete contracts.[10]

Vertical Coordination

Common to all three of these streams of research is the view that firms exist because the hierarchical coordination of the inputs of a large number of participants leads to a greater output than can be obtained from those same inputs when the transactions among them are governed in a decentralized manner by markets and the price system. The focus of economists, who generally model the firm as a hierarchy, is on *vertical* coordination. Transactions cost economics argues that, within firms, transactions are most economically governed by a hierarchical form of organization in which management coordinates the gathering and processing information from lower levels of the organization and uses knowledge concentrated at higher levels of the organization to make decisions based on this information.[11]

8. Coase (1937).

9. Putterman and Kroszner (1996, p. 9); Alchian and Demsetz (1972); Williamson (1975, 1985).

10. Blair and Stout (1999).

11. Thus, economists who take a transactions cost approach to the economics of organizations (Alchian and Demsetz [1972]; Jensen and Meckling [1976]; Williamson [1985]) come down on the side of an older generation of organizational theorists who argued that the benefits of vertical coordination at the highest levels of the hierarchy outweighed the inefficiencies associated with this type of bureaucratic organization. Barnard (1938); Taylor (1911); March and Simon (1958); Weber (1978);

There are few opportunities for ideas to flow upward from front-line workers. Once decisions have been made, orders are relayed back down the chain of command, to be carried out by front-line workers doing routine tasks.

The firm uses a variety of means to ensure that these commands are carried out. When the performance of individual workers is easily measured, firms may offer employment contracts with explicit pay incentives (for example, piece rates). If measured output depends not only on worker effort but on circumstances beyond the control of the worker (weather, quality of raw material, delivery of required inputs), the income risk may be shared between employer and employee with the employment contract specifying a fixed-pay component that includes a risk premium and a piece rate component. Where the pay of these workers cannot be directly related to performance, either because the output they produce is not easily measured or because it is produced jointly by a group whose individual contributions cannot be separated out, the assumption is that workers will reduce work effort. To reduce shirking, lower-level managers and supervisors are employed to act as monitors. Besides disciplining workers to prevent shirking, monitors measure output performance, observe the behavior of workers in order to estimate marginal productivity, recommend promotions and pay raises, and give assignments or instructions in what to do and how to do it.[12] The transactions cost argument is that it is more efficient for supervisors to assign tasks to individual workers and to monitor their performance than for self-directed teams to meet to deal with these issues. Traditional manufacturing in large, bureaucratic corporations is probably the canonical case of the firm as vertical hierarchy.

Chandler (1989). Vertically coordinated organizations are inefficient in at least two key respects: they respond slowly to changes in the organization's environment, and they sacrifice the potential gains from collaboration among employees at lower levels of the hierarchy. These disadvantages are outweighed, in the view of these writers, "by the relative efficiency of coordination at the highest levels of the organization to achieve control and unity of purpose." Gittell (1995, p. 10). Marxist theorists have emphasized the control aspect of bureaucracy. Edwards (1979); Bowles (1985). They argue that bureaucratic control and vertical coordination of the production process are designed to prevent collaboration among workers, whose interest are antagonistic to those of managers and owners, even when such collaboration can increase the firm's profits. In some ways, these arguments parallel those put forward in principal-agent models of the firm. In these models, appropriate use of incentives (stock options, promotion tournaments, bonuses tied to share price or return on assets) can align the interests of high-level managers with those of owners (shareholders). Owners can have confidence that decisions made at the highest levels of the corporate hierarchy will reflect their interests and concerns. The role of managers and supervisors at lower levels of the organization is to operationalize these decisions and make sure they are carried out. See Gittell (1995, pp. 2–15) for a summary of these issues.

12. Alchian and Demsetz (1972).

Governance issues in these corporations are framed in terms of the relationship between the shareholders of the firm, who have made the investments in firm-specific physical assets and are assumed to be the only group with ownership claims on the firm and its residual income, and high-level managers, who are the firm's decisionmakers. This relationship between shareholders and managers is modeled using the principal-agent theory of the firm, in which the central problem is to provide managers (the agents) with appropriate incentives to act in the interests of the shareholders (the principal). Executive compensation includes stock options and other claims on the firm's earnings and is structured to align the interests of top managers with those of shareholders. Incentive pay that is correlated with the residual income of the firm—profit sharing or bonuses, for example—is used to reward lower-level managers and supervisors responsible for monitoring workers and gathering information for use in decisions taken at higher levels. Providing them with a claim on the firm's residual income is assumed to significantly reduce the need to monitor the monitors.

In contrast, front-line workers are linked to the firm via employment contracts that specify the wage-effort bargain. Piece rate or other incentive pay contracts may be used when output or performance is easy to measure. When this is not the case, firms offer workers—whom they view as largely interchangeable groups of operators, mechanics, clerks, and so on—flat wages equal to their respective opportunity costs in exchange for work effort, and then utilize monitors to enforce the employment contract. Where monitoring work effort is especially difficult or costly, firms may pay workers a premium over their opportunity cost either to raise the cost to them of losing their job if they are discovered withholding effort and, in this way, to reduce shirking and improve productivity; or to induce them, by means of a gift exchange, to provide appropriately high levels of effort.[13]

Additionally, firms that want to encourage workers to make investments in firm-specific skills may supplement the wage contract with internal labor markets. Once hired, workers in firms with internal labor markets are protected from competition from the external job market. They move up a job ladder as they invest in firm-specific skills, earning less in the early years while acquiring these skills and enjoying payoffs to these investments in their human capital in later years in the form of promotions, higher pay, and job security. Such implicit contracts are not legally binding, however. Workers may leave the firm, depriving the firm of the higher productivity

13. Stiglitz (1987); Akerlof and Yellen (1988); Akerlof (1984); Bowles (1985).

that results from investments in worker skills; and firms may close plants, depriving workers of the return to their investments in these assets. The payment of wages below the worker's marginal productivity in the early years and above his or her productivity in later years encourages workers to remain with the firm and provides firms with some protection for their investments. Workers, however, have no similar means of protecting their investments in firm-specific skills. Collective bargaining by unions creates internal governance structures such as established pay scales that protect workers from being penalized by the subjective judgment of supervisors, grievance procedures that provide a voice mechanism for workers who may have been treated unfairly by management, and job structures and employment security agreements that limit employers' ability to hire and fire at will. These governance structures provide some protection for workers' investments in firm-specific skills by protecting individual workers against arbitrary or opportunistic behavior by managers. But workers have no protections against layoffs and no means of enforcing any claims to a long-term employment relation.

Horizontal Coordination

The role of *horizontal* interactions among the resources whose production activities are coordinated by the firm has received relatively little attention in the new economics of organizations, apart from discussions of pathologies such as collusion and side contracting that need to be controlled to discourage wasteful rent-seeking behavior by team members and ensure that resources are deployed in the interests of the principal.[14] In this view, horizontal interactions need to be constrained so that team members remain focused on the goals set by the principal. Margaret M. Blair and Lynn A. Stout suggest, however, that these horizontal interactions may also play a positive role in explaining how teams produce a greater output than can be achieved by employees individually, since team members are probably better situated to assign tasks, solve problems, and regulate or improve the production process than is a supervisor.[15] Thus, horizontal

14. Aoki (1990, p. 27), notes "the emergence of a new mode of intra-organizational coordination which is somewhat at odds with the traditional economists' modeling of the firm as a hierarchy. This emerging mode relies more upon participatory information processing by, and the communications among, workers (shops) than does the traditional hierarchical structure, which is characterized by the specialized separation between coordination and operating tasks as well as among different operating tasks."

15. Blair and Stout (1999).

information processing and communication can create value, although these gains need to be weighed in particular settings against the costs of increased communication.

The complementarities that exist among activities in modern manufacturing increase the payoff to the firm from coordinated actions across functions such as engineering, manufacturing, and design. This leads to an increase in horizontal interactions of the type envisioned by Blair and Stout among lower- and mid-level managers who, in a traditional corporation, would commonly address interdepartmental problems through vertical communication with managers at higher levels. Eileen Appelbaum and Rosemary Batt provide evidence for two distinct modern strategies for organizing production.[16] The first is American lean production, which somewhat resembles the description of modern manufacturing in Paul Milgrom and John Roberts.[17] It includes the types of horizontal interactions among managers at various levels of the company described by Blair and Stout, as well as extensive involvement of front-line workers in decisionmaking through their participation in offline problem-solving and quality improvement teams. The second is American team production, which extends the need for horizontal communication and coordination to front-line workers. It is distinguished by participatory management and the real-time regulation of the work process by self-directed work teams that engage in problem solving, make decisions, and have responsibility for coordinating the production process. Both of these new forms of work organization increase horizontal communication across functions and vertical communication across levels of the organization. This contrasts sharply with Taylorist work organization and vertical coordination in factories which, as Masahiko Aoki observed, minimizes the need for communication among front-line workers.[18]

16. Appelbaum and Batt (1994).
17. Milgrom and Roberts (1990).
18. Aoki (1988, p. 16). In a vertically coordinated organization, coordination across functionally specialized production processes takes place near the top of the hierarchy. Different parts of the production process are separated by buffers of time or of work-in-process inventory. These buffers enable workers to carry out their parts of the production process largely unaffected by problems or delays that arise elsewhere in the production system. Standardization of organizational routines and conformance to rules allows work to be carried out in predictable ways and simplifies the requirements of coordination. Communication across the internal structures of the firm is minimized and functional areas of the organization operate at arm's length from each other.

These more participatory forms of work organization also contrast with the stylized notion of teams encountered in agency theory. The assumption made in the earliest work on teams in this tradition is that workers are undifferentiated inputs without distinctive skills or firm-specific investments in human capital who could be hired as needed in the external labor market.[19] A more recent article begins with the assumption that there are no differences among workers (agents) and no complementarities among task assignments and derives the proposition that "it is never optimal for two agents to be jointly responsible for any task."[20] Both the assumptions and conclusion are typically violated when teams are implemented as part of a set of high-performance manufacturing practices. In particular, the jobs of operators often involve overlapping responsibilities, cross-training is common, and communication of abstract information necessary for team decisions is easier when multiple operators share joint responsibility.[21]

Agency theory also argues that firms should provide *individual* performance incentives to motivate workers to pay appropriate attention and effort to their assigned tasks—piece rates for operators. The Lincoln Electric Company and Safelite Glass Corporation cases are often cited as examples of the successful use of explicit pay incentives for operators.[22] But a basic incompatibility may exist between the requirements of team production and individual piece rates for operators.

Apparel operators in the traditional bundle system are paid piece rates for performing a single task repetitively—pocket setting, collars, hems, seams, and so on. Costs are reduced in this system by maximizing the output of individual operators. The bundle system maximizes labor productivity and utilization of machines at each stage of the production process, but it has many weaknesses. The accumulation of inventory buffers adds time and cost to the production cycle; it can take weeks before a plant can switch from one color or style to another; and the minute engineering of each small step makes it more difficult to change styles. The system is inflexible and cannot respond to the demands of retailers for quick delivery of perfect quality garments. The goal of the team sewing system is to minimize the time between an order at the retail level and the final delivery of the goods

19. Alchian and Demsetz (1972).
20. Holmstrom and Milgrom (1991, p. 45).
21. Preuss (1998).
22. Harvard Business School (1975); (Lazear 1996).

while largely eliminating defects and rework.[23] As the focus shifts from increasing the efficiency of individual operators to increasing the efficiency of the system, piece rates become counterproductive and are replaced by a fixed hourly wage plus a group quality, production, or profit-sharing bonus.

Horizontal interactions among employees do not negate the role of hierarchy in coordinating production, but they certainly modify it.[24] The separation of thinking from doing in Taylorist work organization was assumed to improve efficiency by increasing the division and specialization of labor, economizing on scarce information processing and decisionmaking skills, avoiding the time lost in group discussions, and centralizing all decisionmaking in management planning bodies near the top of the organizational hierarchy. On these assumptions, economists expect hierarchy and centralized planning to achieve greater productivity than more participatory forms of work organization.[25]

Evidence is accumulating, however, that centralized control of shop floor decisions tends to become less efficient as batch sizes fall, product variety increases, and lead times are reduced. As firms eliminate inventory buffers, as the bar on conformance quality and defect rates is raised, and as firms compete by reducing time to market of new products, modern manufacturing practices that rely on horizontal coordination can improve firm performance.[26] Sometimes, as in auto assembly, horizontal coordination among front-line workers increases productivity. But in other cases, the effects on productivity tend to be fairly small. The real payoff to companies from an increased emphasis on horizontal coordination of the production process comes on the revenue side of the equation as companies that consistently deliver perfect quality products in a timely fashion develop long-term relationships with their customers and land lucrative long-term contracts. In all of these situations, the information rents are positive—which raises the question of who appropriates these collectively produced rents.[27]

23. The results can be dramatic. At one plant the changeover to team production allowed the company to compete effectively for orders from retailers such as Walmart, Sears, and Lane Bryant. As a result, shipments increased from 750 dozen units a week in 1989 to 3,500 dozen in 1993 and nearly 4,000 dozen units per week in 1994. Work-in-process inventory as a percent of shipments at wholesale price decreased 69 percent, from 3.03 to 0.93 percent from 1989 to 1993. Berg and others (1996).

24. Blair and Stout (1999).

25. Williamson (1975); Williamson (1985, chap. 9).

26. Berg and others (1996); Black and Lynch (1997); Ichniowski, Shaw, and Prennushi (1997); Kalleberg and Moody (1994); Huselid (1995).

27. Information rents are defined as the difference between the value created by the horizontal processing and communication of information on the one hand and the productive losses owing to greater

In addition, both offline and production teams associated with the new forms of work organization require greater investments in general and firm-specific worker skills. Firm-specific skill requirements increase because firms share business and financial information with employees, and frontline workers are expected to be knowledgeable about the firm's products and markets. Workers are also expected to develop the ability to meet with customers and to be sufficiently knowledgeable about how the organization operates to help solve customer problems. The same is true if workers are to address shop floor problems effectively. The team building, problem-solving, and decisionmaking activities they undertake, as well as their coordination and communication with coworkers, must be carried out in a manner consistent with the organization's corporate culture. Furthermore, team members must be able to carry out supervisory tasks, such as assigning tasks and dealing with absences, and do routine maintenance tasks. Finally, some skills have general as well as firm-specific characteristics. Workers in self-directed production teams are also required to increase their technical skills in order to perform multiple tasks, carry out statistical process control, and do quality inspections. Investments in these various types of skills increase the "asset specificity" of workers' human capital—that is, the extent to which their human capital is valuable in this firm and the degree of difficulty in transferring these skills to other settings.[28] Workers have a stake in safeguarding their investments in human capital and in protecting future returns to these investments against opportunistic expropriation by managers or shareholders.[29] This raises the question of whether workers in more participatory workplaces, as owners of

---

time spent in learning and communicating on the other. See Aoki (1990, pp. 42–43). In principle, the distribution of information rents should be subject to collective bargaining since workers can mount an effective threat to collectively withhold participation and communication and thereby reduce the firm's output unless they are guaranteed a share in the information rents (Aoki, 1990, p. 44). In practice, very few private sector U.S. workplaces are unionized, and those that are cannot credibly propose actions that would reduce productivity because any reduction in competitiveness could lead management to close the plant.

28. Williamson (1985).

29. This problem has been recognized in the literature as dual moral hazard. Dual moral hazard is defined as follows: "An opportunistic firm may renege on a promise to give its worker a higher wage, by claiming that the worker has not acquired the required skills even when she did; anticipating this, a worker has of course no incentive to collect firm-specific skills. Most solutions to this problem rely on discrete incentives and internal labor markets: wages are linked to jobs rather than performance, and diligent employees are rewarded through assignments and promotions." Sinclair-Desgagné and Cadot (1997, p. 2). Tournament-based promotions are one means through which firms seek to address this problem, but this approach may not be compatible with cooperation among workers.

human capital with a high degree of asset specificity, need a legally protected role in corporate governance, parallel to that of shareholders, in
order to protect these investments in human capital.

For firms that adopt modern manufacturing practices and more participatory types of work organization, the departure of any individual worker
is far more disruptive than in the old work organization, where work is frag-
mented and routinized and front-line workers receive little technical training and less education in interpersonal and decisionmaking skills. For the
worker, payoffs to investments in skills that are costly in the effort, time, and
resources necessary to acquire them can only be realized in a long-term
employment relationship. Explicit contracts cannot resolve these problems.
It is impossible to write contracts in which firms require workers to develop
and use these skills to supply appropriate levels of discretionary effort—a
concept that is difficult to define, let alone measure.[30] Nor can employees
require firms to make a long-term commitment to them.

It is somewhat easier for firms to take steps to encourage employees to
commit to a long-term relationship than the other way around. Firms may
choose to implement human resource and industrial relations practices
intended to increase trust, such as sharing business information or consulting workers before major changes are made. They may provide workers with opportunities to share in the rents and risks of the firm by making
pay partly contingent on firm performance through profit sharing, subsi-
dized stock purchases, and quality or production bonuses. Putting part of
a worker's pay at risk in these ways has three effects: it provides incentives
for sharing knowledge, making decisions, and carrying out production
tasks; it encourages employees to take steps under their control to protect
their investments in human capital, for example, through retraining if current skills become less useful to the firm; and it rewards workers' investments in firm-specific human capital by providing them with a current
claim (and, in some cases, a future claim) on the firm's residual earnings.

Nevertheless, it is still unclear whether new forms of work organization require higher levels of at-risk pay. One source of skepticism about
the incentive effects of profit sharing or bonuses linked to meeting team
quantity or quality targets centers on the concern that the output due to
greater effort by any individual contributes very little to that individual's
compensation—hence the presumed incentive of individuals to shirk and

---

30. Bailey and Merritt (1992).

free ride, rather than to expend appropriate effort.[31] Peer pressure may operate to overcome the incentive for free riding and to increase the effort of a group of workers. Workers may feel bad about working in such an environment, however, and may be worse off as a result.[32] Alternatively, gift exchange and reciprocity can explain how the gift of a share of the firm's rents can be exchanged for greater effort via a shift in the individual worker's cost of effort function.[33] When a significant portion of pay is at risk, allowing workers to share in the rents earned by the firm makes it costly for workers to leave since the high degree of firm specificity of their skills makes it unlikely they can earn similar rents elsewhere. Importantly, these pay arrangements also signify a partial recognition that workers have ownership claims on the firm because of the high level of their investments in firm-specific human capital, and that their claims to be stakeholders, like those of the investors who financed the firm's physical capital, are legitimate.[34]

While companies can provide incentives to workers to commit to a long and stable relationship with the firm, it is far more difficult for workers to extract such a commitment from the firms that employ them. Implicit understandings about employment security that depend on firms' concerns about their reputations have been greatly weakened by the waves of plant closings in the 1980s and downsizing of employees in the 1990s. Nevertheless, companies that adopt modern manufacturing practices still tend to offer promises of employment security, including explicit commitments in some unionized firms. This promise of employment security serves several purposes: building trust; providing workers with confidence that abandoning old work rules and making the production process more efficient will not lead to layoffs; and providing some assurance of long-term employment. All such agreements provide loopholes, however, in case of downturns in demand or poor decisions by top managers.

The problem of safeguarding investments in firm-specific human capital and providing long-term continuity in employment has been recognized in the transactions costs literature, which specifically mentions the need to embed these investments in human capital in a protective governance

31. Lazear (1995).
32. Kandel and Lazear (1992).
33. Burks (1997).
34. Blair (1999).

structure.[35] As noted above, unions have affected corporate governance structures through collective bargaining agreements that establish pay scales, grievance procedures, and protections against arbitrary dismissal. This may not be sufficient, however, to protect the more extensive investments in firm-specific human capital made by workers in more participatory workplaces. Enforceable rights to employee participation in corporate governance may be required to safeguard the continuity of the employment relationship. Works councils in Germany, for example, have legally enforceable rights to comanagement on such issues as firm-sponsored training, work organization, and plans for layoffs. The councils can veto the dismissal of workers and have consultation and information rights about health and safety, business plans, new equipment, and changes in work processes.[36] Without such legally enforceable rights, U.S. labor-management partnerships are in a much weaker position to protect workers' investments in human capital.

Evidence on Horizontal Coordination

In our study, we examined two broad questions about horizontal coordination in the production process. One, do front-line workers participate in coordinating the production process and in making decisions? To find out, we asked the following questions:

—How widespread are self-directed work teams in this study? Do the responsibilities of workers in such teams differ substantially from those of other workers? (See table 4-2 for the questions used to define "self-directed teams.")

—How do such teams affect the supervisors' job?

—How widespread is the use of offline quality improvement and problem-solving teams? (See table 4-2 for the questions used to define offline teams.)

—Do these offline teams meet regularly? How do they function?

—Do their recommendations affect the jobs of other workers in the factory?

—How extensive is daily or weekly communication by workers with other workers, supervisors, and managers and with subject matter experts?

35. Williamson (1985); Blair (1999).
36. Baethge and Wolf (1995).

Table 4-2. *Questions Used to Define Team Variables*

Self-directed teams

- In your daily work activities, are you part of a team of people who work together? (This is usually 12 or fewer people but it could be more.) Is this team a self-directed team of people who work together and jointly make decisions about task assignments? (Asked of steel and medical blue-collar workers.)

- In your daily work activities, do you work in a module or team of people who work together and jointly make decisions about task assignments? (Asked of apparel blue-collar workers.)

- Do you have a self-directed team (module) of people who work together and jointly make decisions about task assignments that reports to you? (Asked of supervisors in steel and apparel.)

- Do you work in a team? If not, do you work with others or do you work alone? (Asked of medical white-collar employees.)

Offline teams

Now I would like to ask about other teams, committees, or task forces that you work on with other employees or managers. This includes employees and managers other than those you work with in conducting your normal job duties.

- Do you work on a team, committee, or task force that deals specifically with product development and product redesign?

- Do you work on a team, committee, or task force that deals specifically with product quality?

- Do you work on a team, committee, or task force that deals specifically with reducing cost?

- Do you work on a team, committee, or task force that deals specifically with purchases or modifications of equipment?

- Do you work on a team, committee, or task force that deals specifically with working conditions?

- Do you work on a team, committee, or task force that deals specifically with training?

- Do you work on a team, committee, or task force that deals specifically with other work-related problems or issues?

- Of all of the teams, committees, or task forces you mentioned you serve on, please tell me which one you spend the most time on.

- Now we'd like you to answer the following questions referring to this team, committee, or task force you spend the most time on.

—Does frequency differ by whether workers participate in self-directed or offline teams?

Two, how widespread are contingent pay arrangements? We examine the extent to which firms compensate workers using individual piece rates, group piece rates, profit sharing, or bonuses for meeting quality goals or production goals and whether firms are more likely to use contingent compensation for workers in self-directed or offline teams. Finally, we examine the relationship between contingent pay and communication.

Sample

During 1995–97, our research team conducted interviews with managers and, when relevant, with union leaders at 44 manufacturing facilities across the country. We obtained employee lists at 41 of these facilities. At the time this chapter was written, more than 4,000 employees at 38 plants (14 in steel, 14 in apparel, and 10 in medical electronic instruments and imaging) had been surveyed.

Our sampling frame in steel focused on facilities with rolling mills and steelmaking capacity that produced either carbon sheet or bar products. We did not include superprocessors or stand-alone rolling facilities that may specialize in cold rolling or galvanizing. Our intent was to capture a large part of the steel production process that could be compared across integrated and minimill producers of sheet and bar products. Whereas steelmaking processes differ across integrateds and minimills, the hot and cold rolling and cold finishing operations are quite similar. Using standard industry guidebooks, and after eliminating new start-ups and worker-owned mills, we identified 18 bar mills and 19 sheet mills that were eligible for inclusion in the study. Of these, nine bar mills and eight sheet mills (twelve separate companies) participated.

In apparel, our strategy for selecting plants was driven by our interest in comparing the performance of module and bundle production systems. This requires us to make direct comparisons between module and bundle production of the same product. With the help of the Textile/Clothing Technology Corporation, an organization that is sponsored by firms and unions in the apparel industry and provides consulting services and advice, we identified plants producing the same or very similar products under the two different regimes. The sample of eighteen plants includes manufacturers of a variety of basic products plus some that produce more varied products.

These products represent a majority of the types of production that remain in the United States. The highly varied women's wear segment, which has the highest import penetration ratio, is least represented in our sample.

Medical electronic instruments and imaging consists of companies that manufacture electrodiagnostic equipment, such as electrocardiographs, and companies that manufacture medical imaging equipment, such as ultrasound, X-ray, computed tomography, and magnetic resonance imaging equipment. Using standard industry guidebooks, we identified 328 firms listed as doing business in these industry segments. Through telephone contact, we identified 144 companies that actually manufacture such devices in the United States. Forty-four of these companies employ 100 or more people. These 44 companies constituted our potential sample. Of these, 9 companies (10 plants) participated in the study.

We emphasize that the plants that participated in this study do not constitute a random sample of producers. A disproportionate number of the plants have taken steps, or plan to take steps, to introduce some types of high-performance workplace practices. However, the research team consciously worked in each industry to include plants in which all or a significant part of the work of blue-collar workers is traditionally organized and managed.

Top managers (that is, the plant or human resource manager) at 27 of the plants in the sample report that they have formally introduced self-directed teams at their facilities. This includes 15 of the 18 apparel plants in our sample (some of which continue to operate both team and bundle production systems), 8 of the 10 medical plants, and a quarter of the steel mills. Team production was introduced earliest in the assembly operations of the medical electronic instruments and imaging plants in our sample. Production cells in the assembly stage of the production process were implemented between 1987 and 1991, with most introduced before 1989. Module production in the apparel plants in our sample was implemented between 1991 and 1996. Team production in the medical and apparel plants requires a distinctive reorganization of workers and machinery on the shop floor. As a result, there is little ambiguity about whether team production has been introduced in these plants. In steel, where the shift from production crews to production teams is not associated with a rearrangement of equipment, the question of whether team production exists in the mill is more ambiguous. At only four of the steel mills in our sample, all unionized, did managers report the formal introduction of team production in steel rolling or finishing operations—mainly in conjunction with the partnership agreements negotiated with the United Steel Workers of America (USWA) in 1993 and 1994. We emphasize that while our methodology allows us to examine the nature of workplace practices such as production teams or offline teams and to determine whether they are "real," it does not permit us to make any generalizations about how widespread these practices are in the industries we have examined.

At each plant, we conducted interviews over a two-day period with a variety of managers (plant manager, human resource manager, training manager, marketing manager, production manager or superintendent, department managers and, as needed, with accountants and engineers). When a union was present, we also interviewed union officials. We collected data on business strategy, formal workplace and human resource practices, technology, computer use, and plant performance. A stratified random sample of hourly workers at each site was drawn and a thirty-minute telephone survey with these individuals was conducted. Finally, separate surveys of first-line supervisors in steel and apparel and of white-collar professionals in engineering, marketing, and purchasing in medical electronic instruments and imaging were conducted.

Our sample consists of 4,081 employees of which 3,250 are blue-collar workers, 610 are white-collar employees in medical, and 221 are supervisors in steel and apparel plants (table 4-1). The industry breakdown of the employees is 51.0 percent in steel, 24.4 percent in apparel, and 24.6 percent in medical. Demographic and educational characteristics are given in appendix table 4A-1. Means of variables used in the analysis are given in appendix table 4A-2.

Horizontal Coordination and Communication

We find evidence of substantial lateral coordination and communication among front-line workers in our sample. A very high percentage of blue-collar workers report that they work in a self-directed team—57.0 percent in steel, 63.1 percent in apparel, and 59.6 percent in medical.[37] Even when

37. In steel, we also examined the use of self-directed teams and offline teams in minimills, which tend to be smaller greenfield facilities, and in the larger and older integrated mills. We found no significant difference in participation in offline teams. Approximately 50 percent of workers in both settings (50.5 percent in minimills and 49.2 percent in integrateds) report that they currently participate in an offline team. Workers in minimills are somewhat more likely than those in integrated mills to report that they work in a self-directed team—61.5 percent compared with 54.2 percent, but both figures are quite high.

Table 4-3. *Participation in Self-Directed and Offline Teams, by Type of Worker and Industry*

	Percent of Nonsupervisory Workers by Industry Who Participate in Self-Directed Teams	
Industry	*Self-directed team*	*Self-directed team that does key tasks*[a]
Steel	57.0	24.8
Apparel	63.1	29.5
Medical	59.6	39.1
N		3,837

	Percent of Blue-Collar and White-Collar/Supervisory Workers by Industry Who Participate in Offline Teams	
Industry	*Blue collar*	*White collar/supervisory*
Steel	49.7	72.5
Apparel	43.8	84.0
Medical	67.3	79.3
N	3,249	831

a. Self-directed team does its own quality control, meets to solve problems, and assigns daily tasks.

we restrict the definition to teams that do their own quality control, meet to solve problems, and assign daily tasks, a surprisingly high percentage of blue-collar workers are in a self-directed team—24.8 percent in steel, 29.5 percent in apparel, and 39.1 percent in medical (table 4-3). Participation in offline teams is also very high. Approximately three-quarters of blue-collar workers (76.4 percent) participate in a self-directed team or an offline team of some kind, and about one-third (32.7 percent) participate in both (table 4-4). The function of the supervisor in many of the plants in our sample is shifting from monitoring workers and running daily production operations to focusing on problem solving across functional areas. This objective is reflected in the high levels of participation by supervisors in offline teams—72.5 percent of supervisors in steel and 84.0 percent in apparel.

Table 4-4. *Extent of Participation by Nonsupervisory Workers in Self-Directed or Offline Teams*

Percent

Item	All	Blue collar	White collar medical
No participation	21.3	23.6	8.7
Self-directed team only	24.2	26.5	12.0
Offline team only	16.6	17.2	13.0
Both self-directed team and offline team	38.0	32.7	66.2
	100	100	100
N	3,836	3,229	607

Self-Directed Teams

The introduction of modular production in apparel and cell production in assembly operations in medical electronic instruments and imaging has meant a formal shift in authority and responsibility to front-line workers and increased investment in workers' firm-specific technical and team-building skills. In steel, even without the formal introduction of team production, many plants have eliminated supervisors on the night shifts, with the result that steel workers in these plants (all of whom work rotating shifts) work either one or two out of every three weeks without a supervisor present and have increased responsibility for regulating and monitoring the production process themselves.

If these teams are actually managing day-to-day operations, we would expect them to take over many of the functions of traditional supervisors. In particular, we would expect them to participate in setting performance goals for the team, do their own quality control, meet to solve work-related problems, do routine maintenance on their machinery, assign daily tasks to team members, and deal with scheduled absences of team members from work. Tables 4-5 and 4-6 show that workers in self-directed teams report that their teams do, indeed, carry out many of these functions. In steel, the proportion of team members who report that their team performs these tasks varies from 60 to 79 percent, while in apparel, the proportion varies from 75 to 89 percent. For medical blue-collar workers, the proportion whose teams perform these tasks ranges from 75 to 93 percent. It is much

Table 4-5. *Tasks of Self-Directed Teams of Blue-Collar Workers, according to Workers and Supervisors*

Question and response	Steel[a]		Apparel[a]	
	Worker	Supervisor	Worker	Supervisor
What do self-directed teams of blue-collar workers do?				
Choose team leader	19.0	46.9	47.3	77.8
Participate in setting performance goals	60.8	75.7	78.5	100.0
Do own quality control	76.5	63.5	80.6	83.3
Meet to solve problems	73.3	86.0	82.2	94.4
Do routine maintenance	78.9	92.1	84.0	100.0
Assign daily tasks	78.9	59.7	74.7	83.3
Schedule time away from work	59.1	71.4	88.5	88.9
N	1,066	132	610	18

a. Reports responses of workers in self-directed teams and of supervisors who have at least one self-directed team reporting to them.

less common for these teams to choose their own team leader than to perform other tasks.

We tried to determine whether supervisors shared the view of blue-collar workers about what self-directed teams do. Supervisors who have a self-directed team reporting to them were asked whether the team performs these various functions. Their responses are reported in table 4-5. Although some differences show up in perceptions between workers and supervisors, what stands out in table 4-5 is that similarly high percentages of supervisors and workers indicate that self-directed teams perform these functions. This consistent assessment by supervisors and workers reinforces the notion that self-directed teams perform significant functions.[38]

Workers not in teams were also asked whether their work group or department performed these functions. Most apparel workers in the traditional bundle system work alone, and the overwhelming majority responded that these questions did not apply to them. For blue-collar workers in medical and steel, however, we are able to compare the responses of workers in work groups with those of workers in self-directed

38. We also compared responses of workers and supervisors in the same mills and plants, and found results similar to those reported in table 4-5.

Table 4-6. *Blue-Collar Workers in Steel and Medical Industries: Differences between Self-Directed Teams and Traditional Work Groups*
Comparison of means

| | Blue-collar workers | | | | |
| | Steel | | Medical | | Apparel[a] |
Question and response	Work group	Self-directed team	Work group	Self-directed team	Self-directed team
Does your team or work group					
Choose team leader	9.8	19.0[b]	9.9	22.6[b]	47.3
Participate in setting performance goals	33.1	60.8[b]	38.6	74.9[b]	78.5
Do own quality control	58.1	76.5[b]	74.7	84.5[b]	80.6
Meet to solve problems	76.9	73.3	87.4	85.3	82.2
Do routine maintenance	66.8	78.9[b]	80.3	88.7[b]	84.0
Assign daily tasks	58.3	78.9[b]	70.6	93.1[b]	74.7
Schedule time away from work	46.6	59.1[b]	73.0	78.4	88.5
N	1,869		394		582

a. Questions do not apply to workers in the bundle system in apparel who work alone and not in a work group. The vast majority of these workers responded "not applicable."

b. Self-directed team significantly higher at 5 percent level.

teams. Table 4-6 shows the results of means comparisons between those who work in a self-directed team and those who work in a more traditional work group. We find that workers in self-directed teams are more likely to report that they choose a team leader, participate in setting performance goals, conduct quality inspection, conduct routine maintenance, and assign daily tasks. In steel, workers in self-directed teams are also more likely to report that they schedule time away from work. Notably, no significant difference occurs between self-directed teams and work groups in either industry in meeting to solve problems. Three-quarters of both groups of workers in steel and four-fifths of both groups in medical report that they meet to solve problems.

Finally, we examine how supervisors who have at least one self-directed team that reports to them assess the impact of these teams on their jobs (table 4-7). These supervisors recognize that self-directed teams allow them to supervise more workers and that this may reduce the number of super-

Table 4-7. *Effect of Self-Directed Teams on Supervisors,
according to Supervisors*

Percent of supervisors who have a self-directed team reporting to them who agree or strongly agree

Question and response	Steel	Apparel
How do self-directed teams affect the job of supervisor?		
Reduces the authority of supervisors	31.9	66.7
Makes the supervisor's job easier	91.1	77.8
Makes the supervisor more effective	92.9	100.0
Allows the supervisor to supervise more workers	80.4	94.4
Lines of responsibility are clearly defined	92.1	94.4
Seek agreement from workers before I change things	76.1	88.9
N	132	18

visors in the plant. They also report that teams make their jobs easier and make them more effective. Most supervisors seem to be adapting to their new roles. We find that most supervisors believe that lines of responsibility are clearly defined, and most report that they seek agreement from workers before they change things.

Offline Teams

How extensive is participation in offline teams? Well over half of all employees—blue-collar workers, white-collar workers, and supervisors—report that they currently serve on an offline team. Table 4-8 examines how many employees are on teams that meet regularly. Almost 24 percent of the sample participate in an offline team that meets four or more times a month and 37 percent are in teams that meet two or more times a month. Table 4-9 examines how offline teams function. We find that among blue-collar workers 77 percent of employees in offline teams report that their teams include managers while 70 percent report that offline team meetings are run by managers. Offline teams are primarily management led across all three industries; this is especially true in the apparel industry where even teams that do not include a manager as a regular member have meetings that are run by a manager. Offline teams are systematic in their approach to problem solving. Nearly all offline teams develop plans to solve problems and then evaluate how well these plans worked. Whether nonsupervisory workers believe their plans are very likely to be carried out

Table 4-8. *Frequency of Offline Team Meetings*

Question and response	Percent[a]
How frequently does your offline team meet?	
Not in offline team	44.3
Less than once a month	3.0
Once a month	16.0
Two or three times a month	13.0
Four or more times a month	23.7
	100.0
N	4,080

a. Includes supervisors in steel and apparel industries and white-collar employees in medical industry.

depends on the industry and occupational group, with the percentage varying from a low of 40.3 percent in apparel to a high of 71.0 percent of white-collar workers in medical industries. The opportunity to challenge a rejected recommendation by an offline committee also varies by industry, with higher percentages of both blue- and white-collar workers in the medical electronic instruments and imaging industry maintaining that it is very likely they would have the opportunity to challenge a rejection.

Table 4-9. *How Offline Teams Function*
Percent of participants in offline teams who answer yes

	Blue collar				White collar medical
Question and response	All	Steel	Apparel	Medical	medical
How do offline teams function?					
Team includes managers	77.3	79.9	68.3	81.0	86.3
A manager runs meetings	70.2	68.5	80.2	64.3	65.5
Team develops plan to solve problem	88.7	90.1	83.5	91.2	93.8
Team evaluates how well plan worked	84.4	83.0	87.4	85.2	73.1
Plans developed by this team are very likely to be carried out	46.4	45.8	40.3	56.8	71.0
When plan is rejected, team very likely to have opportunity to challenge	28.5	28.7	22.0	37.0	39.0

Not surprisingly, 80 to 95 percent of participants in offline teams believe their offline team is very or somewhat effective. We also asked workers whether the recommendations made by problem-solving or quality improvement teams at their facility have affected their work. Here, the high proportion that responded that these recommendations have affected their jobs to some or a great extent is quite unexpected. Of those blue-collar workers who do not participate in offline teams, a surprisingly high 59 percent (72 percent of medical blue collar, 82 percent of medical white collar) believe that the recommendations of quality improvement or problem-solving teams have affected their work.

Communication

We examine next the extent to which blue-collar workers communicate regularly about work issues with workers, managers, or other professional workers outside their work group. Table 4-10 shows that a substantial proportion of workers in our sample communicate regularly with managers and professionals. Two-fifths of the workers communicate regularly with managers outside their work group or team and nearly a third with technical experts. In addition, two-thirds communicate frequently with workers outside their work group or team. We find that communication is greater for those who work in a self-directed team or participate in an offline team compared with other workers, and the differences are statistically significant. The results suggest that communication is not just horizontal, with other workers, but vertical across levels of the organization too.

Contingent Pay and Participation

Group incentives are widely used by the plants in our sample. Human resource managers report profit sharing for blue-collar workers at 80 percent of the steel mills, 56 percent of the apparel mills, and 40 percent of the medical electronic instruments and imaging plants. This finding was confirmed in our survey of blue-collar workers, where 84 percent of steel workers, 39 percent of apparel workers, and 47 percent of medical workers reported receiving part of their pay as profit sharing (table 4-11). A much larger proportion of white-collar workers than blue-collar workers in medical receive profit sharing.

We also asked human resource managers how the wages paid to blue-collar workers at their facilities compared with wages in their local labor

Table 4-10. *Nonsupervisory Workers and Discussion of Work Issues*

Percent who communicate personally daily or weekly

Question and response	All	Steel	Apparel	Blue collar medical	White collar medical	Self-directed team		Offline team	
						Yes	No	Yes	No
Do you discuss work issues with									
Managers or supervisors in your work group or work team	82.5	79.6	81.0	86.8	91.0	85.6[a]	77.1	87.1[a]	76.9
Outside of your work group or work team	40.9	37.5	40.7	42.0	50.7	43.8[a]	36.0	49.2[a]	30.7
Workers outside of your work group or work team	67.1	62.7	59.9	76.9	85.7	70.4[a]	61.8	74.6[a]	58.0
Technical experts outside of your work group or work team, such as engineers, technicians, accountants, or consultants	31.9	21.7	23.7	59.9	58.2	36.1[a]	25.2	41.6[a]	20.2
N	3,859					2,381[b]	1,446[b]	1,744[b]	2,109[b]

a. Significantly higher at the 1 percent level.
b. Numbers do not match total because not everyone answered the question.

Table 4-11. *Contingent Pay for Blue-Collar Workers*
Percent who receive contingent pay

Incentive for contingent pay	All	Steel	Apparel	Medical	Self-directed team		Offline team	
					Yes	*No*	*Yes*	*No*
Individual piece rate	10.2	2.9	28.0	0.76	4.4	18.6[a]	7.5	12.8[a]
Group piece rate	20.9	15.4	39.9	1.0	29.6[a]	8.4	19.7	22.2
Profit sharing	65.7	83.5	38.5	46.9	67.2	63.5	67.1	64.4
Meet work group/department quality goals	43.4	50.3	38.5	22.4	50.5[a]	33.3	46.8[a]	40.1
Meet work group/department production goals	52.7	65.7	39.4	23.1	58.0[a]	44.6	54.3	51.2
N	3,240	1,880	966	394	3,222		3,239	

a. Significantly higher at 1 percent level.

market and to wages in their industry. In apparel, 70 percent of managers reported that their plants paid wages above the average for the industry, and 30 percent reported paying wages above the average for the local labor market. In steel the situation was reversed, with human resource mangers reporting that 94 percent of the mills paid wages above the average for the local labor market, but only 20 percent paid wages above the average for the industry. In medical, human resource managers reported that 70 percent of plants paid wages above the average for the local labor market and 40 percent paid wages above the average for the industry.

We then compared the average wages reported by workers in our sample with Current Population Survey (CPS) data on average wages by industry and occupation and found that the average hourly pay of blue-collar workers is higher in our sample. Medical operators in our sample earn $13.50 an hour on average, compared with hourly earnings in 1996 of $10.15 for all electromedical equipment operators. Apparel operators in our sample earn $7.17 an hour on average, compared with $6.40 an hour in 1996 for all apparel operators. Blue-collar workers in our steel sample include maintenance workers and operators. Average hourly pay of these workers was $15.20. Hourly earnings in 1996 of steel operators was $12.37 and of steel maintenance workers was $14.74 according to the CPS.[39] Thus, in each industry, workers reported substantially higher earnings than the national average for their occupation. This may be because of profit sharing and bonus payments that put a significant part of the pay of some workers at risk, or to premium base pay associated with rent sharing or unionization.

Our survey provides evidence that a much larger proportion of workers in self-directed teams, compared with those not in such teams, have part of their pay contingent on group performance. This is far less likely to be true of workers in offline teams. Workers in self-directed teams are far less likely to be paid individual piece rates (4.4 percent compared with 18.6 percent) and far more likely to be paid group piece rates (29.6 percent compared with 8.4 percent). This result is mainly driven by apparel, where 28 percent of workers are paid individual piece rates and 39.9 percent are paid group piece rates. However, 15.4 percent of steel workers also report that they are paid group piece rates. Half of the workers in self-directed

---

39. Average wages by industry and occupation were tabulated from the Outgoing Rotation Group file of the Current Population Survey.

teams report that part of their pay depends on meeting work group or department quality goals, compared with a third of workers not in such teams. For pay partly dependent on meeting production goals, the proportions are 58.0 percent and 44.6 percent respectively. There are no significant differences in the prevalence of profit sharing. For offline teams, it makes sense that the only group incentive that is significant is pay related to meeting work group or department quality goals, since that is what many of these teams work on.

Finally, while group incentives are used by firms to motivate participation in self-directed teams, and workers in such teams are significantly more likely than workers not in such teams to communicate with other actors in the firm, we do not find evidence that firms rely on contingent pay to motivate these types of communication and coordination.

Conclusion

The competitive pressures pushing companies to produce defect-free and reliable products, to reduce buffers of work-in-process inventory and carefully manage inventories of finished products, and to provide consistent on-time delivery are changing the role of blue-collar workers in the production process. A common theme among the plants that agreed to participate in this study is the recognition of these competitive pressures and, as a result, a recognition of the need to adopt work organization and human resource practices that more fully engage the capabilities of their employees in decisions about production and in quality improvement. The plants in our sample vary widely in the extent to which they have adopted a full set of complementary modern manufacturing practices. Many of these plants are industry leaders in this regard. Some are in a process of transition, operating team and traditional work systems in the same facility. And some recognize that they need to change but are uncertain about how to go about it or what practices really pay off in their industry.

The plants that participated in this study are vertically organized, although some have only four layers from operator to CEO. Most are part of large corporations, many with multiple plants in the same industry. Yet, there are important differences between these plants and traditional hierarchies. In traditional hierarchical organizations, information flows vertically. At the bottom of the organization, this means that information flows vertically between front-line workers and supervisors while horizontal coordination of production is the task of supervisors. In the plants in this study, however, the view that supervisors are necessary to assign daily tasks, monitor worker effort and prevent shirking, inspect the quality of the work and monitor performance, gather information to pass up to higher level managers for action, and enforce decisions made at higher levels of the organization is changing. Where there are self-directed teams, the tasks of monitoring and coordination have been shifted to front-line workers, with a consequent flattening of the hierarchy at the bottom and a reduction in the number of supervisors and changes in their responsibilities. In some steel mills, the number of supervisors has been radically reduced without the formal introduction of team production. The evidence from the worker survey suggests that even in these cases, where other formal changes have not been made, monitoring and coordination tasks have effectively been shifted to front-line workers.

In many of the plants in the three industries in our sample, workers are expected to engage in problem-solving activities whether or not there are self-directed teams, and firms have tried to motivate such participation through the introduction of profit sharing. Front-line workers have increased responsibility for coordinating production activities. Offline teams with problem-solving and decisionmaking responsibility are widespread. Even in plants with traditional organizational structures, workers are more engaged in horizontal coordination and communication than is usually assumed in transactions cost or principal-agent theories of the firm. Nevertheless, workers in self-directed teams have responsibilities that go beyond these problem-solving activities.

The very high proportions of workers who report that they work in self-directed teams is a function of the way in which firms self-selected into this study. But the evidence from the worker survey, confirmed in the supervisor survey and in the manager interviews, is that much of the information about production and quality problems in these plants is collected and remains at the bottom levels, where it is acted on directly by workers who call on subject matter experts, confer with workers and managers outside their work groups, and make decisions about organizational routines that affect product quality, maintenance of production equipment, and adherence to production schedules.

Workers' reports of profit sharing and production and quality bonuses, and their higher average earnings compared with national averages suggest that firms may be putting in place contingent pay systems that provide members of self-directed teams with a claim on the firm's rents. For most workers in our sample, however, contingent pay is a small fraction of earnings. Since each worker bears the full cost of his or her own effort but gains only a small share of the resulting increase in profit or output, economic theory suggests that workers have an incentive to be free riders and not contribute difficult-to-measure discretionary effort in production and offline teams).[40] Yet workers in high-performance work organizations do appear to be contributing discretionary effort to improving efficiency and quality, and contingent pay practices correlate with participation in self-directed production or offline teams.

We propose an alternative explanation for the effectiveness of contingent pay schemes. Workers are more likely to make the necessary investment in skill attainment, expend the additional effort to gather and share information, and participate in decisionmaking and in regulating the production process when they have a stake in the long-term success of the enterprise, and when management recognizes this stake. In this context, profit sharing and other forms of contingent pay can be understood as a recognition by shareholders and managers of workers' claims on the enterprise's residual income, directly analogous to the claims of managers and CEOs whose pay is contingent on performance. By making pay partly contingent on firm performance, companies may provide workers with opportunities to share in the rents and risks of the firm. It is the recognition of workers as stakeholders in the firm, and not the size of the incentive, that is significant and that provides incentives for workers to expend appropriate levels of discretionary effort.

Our survey results show that firms' responses to competitive pressures are changing the relationships among actors within firms. The evidence suggests that companies that strive to meet world class standards for quality, reliability, and on-time delivery have given front-line workers major responsibility for horizontal coordination of the production process previously carried out by supervisors and lower level managers, and have changed their compensation systems to reflect participation by front-line workers in management decisionmaking.

---

40. Alchian and Demsetz (1972); Bowles (1985); Kandel and Lazear (1992); Lazear (1995).

Table 4A-1. *Means of Demographic and Education Variables,*
by Industry and Occupational Category
Percent unless noted otherwise

Variables	All	Steel Blue collar	Steel Super-visor	Apparel Blue collar	Apparel Super-visor	Medical Blue collar	Medical White collar
Gender							
Female	32.3	6.2	3.1	92.7	92.0	35.5	21.5
Male	67.7	93.8	96.9	7.3	8.0	64.5	78.5
Age (years)	43.9	45.8	47.1	41.8	48.8	42.6	40.8
Race							
White	77.9	76.2	93.3	73.0	92.0	77.2	86.3
Black	11.4	15.8	3.6	13.1	4.0	5.4	1.8
Hispanic	4.6	4.7	1.5	7.4	4.0	2.8	2.2
Other	6.0	3.3	1.5	6.5	0.0	14.6	9.8
Education							
Less than high school	11.1	6.7	1.5	30.2	28.0	5.1	0.5
High school graduate	44.1	54.3	36.4	55.9	56.0	31.5	4.4
High school plus	29.5	34.3	30.3	12.7	16.0	50.4	27.9
College graduate	15.4	4.8	31.8	1.5	0.0	13.0	67.2
Classroom or structured training	69.4	71.2	80.1	53.4	60.0	84.8	58.3
Job tenure (months)	77.6	97.9	100.6	56.9	89.1	60.0	51.1
Union	53.7	77.9	. . .	26.8	. . .	3.8	. . .
Hourly pay (blue collar)	$12.50	$15.20	. . .	$7.17	. . .	$13.50	. . .

Table 4A-2. *Means of Variables Used in the Analysis*
Percent

Variables	Means
Industry	
Steel	51.0
Minimill	40.8
Integrated	59.2
Apparel	24.6
Medical	24.6
Occupational category	
Blue collar	79.6
White collar	14.9
Supervisor	5.4
Self-directed team	
Blue collar	59.2
White collar	78.3
Supervisor (a self-directed team reports to him/her)	87.3
Offline team	55.7
Communications	
With workers in work group	94.3
With workers outside work group	67.1
With own managers/supervisors	82.5
With managers/supervisors outside work group	40.9
With experts outside work group	31.9
Incentive pay	
Piece rate (blue collar)	10.2
Group piece rate (blue collar)	20.9
Profit sharing	65.2
Meet quality goals	40.3
Meet production goals	51.9

COMMENT BY

Kathryn Shaw

Eileen Appelbaum and Peter Berg address the following general question: as firms alter their production environments to improve performance, are they adopting human resource practices that produce more horizontal control? In firms with more horizontal control, production workers have greater decisionmaking power on the job and in team activities, and production workers communicate more often with workers across crews and directly with managers. To assess these changes, the authors collect data by visiting plants—16 in steel, 14 in apparel, and 9 in medical electronic instruments and imaging—and surveying approximately 4,000 employees, mostly blue collar. As the authors turn to their survey data, they ask two questions:

—Are front-line employees participating more extensively in management-like activities?

—Does the incentive structure complement these changes (or motivate these new participatory behaviors)?

Overall, they find that blue-collar employees are very involved in teams and decisionmaking—more than would be expected perhaps—and that these involved workers are more likely to have a complementary form of incentive pay.

I find this chapter interesting and important for several reasons. First, the authors have gathered the first available data set assessing how workers believe their jobs have changed as firms have adopted more innovative human resource managment (HRM) practices. Previous surveys have already shown that managers say they are using more innovative HRM practices, for example, teams.[41] No prior survey, however, has asked workers whether they are truly participating in teams of any kind and how their jobs have changed. Prior research has shown too that plants with more innovative HRM practices tend to be more productive, but this research has not documented how worker behavior has changed with the adoption of such practices. Thus these new survey data fill in a missing link in our knowledge by showing that workers have indeed changed their behavior as innovative practices are adopted. The data also suggest that innovations in pay practices complement innovations in team use, rein-

---

41. See, for example, Osterman (1994); Lawler, Mohrman, and Ledford (1995).

forcing previous evidence pertaining to production units rather than to individual workers.[42]

The analysis has been carefully conducted, making this a substantial piece of research. The cross-industry analysis is very valuable. The industries studied are varied and yet similar confirming results occur. A cross-industry analysis is something that previous industry studies have lacked. The Appelbaum and Berg study was implemented very carefully in execution and in writing. The survey questions are well-crafted and nicely cover a range of key issues. And though the authors clearly state that they do not have a random sample of firms, they present evidence on how the sample might be biased, by matching their data to CPS data and showing that they tend to have a higher-paid sample than what appears in the more representative CPS data. Within their industries Appelbaum and Berg sought to include a range of producers. This study was extremely time consuming, and its authors took the time and care to involve the management, the union, and the employees.

The introductory discussion about the theory of the firm is a valuable summary of the issues that frame the survey. The authors reinforce issues that other chapters in this volume also introduce. For example, the authors describe the model of Armen A. Alchian and Harold Demsetz in which firms are hierarchical, with managers getting the residual pay and workers a fixed wage, because team effort is likely to otherwise result in shirking.[43] In contrast, more recent research suggests a need for horizontal organizations because modern manufacturing methods suggest several reasons for pushing more decisionmaking into the hands of production workers. Speed is important, quality is important, and information technology makes lower-level decisionmaking more feasible.[44]

As with most provocative papers, the results raise a number of questions that should be explored further and that suggest how the current results might be reinforced. These cross-sectional data show that today many workers are in team environments where they have greater decisionmaking power, but I now want to know how much power blue-collar workers really possess and how much that power has changed over time. I am most familiar with the steel industry, so let me give an example from my plant visits.

42. I have coauthored separate studies of steel mills and also find that communication patterns have changed in the ways that Applebaum and Berg have described and that teams reinforce the use of incentive pay. Gant, Ichniowski, and Shaw (1999a, 1999b); Boning, Ichniowski, and Shaw (1998).

43. Alchian and Demsetz (1972).

44. Milgrom and Roberts (1990).

At one mill that did not have team production, my colleagues and I asked the mill manager why he did not adopt it. He responded that he felt only individual managers could truly be held accountable for the performance of the mill—that teams or groups of workers could not be accountable for their actions. He pointed out that it was hard to penalize groups for poor outcomes. His observation raises an important question in the context of the Appelbaum and Berg study—how much responsibility do work teams really have? The authors try to address this concern and show in table 4-6 that workers in teams are more likely to set performance goals, do quality control, and assign daily tasks. However, at the same time, in table 4-7 they report that most teams in the steel industry have not reduced the authority of the supervisor, though they have made his job easier. Thus one tends to conclude that production workers today are more productive than in the past because they are more involved in the day-to-day job assignments and decisions that enable the line to run more smoothly. But they are not very involved in the longer-run decisionmaking or the key short-run decisions that are more critical. They help managers by "making supervisors' jobs easier," but they may not really change the primary decisionmaking power.

To assess the responsibility of the work teams, some questions on how job duties have changed over time, rather than reliance on the cross-sectional evidence, would have been useful. Again, let me reiterate the situation in steel. In some mills, production workers function in self-directed teams that do not have foremen and sit on committees that make long-term decisions (including hiring new workers). In other mills, the members of the production crew have seen their decisionmaking power grow over time, but production workers are still continually monitored by a foreman and are not involved in hiring. According to definitions used by Appelbaum and Berg workers in both situations may report being in self-directed teams, and only more detailed information on changes over time might uncover deeper differences. In steel, only 25 percent of the managers state that production workers are in self-directed work teams, but 57 percent of the workers state that they are in such teams. This difference is explained by the fact that of the workers in teams, only 19 percent state that they can choose their team leader, and less than 80 percent do other standard team tasks like meeting to solve problems. Do these percentages imply that most of the steel workers are now in more participatory "work crews" but not truly in self-directed work teams? Appelbaum and Berg are aware of the "ambiguous" nature of teams in steel, but I feel it is worthy of elaboration. Workers seem to have experienced genuine change, but the extent varies and cannot be pinned down without information on changes over time.

Given the implied evidence that participation has risen over time, it would be nice to have a more systematic discussion of the factors that are driving this change in organization. Is it information technology, or is it other factors, such as the desire to use innovative human resource practices to make greater use of workers' knowledge? This question is addressed in this volume by Timothy F. Bresnahan, Erik Brynjolfsson, and Lorin M. Hitt, and it would be valuable to have more evidence in Appelbaum and Berg. Appelbaum and Berg offer concrete examples. Attempting to generalize from them would suggest further empirical analysis. Appelbaum and Berg could use their data to run regressions of decisionmaking authority as a function of the use of information technology to find out what "drives" the adoption of innovative HRM practices.

Finally, the authors ought to contrast the participation and incentive mechanisms of their mills with that of employee stock ownership plans (ESOPs) (to tie to other chapters in the volume). If we are seeing much greater control by employees through changes in HR practices, what does that say more broadly about the nature of the employment contract and about the value of ESOPs? Does it imply that the problems with ESOPs discussed in other chapters—the riskiness, the need for financial resources, and the correlation between the returns to financial capital and human capital—are undermining their use relative to the team concept? And in their conclusion, after they have addressed the control and incentive issues, the authors might return to the ESOP comparison for the incentive structure and voice mechanism there. ESOPs give employees a stake in the outcome—can incentives match this claim?

References

Akerlof, George A. 1984. "Gift Exchange and Efficiency-Wage Theory: Four Views." *American Economic Review* 74 (May): 79–83.

Akerlof, George A., and Janet L. Yellen. 1988. "Fairness and Unemployment." *American Economic Review, Papers and Proceedings* 78 (May): 44–49.

Alchian, Armen A., and Harold Demsetz. 1972. "Production, Information Costs, and Economic Organization." *American Economic Review* 62 (December): 777–95.

Aoki, Masahiko. 1988. *Information, Incentives, and Bargaining in the Japanese Economy.* Cambridge University Press.

————. 1990. "The Participatory Generation of Information Rents and the Theory of the Firm." In *The Firm as a Nexus of Treaties*, edited by Masahiko Aoki, Bo Gustafsson, and Oliver E. Williamson, 26–52. London: SAGE Publications.

Appelbaum, Eileen, and Rosemary Batt. 1994. *The New American Workplace: Transforming Work Systems in the United States.* ILR Press.

Baethge, Martin, and Harold Wolf. 1995. "Continuity and Change in the 'German Model' of Industrial Relations." In *Employment Relations in a Changing World Economy*, edited by Richard Locke, Thomas Kochan, and Michael Piore, 231–62. MIT Press.

Bailey, Thomas, and Donna Merritt. 1992. "Discretionary Effort and the Organization of Work: Employee Participation and Work Reform since Hawthorne." Working Paper. Teachers College and Conservation of Human Resources. Columbia University (August).

Barnard, Chester I. 1938. *The Functions of the Executive.* Harvard University Press.

Batt, Rosemary, and Eileen Appelbaum. 1995. "Worker Participation in Diverse Settings: Does the Form Affect the Outcome, and If So, Who Benefits?" *British Journal of Industrial Relations* 33 (September): 353–78.

Berg, Peter. 1997. "The Effects of Workplace Practices on Job Satisfaction in the United States Steel Industry." Technical Working Paper. Washington: Economic Policy Institute.

Berg, Peter, and others. 1996. "The Performance Effects of Modular Production in the Apparel Industry." *Industrial Relations* 35 (July): 356–73.

Berggren, C. 1992. *Alternatives to Lean Production: Work Organization in the Swedish Auto Industry.* ILR Press.

Black, Sandra E., and Lisa M. Lynch. 1997. "How to Compete: The Impact of Workplace Practices and Information Technology on Productivity." NBER Working Paper 6120. Cambridge, Mass.: National Bureau of Economic Research.

Blair, Margaret M. 1999. "Firm-Specific Human Capital and the Theory of the Firm." In *Employees and Corporate Governance*, edited by Margaret M. Blair and Mark J. Roe. Brookings, 58–89.

Blair, Margaret M., and Lynn A. Stout. 1999. "A Team Production Theory of Corporation Law." *Virginia Law Review* 85 (March): 247–328.

Boning, Brent, Casey Ichniowski, and Kathryn Shaw. 1998. "Incentive Pay for Production Workers: An Empirical Analysis."

Bowles, Samuel. 1985. "The Production Process in a Competitive Economy: Walrasian, Neo-Hobbesian, and Marxian Models." *American Economic Review* 75 (March): 16–36.

Burks, Stephen V. 1997. "Origins of a Segmented Labor Market: An Endogenous Gift Exchange Explanation of Good Jobs and Bad Jobs in Motor Freight." University of Massachusetts-Amherst.

Chandler, Alfred D. 1989. *Strategy and Structure: Chapters in the History of the American Industrial Enterprise.* MIT Press.

Coase, R. H. 1937. "The Nature of the Firm." *Economica* 4: 386–405.

Dunlop, John T., and David Weil. 1996. "Diffusion and Performance of Modular Production in the U.S. Apparel Industry." *Industrial Relations* 35 (July): 334–55.

Edwards, Richard C. 1979. *Contested Terrain: The Transformaton of the Workplace in the Twentieth Century.* Basic Books.

Gant, Jonathan, Casey Ichniowski, and Shaw, Kathryn. 1999a. "Getting the Job Done: Production Functions in High-Involvement and Traditional Organizations." *Industrial Relations Research Association 51st Annual Proceedings*, 43–52.

———. 1999b. "Social Capital and Organizational Change in High-Involvement and Traditional Organizations." Paper presented at National Bureau of Economic Research Conference on Organizational Change.

Gittell, Jody H. 1995. "Effects of Coordination and Control on Operating Performance." Industrial Relations Research Seminar, Sloan School of Management, MIT (May).

Harvard Business School. 1975. "The Lincoln Electric Company." *Harvard Business School Case*. Harvard University.

Holmstrom, Bengt, and Paul Milgrom. 1991. "Multitask Principal-Agent Analyses: Incentive Contracts, Asset Ownership, and Job Design." *Journal of Law, Economics and Organization* 7 (Special Issue): 24–52.

Huselid, Mark A. 1995. "The Impact of Human Resource Management Practices on Turnover, Productivity, and Corporate Financial Performance." *Academy of Management Journal* 38 (June): 635–72.

Ichniowski, Casey, Kathryn Shaw, and Giovanna Prennushi. 1997. "The Effects of Human Resource Management Practices on Productivity: A Study of Steel Finishing Lines." *American Economic Review* 87 (June): 291–313.

Jensen, Michael C., and William H. Meckling. 1976. "Theory of the Firm: Managerial Behavior, Agency Costs and Ownership Structure." *Journal of Financial Economics* (October): 305–60.

Kalleberg, Arne L., and James W. Moody. 1994. "Human Resource Management and Organizational Performance." *American Behavioral Scientist* 37 (June): 948–62.

Kandel, Eugene, and Edward P. Lazear. 1992. "Peer Pressure and Partnerships." *Journal of Political Economy* 100 (August): 801–17.

Lawler, Edward E., Susan A. Mohrman, and Gerald E. Ledford. 1995. *Creating High Performance Organizations: Practices and Results of Employee Involvement and Total Quality Management in Fortune 1000 Companies*. Jossey-Bass.

Lazear, Edward P. 1995. *Personnel Economics*. MIT Press.

———. 1996. "Performance Pay and Productivity." NBER Working Paper 5672. Cambridge, Mass.: National Bureau of Economic Research.

MacDuffie, John Paul. 1995. "Human Resource Bundles and Manufacturing Performance: Organizational Logic and Flexible Production Systems in the World Auto Industry." *Industrial and Labor Relations Review* 48 (January): 197–221.

MacDuffie, John Paul, and John F. Krafick. 1992. "Integrating Technology and Human Resources for High Performance Manufacturing: Evidence from the International Auto Industry." *Transforming Organizations*, edited by Thomas A. Kochan and Michael Useem, 209–25. Oxford University Press.

March, James G., and Herbert A. Simon. 1958. *Organizations*. John Wiley and Sons.

Milgrom, Paul, and John Roberts. 1990. "The Economics of Modern Manufacturing: Technology, Strategy, and Organization." *American Economic Review* 80 (June): 511–28.

Osterman, Paul. 1994. "How Common Is Workplace Transformation and Who Adopts It?" *Industrial and Labor Relations Review* 47 (January): 173–88.

Preuss, Gil. 1998. *Committing to Care: Labor-Management Cooperation and Hospital Restructuring*. Washington: Economic Policy Institute.

Putterman, Louis, and Randall S. Kroszner. 1996. "The Economic Nature of the Firm: A New Introduction." In *The Economic Nature of the Firm: A Reader*, edited by Louis Putterman and Randall S. Kroszner, 1–31. Cambridge: University of Cambridge Press.

Sinclair-Desgagné, Bernerd, and Oliver Cadot. 1997. "Career Concerns and the Acquisition of the Firm-Specific Skills." Discussion Papers. Wissenschaftszentrum Berlin.

Stiglitz, Joseph E. 1987. "The Design of Labor Contracts: The Economics of Incentives and Risk Sharing." In *Incentives, Cooperation, and Risk Sharing: Economic and Psychological Perspectives on Employment Contracts*, edited by Haig R. Nalbantian, 47–68. Rowman and Littlefield.

Taylor, Frederick W. 1911. *The Principles of Scientific Management*. Harper.

Weber, Max. 1978. *Economy and Society*. University of California Press.

Williamson, Oliver E. 1975. *Markets and Hierarchies: Analysis and Antitrust Implications: A Study in the Economics of Internal Management*. Free Press.

———. 1985. *The Economic Institutions of Capitalism*. Free Press.

5

TIMOTHY F. BRESNAHAN
ERIK BRYNJOLFSSON
LORIN M. HITT

Technology, Organization, and the Demand for Skilled Labor

O VER THE PAST two decades, wage inequality has grown significantly in the United States. The total effect has been large, as the gap between wages at the seventy-fifth percentile of the distribution and the twenty-fifth percentile has increased by nearly 50 percentage points.[1] The total effect has also been widespread, shifting relative wages in the top, middle, and bottom of the income distribution. The main cause of the growth in inequality appears to be a shift in the demand for workers of different kinds. Demand is growing for workers with exceptional talent, training, autonomy, and management ability much faster than for workers in low- and middle-wage occupations.

Parts of this shift in labor demand are explained by such broader economic patterns as globalization, sectoral shifts in employment, and changes

We thank Alan Krueger for valuable comments. This research has been generously supported by the MIT Center for Coordination Science, the MIT Industrial Performance Center, the National Science Foundation (Grants IIS-9733877 and IRI-9700316) and the Stanford Computer Industry Project under grants from the Alfred P. Sloan Foundation and NationsBanc Montgomery Securities. Incon Research, the Center for Survey Research, Computer Intelligence Infocorp, and Informationweek provided or helped to collect essential data.

1. Murphy and Welch (1993) show percentiles of the wage distribution of prime-age men: the interquartile range has increased from about 1.75 to 1 to about 2.25 to 1. More extreme percentiles have moved even farther from the median, so that the entire distribution of wages is widening over time.

in labor market institutions. Yet these forces appear too small to explain the breadth and depth of the shift, leaving a large residual shift.[2] Economists have concluded that this residual must reflect a "skill-biased technical change" in the way goods and services are produced in the economy.[3] The nature of this technical change is still not well understood, but its size, breadth, and timing have led many observers to link it to the largest and most widespread technical change of the current era, information technology.[4]

In this chapter, we examine the firm-level evidence for a specific theory of how information technology (IT) could cause skill-biased technical change. We argue that the effects of IT on labor demand involve far more than simple automation and substitution. Instead, we highlight the central role of IT-enabled organizational change in a cluster of complementary and mutually reinforcing innovations that change work fundamentally.

Employers adopt IT-based production processes to improve service quality or increase efficiencies and thereby increase profits. In either case, effective use of IT involves changes to organization. Examination of the form of the organizational changes suggests a theory of why IT-based technical change is skill biased.[5] First in service-producing sectors like finance, and then in the service parts of goods-producing industries, firms have found ways to take advantage of new production processes that use IT intensively.[6] They have found it very difficult to profit by just replacing other factors with computers and telecommunications gear while making the same products. Often, the benefit of the new production process is new services or improved service quality. Further, the new production process involves global changes to the organization.[7] This often means replacing low-skilled workers (automation), while passing on to other workers an increased variety of tasks related to the higher level of service. A similar pattern holds for attempts to achieve IT-based efficiencies in pro-

2. Krugman and Lawrence (1993).

3. Griliches (1969); Berndt, Morrison, and Rosenblum (1992); Berman, Bound, and Griliches (1994).

4. See, for example, Autor, Katz, and Krueger (1997, especially references).

5. Bresnahan (1997).

6. Barras (1990).

7. Among the first to predict this effect were Leavitt and Whisler (1958). There are by now many papers that illustrate the role of IT-enabled organizational change at varying levels of detail, notably Attewell and Rule (1984); Crowston and Malone (1988); Malone, Yates, and Benjamin (1987); Milgrom and Roberts (1990); Brynjolfsson, Renshaw, and Van Alstyne (1997); Bresnahan and Greenstein (1996); and Brynjolfsson and Hitt (1997). It has also been an important theme in the management literature (Davenport and Short, 1990; Hammer, 1990).

duction. Only with organizational change, typically of a kind that involves complementarity with high skill as well as substitutability for low-skilled human work, do employers get the benefit they seek from IT.

These observations lead us to an analysis based on a cluster of complementarities that we see as being at the heart of recent changes in labor demand. Intensive use of IT, higher service levels for customers, and organizational change go together and together call for higher-skilled labor. These form a mutually reinforcing cluster of inventions for employers. Critically, the organizational changes associated with IT-based service improvements are skill using. The key skill-biased technical change of the present can thus be seen to consist not only of IT but of the complete cluster of associated complements. The "technical" side of this cluster is the large, ongoing declines in IT prices and large, ongoing improvements in IT performance. It is tightly linked to labor demand through its organizational side. Investments in the complete cluster, including the dollars, time, and effort associated with the organizational change are likely to be substantially larger than the IT investments themselves, even if they are more difficult to quantify.

Aggregate Data Suggest IT Is Behind the Labor Demand Shifts

Broad-based studies of the labor market are consistent with the hypothesis of an IT-based demand shift.

An important body of research looks at wage determination at the level of individual workers or jobs. Many studies have examined individual worker wage equations.[8] Based on large data sets, such as the Current Population Survey, these studies predict wages with both observables—education and experience—and unobservables—the residual in the wage equation. The observables are interpreted as proxies for skills. Changes in their coefficients over time are interpreted as changes in the prices of those skills. When the distribution of the residual spreads out, it is interpreted as an increase in the price of an unobserved skill. The important results from these studies are that the relative demand for more highly educated workers is rising (probably related to general cognitive skill), that the relative demand for more experienced workers is rising (likely specific knowledge or managerial/people skills), and that the relative demand for "residual" highly skilled workers (skills not captured by education or experience) is rising too.

8. The studies are surveyed in Gottschalk (1997).

A related literature classifies occupations by skills and examines the wages and employment changes for work thus classified.[9] These studies also find considerable support for the view that relative demand is shifting toward cognitive and interpersonal interaction skills.

The difficulty with both these bodies of empirical inquiry is the same. While they can reveal the effects of changes in labor demand, they do not examine the demanding unit. They look at the *demanded* unit—the worker or the job. Accordingly, their ability to examine alternative stories of demand is quite limited.

Another body of studies gets closer to the demanding unit by looking at industries. Here there is also a very clear finding. The IT-intensive industries have seen the demand shift earlier and to a larger extent than other industries.[10] This finding appears to be robust to how computer-intensity is measured and is particularly strong in services.

An industry may be simply too wide a unit to capture the relevant flows of causation. Industries vary in their firms' use of IT strategies. Industries vary in service and product strategies. Industries also vary in their organization of work. Our study, focusing on the firm-level behavior, is pointed more closely at the relevant unit of demand.

Plan of This Chapter

In the following pages we use a simple production function framework to explain our view of the relevant complementarities. We then derive the implications for labor demand and summarize the data we use to test our theory. We also present our findings on the correlations among the variables, firm productivity, and managers' opinions about the effects of IT. Finally we derive some implications and summarize our conclusions.

What Does "Computerization" Mean? The Case of White-Collar Bureaucracies

The key to our argument is that computerizing a firm involves far more than installing computers. Typically, success requires that the firm reinvent

9. See, for example, Howell and Wolff (1991).
10. Wolff (1996); Autor, Katz, and Krueger (1997).

its work organization and the nature of its services and products in myriad large and small ways. As a result, the types of workers employed and the skills of those workers are likely to change.

In this section, we look at the implications of computer business systems for labor demand in white-collar bureaucracies.[11] There are two stages. First, we summarize our overall view of the complementarities, as shown in the graphic presentation in figure 5-1. We then discuss the specifics of the relationship between IT-enabled organizational change and the shift in labor demand patterns.

Computer business systems change white-collar work. One way they change it is by organizing, routinizing, and regularizing tasks that people- and paper-based systems did more intuitively but more haphazardly. The systems also change work by changing the nature of the firm's output, especially in the service sectors, and in the white-collar activities of the goods sectors. Computer-based production leads to higher levels of service or even whole new services and products. The labor-demand impact comes at the firm level, as computer business systems form the modern production process for many service industries (and for the service functions of other industries). As computers have grown cheaper, and especially as computer networking has improved, computer-based production has spread more and more widely through white-collar work.

IT, Organizational Innovations, and Improved Services Are Complements

An emerging view of the way IT comes to be used in companies is represented in the bottom half of figure 5-1. This view, which has considerable support in earlier work, emphasizes complementarity among three distinct kinds of technical change.[12] The three complements are as follows:

11. Many of the same implications are present in blue-collar contexts (see, for instance, the case study of "Macromed" in Brynjolfsson, Renshaw, and van Alstyne (1997), but for brevity we do not emphasize them. A very substantial portion of work in modern economies is in purely white-collar industries, such as service industries, or in the white-collar functions of goods-producing industries. We focus on the parts of bureaucracies that are associated with transactions. These are associated not only with a great deal of the IT-related technical change of the past, but also, as electronic commerce grows more important, with the IT-related technical progress of the future.

12. See, for example, Applegate, Cash, and Mills (1988); Barras (1990); Davenport and Short (1990); Levy and Murnane (1996); Malone and Rockart (1991); Milgrom and Roberts (1990); Orlikowski (1992); Scott Morton (1991); Simon (1973); Zuboff (1988).

Figure 5-1. *Causal Flows in Our Framework*

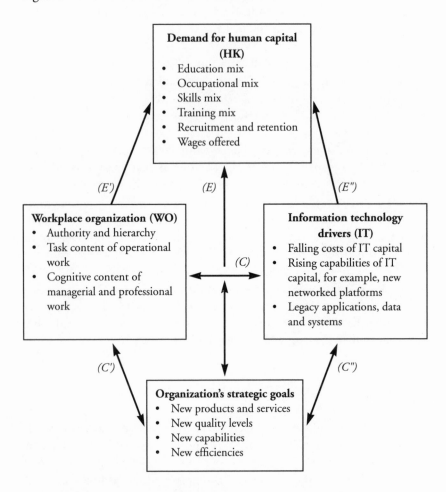

—Cheaper, more powerful IT capital;

—Organizational change; and

—New products, services, or quality.

The theory we will test is that this cluster of three complements represents, *together*, a form of skill-biased technical change. Implementing all three of these forms of technical change together transforms companies and leads to substantial changes in labor demand by type. We need not make any assumption that one of these three uniquely causes the other, only that they tend systematically to go together. Since all three involve

Figure 5-2. *The Production Function Framework*

Detailed inputs		Detailed production process		Detailed outputs
Labor of several types		Tasks for each input		Services
IT capital of several types	▶	Job responsibilities and computer programs	▶	Transactions
Other capital goods of several types		Organizational structure of inputs, hierarchy, and so on		Control

substantial amounts of invention, the complementarity arises in the long run. Taken together, the three forms of technical change are the cluster of driver technologies for labor demand that we study.

Production Function Framework

The next step moves us toward specificity by having a simple framework for the inputs and outputs of white-collar work. We show our framework in a descriptive way in figure 5-2 and in a more analytical way in figure 5-3.

The view we take of the production function is one that has a detailed presentation of inputs, processes, and outputs. Labor and capital of several different types are the inputs. This gives us the opportunity to represent our fundamental long-run driver, declines in the price of IT capital goods. It also gives us the opportunity to represent our fundamental dependent

Figure 5-3. *Short-Run Production Function Notation*

Detailed inputs		Detailed production process		Detailed outputs
$L_1 \ldots L_M$	▶	Indexed by T, S	▶	X
$K_1 \ldots K_M$				Q

variable, demand for labor of different skill levels. The detailed production process and detailed outputs play a different role. They permit us to state a specific theory about the mechanisms by which changes in the price of IT affect the demand for labor in the intermediate run. They also offer some further dependent variables tied to the mechanisms of the theory.

The production of detailed outputs is particularly important and illustrates why we take a detailed view of the production process. A white-collar bureaucracy's outputs do not only consist of what the bureaucracy literally does—the services it makes for customers or the transactions it processes with customers or suppliers. Above and beyond the simple completion of its task, a bureaucracy produces managerial control of the task.

Simple examples illustrate what we mean. Consider a department with responsibility for accounts receivable. What does it produce? It produces, in a literal sense, transactions in which the firm collects money and a record of those collections. If we think literally about the "service quality" associated with those tasks, it suggests collecting most of the money owed the firm, not annoying customer-debtors too much, and so on. A broader view includes the firm's control of its receivables and of the collection process in the output. Can the firm identify problem accounts for special attention? In allocating new trade credit associated with new sales, can the firm discriminate between rapid payers and slow ones? Can it do this unobtrusively and quickly?

Both the narrow and the broad view of output suggest a changed role with computerization. Better record-keeping clearly makes it possible to collect each bill once and only once. Combined with some changes in policies and procedures, records also make it possible for salespeople to know the credit status of an account while in the process of making a sale.

More generally, these examples reveal two things about the IT-based production process from an operational perspective. First, as IT has grown cheaper and more powerful, the number and kind of white-collar processes it can automate in this way has grown. More and more interactions in the business world are undertaken with this kind of computer support. That means more and more substitution away from certain kinds of human effort. Computers have been especially successful in automating routine, repetitive tasks, which are typically those that have not been highly rewarded historically. Second, computerizing tasks makes it much easier to accumulate data, both intentionally and as a by-product of other tasks.[13] A

13. The introduction of bar code scanners to supermarkets might seem to be primarily a way to save labor by cashiers. However, this benefit is vastly outweighed by the benefit of analyzing scanner-

firm can decide to retain a systematic record of all its interactions with a customer, or all of a given employee's interactions with customers, for example. This is a much lower-cost decision given that the interactions are mediated through IT. As more and more interactions are so mediated, the complexity of record-keeping and record analysis can grow. This offers opportunities for the new uses of human intelligence.

In figure 5-3 we show how we represent the detailed outputs and inputs. L and K are vectors of labor and capital types, respectively. X measures the quantity of various services or transactions, and Q represents the service level or degree of control over those transactions that the bureaucracy offers. T and S index the technologies used in production and the organizational structure of production, respectively. These are the things usually left in the black box.

The link to factor demand is via a short-run production function:

$$0 = F(L_1 \ldots L_M, K_1 \ldots K_M, X; Q, T, S)$$

That is, the detailed labor and capital requirements are determined by the level of output, output qualities, and the technology and organizational structure used in the firm. This is a short-run production function because it conditions on the organizational variables fixed by the firm in the intermediate run.

Our analysis will focus on the short run and the intermediate run. The short run has Q, T, and S fixed, and we look at the relationship between the capital (IT) and labor factors of production. In the intermediate run, Q, T, and S can be improved by the firm, perhaps because of the complementarities associated with (C), (C'), (C''), and so on. The relationship between the two runs and figure 5-1 is as follows. In the short run, Q, T, and S are fixed, and only flow of causation (E'') is available to change labor demand. In the intermediate run, organizational structure and service are flexible, so that flows of causation (E) and (E') also come into play. We believe that both the short- and intermediate-run causal flows can be seen in our data. We are less certain that they can be distinguished.

It is worth noting at this stage that this framework is designed to look at the individual firm. Further organizational changes associated with changes in the boundary of the firm will not be fully captured in firm data, nor will they enter our framework. We conjecture that we are, as a result,

---

derived product data to improve inventory control, supply-chain management, marketing and promotion programs, and pricing strategies.

leaving out one of the important flows of causation from IT-based organizational change to labor demand. We will miss, both theoretically and empirically, much of the impact of the creation of new specialty firms employing highly paid workers, for example.

Implications of the Theory for Labor Demand

In this section we consider two theories for how IT relates to labor demand: limits or substitution of IT for high-skilled work and changes in information processing requirements that increase the demand for cognitive skills.

Limited Substitution

Computer business systems involve the regularization and routinization of white-collar tasks. Simple, repetitive tasks are far more amenable to regularization and routinization than more complex and idiosyncratic ones. The result has been the systematic substitution of computer decisionmaking for human decisionmaking in clerical (and similar bureaucratic) work. Decisions that were once reached by humans in a paper- and people-based system are now reached by software. Advances in artificial intelligence notwithstanding, the scope of this substitution has been limited. Simple decisions, closely related to individual transactions or other operational actions, have been most amenable to computerization. More complex and cognitively demanding work, such as that of managers and professionals, has proved remarkably difficult to automate with computers. Similarly, tasks that require judgment, creativity, and frequent exceptions are much more difficult to computerize than well-defined and repetitive tasks. Computer automation of white-collar work has been correspondingly limited in its scope, affecting demand for clerks and expediters far more than for managers and professionals.

This limited substitution is related to all three of the causal arrows (E), (E'), and (E'') in figure 5-1. First, but probably least important empirically, is the narrow flow of causation from the use of IT capital alone to substitution out of low-cognitive-skill labor; this is (E''). In the short run, holding Q and S constant, it is sometimes possible to literally replace people with IT, holding other aspects of the organizational system constant. A telephone-switching computer replaces a telephone operator in a variety of tasks, an automatic teller machine replaces a bank teller, and documents once organized and filed by clerks are instead handled entirely by machine. Yet these examples—and even they are imperfect, involving considerable change in Q and S as well as T—are rare.

Far more important is substitution of computer for human decision-making in the intermediate run, with corresponding changes in T, Q, and S. This reflects the fact that job design and the allocation of tasks to workers combine tasks that use similar information sets, that are more efficient to monitor together, that have similar skill requirements, or that should be performed geographically close together.[14] Yet computers have very different strengths and weaknesses than humans. As a rule, computerization significantly changes at least one, and more often all, of these factors influencing job design. As a result, successful computerization also requires a rethinking of how work is organized and the types of workers required.

This can perhaps be most simply seen in a homey example from accounts receivable (AR). Almost everyone has heard of how early applications lacked the common sense of human clerks, for example, bills were sent out for $0.00. A computer needs to be told not to send a bill for $0.00, whereas (many) clerks could be relied upon to make this decision without explicit instruction. After a while, the software system in an AR application improves and the system stops making these silly mistakes. Or the company adopts an organizational change, such as a human clerk who can override the system when it is obviously doing something silly. Improvements in T—better software systems—made the computer a better substitute for a clerk. Improvements in S, such as using the fact that the clerk's actions are now well recorded to permit autonomy, or using the computer's memory to permit any of a wide variety of clerks to deal with a particular account in a teamwork fashion, make the clerk plus the computer an improved production process. These improved rules draw on the very distinct capabilities of IT and humans. They can only affect labor demand with some invention by the firm. The invention is one of improved work organization as much as it is of improved software.

This tendency for improvements in T and S to offer opportunities to substitute out of L into K is quite general. There are some commonsense rules in any bureaucracy. When common sense can be reduced to rules, or when the business can get by with a little less common sense, or when common sense can be reorganized into a human-override, IT systems can

14. Holmstrom and Milgrom (1991); Jensen and Meckling (1992); Williamson (1979).

be made to substitute for simple human decisionmaking. It is especially true when S changes.

There are, however, strict limits to this substitution, for all its power. As a result, some types of work are affected far more than others.

Increased Demand for Cognitive Skills

The IT-related cluster of innovations is not merely a substitute for low-cognitive-skill labor. It is also a complement for high-cognitive-skill labor. These two effects of computerization combine to change the demand for skilled labor. We now look at the more complex causal relationship between the IT-related cluster and high-cognitive-skill workers such as managers and professionals.

DIRECT CAUSAL FLOWS. There is an important causal flow directly from IT capital to use of very skilled technical workers of an (E'') form. Computer departments employ highly skilled people. So does the computer services industry. (This industry is an extension of company computer departments. It offers custom programming, consulting, and systems integration to user companies.) Finally, there is a related effect on demand in the computer hardware, software, and networking industries themselves. In the United States, though not to any large extent in other countries, this represents a substantial demand for cognitive skill. Aggregating all these flows will not, however, amount to a very large fraction of employment.[15] We need to look elsewhere for a substantial complementarity between the IT-based cluster and high cognitive skill.

Another direct causal flow of the (E'') variety has been widely discussed but is likely to be of limited importance. This is the direct use of personal computers (PCs) by individual workers in organizations. By far the largest single use of PCs is for word processing.[16] Anecdotes about excessive font-futzing and lost data notwithstanding, typists and secretaries have clearly become much more productive as a result. However, this is an implausible source of wage dispersion. Meanwhile, managers and professionals who do their own typing may also become somewhat more productive with PCs, but this is also an unlikely explanation for their higher relative wages.

---

15. Bresnahan (1997).
16. The statements about the relative importance of various PC applications are based on data from Computer Intelligence Infocorp.

Similar arguments apply to the other dominant PC applications: spreadsheets, and graphics. However, a minority of more specialized applications, such as PC-based computer-aided design and project management, are more promising candidates for skill complementarity. The growing organizational uses of PCs, which can affect the wages of even those managers who do not literally use computers, are likely to be especially important.[17]

CAUSAL FLOWS THROUGH ORGANIZATIONAL CHANGE. Many effective uses of computers make use of IT's comparative advantage in doing simple tasks quickly and in remembering a large volume of simple information and recalling it rapidly. Many times, these features of computers are most effective when combined with human intelligence. For example, a typical "analytical" application consists almost entirely of complex data storage and recall. Rapid, detailed memory by computers is often a complement for human judgment in decisionmaking. In our accounts receivable example, the computer may quickly report a summary of a particular customer's payment history. That is an "analytical" application. As a result, firms like Capital One (a major credit card issuer) are hiring more people with master's degrees in business administration and even Ph.D.'s to help them analyze customer data that they collect so easily with IT. Human judgment might have the final say in whether a particular account's value to the firm warrants extending trade credit in particular circumstances or whether a new type of product or service is likely to be successful with a particular customer segment.

A related kind of effective use of the computer's detail and completeness turns the "analytical" lens on workers and departments in the firm. Detailed reports on the success—measured by anything the computer system knows systematically—of individual workers or departments are a kind of management tool that has grown cheaper with the falling costs of computerization. In figure 5-1 this kind of increased demand for highly skilled labor shows up as an (E) flow, that is, one that involves changes in computerization and in organization.

This complementarity between machine and human capabilities leads to a wide variety of organizational structures, but certain ones are worth mentioning. One is the information-enabled decentralized worker. In the most extreme form, this involves use of a worker who is supported by

---

17. See further discussion in Bresnahan (1997).

analytical applications that let her know everything she needs to know to accomplish her task. She is in turn monitored by a computer analytical application that permits her superiors to monitor her performance quickly and efficiently. Less extreme examples vary in a number of ways. They might have the human unit that is supported and monitored be a team rather than an individual worker. They might use only one of the support/monitoring flows of information.

This tendency toward computer-based reorganization calls for several very different changes in worker capabilities. The first is cognitive. Individual workers or teams supported by analytical applications must be able to interpret the information that is presented. Often, this involves bridging from the quantitative data provided by computers to complex decisions involving many factors. In a wide variety of applications, computers have made information vastly cheaper and more abundant. This increases the demand for humans who can process information in ways that machines cannot. Indeed, it creates an information-overload bottleneck. Herbert Simon noted this not long after the first widespread use of computers in business. "The scarce resource is not information, it is processing capacity to attend to information. Attention is the chief bottleneck in organizational activity, and the bottleneck becomes narrower and narrower as we move to the tops of organizations."[18] Thus, besides a general increase in demand for human cognitive skills, computerization can lead to attempts to bypass the managerial bottleneck via new organizational forms that favor increased lateral communication and coordination.

A second set of human capabilities associated with this kind of organizational change has to do with autonomy more than with any specific cognitive skill. Monitoring technologies in general are useful for moving responsibility and authority. The monitoring technology associated with computer-based work appears to be systematically related to incentives, at least long-run incentives, which are more closely tied to measurable performance. Not all workers come with equal tolerance for or capability to respond to these kinds of incentives. The change in the mode of supervision calls for changed talents.

A third set of human capabilities associated with this kind of organizational change involves the skills associated with dealing with customers and suppliers, influencing teammates and colleagues, and inspiring and

18. Simon (1973, p. 270).

coaching subordinates. More generally, they involve providing the people skills that computers lack.

Additional complementarities of the (E) form, that is, involving the three-way complementarity with organization, IT, and product change, arise from the inventive dynamics of computer-based organizations. As emphasized above, effective use of computer systems involves a great deal of invention by the firms using them. Discovering and implementing ways to gain from computers' capabilities is a complex activity. As computers have become more powerful, more flexible, and more user friendly, the largest and growing fraction of this inventive activity occurs outside of the programmers' job function. Organizational innovation is now the duty of those who use computers, directly and indirectly, in large ways and in small ways. Thus more pressure is put on the cognitive capabilities of managers and professionals.

The most computer-intensive businesses typically use computers for improved customer service and as the basis for new and improved services. Invention of the new products those processes will deliver and of the human side of the delivery mechanism are very difficult cognitive tasks. They call for managers who can take advantage of the new production processes offered by computing, which calls for new cognitive skills and a deep understanding of one's own organization and customers' needs.[19]

Some of these new demands on highly skilled workers call for a great deal of human capability. It can be quite difficult to think about one's customers, for example, both through the lens of knowing them and the more analytical lens of their behavior systematically shown in databases. Once the firm knows new and interesting things about its customers, it must invent new ways to interact with them.

As more and more of business is mediated through computers, more and more opportunities arise for managers and professionals to undertake two activities. The first is research-like, combining IT-based quantitative information about customers or employees with deep knowledge of the business. The second is designing organizations, products, and so on, taking advantage of the new research findings. This, too, combines hard quantitative skills with deep business knowledge. To the extent that the new

---

19. Bartel and Lichtenberg (1987) suggest that high levels of cognitive skills may be particularly important in creating and adapting to change, notably in implementing new technology. The managerial side of computer-based production processes is an excellent example of this story. The constant improvements in computer technology mean that organizations that use IT intensely have this demand for high levels of cognitive skill on a standing basis, not just for a single transition.

organization or product will be enabled by computer, the firm is specifying a new computer "program." Even those managerial and professional workers who never touch computers have their work transformed in this way, as they must use more and more complex bodies of skill and knowledge and participate in new organizational structures. Thoughtful designers of business information systems recognize the information overload bottleneck. As one corporate executive said, "While we've seen a great revolution in bandwidth and computing power, unfortunately the input/output capability of human beings hasn't changed much over the last decade."[20]

The Net Impact of IT and IT-Enabled Organizational Change

In computerized work environments, high levels of human information processing skills should be getting more valuable. In part, this value reflects the potential of present-day computers to substitute more effectively for routine information processing tasks than for complex or ill-structured cognitive tasks. It also reflects a potential complementarity between some of the strengths of computers—storing, communicating, and executing instructions on a flood of data—and many types of human judgment and decisionmaking. As Herbert A. Simon has noted, "What information consumes is rather obvious: it consumes the attention of its recipients."[21] In an information age, the scarce resource is human information processing.

One implication is that computerized firms will seek to address the increased relative demand for high-cognitive-skill labor by hiring more skilled and educated workers and by investing more heavily in training for existing workers. Another implication is that the information overload bottleneck is likely to be especially severe higher up in the hierarchy. Human capital should be at a premium here. But firms will also seek nonhierarchical forms of organizing to bypass the bottleneck (for example, "self-managing teams"). As a result, computerized firms should make greater use of self-managing teams and decentralized decisionmaking. Furthermore, in these firms, employees with "team" skills and "autonomy" skills should become more valuable.

To summarize the implications of our theory for labor demand, information technology has an impact on the optimal organization of work and the demand for skills directly and through changes in the organization of the workplace.

20. Robert Walker, CIO of Hewlett Packard, quoted in Mendelson and Pillai (1998, p. 3).
21. Simon (1971, p. 40).

Data Description

The data set used for our analyses is a cross-sectional survey of organizational practices and labor force characteristics conducted in 1995 and 1996 matched to a panel detailing IT capital levels and mix over the 1987–94 period. For some analyses, we will also use data on other inputs and outputs, including non-IT capital, total employment, sales, and value added. Data cover approximately four hundred large U.S. firms. Approximately 55 percent of the sample are from the manufacturing, mining, or construction sectors and 45 percent are in services.[22]

Measures of Key Variables

In our empirical work, we used a simplified and streamlined version of figure 5-1.

HUMAN CAPITAL. Our richest set of measures falls in the upper box labeled "demand for human capital." We measure human capital (HK) in several direct ways: via the manager's assessment of work force skill, the educational composition of the firm's work force or the percentage of employees who are professionals, managers, clerical, and so on. We also construct a broader measure of information work based on the percentage of all employees who are managerial, professional, or clerical—precise definitions of all constructed variables are in table 5-3. Our interpretation is that these are alternative measures of the same broad concept—a tendency at the firm level to use, or to attempt to use, more highly skilled workers.

While we observe those human capital measures only once in cross section, we also have a measure of the firm's policies toward human capital investment (HKI). HKI is defined as a mean zero, standard deviation one variable that is created from the percent of workers receiving training, the extent to which the firm screens for education in hiring, and the firms' use of cross-training (definition, table 5-3). This variable is more dynamic: it shows where human capital levels are changing, whereas others reveal where they are high.

All these data were gathered through a survey administered to senior human resource managers or their designees. The survey was based on

22. More detail on the survey can be found in Brynjolfsson and Hitt (1997); Bresnahan, Brynjolfsson, and Hitt (1998).

questions from prior surveys on workplace organization and human resource practices.[23] In particular, the approach of Paul Osterman was followed in focusing on a single class of employee called "production employees" (which corresponds to Osterman's "core employee") and focused on the organizational practices at the most typical establishment.[24] A total of 416 firms provided at least some data for the study. Descriptive statistics are in table 5-1.

WORKPLACE ORGANIZATION. On the left of figure 5-1 lies the concept of workplace organization(WO). Workplace organization is notoriously difficult to measure, and the changes in organizational structure that are complementary to IT capital might be particularly so. Gathering new data on workplace organization and linking these variables to IT capital at the firm level is one of the advances that permits this study and the earlier ones by Brynjolfsson and Hitt.

In a general sense, it is well established that organizational change and information technology are complements. However, only a subset of the relevant organizational changes is captured in our survey and used in our empirical work.[25] We focus on one particular type of organizational change that has been found important in earlier work by Erik Brynjolfsson and Lorin M. Hitt.[26] Our variable WO is defined as a mean zero, standard deviation one variable reflecting the several distinct measures of greater use of teams, greater delegation of a variety of decision rights to line workers, and activities that support the use of teams such as team building (definition, table 5-3).[27] These variables have a clear interpretation as measures of

23. Ichniowski, Shaw, and Prennushi (1997); Osterman (1994).

24. Osterman (1994). Because we are especially interested in firm-level effects, one difficulty of our sampling approach is that the practices reported by the respondent may not be representative of the work practices across the entire firm. To address this issue, the revised instrument contained questions about how representative production workers were in terms of total employment and the uniformity of work practices for this category of workers. For the average firm in the second survey subsample, production workers account for about two-thirds of total employment, and organizational practices are found to be fairly uniform: 65 percent of respondents said that all production workers have the same work practices. Furthermore, 82 percent reported that at least 80 percent of workers had the same work practices.

25. For instance, we do not have any data on changes in outsourcing that might plausibly change the skill mix of remaining employees. Nor do we attempt to catalog and measure all the types of internal reorganization that might occur. Omitting these other forms of organizational change probably leads us to understate the role of organizational factors.

26. Brynjolfsson and Hitt (1997).

27. This choice of measures reflects the first principal component of a factor analysis of responses to the organizational practices survey. Interestingly, Osterman (1994) reports that a similar set of team-oriented practices loaded on the first principal component in his survey of 694 establishments.

Table 5-1. *Organizational Practice Survey Variables*

Item	Range	Variable	N	Mean	Standard deviation
Team-based work organization					
Use of self-managing teams	1–5	SMTEA	345	2.11	1.13
Use of employee involvement groups	1–5	QUALC	345	2.85	1.21
Use of team-building activities	1–5	TEAMB	345	2.95	1.17
Promote for teamwork	1–5	PROTE	345	3.59	0.95
Breadth of jobs	1–5	BROAD	345	3.25	0.99
Individual decision authority					
Who decides pace of work (3=workers)	1–3	PACE	345	1.33	0.37
Who decides method of work (same)	1–3	METH	345	1.39	0.38
Human capital (levels)					
Skill level of work	1–5	SKILL	345	3.60	0.86
Education level	1–5	EDUC	345	2.48	0.66
Workers w/high school or less education	0–100%	%HSED	263	59.3%	27.8%
Workers with some college education	0–85%	%SCED	263	23.3%	17.5%
Workers completed college	0–100%	%COLL	263	17.4%	21.0%
Human capital investment					
Pre-employment screen for education	1–5	SCNED	345	3.31	0.89
Training (percent workers involved)	0–100%	TRAIN	345	48.0%	36.1%
Cross-train workers	1–5	XTRAI	345	3.16	0.98
Production worker composition					
Blue collar (fraction of jobs listed)	0–100%	PRBL	345	61.9%	46.2%
Clerical (fraction of jobs listed)	0–100%	PRCL	345	31.4%	43.4%
Professional (fraction of jobs listed)	0–100%	PRPF	345	4.6%	17.5%
Work force composition					
Unskilled blue collar (percent)	0–95%	%US	337	18.4%	21.4%
Skilled blue collar (percent)	0–85%	%SK	337	24.7%	21.1%
Clerical (percent)	0–80%	%CL	337	19.4%	17.6%
Professionals (percent)	0–90%	%PF	337	20.7%	16.8%
Managers (percent)	0–50%	%MG	337	16.8%	8.5%

Source: Authors' survey. Survey details appear in Bresnahan, Brynjolfsson, and Hitt (1998).

decentralization. Our concept of workplace organization is narrow and specific.

Our data on organizational characteristics were gathered from the same survey used for our human capital data. Since these data are based on a snapshot at the end of the sample period, we do not know whether each firm had the same organizational characteristics throughout the sample period, and in contrast to the human capital data, we do not have information on the levels of "investment" that firms were making in organizational change. The reasonable interpretation based on aggregate data, however, is that many of the firms have only recently adopted these practices.[28] In a measurement sense, our measure of WO (a level at the end of the sample period), can also be interpreted as ΔWO (the amount of organizational change in the organization during the sample period).

INFORMATION TECHNOLOGY. At the right of figure 5-1 is the concept of IT drivers. Our IT measures are stocks of computer hardware at the firm level and also stocks of specific types of hardware (for example, PCs).[29] Empirically, we view them largely as alternative measures of the same concept. A distinction among the types of computers between those suitable for organizational computing (mainframe and minicomputers) and those for personal computing (PCs) sharpens this somewhat. In the period of our data, however, PCs could be an indicator either of a tendency to personal computing or of new-architecture organizational computing. Thus the sharper interpretation is ambiguous, and most of our interpretation is the broad one that some firms are more IT intensive than others.

The measures of IT use were derived from the Computer Intelligence Infocorp installation database that details IT hardware spending by site for companies in the Fortune 1000 (approximately 25,000 sites are aggregated to form the measures for the set of companies that represent the total pop-

28. The practices we use to define WO are very similar to the ones that, according to Ichniowski and others (1996. p. 300), "have become increasingly common among U.S. businesses in recent years." In fact, Osterman (1994) asked about a similar cluster of work practices in a survey of 694 managers and found that 49.1 percent of the establishments in his sample reported introducing "teams" in the five years prior to his survey year of 1992. He also reports that 38 percent introduced job rotation practices, 71 percent total quality management programs, and 67.9 percent problem-solving groups in the years between 1987 and 1992, each of which also reflects increased decisionmaking by line workers (p. 186).

29. It is more difficult to observe the portions of IT expenditure that are distributed throughout the firm (personal computers, small web servers, and so on). It is also more difficult to observe software investments than hardware investments, and it is particularly difficult to observe applications software that would reveal the purposes of business computer systems.

ulation in any given year). This database provides details on the ownership of specific pieces of IT equipment and related products. These data include variables capturing the total capital stock of IT (central processors, PCs, and peripherals) as well as measures of computing capacity of central processors in millions of instructions per second (MIPS) and the number of PCs. The IT data do not include all types of information processing or communication equipment and are likely to miss a portion of computer equipment that is purchased by individuals or departments without the knowledge of information systems personnel.

STRATEGIC GOALS. The most difficult observable in terms of the cluster of driver technologies is the change in product and service quality and the invention of new products and services, the box at the bottom of figure 5-1. Success, which is related to one interpretation of our production function results, may be an observable indicator of these results. Our interpretation is that firms with high levels of measured productivity have achieved one or more of the subgoals at the bottom of the figure.

To calculate productivity, we combined the above data with data from Standard and Poor's Compustat. Measures were created for output, capital, labor, and value added. These let us estimate a production function relationship between value added and the various inputs following the procedures in Bronwyn Hall and Erik Brynjolfsson and Lorin Hitt.[30] Table 5-2 provides sample means for these variables.

Empirical Results

If IT is a complement for HK, we should see firms that have a greater level of IT than their competitors making greater investments in human capital. These investments can take the form of training or increased use of preemployment screening.

Our hypothesis that IT, human capital, and decentralized organizational structure are all complements has a number of testable implications for the firm-level data. What we do in this chapter is focus on the overall patterns in the data to build a case that IT, WO, and HK all "go together."[31]

30. Hall (1990); Brynjolfsson and Hitt (1997).

31. In a related paper, we build more structured models of firm-level demand functions for IT and human capital and also examine a variety of production functions which enable more formal tests of the theory. See Bresnahan, Brynjolfsson, and Hitt (1998).

Table 5-2. *IT and Other Inputs and Outputs*

Item	Variable	N	Mean	Standard deviation
CII survey				
Log(IT capital)	LITCAP	333	3.07	1.66
Total MIPS (millions of instructions/second)	MIPS	333	2,624	8,737
Total PCs	TOTPC	333	4,560	10,997
Organizational survey				
Degree of computerization of work	COMP	343	3.28	1.11
Percent workers using general purpose computers	%GP	290	53.0	33.8
Percent workers using E-mail	%EMAIL	290	31.0	32.2
Compustat (all years pooled)[a]				
Log(output)	LOUTPUT	2466	2,431.59	0.99
Log(value added)	LVA	2466	946.53	1.02
Log(labor expense)	LLABOR	2466	530.33	1.08
Log(non-IT capital)	LNITCAP	2466	1,771.53	1.39
Log(employment)	LEMPLOY	2466	14.41	1.09
Log(IT capital)	LITCAP	2466	11.86	1.42

a. Standard deviation is in log (millions of dollars), while the geometric mean is reported in millions of dollars.

First, under plausible assumptions, we would expect levels of each of them to covary in cross-sectional/time series data.[32] Similarly, if IT is a complement for WO, we should expect IT-intensive firms to be more likely to organize production by using self-managing teams and delegated decisionmaking than other firms in the same industry. High levels of HK or WO should, all else being equal, be predictive of high levels of the other hypothesized complements.

Second, productivity should be higher in firms that successfully match IT, organizational structure, and human capital investments than in those

32. Holmstrom and Milgrom (1994) offer a theory of complementarity and a series of observations about the conditions under which comovements of different organizational practices and factors of production are indicators of complementarity. Athey and Stern (1998) are rightly critical of interpreting comovements in a cross section of firms as indicating complementarity when there is a possibility of omitted common factors.

Table 5-3. *Definitions of Composite Variables*

Description	Variable[a]	Formula
Work organization	WO	SMTEA + QUALC + TEAMB + PROTE + PACE + METH
Human capital investment	HKI	SCNED + TRAIN + XTRAI
Composite decision authority	DA7	PACE + XSCHED + XDIST + METH + XPROB + XCUST + XCOMPL

a. All composites are formed by summing standardized values (except the information worker percentage). The sum is then restandardized to mean 0, unit variance.

that cannot make such matches. Specifically, productivity should, on average, be higher in firms that have above-average levels of *both* IT and HK compared with firms that are above the industry average on one dimension and below average on the other. Other pairwise combinations should also predict productivity levels.

Third, in light of the productivity predictions, one can also make some predictions about how the levels of IT, HK, and WO should change over time in different firms. Firms with high levels of one or more of the three complements should find it more profitable to invest more aggressively in the remaining elements of the hypothesized complementary system. For instance, for any observed level of IT capital stock, we should see more rapid IT investment in firms with high levels of HK. We should also see more investment in training in firms with high levels of IT.

Correlations Among IT, Human Capital, and Workplace Organization

As discussed in the data section, we have numerous different measures of firms' IT capital, their employees' human capital, and overall workplace organization. The first way we examine the data is simply to consider correlations among these measures. We begin by examining Spearman rank-order correlations among pairs of the relevant variables while controlling for industry, firm size (employment), and the composition of the principal production workers in each firm. The last control is really a production-process one. At the risk of "over-controlling" for factors that may be endogenous to our theory, we include these controls to reduce the role of unobserved heterogeneity in the sample.

Table 5-4. *Correlations between IT and Human Capital*

Measure	%GP	% EMAIL	COMP	ITCAP	MIPS	TOTPC
Skills/education (N = 371)						
Skill levels (SKILL)	(+)***	(+)***	(+)***	(+)	(+)***	(+)**
Education (EDUC)	(+)**	(+)***	(+)***	(+)	(+)	(+)
Education distribution (N = 237)						
High school education (%HSED)	(–)***	(–)***	(–)***	(–)*	(–)***	(–)***
College graduate (%COLL)	(+)***	(+)***	(+)***	(+)	(+)	(+)
Skill acquisition (N = 370)						
Training (TRAIN)	(+)***	(+)**	(+)***	(+)**	(+)***	(+)**
Screen for education (SCNED)	(+)*	(+)***	(+)***	(+)***	(+)***	(+)***
Skill acquisition (controlling for SKILL and EDUC)						
Training (TRAIN)	(+)**	(+)*	(+)***	(+)***	(+)***	(+)***
Screen for education (SCNED)	(+)	(+)	(+)**	(+)***	(+)***	(+)***

Note: Spearman partial rank order correlations controlling for industry (9 sector dummy variables), employment (EMPLOY), and production worker composition (PRBL, PRCL). Sample size varies due to non-response.

Key: (+) positive correlation; (–) negative correlation; * $p < .1$, ** $p < .05$, *** $p < .01$; test is against the null hypothesis that the correlation is zero.

In tables 5-4 through 5-8, we show that IT, HK, and WO are all highly correlated with each other in our data, regardless of how each concept is measured. One can thus make predictions about, say, a firm's work organization relative to its competitors, if one knows its IT-intensity or human capital levels, and vice versa.

IT USE IS CORRELATED WITH EMPLOYEES' HUMAN CAPITAL IN FIRM-LEVEL DATA. We find that most measures of IT are significantly correlated with most measures of employees' human capital in our sample of firms (table 5-4). The correlation is stronger when the measures of IT are taken from the same organizational survey as the human capital data (first three columns) than when we use the IT measures from the separate CII survey. This probably reflects a better match of the unit of observation.[33] The find-

33. The respondents for the organizational practices survey were explicitly asked to consider a representative site for both the HK and IT questions. In contrast, the CI data were for the company as a whole.

Table 5-5. *Correlations between IT and Work Force Composition*

Measure	%GP	% EMAIL	COMP	ITCAP	MIPS	TOTPC
Work force composition (N = 303)						
Clerical (%CL)	(–)	(+)	(–)	(–)	(–)	(–)
Unskilled blue collar (%US)	(–)***	(–)***	(–)***	(–)	(–)**	(–)
Skilled blue collar (%SK)	(–)	(–)	(+)	(+)	(+)	(+)
Managers (%MG)	(+)**	(+)**	(+)*	(+)**	(+)**	(+)
Professionals (%PF)	(+)**	(+)***	(+)***	(+)***	(+)***	(+)***

Note: Spearman partial rank order correlations controlling for industry (9 sector dummy variables), employment (EMPLOY), and production worker composition (PRBL, PRCL).

Key: (+) positive correlation; (–) negative correlation; * $p < .1$, ** $p < .05$, *** $p < .01$; test is against the null hypothesis that the correlation is zero.

ing of a correlation between IT and HK in firm-level data extends findings in previous work, which used more aggregate data.[34]

Classification of employment by job title is also correlated with IT. Firms that employ more managers and especially professionals are more likely to have high levels of IT relative to their industry competitors, while those with a greater proportion of blue-collar workers tend to have less IT, and vice versa (table 5-5). In our framework, the employment job titles can be interpreted as proxies for employee skills, as is common in earlier work, or as characteristics of workplace organization.

IT USE IS CORRELATED WITH SPECIFIC CHARACTERISTICS OF WORK-PLACE ORGANIZATION. In table 5-6 we examine the correlations of various measures of IT with our summary measure of decentralization, WO, and with the measures that underlie it. All of the components of WO are individually correlated with IT measures. Interestingly, the strong correlations with self-managing teams and team-building exercises suggest that "people" skills, not just decisionmaking skills, are important complements of IT.

In these tables, one would conclude that significant relationships exist between IT and human capital and between IT and workplace organization, whichever measure of IT was used. Two further points are notable. First, PCs are not the strongest correlate for most measures of human capital. Instead, central computer use appears to be a slightly better predictor,

34. For example, see Autor, Katz, and Krueger (1997).

Table 5-6. *Correlations between IT and Work Organization*

Measure	%GP	% EMAIL	COMP	ITCAP	MIPS	TOTPC
Our main measure						
Decentralization (WO)	(+)***	(+)***	(+)***	(+)***	(+)***	(+)***
Subcomponents of WO						
Self-managing teams (SMTEA)	(+)***	(+)***	(+)***	(+)***	(+)***	(+)***
Employee involvement groups						
(QUALC)	(+)***	(+)***	(+)	(+)	(+)	(+)
Team building (TEAMB)	(+)***	(+)***	(+)	(+)***	(+)***	(+)***
Promote for teamwork (PROTE)	(+)**	(+)**	(+)**	(+)	(+)*	(+)
Pace of work (PACE)	(+)*	(+)*	(+)**	(+)	(+)	(+)
Method of work (METH)	(+)***	(+)***	(+)***	(+)***	(+)***	(+)***
Other organizational						
structure measures						
Broad jobs (BROAD)	(+)***	(+)***	(+)***	(+)	(+)**	(+)*
Scheduling of work (XSCHED)	(+)***	(+)***	(+)***	(+)*	(+)***	(+)**
Distribution of work to workers						
(XDIST)	(+)*	(+)***	(+)***	(+)*	(+)**	(+)**
Production problems (XPROB)	(–)	(+)	(+)	(+)	(+)	(+)
Customer interaction (XCUST)	(+)**	(+)*	(+)	(+)	(+)	(+)
Handling complaints (XCOMPL)	(+)***	(+)***	(+)**	(+)	(+)	(+)
Composite of seven measures						
(DA7)	(+)***	(+)***	(+)***	(+)*	(+)**	(+)***
Individual control (ICDA)	(+)**	(+)***	(+)***	(+)*	(+)**	(+)**

Note: Spearman partial rank order correlations controlling for industry (9 sector dummy variables), employment (EMPLOY), and production worker composition (PRBL, PRCL). $N = 240$–372, due to non-response and some measures limited to second and third wave surveys.

Key: (+) positive correlation; (–) negative correlation; * $p < .1$, ** $p < .05$, *** $p < .01$; test is against the null hypothesis that the correlation is zero.

which is consistent with an important role for organizational computing and, by inference, organizational impacts. Second, e-mail use is a particularly strong indicator of teams and related practices, as well as of high levels of human capital. This could suggest an important role for communication, as opposed to automation, in driving skill upgrading. It may also simply reflect some residual unobserved heterogeneity in the sample, as do the other correlations.

Table 5-7. *Correlations between Human Capital and Work Organization*

Measure	SKILL	EDUC	%COLL	SCNED	TRAIN
Our main measure					
Decentralization (WO)	(+)***	(+)***	(+)***	(+)***	(+)***
Subcomponents of WO					
Self-managing teams (SMTEA)	(+)***	(+)**	(+)***	(+)***	(+)***
Employee involvement groups					
(QUALC)	(+)***	(−)	(+)	(+)	(+)***
Team building (TEAMB)	(+)***	(+)	(+)**	(+)***	(+)***
Promote for teamwork (PROTE)	(+)**	(+)	(+)	(+)	(+)
Pace of work (PACE)	(+)**	(+)***	(+)***	(+)***	(+)
Method of work (METH)	(+)***	(+)***	(+)***	(+)***	(+)*
Other measures of organizational					
structure					
Broad jobs (BROAD)	(+)***	(+)***	(+)**	(+)***	(+)
Scheduling of work (XSCHED)	(+)***	(+)	(+)	(+)**	(+)**
Distribution of work to workers					
(XDIST)	(+)***	(+)*	(+)	(+)**	(+)*
Production problems (XPROB)	(+)**	(−)	(−)	(+)	(+)
Customer interaction (XCUST)	(+)	(−)	(−)	(+)	(+)***
Handling complaints (XCOMPL)	(+)	(+)*	(+)	(+)	(+)***
Composite (DA7)	(+)***	(+)	(+)***	(+)**	(+)***
Individual control (ICDA)	(+)***	(+)	(+)***	(+)***	(+)*

Note: Spearman partial rank order correlations controlling for industry (9 sector dummy variables), employment (EMPLOY), and production worker composition (PRBL, PRCL). N = 240–372, due to non-response and some measures limited to second and third wave surveys.

Key: (+) positive correlation; (−) negative correlation; * $p < .1$, ** $p < .05$, *** $p < .01$; test is against the null hypothesis that the correlation is zero.

HUMAN CAPITAL IS CORRELATED WITH WORKPLACE ORGANIZATION. In turn, the same decentralized workplace organization that is correlated with IT is also highly correlated with employee human capital (table 5-7). Our finding that certain workplace systems are correlated with higher levels of human capital extends and amplifies a result reported by Paul Osterman, who observes, "As the skill levels required by an enterprise's technology increase, so does the use of the various work organization innovations."[35]

35. Osterman (1994, p. 182). The workplace innovations tracked by Osterman were teams, job rotation, total quality management, and quality circles. His measure of skills was a dummy variable for whether the "core job is very or extremely skilled" (p. 181).

Table 5-8. *Correlations between IT and Human Capital,*
Controlling for Work Organization (WO)

Measure	%GP	% EMAIL	COMP	ITCAP	MIPS	TOTPC
Skills/education (partialling WO)						
Skill levels (SKILL)	(+)*	(+)***	(+)***	(+)	(+)	(+)
Education (EDUC)	(+)**	(+)***	(+)***	(−)	(+)	(−)
High school education (%HSED)	(−)***	(−)***	(−)***	(−)	(−)**	(−)**
College graduate (%COLL)	(+)***	(+)***	(+)***	(+)	(+)	(+)
Same analysis without controls						
Skill levels (SKILL)	(+)***	(+)***	(+)***	(+)	(+)***	(+)**
Education (EDUC)	(+)**	(+)***	(+)***	(+)	(+)	(+)
High school education (%HSED)	(−)***	(−)***	(−)***	(−)*	(−)***	(−)***
College graduate (%COLL)	(+)***	(+)***	(+)***	(+)	(+)	(+)

Note: Spearman partial rank order correlations controlling for industry (9 sector dummy variables), employment (EMPLOY), and production worker composition (PRBL, PRCL). First four rows also include WO as a covariate.

Key: (+) positive correlation; (−) negative correlation; * $p < .1$, ** $p < .05$, *** $p < .01$; test is against the null hypothesis that the correlation is zero.

Some, but not all, of the correlation between IT and human capital that we found can be "explained" through their common covariance with differences in organizational structure. When we partial out workplace organization, the correlation between IT and most measures of human capital drops somewhat (table 5-8). While the three move together, there is also substantial separate movement and comovement of the pairs. This is consistent with the view that all three are complements.

Alternative theories in which highly skilled workers or successful managers in particular firms are given IT for nonproductive reasons are implausible here.[36] WO and mainframes are very odd ways to consume a managerial rent or to reward favored classes of workers. This is notably true given that most of WO is ΔWO and that these organizational changes are notoriously difficult and unpleasant. Mainframes and servers make terrible toys. When queried, the managers in our sample provide a simpler explanation: IT use tends to require more skilled workers and more decentral-

36. If highly skilled workers and managers cause IT and WO in the cross section of firms (rather than the reverse) for *productive* reasons, then they are complements in production and our argument is correct.

ized decisionmaking. Indeed, as reported in more detail in our companion paper, the greater a firm's experience with IT, the more likely it is to report these effects, and vice versa.[37]

This argument will be strengthened by the observation that coordinated investments in HK, WO, and IT are more productive than uncoordinated investments.

How Do Various Combinations of IT, Human Capital, and Workplace Organization Contribute to Output?

If all managers fully understood the potential complementarities among IT, workplace organization and human capital; if their decisions always reflected the profit-maximizing strategies for their firms; and if there were no lags, adjustment costs, or mistakes in implementing these strategies, then the demand equations for IT and HK would fully reflect the optimal relationships among these factors. Furthermore, under these assumptions, we would not expect to observe any firms that were *not* implementing the optimal combinations of these practices. Of course, one of the reasons that we think studying these relationships is interesting is that we believe that they are not fully understood. With the benefit of hindsight, it is clear that many firms make significant mistakes in their IT investments, organizational strategies, or human capital policies.[38] Furthermore, a large number of firms actively experiment with these policy levers in a conscious effort to understand how best to use the cheaper processing, storage, and communications power delivered by IT. As with any important general-purpose technology, a tremendous amount of organizational and strategic co-invention must accompany technological advances in computing, and most managers are fully aware of this need.

Under these conditions, different combinations of inputs will lead to differences in product and service quality in our sample of firms. Under the assumption that higher quality levels will be manifested in increased revenues (owing to greater sales, higher unit prices, or both), a production function can help to identify complementarities. Indeed, the production function approach will be most effective to the extent that not all firms are

37. Bresnahan, Brynjolfsson, and Hitt (1998).
38. See, for instance, Kemerer and Sosa (1991) for a catalog of disastrous IT projects, some running into the tens of millions of dollars. Most of the failures are linked to organizational and strategic errors.

employing a well-matched combination of inputs. Thus, this approach provides a valuable counterpart to the correlation results and demand equations, which both provide the strongest results when firms are successfully optimizing.

The theory is quite specific about what we should expect to see. As noted by Paul Milgrom and John Roberts, it is not enough to find that firms that invest heavily in all the posited complements have greater output than those that do not.[39] Instead, the theory requires that the increase in output associated with the investment in one complement be greater when other complements are present than when they are not. IT, for example, may be productive on its own, but our theory predicts that it will be *more* productive in firms with high levels of HK, WO, or (especially) both.

While the productivity analyses depend on at least some firms making the "wrong" choices by investing in one complement without the others, we need not assume that all combinations of inputs are equally likely to be observed. Specifically, suppose that managers are attempting to increase firm output, quantity and quality by choosing the optimal combinations IT, WO, and HK. Suppose further that they are imperfect in these attempts but do better than mere chance. Then we would expect to find evidence of complementarities both in the correlations, which reflect the partial success in combining IT, WO, and HK, and in the estimated production functions, which reflect the increased value of output generated by the firms that get the combinations "right" relative to those who do not. In this way, we can link differences in firms' choices of IT, WO, and HK to their degree of success in achieving their organizational goals.

A natural way to study this question is to estimate a production function and examine how various combinations of organizational characteristics affect productivity. We follow common practice and focus on a log-linear specification and its variants. This functional form has the advantage of its simplicity and straightforward interpretation. It is the interaction effects between different inputs that measure complementarities in this framework. Accordingly, we build a model starting from a very simple specification (consistent with Cobb-Douglas production) and adding various sets of interactions. The baseline production function includes controls for industry and year and two types of productive inputs: labor and capital.

We can now easily explore complementarities among various combinations of inputs. For instance, to study how IT and HK combine to affect

39. Milgrom and Roberts (1990).

output we split the sample into four quadrants: 1) High IT-High HK, 2) High IT-Low HK, 3) Low IT-High HK and 4) Low IT-Low HK, and define dummy variables for the quadrants, D.

We then run a regression of the form:

$$\log(\text{Output}) = \alpha \log(\text{Labor}) + \beta \log(\text{Capital}) + \delta_{hh} {}^* D_{\text{high-IT*high-HK}} + \delta_{hl} {}^* D_{\text{high-IT *low-HK}} + \delta_{ll} {}^* D_{\text{low-IT*high-HK}} + \epsilon.$$

The first two terms control for the contributions of the traditional inputs, labor and capital, to output while the next three terms interact a dummy variable for IT intensity with one for human capital. In this way, we can estimate the average productivity levels of firms in each quadrant relative to the baseline case of low IT-low HK. The results for δ are shown in table 5-9.

As we expected, those firms that combine high levels of IT with high levels of HK are more productive than those that are low on both dimensions (table 5-9, part A). And the differences are not small. The measured output of firms with high levels of IT and more skilled workers is more than 4 percent higher than their industry competitors' with similar levels of labor and capital inputs.[40]

What is striking, however, is that low-low also tends to be a relatively high-productivity outcome. We normalize the omitted category low-low to zero, so the negative estimates for δ_{hl} and δ_{lh} mean that firms in the off-diagonal cells (low-high or high-low) are less productive than those with low IT and low HK. Thus, high HK is associated with high productivity but only in firms that also have high IT. HK is not associated with high levels of productivity for firms with low IT. The productivity kick comes from matching IT and HK. This suggests that high levels of IT are most effective in the presence of a trained and educated work force, and the converse is also true.

As noted, this is exactly the pattern predicted by the complementarities notion. There is a perfectly workable cluster of low-low, old-style firms. They have internal consistency in their mix of complements, what Milgrom and Roberts call a coherent combination of practices.[41] Further, this result argues against heterogeneity arguments as an explanation for the results. While some unobserved firm-level shock (free cash flow is the obvious one)

---

40. The table shows sample splits for only one measure of HK, namely SKILL. Qualitatively similar results obtain for other measures, such as %COLL, and for related specifications with the output elasticities varying between high- and low-IT firms.

41. Milgrom and Roberts (1990).

Table 5-9. *Productivity with Matches and Mismatches on Complements*

Part A: IT × HK (as measured by ITCAP and SKILL, respectively)

	IT	
HK	Low	High
High	−.0293	.0422
	(.0221)	(.0199)
	N = 552	N = 762
Low	0	−.0321
	n.a.	(.0174)
	N = 561	N = 358

Standard error in parentheses; estimates are the δs as shown in the equation.
Pearson chi-square test for association: $\chi^2 = 82.4$ ($p < .001$).
Number of firms in each half of the table is unbalanced because of ties and discrete scales (SKILL).

Part B: HK × WO (as measured by SKILL and WO, respectively)

	IT	
HK	Low	High
High	−.0481	.0372
	(.0208)	(.0165)
	N = 492	N = 822
Low	0	−.0522
	n.a.	(.0178)
	N = 627	N = 284

Standard error in parentheses.
Pearson chi-square test for association: $\chi^2 = 211$ ($p < .001$).
Number of firms in each half of the table is unbalanced because of ties and discrete scales (SKILL, WO).

Part C: IT × WO (as measured by ITCAP and WO, respectively)

	IT	
HK	Low	High
High	.00356	.0664
	(.0179)	(.0197)
	N = 448	N = 664
Low	0	.00153
	n.a.	(.0199)
	N = 671	N = 442

Standard error in parentheses.
Pearson chi-square test for association: $\chi^2 = 89.0$ ($p < .001$).
Number of firms in each half of the table is unbalanced because of ties and discrete scales (WO).
n.a. Not applicable.

could yield positive effects on human capital, IT, and productivity at the same time, it would not explain why firms with both low IT and low HK have *higher* productivity than those with one but not the other. Similarly, this result argues against a "fad" interpretation. The cluster of inputs that go together are clearly related to increases in output quantity or price (perhaps because of service quality). Thus they cannot be merely an inefficient fad.[42]

Similar results also hold when the regression includes WO and its interaction with HK (in table 5-9, part B) instead of IT and HK. Firms with more of the characteristics of the new work organization are more productive if they also have highly skilled workers. However, firms that attempt the new work organization without more skilled workers than their industry peers, or which employ more skilled workers but not the new work organization, are notably *less* productive than firms that simply adopted a low-WO-low-HK strategy. As before, this is most easily explained as evidence of complementarities.

Finally, comparing interactions of WO and IT (in table 5-9, part C) leads to a similar story. In this case, the off-diagonal firms (high-low and low-high) are not actually less productive than the low-low firms. Instead, the productivity advance to getting one but not the other is positive but small and insignificant. Shifting from low levels of IT to higher levels of IT is associated with a greater increase in productivity for high WO firms than for low WO firms, and conversely, WO appears to be most productive in the presence of high levels of IT.

As noted, in each table the sample is split at the median firm so that approximately half of the firms are in each "high" group and half are in each "low" group. However, it is clear that the firms are not evenly distributed among all four quadrants. As one might expect if our explanation is correct, a majority of firms avoid the low productivity quadrants in favor of the "high-high" or "low-low" quadrant. For instance, there are more than twice as many firms in the "high-IT-high-HK" quadrant as in the "high-IT-low-HK" quadrant." This is of course consistent with the earlier correlation analyses, but we can now see that this pattern is also consistent with the hypothesis that firms choose their practices at least in part to increase productivity.

While analyses presented in table 5-9, parts A, B, and C, present a simple way to see the productivity levels associated with various combinations

---

42. We exclude the fancier theory of an inefficient fad whose incidence is somehow confined to successful firms. That is, of course, possible, if peculiar.

of IT, HK, and WO, much the same story is evident in more structured models such as those we explore in our companion paper.[43] When various interaction terms are included in a log-linear specification, alone or in combination, the results indicate that IT, HK, and WO are complements. This is true when alternative measures of each of the basic work practices are examined, when we instrument the endogenous variables to control for endogeneity, and to a limited extent even when three-way interactions are explored, although collinearity limits the reliability of such analyses.

How Are IT, HK, and WO Changing over Time?

Levels of investment in both IT and HK are well known to be increasing over time. The biggest changes are in IT, where impressive advances in the underlying science and engineering of the technology have led to sharp improvements in both capabilities and costs. As a result, real investment in IT has grown at double-digit rates for several decades and current levels dwarf those of even a few years ago. Meanwhile, the skill levels of the work force have also increased, at least according to such metrics as the proportion of college graduates in the work force. Data on changes in WO are harder to come by, although there seems to be a consensus that many of the practices we measure are becoming more common.[44] While the levels of IT, HK, and WO may all be increasing, all firms do not necessarily adopt them at the same rate. In fact, the complementarities theory predicts that firms which are further along in one practice should be more likely to adopt the other practices, other things being equal. The productivity analyses empirically support the notion that such a policy will have the greatest rewards.

We can test this implication more directly by looking at investments, not just levels, of the work practices. We do not have direct measures of HK or WO over time, but we do have measures of investments in training and policies of screening new employees based on education at the end of the sample period. These measures can be interpreted as investments in HK. As noted earlier, we find that most measures of IT are correlated with greater *investments* in human capital (table 5-4, middle rows). IT can predict greater investments in human capital even when we control for current levels of human capital (by including SKILL and EDUC as partial covari-

---

43. Bresnahan, Brynjolfsson, and Hitt (1998).
44. See, for example, Ichniowski and others (1996); Osterman (1994).

ates in the bottom rows of the table). Although HK is changing much more slowly than IT, this result is consistent with the hypothesis that IT-intensive firms are attempting to move toward a new cluster of complements, relative to less IT-intensive firms.

The earlier results indicated that firms with high levels of human capital and work organization are more likely to also have high levels of IT. We can also examine a dynamic version of this question by adding interaction terms between a time trend and two human capital and organizational structure measures. We can undertake this partially dynamic analysis as we have IT data for each year of our sample period, but our measures of human capital and workplace organization are only available for the end of the period. In table 5-10 we see that for any given set of prices and business conditions, firms with more decentralized decisionmaking (WO) tend to invest more rapidly in IT than their competitors. However, we do not find that HK is a particularly strong predictor of IT investments (as opposed to IT levels) even though IT levels can predict HK investments.

As with our other results, the most direct interpretation is complementarities. The interactions with time pick up changes in IT over time. WO is changing in many of our sample firms and, where it is changing, IT is growing. In one story, WO is a new organizational invention (or IT-enabled WO is a new organizational invention).[45] By this interpretation, those firms that have moved forward in WO have also moved forward on the other complements.[46] HK is more stable, and so the level of HK at the end of the period is not a good predictor of changes in IT. This would suggest that the IT-HK complementarity is closer to equilibrium while we are observing firms actively investing in both WO (narrow definition) and complementary IT.

In summary, we view these dynamic results as consistent with the complementarity story. While not all of the complements are changing at the same rate, it appears that one can make some predictions about a firm's investment rates in one complement by looking at the levels of other complements in that firm.

45. This is essentially the view that Ichniowski and others (1996) put forth in their summary of the literature on innovations in workplace organization.

46. Accordingly, it is not a criticism to note a weaker correlation between WO and IT in the early part of the sample (since our WO data are only contemporaneous with IT at the end of the sample period). Similarly, it is not an econometric criticism that WO (1995) is a measure of WO(t) with an error that declines over time, rather, this econometric remark is closely linked to the economics of our interpretation.

Table 5-10. *Changes in IT Demand as a Function of Human Capital and Organization, Controlling for Work Force Composition*

Dependent variable	log(ITCAP)		
Specification			Base + ed. +
	Base +	Base +	WO w/o
(Variable)	WO	education + WO	WO × time
Worker skill × time	.000255	−.0194	−.00557
(SKILL × YEAR)	(.00759)	(.0220)	(.0203)
College ed. × time		.00656	.0109
(%COLL × YEAR)		(.0210)	(.0207)
WO × time	.0183***	.0358	
(WO × YEAR)	(.00766)	(.0219)	
Worker skill	.0438***	.0560***	.0543***
(SKILL)	(.0191)	(.0247)	(.0247)
College education		.0388	.0392
(%COLL)		(.0276)	(.0277)
Decentralization	.0668***	.0876***	.0890***
(WO)	(.0186)	(.0238)	(.0238)
Log(value-added)	.647***	.600***	.599***
Log(VA)	(.0186)	(.0219)	(.0219)
Professionals	.133***	.0967***	.0958***
(%PF)	(.0206)	(.0291)	(.0291)
Controls	Sector year composition (PRBL, PRPF %MG, %CL, %SK) %SCED	Sector year composition (PRBL, PRPF %MG, %CL, %SK) %SCED	Sector year composition (PRBL, PRPF %MG, %CL, %SK) %SCED
R^2	53.7%	51.0%	50.9%
N	1,854	1,331	1,331

Key: $* p < .1$, $** p < .05$, $*** p < .01$.

All variables standardized to mean 0, unit variance except interaction terms which represent a standardized variable multiplied by a mean 0 time measure (units are years).

Relationship to Earlier Work

Most earlier work at the *industry level* finds complementarity between IT and HK.[47] The incompleteness, there, and the advance here, is getting inside the black box of the firm first with the WO data and second with the managerial queries just reported. This illuminates the mechanisms at work in a way that makes the technological causation story more complete and thus more refutable; when unrefuted, more convincing.

Earlier work at *the individual worker* level has been at best ambiguous in its results about IT-HK complementarity. Individual workers who use computers do command higher wages.[48] Yet it appears that both the higher wages and the computers may be given to workers who are already particularly productive, rather than (or in addition to) the computer making the worker more productive.[49] Here we have considerable evidence against a nonproductivity alternative direction of causation argument at the *firm* level. The firm-level equivalent would be that *firms* with particularly high levels of HK got, for some reason not related to production complementarities, WO and IT. The analogy to the individual-worker theory is obviously false. WO and mainframes make poor "rewards" for the reasons we just argued. Finally, at the firm level we have more direct evidence on the productivity of using the factors together. Moving closer to the actual demanding unit, the firm, permits investigation of the hypotheses better than at the worker or industry level.

Implications

Strong complementarity among human capital, new forms of workplace organization, and IT is a finding with important implications for the whole economy. The three complementary factors play different roles.

—(IT) The real price of IT has been falling rapidly and will continue to fall for at least a decade. This shifts firms in the direction of using all three complements. This is the route by which IT and the workplace organization changes it enables become skill-biased technical change.

47. Autor, Katz, and Krueger (1997).
48. Krueger (1993).
49. DiNardo and Pischke (1997).

—(HK) The supply curve for more skilled workers is rising. The IT-driven skill-biased technical change has driven changes in relative wages, hours, and earnings.

—(WO) Finally, the third complement, workplace organization, is characterized by very substantial adjustment costs, as is change in output quality. Firms must co-invent the specific organizational changes and specific new product qualities that work in their particular circumstances, a nontrivial challenge.

Computer and other information technology prices have been falling steadily, tending to raise demand not only for IT capital but also for the invention of new organizational forms and for new services or new levels of quality. The demand for all three is by no means automatic, however, because of those substantial adjustment costs. At any given moment, we expect to see variety in a cross section of firms in the degree to which they have adopted the three complements. Leading firms will have high levels of all three complements; trailing firms will have low levels of all three complements. Some firms will be further along on some dimensions than on others owing to mistakes or random factors that influence their adoption.

What's more, the underlying complementarities in the systems adopted by the leading firms are undoubtedly far more complex and intricate than those we can observe in our data. For instance, Erik Brynjolfsson, Amy Renshaw, and Marshall Van Alstyne studied one firm's transition from traditional manufacturing to modern, computer-intensive manufacturing and found not only dozens of complementarities but also several mistakes, reversals, and abortive attempts to implement incomplete clusters of complements.[50] When the firm finally got the new work system working smoothly, they literally painted the factory windows black to prevent competitors from quickly imitating their success. This supports the hypothesis that one of the barriers that prevents competitors from quickly imitating the most successful computer users is the subtlety and complexity of the organizational co-inventions needed to harness this revolution in computer power.[51]

Like econometricians, rival managers may be able to discern the broad outlines of a successful strategy even though they do not know the myriad

50. Brynjolfsson, Renshaw, and Alstyne (1997).

51. Indirect evidence for this fact is the high gross marginal products found for IT when standard production functions are estimated using firm-level data. Brynjolfsson and Hitt (1995, 1996); Lichtenberg (1995).

details necessary to implement the strategy effectively. This observation is consistent with the large adjustment costs associated with IT, which have been found to be primarily the costs of adjusting the complementary WO, not the IT itself.[52] The research suggests that merely pointing the way toward a "high-performance work organization" will rarely be sufficient to get trailing firms to adopt the new system.

Besides these adjustment costs, rising wages of highly skilled labor also slow the diffusion of the cluster of complements (and presumably offer a powerful incentive for inventing ways to use IT and organizational forms that economize on skill.) Neither of these countereffects, however, reverses the trend to the cluster of complements. They simply slow it, in large measure by limiting the number of firms using the cluster of complements.

We therefore believe that the current cross-firm variety in adoption of the three-way cluster of innovations embodies a forecast of the future. An easy prediction is that IT prices will continue to fall and IT performance will continue to improve (notably in the data networking area). As a result, more and more firms will find the cluster of complements worth adopting. In parallel, firms that are now experimenting or unsure will increasingly overcome the costs and delays associated with the organizational change. Over time, therefore, more firms will come to look like those using the cluster of complements: IT-intensive, changed workplace organization, and high human capital. The aggregate implication is that the recent tendency toward skill-biased technical change will continue.

Conclusion

In this chapter, we combine and extend two distinct research streams. One, developed primarily by labor economists, links IT to the increased demand for skills. Another, developed primarily by information systems researchers,

---

52. See Bresnahan and Greenstein (1996); Brynjolfsson and Hitt (1997); and especially Ito (1996) on this point. If we were to expand the definition of IT to include applications software and the training and reorganization needed to use it effectively, it would become more fixed in the short run. Our observables, however, correspond to the adjustment cost relationships described in the text. There might well be a different way to divide the cluster of complements, focusing on applications of IT rather than IT hardware, which would yield a more detailed and nuanced view of the pattern of adjustment costs than we can provide here. That, however, would call for more detailed data on the software side of IT.

links IT to changes in organization and output quality. We hypothesize that the increased demand for skilled labor is related to a particular *cluster* of technological change involving not only increased use of IT but also changes in workplace organization and changes in product and service quality. The most common combinations of IT-enabled organizational and strategic change increase the relative demand for skilled workers.

We find that the empirical evidence is broadly consistent with our hypothesis as well as prior theoretical and empirical work on IT and labor demand and IT and organization. In particular, our analysis of firm-level data suggests that IT use is correlated with increases in the demand for various indicators of human capital and work force skills. IT use is also correlated with a pattern of work organization involving more decentralized decisionmaking and greater use of teams. Increases in firms' IT capital stock are associated with the greatest increases in output in firms that also have high levels of human capital or decentralized work organization, or both. However, firms that implement only one complement without the others are often less productive than firms which implement none at all. Firms with high levels of some complements are more likely to invest in other complements. In addition, in our companion paper we show that these empirical facts are consistent with the widespread perception among the managers in our sample.[53] When asked directly, these managers reported that IT is skill increasing, and this tendency is particularly pronounced in high human capital, IT-intensive, and decentralized firms.

The combination of computerization, workplace organization, and increased demand for skilled workers appears as a cluster of changes in modern firms, almost certainly because they are complements. This has two implications. First, many of the recent changes in the structure of the corporation and the demand for human capital have a common origin in technological change, which shows no sign of abating. As a result, the specific mechanisms of skill-biased technical change now and in the future can be better understood by more closely studying the nature of IT-enabled organizational change in firms.

---

53. Bresnahan, Brynjolfsson, and Hitt (1998).

COMMENT BY
Gary Burtless

In the introduction to this chapter, the authors motivate our interest by
describing the growth of income and wage inequality in the United States.
Growing wage inequality is a hotly debated topic among scholars and policymakers. The question is, how much can the authors' results tell us about
nationwide trends in wage inequality? I think they tell us a great deal about
current trends (and likely explanations for those trends) in the nation's
largest companies. I am less certain they tell us as much about trends in
smaller and mid-size companies, which account for a growing percentage
of the nation's employment.

Pay premiums for worker skill increased dramatically between 1979 and
1993. At the same time, U.S. employers' utilization of skilled workers also
rose. In other words, American employers paid an increasing relative price
in order to hire skilled workers, but they nonetheless hired more of them.
What can the authors' data tell us about this phenomenon? The data come
from several sources: a survey of information technology (IT) spending in
Fortune 1000 companies; a new survey on workplace organization and
human resource management practices; and Compustat records on company employment levels, output, capital, labor, and value added.

In their sample of firms, the authors find that IT investment and the
intensity of use of IT is correlated with higher levels of human capital and
labor skill in the company's work force. That is, a company with a bigger
installed base of mainframe and personal computers typically has a more
educated and better-skilled labor force. Technical innovations in IT do not
push the sample companies to substitute better or cheaper machines for
highly skilled (and highly paid) workers; they induce companies to hire
more skilled workers.

The authors' cross tabulations also shed light on the influence of new
workplace management techniques. Their estimates show that new patterns of work organization—greater use of teams in production and more
decentralized decisionmaking—are correlated with more intensive use of
highly educated workers and with above-average use of IT. The authors
sensibly interpret this finding to mean that companies' adoption of new
kinds of work organization and their investment in IT are tightly linked
with companies' choices about the average level and distribution of worker

skill. All three aspects of the company environment are part of an overall management plan, which, if it is effective, must integrate new investment in IT, human capital, and new management practices.

The statistical correlations suggest that innovations and new investment in information technology may be a source of higher demand for skilled workers in these corporations. New forms of workplace organization probably reinforce the effects of IT innovations in these firms.

Many people who follow corporate management practice may feel that these observations are not new. In fact, they may feel the connection found by the authors is fairly obvious from first principles. I am not sure this is true. When we look inside the black box of the firm, should we always expect to turn up evidence that firms' investment in IT is correlated with more intensive use of skilled workers?

Some technical innovations may permit companies to use less skilled workers to perform tasks formerly done by workers with midlevel skills. For example, some retail outlets have introduced smart cash registers with separate keys representing each item offered for sale. People who operate these machines do not have to be terribly skilled. Many retailers now use computer-assisted scanning devices for final sales and inventory control, reducing the chances a careless clerk will charge an incorrect price or forget to notify a manager that the supply of some product is running low. These kinds of innovations may *reduce* the average skill needed by retail clerks. The innovations should make it possible for retailers to substitute a less skilled and less well-paid class of workers for the semiskilled workers formerly needed to perform the same tasks. The innovations may thus reduce employer demand for a (moderately) skilled class of worker at the same time it increases job opportunities for the least skilled. To be sure, the sophisticated equipment increases the demand for technically accomplished technicians and managers who are responsible for ensuring the new machines operate effectively. But it is not obvious why it would cause demand for *both* the least skilled *and* the moderately skilled to fall in comparison with demand for the very highly skilled. Yet a characteristic pattern of rising inequality is that the pay gap between skill classes has widened at every step of the economywide wage ladder; it has not widened only between the very highly skilled and everyone else.

What can we infer from this study about the overall demand for different classes of labor? Can we infer anything about the economywide link between technology, innovations in IT, new forms of workplace management, and the demand for different kinds of workers?

I am cautious about drawing broad inferences on the shifting demand for different classes of U.S. workers. One point to bear in mind is that firms may not only change the way they produce value added *within* the company, they may also change the way they divide production between company insiders and outsiders. Focusing on what is happening within four hundred or so large companies cannot tell us much about how these companies are dividing work between employees and nonemployees.

Fortune 500 companies account for a sharply lower percentage of total employment today than was the case in, say, 1970. I have been told that senior corporate managers now focus like a laser beam on the question, "make or buy?" Should the company produce an essential component inside the company? Or should it purchase it from outside suppliers, possibly by contracting out? My impression is that, compared with twenty-five years ago, big firms are less likely to make and more likely to buy.

They buy cafeteria services from Marriott rather than using company workers to produce coffee and hot lunches. They contract with Purolator to supply protective services rather than hire company guards. They buy office cleaning services from Gen-X Office Cleaners rather than hire their own janitors.

My guess is that this trend has reduced the number of unskilled workers on big company payrolls, but it does not follow that it has reduced the economywide demand for unskilled worker services. A study focusing only on the company payrolls of Fortune 1000 companies will capture the reduced direct demand for low-skilled workers on these companies' payrolls while missing the fact that overall utilization of unskilled workers may be essentially unchanged.

Let me suggest an alternative interpretation of what is going on. Big companies have historically favored paternalistic pay structures. Personnel managers are uncomfortable seeing big pay gaps between workers on company payrolls. (Bear in mind that I am describing company practices in 1970, not in 1999.) This may mean the company must pay higher wages for unskilled or semiskilled labor services than the spot market price for these services would require. Baggage handlers were paid $18.00 an hour at Eastern Airlines, even though the airline could easily hire a worker to move bags for $10.00 an hour (or less). As long as the firm makes a profit, and the company manager faces little prospect of dismissal from his or her job, this "overpayment" is affordable and sustainable.

Now assume either of two changes occurs. One, the company faces an imminent threat of bankruptcy. Or two, new institutional arrangements in corporate finance or corporate ownership and control permit aroused stockholders to remove managers who fail to minimize costs. One of three things must then happen: managers will force "overpaid" unskilled and semiskilled workers to take a pay cut. Managers will look for a way to "buy" rather than "make" the good or service formerly produced by "overpaid" unskilled and semiskilled workers. Or managers will get fired.

Consider the second outcome. Managers go to the spot market for janitorial or cafeteria or protective services and contract for the service at the lowest market price consistent with minimal acceptable quality. Unskilled workers will become less numerous on big company payrolls, but they will still find jobs . . . with small, low-paying firms.

I do not claim that this is the main story accounting for lower wages to the less skilled, but it is probably part of the story. And it is a part that will be missed when we focus solely on workers who are on the current payrolls of a sample of big companies.

Let's step back for a moment from the particular focus of this chapter. Ignoring for a moment changes in information processing technology and the evolution of workplace practices, let us consider the big question: what forces have pushed down the wages of less skilled workers and pushed up wage disparities across the American labor force? Weaker unions have reduced the bargaining clout of unskilled and semiskilled workers. Lower trade barriers and reduced communication and transportation costs have made poorly paid Asian and Latin American workers better substitutes for unskilled U.S. workers. Higher flows of immigrants—particularly of unskilled immigrants—have depressed the wages of the least skilled U.S. workers. Most informed economists share the authors' view, however, that biased technical change is the most persuasive explanation for declining relative wages among the unskilled. This chapter provides hard evidence from big companies that tends to support this interpretation, at least with information that can be gleaned from big companies' payrolls.

But even though technological change is economists' favorite explanation for the growth in wage disparities, it is not a particularly satisfying explanation. The direct evidence in support of it (up to now) has been pretty weak. Economists do not conclude that technical change has caused recent inequality trends because they directly observe the skill requirements embodied in specific technological advances. In fact, they have little evidence about the skill requirements embodied in any production process (although the evidence in this chapter is certainly suggestive). What they observe instead is the skill distribution of workers employed in different plants or industries and the absolute levels of pay received by workers in different skill classes.

The changing pattern of use of workers in different skill classes and the changing pattern of their pay is easy to explain by saying that the production technology has changed in a way that makes production more intensive in its requirement for skill. But this statement simply means that other explanations of changing pay patterns (such as growing international trade or weaker labor unions) cannot satisfactorily account for a big percentage of the trend in the wage structure or the relative intensity of use of workers at different skill levels. The explanation is analogous to explaining the slowdown in productivity growth after 1973 by saying that there has been a slowdown in technical advance. In both cases the explanation would be more useful and persuasive if we could point to specific evidence about technical change that would tend to support it.

The authors have tried hard to clarify the link between IT investment, new management practices, and the skill mix of a company's work force. They show that adoption of new technologies connected to information processing may push companies to adopt new personnel policies and management techniques. The personal computer is certainly an example of a technical advance that can have major effects on personnel policies and management practice. The dramatic decline in the cost of stand-alone computers has influenced the way goods and services are produced in a wide variety of industries and occupations. Arguably, this change has put a premium on the ability of workers to acquire the skills needed to operate computers. Workers who possess this ability are favored; workers who lack it, suffer.

But a good case can be made that another kind of technical advance has had consequences just as profound for personnel and management practices. As recently as the early 1970s many observers believed that senior corporate managers could not be replaced by dissatisfied but hapless stockholders, who were too numerous and poorly organized to exert a decisive influence on company management. As a consequence, lax, foolish, or unprofitable company management could survive as long as managers could keep their companies out of bankruptcy. By the middle of the 1980s this view was seriously incomplete. Innovations such as leveraged buyouts and junk bonds made it possible for a small number of well-organized stockholders and lenders to take over a company's management and fundamentally change the direction of the corporation—for example, by modifying historical pay patterns in the company, by selling off unprofitable operations, or by outsourcing the production of important company inputs. These innovations, too, may have caused big increases in pay disparities, within and between companies, but they are not the kind of innovation most people have in mind when they are told that technical change is the most important single source of rising wage inequality.

This chapter sheds light on two of the most important sources of change in the demand for unskilled workers in big companies. It suggests that investments in IT and adoption of new kinds of workplace management can boost the relative demand for highly skilled workers in these companies. It does not tell us whether this will result in a shrinkage in the *overall* utilization of unskilled and semiskilled workers or only a reallocation of workers across different kinds of companies. My guess is that both kinds of change will occur: The demand for unskilled and semiskilled workers on *big company* payrolls will shrink, and the economywide demand for these workers' services will shrink, too.

References

Applegate, Lynda M., James I. Cash, and D. Quinn Mills. 1988. "Information Technology and Tomorrow's Manager." *Harvard Business Review* 66 (November–December): 128–36.

Athey, Susan, and Scott Stern. 1998. "An Empirical Framework for Testing Theories about Complementarity in Organizational Design." NBER Working Paper 6600 (June).

Attewell, Paul, and James Rule. 1984. "Computing and Organizations: What We Know and What We Don't Know." *Communications of the ACM* 27 (December):1184–92.

Autor, David, Lawrence F. Katz, and Alan B. Krueger. 1997. "Computing Inequality: Have Computers Changed the Labor Market?" NBER Working Paper 5956. Cambridge, Mass.: National Bureau of Economic Research (March).

Barras, Richard. 1990. "Interactive Innovation in Financial and Business Services: The Vanguard of the Service Revolution." *Research Policy* 19 (June): 215–38.

Bartel, Ann P., and Frank R. Lichtenberg. 1987. "The Comparative Advantage of Educated Workers in Implementing New Technology." *Review of Economics and Statistics* 69 (February): 1–11.

Berman, Eli, John Bound, and Zvi Griliches. 1994. "Changes in the Demand for Skilled Labor within U.S. Manufacturing: Evidence from the Annual Survey of Manufacturers." *Quarterly Journal of Economics* 109 (May): 367–97.

Berndt, Ernst, Catherine J. Morrison, and Larry S. Rosenblum. 1992. "High-Tech Capital Formation and Labor Composition in U.S. Manufacturing Industries: An Exploratory Analysis." MIT Working Paper 3414-92.

Bound, John, and George Johnson. 1992. "Changes in the Structure of Wages in the 1980s: An Evaluation of Alternative Explanations." *American Economic Review* 82 (June): 371–92.

Bresnahan, Timothy F. 1997. "Computerization and Wage Dispersion: An Analytic Reinterpretation." Mimeo. Stanford University.

Bresnahan, Timothy, and Shane Greenstein. 1996. "Technical Progress and Co-Invention in Computing and in the Uses of Computers." *Brookings Papers on Economic Activity, Microeconomics:* 1–83.

Bresnahan, Timothy, Erik Brynjolfsson, and Lorin Hitt. 1998. "Information Technology, Workplace Organization, and the Demand for Skilled Labor: Firm Level Evidence." Mimeo. MIT, Stanford University, and Wharton.

Brynjolfsson, Erik, and Lorin Hitt. 1995. "Information Technology as a Factor of Production: The Role of Differences among Firms." *Economics of Innovation and New Technology* 3 (3–4): 183–99.

———. 1996. "Paradox Lost? Firm-Level Evidence on the Returns to Information Systems Spending." *Management Science* 42 (April): 541–58.

———. 1997. "Information Technology and Organizational Design: Evidence from Firm-Level Data." MIT Sloan School Working Paper.

Brynjolfsson, Erik, Amy A. Renshaw, and Marshall Van Alstyne. 1997. "The Matrix of Change." *Sloan Management Review* 38 (Winter): 37–54.

Crowston, Kevin, and Malone, Thomas W. 1988. "Information Technology and Work Organization." In *Handbook of Human-Computer Interaction,* edited by Martin Helander, 1051–70. Amsterdam: Elsevier Science.

Davenport, Thomas H., and James E. Short. 1990. "The New Industrial Engineering: Information Technology and Business Process Redesign." *Sloan Management Review* 31 (Summer): 11–27.

DiNardo, John E., and Jörn-Steffen Pischke. 1997. "The Returns to Computer Use Revisited: Have Pencils Changed the Wage Structure Too?" *Quarterly Journal of Economics* 112 (February): 291–303.

Gottschalk, Peter. 1997. "Inequality, Income Growth, and Mobility: The Basic Facts." *Journal of Economic Perspectives* 11 (Spring): 21–40.

Griliches, Zvi, 1969. "Capital-Skill Complementarity." *Review of Economics and Statistics* 51(November): 465–68.

Hall, Bronwyn H. 1990. "The Manufacturing Sector Master File: 1959–1987." Working Paper 3366. Cambridge, Mass.: National Bureau of Economic Research.

Hamermesh, Daniel S. 1993. *Labor Demand.* Princeton University Press.

Hammer, Michael. 1990. "Reengineering Work: Don't Automate, Obliterate." *Harvard Business Review* 68 (July): 104–13.

Holmstrom, Bengt, and Paul Milgrom. 1991. "Multitask Principal-Agent Analyses: Incentive Contracts, Asset Ownership, and Job Design." *Journal of Law, Economics, and Organization* 7 (Spring): 24–52.

———. 1994. "The Firm as an Incentive System." *American Economic Review* 84 (September): 972–91.

Howell, David R., and Edward N. Wolff. 1991. "Trends in the Growth and Distribution of Skills in the U.S. Workplace 1960–1985." *Industrial and Labor Relations Review* 44 (April): 486–502.

Ichniowski, Casey, and others. 1996. "What Works at Work: Overview and Assessment." *Industrial Relations* 35 (July): 299–33.

Ichniowski, Casey, Kathryn Shaw, and Giovanna Prennushi. 1997. "The Effects of Human Resource Management Practices on Productivity." *American Economic Review* 87(June): 291–313.

Ito, Harumi. 1996. *Essays on Investment Adjustment Costs.* Ph.D. dissertation. Stanford University (September).

Jensen, Michael C., and William H. Meckling.1992. "Specific and General Knowledge and Organizational Structure." In *Contract Economics*, edited by Lars Werin and Hans Wijkander, 251–74. Basil Blackwell.

Katz, Lawrence F., and Kevin M. Murphy. 1992. "Changes in Relative Wages, 1963–1987: Supply and Demand Factors." *Quarterly Journal of Economics* 107 (February): 35–78.

Kemerer, C. F., and G. L. Sosa. 1991. "Systems Development Risks in Strategic Information Systems." *Information and Software Technology* 33 (April): 212–23.

Krueger, Alan B. 1993. "How Computers Have Changed the Wage Structure: Evidence from Microdata." *Quarterly Journal of Economics* 108 (February): 33–60.

Krugman, Paul, and Robert Z. Lawrence. 1993. "Trade, Jobs, and Wages." Working Paper 4478. Cambridge, Mass.: National Bureau of Economic Research (September).

Leavitt, Harold. J., and Thomas L. Whisler. 1958. "Management in the 1980s." *Harvard Business Review* 36 (November–December): 41–48.

Levy, Frank, and Richard J. Murnane. 1996. "With What Skills Are Computers a Complement?" *American Economic Review* 86 (May): 258–62.

Lichtenberg, Frank R. 1995. "The Output Contributions of Computer Equipment and Personnel: A Firm-Level Analysis." *Economics of Innovation and New Technology* 3 (3–4): 201–17.

Malone, Thomas W., and John F. Rockart. 1991. "Computers, Networks and the Corporation." *Scientific American* 265 (September): 128–37.

Malone, Thomas W., Joanne Yates, and Robert I. Benjamin. 1987. "Electronic Markets and Electronic Hierarchies." *Communications of the ACM* 30 (June): 484–97.

Mendelson, Haim, and Ravindran R. Pillai. 1998. "Clockspeed and Informational Response: Evidence from the Information Technology Industry." Stanford University.

Milgrom, Paul, and John Roberts. 1990. "The Economics of Modern Manufacturing: Technology, Strategy, and Organization." *American Economic Review* 80 (June): 511–28.

Murphy, Kevin M., and Finis Welch. 1993. "Inequality and Relative Wages." *American Economic Review* 83 (May): 104–09.

Orlikowski, Wanda J. 1992. "Learning from Notes: Organizational Issues in Groupware Implementation." Sloan School Working Paper 3428-92. MIT Sloan School of Management, Center for Coordination Science.

Osterman, Paul. 1994. "How Common Is Workplace Transformation and Who Adopts It?" *Industrial and Labor Relations Review* 47 (January): 173–88.

Scott Morton, Michael S., ed. 1991. *The Corporation of the 1990s: Information Technology and Organizational Transformation.* Oxford University Press.

Simon, Herbert A. 1971. "Designing Organizations for an Information-Rich World." In *Computers, Communications, and the Public Interest*, edited by Martin Greenberger, 37–72. Johns Hopkins Press.

————. 1973. "Applying Information Technology to Organization Design." *Public Administration Review* 33 (May–June): 268–78.

Wolff, Edward N. 1996. "The Growth of Information Workers in the U.S. Economy, 1950–1990: The Role of Technological Change, Computerization, and Structural Change." New York University, C.V. Starr Center for Applied Economics.

Williamson, Oliver E. 1979. "Transaction-Cost Economics: The Governance of Contractual Relations." *Journal of Law and Economics* 22 (October): 233–61.

Zuboff, Shoshana. 1988. *In the Age of the Smart Machine: The Future of Work and Power.* Basic Books.

6

AVNER BEN-NER
W. ALLEN BURNS
GREGORY DOW
LOUIS PUTTERMAN

Employee Ownership:
An Empirical Exploration

IN THIS CHAPTER we study the empirical determinants of employee participation in decisionmaking, financial returns, and ownership, using a unique data set that includes information about the extent of employee involvement in firm decisionmaking, the existence of employee stock ownership plans (ESOPs), and the use of profit sharing (PS) in a large number of Minnesota firms from a cross section of industries. In our sample, 10 percent of firms have ESOPs covering 69 percent of employees on average, and 52 percent of firms have profit sharing covering 65 percent of employees on average. These figures are similar to those reported in other studies.

Our focus is on causes of employee participation rather than its consequences. That is, we regard the use of a profit-sharing or other participatory plan as something to be explained by observable factors that are tied in to the concepts of economics and organization theory, whereas it is not

We thank Derek Jones and Richard Freeman for their helpful suggestions on earlier versions of this chapter, not all of which we have been able to follow. Ben-Ner acknowledges support for the data collection effort by the Sloan Foundation, the Sloan Foundation's Retail Food Industry Research Center at the University of Minnesota, and by the University of Minnesota's Center for Urban and Regional Affairs, Carlson School of Management, and the Industrial Relations Center. Dow would like to thank the Social Sciences and Humanities Research Council of Canada.

our purpose to trace the impacts of such plans upon labor productivity and other outcomes.[1] Of course, to the extent that worker participation is driven by anticipated productivity benefits, it is not entirely possible to maintain a clean separation between causes and consequences.

Theory and Hypotheses

There is an enormous literature on the topic of employee involvement. In this chapter, we do not propose any new theory to explain the phenomenon but instead look for evidence on a few of the main theories that have been proposed elsewhere. We draw upon literatures asking two types of questions. One, why do most workers accept employment with firms owned by investors, rather than organizing their own firms?[2] Two, what are the effects of adoption of modest levels of profit sharing, employee ownership, or employee involvement schemes by otherwise conventional firms?[3] The hypotheses considered are culled from a variety of sources, including the new institutional economics, the economic theory of the labor-managed firm, and the broader literature on organization theory.[4] The hypotheses derived from these diverse literatures are highly heterogeneous, and we do not attempt to synthesize them here.

To streamline presentation, hypotheses about what drives the adoption of employee participation in decisionmaking, profit sharing, and ownership are grouped into five principal categories, depending on whether they center on problems of information flow and coordination of the work process; problems of eliciting effort; financing; problems of rent seeking in the face of asset specificity; or institutional features of the firm, such as unionization and whether the firm is publicly traded. The effect of these categories on the desirability of employee participation in decisionmaking

1. The consequences of different forms of organizing work have been investigated in other work by members of the Minnesota Organization of Work project, including Han (1995), who focuses on productivity; Park (1997), who concentrates on work place safety; and Liu (1998), who analyzes the determinants of the choice of work systems. Excellent surveys of the literature on the effects of employee participation on productivity are found in Blinder (1990). More recent research on the effects of profit sharing on labor productivity includes Wadhwani and Wall (1990); Kruse (1993); Jones and Kato (1995); and Ben-Ner, Han, and Jones (1996).

2. As surveyed by Dow and Putterman (1999).

3. The question is addressed by Ben-Ner and Jones (1995).

4. For the new institutional economics see Williamson (1985); Milgrom and Roberts (1992); Hart (1995).

or financial returns is generally influenced by the production technology a firm employs and the implications of this technology for the nature of employees' tasks.[5]

Information and Coordination

Production technology involves the processes through which labor, equipment, raw materials, and other inputs are transformed into useful goods and services. The technology of production is partly embedded in machinery and computers but also in the related ways in which work is organized, such as the physical location of employees, whether the flow of work involves serial or parallel processing, what sort of communication channels are available to workers, how work is scheduled, and so on. Two attributes of production technology are especially salient for our purposes: the complexity of the tasks that employees have to execute and the degree of interdependence among the tasks of different employees.[6] Here we focus primarily on implications for managerial coordination within the firm; we will also explain the incentive implications of these factors.

First, information transmission across different levels of a hierarchical organization is costly and difficult.[7] Bounded rationality limits the capacities of decisionmakers at upper levels to make proper decisions and exercise effective control over day-to-day operations, particularly when tasks at the lower tiers of the hierarchy are variable and complex. For these reasons, centralization of decisionmaking can lead to efficiency losses, which may motivate some delegation of authority to lower echelons. Second, making decisions about the execution of complex tasks often requires cooperation among individuals with different and complementary skills, or with complementary judgments. This suggests that complexity calls for consultation among employees. (In contrast, when problems are routine and predictable, tasks can be preprogrammed and formalized in ways that reduce the information load on upper echelons and reduce the need for delegation. And to the extent that delegation is necessary, it can be

---

5. Clearly any typology of this kind has some arbitrary features and important areas of overlap: for instance, incentive issues arise in large part because information is unevenly distributed, and asset specificity tends to matter because asymmetric information facilitates opportunistic behavior with respect to quasi-rent distribution. But it does seem meaningful to distinguish between problems of coordinating the flow of work, eliciting effort, and avoiding opportunistic rent-seeking.

6. Perrow (1986).

7. Marschak and Radner (1972).

confined to individual employees rather than to groups such as teams.) These considerations suggest that employee participation in decision-making will increase with greater complexity of tasks, but that such complexity will not have a direct effect on the use of profit-sharing or employee ownership plans.[8]

Interdependence among tasks has two possible effects. First, it makes metering of individual input and output difficult and therefore coordination and mutual monitoring among employees has to replace at least partially direction, supervision, and monitoring from above.[9] Second, it requires rewarding financially the group of employees whose tasks are interdependent because it is difficult to reward individuals (we return to this point in the context of incentives). Thus, we predict that greater task interdependence will be associated with greater likelihood to adopt plans that entail sharing of financial returns with employees, as well as employee involvement in decisionmaking.

Firm or establishment size can have two opposite effects on organization structures. First, larger organizations may be associated with structural differentiation, where differentiation increases the heterogeneity of work among various subunits and individuals. Employee participation programs may be a useful coordinating device in large firms for this reason. Large organizations, however, also tend to have a more elaborate hierarchy, with more formal rules and routines, and their owners and managers may therefore view additional channels of worker participation as unnecessary, inconvenient, or distracting. Such bureaucratic firms may see employee participation as an alternative to conventional administrative procedures rather than a supplement to them, suggesting that smaller size may be more conducive to worker involvement.

Work Incentives

In an influential article, Armen Alchian and Harold Demsetz asserted that team production leads to monitoring problems because it is hard to gauge the contribution of an individual team member.[10] If simple profit sharing

---

8. We empahsize the absence of a *direct* effect. An indirect effect may exist because of the desire to complement decisionmaking plans with financial returns plans (see Ben-Ner and Jones (1995) for a detailed discussion of this issue).

9. Appelbaum and Batt (1994).

10. Alchian and Demsetz (1972).

were used, each team member would be tempted to shirk, because each would bear the full cost of his or her own effort, while receiving only a per capita share of the resulting benefits. This free rider problem becomes more severe in larger production teams. Alchian and Demsetz argue that the solution is to appoint a specialist to monitor other team members. The monitor will be the sole residual claimant in order to avoid shirking in the monitoring activity itself, will have decisionmaking authority because monitoring yields information that can be used for other managerial purposes, and will own the physical assets of the firm in order to curb possible misuse of equipment.

Many criticisms have been aimed at this theory, and we will not rehearse them all here.[11] Since our focus is empirical, it suffices to identify the predictive content of the story. First, the theory implies that more interdependence of tasks (other things equal) is likely to motivate intensified central monitoring rather than profit sharing or other group financial incentives, because residual claims must go to the monitor rather than frontline production workers when team production is important. Second, the size of the firm or establishment should be negatively related to profit sharing or employee ownership owing to the increased free rider problem in larger teams. Third, interdependence and establishment size should be associated with less worker participation in decisionmaking because they lead to greater reliance on centralized monitoring, which yields information that can be used to solve coordination problems. Fourth, increased reliance on physical assets that are easily abused, or where abuse is hard to detect, should lead to less employee participation in profit, ownership, and management because it is more important to have a central monitor who supervises asset use in such situations.

A line of argument with very different predictive content runs as follows. Suppose that there is a high level of task complexity and perhaps interdependence among workers. This sort of situation is likely to impede direct central monitoring by weakening managers' knowledge of cause-and-effect relations between worker actions and outcomes.[12] Rather than appointing a central monitor, a better response may be to use group financial incentives, including profit sharing and employee ownership, to motivate effort.[13] This encourages cooperation among employees and perhaps the evolution of group norms favoring increased productivity. Apart from

11. For example, Putterman (1984).
12. Eisenhardt (1985,1988); Snell (1992).
13. FitzRoy and Kraft (1995).

effort incentives in themselves, such group incentives may help to elicit private information from shop floor employees that is valuable for managerial purposes. Group incentives may therefore be associated with programs of employee consultation when production processes are complex and tasks are highly interdependent. Financial incentives are expected to be more effective in smaller firms since the return to the worker's effort and to her encouragement or monitoring of fellow workers' efforts is diluted over a smaller number of participants.

A final argument about work incentives and firm organization is more in the spirit of modern principal-agent theory. The premise is that output depends stochastically on the effort of one or more workers, where workers are risk averse and the owner is risk neutral, perhaps because of the owner's ability to diversify investments across many firms.[14] The theory predicts that more intrinsically risky production activities will be associated with less use of profit sharing or employee ownership, since such activities would otherwise require workers to bear more risk. A reduction of employee involvement in decisionmaking follows indirectly, in this case, if the separation of the workers from risk bearing is viewed as removing their incentive to deploy organizational resources in such a way that total returns are maximized.

Finance and Investment

A third group of theories develops the implications of limited worker wealth and risk aversion for financing firms. The starting point is an argument that firms can rarely obtain the services of all required assets through leasing. Some assets must be owned by the firm itself, perhaps because they are subject to misuse because they are firm specific and yield quasi rents that provoke costly bargaining; or simply because they are intangible in nature, such as technological know-how and reputation. Such assets must somehow be financed in advance of production.[15] It is not usually feasible

14. See Sappington (1991) and Holmstrom and Milgrom (1991); elements of the theory can be traced to Frank Knight (1964 [1927]). In the Knight version, entrepreneur-owners sell insurance to workers through the employment contract, in exchange for which workers, whose incentives are now weakened by moral hazard, agree to hand control to the entrepreneur. In the principal-agent approach a trade-off takes place between incentives and insurance, because greater insurance for workers reduces effort while high-powered incentives expose workers to more income variability.

15. Alchian and Demsetz (1972); Klein, Crawford, and Alchian (1978); Williamson (1985); Hart (1995); Jensen and Meckling (1979).

to finance a firm entirely by debt due to the presence of adverse selection and moral hazard problems in the credit market.

According to this view, workers are unlikely to own and control firms unless they can put up some of their own money. But this is difficult if workers have limited wealth, especially since it is hard to borrow against future labor income.[16] Moreover, if workers are risk averse they will be reluctant to hold undiversified financial portfolios, as large personal investments in a single firm would require. This problem may be even more serious when workers have firm-specific human capital, because then their financial and human assets are tied up in the same firm.

What are the predictions emanating from this theoretical perspective? First, worker wealth in relation to the per-worker equity-financing requirements of the firm should matter. Other things being equal, workers who are poorer should invest less financial wealth in their firms, either because current consumption is very important relative to future consumption, or because they are more risk averse. Second, holding worker wealth and risk aversion constant, firms with higher capital-labor ratios should have larger per-worker financing requirements and thus a lower percentage of total equity financing coming from employees. Third, these financing constraints should be relaxed when physical assets are less specific to the firm, because generic assets have more value as collateral, thus making debt finance easier and increasing the ability of workers to participate in financing the firm's remaining equity.[17] Finally, if firm-specific human capital aggravates the problem of nondiversification, we might see reduced financial investment by workers when such human capital is substantial— although protection of their quasi rents provides a countervailing reason why workers might want ownership and control in such situations.

Asset Specificity

We alluded above to the role of asset specificity in connection with financing, but the degree of specialization in physical and human assets is often claimed to have broader implications. For instance, job incumbents often have more skill and knowledge than new recruits, so the departure of these employees would impose significant search and training costs on the firm.[18]

16. Hart and Moore (1994).
17. Williamson (1988).
18. Williamson (1985).

This can lead the firm to offer stock ownership and deferred profit sharing, which tie current actions to future benefits and thus provide an incentive to workers to protect their investments by acting on behalf of the firm's long-term interests. As greater skills and knowledge are highly correlated with task complexity,[19] those workers who are likely targets for inclusion in stock ownership and profit-sharing plans will also be targets for participation in decisionmaking in their firms (according to the argument presented under "Information and Coordination"). Workers may also seek increased control to protect their firm-specific skill investments. Furthermore, employee ownership and profit sharing may be useful tools in getting specifically skilled employees to share information or to refrain from opportunistic seizures of quasi rent. As noted earlier, however, such policies can have disadvantages if workers are risk averse and have difficulty diversifying their assets.

Physical asset specificity may also matter independently of its financial implications. This, it will be recalled, may make debt financing more difficult, thus making worker ownership less likely for reasons of risk aversion or limited liquidity. Highly specialized physical equipment, however, is likely to be associated with complex, uncertain, and idiosyncratic production processes, so that shop floor workers must be encouraged to maintain valuable machinery, share information willingly, refrain from strategic behavior aimed at appropriating quasi rents, and so on. In general we would expect incentive alignment problems of this sort to arise whenever physical assets are highly specialized, even if employees themselves do not appear to have highly firm-specific human capital.

Institutional Factors

Apart from the causal mechanisms discussed above, a number of factors connected with the structure of firms may have some bearing on employee involvement in decisionmaking or financial participation. In this chapter we do not develop hypotheses about the relationship between such factors (unionization and the form of ownership) and employee involvement in decisionmaking and financial returns. For our empirical work, therefore, we treat these institutional factors as exogenous and control for them.

Table 6-1 summarizes the potentially testable implications of this section's discussion. The lefthand column lists the five sets of issues considered

19. In our sample, the correlation between worker skills and task complexity is 0.70.

Table 6-1. *Issue Areas and Predictions for Three Dimensions
of Employee Participation*

Issues	ESOPs	Profit-sharing	Employee involvement
Information and coordination			
Complexity	?	?	+
Interdependence	+	+	+
Establishment size	?	–?	+/–?
Work incentives			
(a) Alchian/Demsetz framework			
Interdependence	–?	–?	–
Establishment size	–	–	–
Physical asset specificity	–?	–?	–?
(b) Mutual monitoring framework			
Complexity	+	+	+
Interdependence	+	+	+
Establishment size	–	–	–
(c) Principal-agent framework			
Riskiness of firm net income	–	–	–?
Finance and investment			
Average wage	+	+	?
Average tenure	+	+	?
Riskiness of firm net income	–	–	?
Capital/labor ratio	–	–?	?
Physical asset specificity	–	–?	?
Human capital specificity	+/–?	–	+/–?
Transaction costs			
Physical asset specificity	+/–?	+/–?	+/–?
Human capital specificity	+	+	+
Institutional factors			
Publicly/privately held	No a priori theoretical expectations		
Unionization	(exogenous variable to be controlled)		

above and the key variables relevant to each issue.[20] In the remaining three columns, we summarize the predicted effect of each variable upon the incidence of worker participation in ownership, profit sharing, and decisionmaking. For example, the plus (+) sign under complexity in the employee involvement column reflects our expectation that the more complex the work process, the more likely it is that employees will play a role in its management. The minus (–) sign under riskiness of firm net income in the ESOPs column follows from our expectation that risk-averse employees will more likely eschew worker ownership the more variable the firm's earnings stream. In some cases, for instance the effect of establishment size on employee involvement, different lines of theoretical reasoning suggest different effects, and we list both signs with a question mark (?). Where theory loosely suggests a particular effect, but does not necessitate it in a tighter or more logical fashion, we list only the one relevant sign with a question mark. A last possibility, illustrated by the impact of complexity on worker ownership, is that no specific hypothesis has been advanced; in such cases, a question mark alone appears.

Of course, this way of summarizing matters collapses complex considerations, already much abbreviated in our discussion, into overly simplified categories. Since it is impossible to review each hypothesis again here, simply return to the discussion above for guidance on the individual categories. In one issue area, work incentives, we are able to identify distinct frameworks with different implications for some of the variables. Table 6-1 breaks these out for ease of identification.

The remainder of this chapter is devoted to examining the empirical validity of these theoretical predictions. We first describe the data and discuss their limitations in the next section; clearly, the variables we use to proxy certain concepts are often far from ideal. In the following section we discuss the empirical strategy, which is not formal testing of hypotheses, but an exploratory attempt to bring empirical data to bear on theoretical questions. Our findings are tentative because it is often difficult to draw sharp distinctions between alternative causal mechanisms in our empirical analysis, given the limited array of variables that are available to us.

---

20. We hope the variable names are in most cases transparent from our earlier discussion. We include average wage and average tenure on the assumption that these variables, available in the data to be described, are correlates of worker wealth, about which some hypotheses were advanced.

Description of the Data

Four main data sources are used in our analysis: the Compustat database of publicly held companies, the Minnesota Department of Economic Security database on employment and wages in Minnesota firms, the Internal Revenue Service/U.S. Department of Labor database on tax-qualified deferred compensation as reported on form 5500, and the Minnesota Human Resources Management Practices Survey. Each of these has provided several key variables in the analysis. We have also taken a measure of capital specificity from the 1992 U.S. Census of Manufacturers.

THE MINNESOTA HUMAN RESOURCES MANAGEMENT PRACTICES SUR-VEY (MHRMPS).[21] Our sample consists of 656 private for-profit firms with at least twenty employees in diverse industries outside agriculture, head-quartered and operating in the state of Minnesota. The choice of a single state, and Minnesota in particular, offers several important advantages. First, the work force in these firms is likely to be more homogeneous than in firms operating in many states. Second, all firms are subject to the same state laws and regulations. Third, crucial firm-level data that are not in the public domain are available from the State of Minnesota agencies.

The survey was administered in two rounds (because of funding considerations), the first in mid-1994 to early 1995 to 587 firms, and the second in early 1996 to 1,434 firms.[22] The overall response rate for the survey was about 43 percent, which compares favorably with previous work of similar sample size. Of 874 respondents, 68 were dropped either because they were duplicates (7); because they do not operate principally in Minnesota (11); or because there were fewer than twenty employees at the time of the survey (50). A further 150 firms do not appear in this chapter's analysis because data for one or more of the variables used are missing.[23]

21. The survey instrument was developed as part of the project directed by Ben-Ner at the Industrial Relations Center at the University of Minnesota, "The Organization of Work: Determinants and Consequences." For a detailed description of the data, see Ben-Ner (1997).

22. The data that we analyze pertain to the same years, regardless of which year they were collected in. In the case of the participation measures, for which the surveys asked about current situation, we must assume that responses in early 1996 are a reasonable proxy for the information that would have been given a year earlier.

23. Comparison of the descriptive statistics of the 804 firm sample left before the last-mentioned cut and those of the smaller sample of 656 firms for which our analysis can be carried out suggests that the latter firms do not differ in noticeable ways from the larger universe from which they are drawn.

Most of the responding firms had been in operation for more than fifteen years.[24]

SURVEY VARIABLES IN THE ANALYSIS. Several variables in our analysis come directly from the survey, including the average tenure of workers in the firm (TEN), the unionization status of the firm (UNION), and whether the firm is publicly or privately held (STATUS). Also directly from the survey are the respondents' estimates of the level of task complexity, task interdependence, and skill transferability in the work of the core workers of the firm (CMPLX1, DEPND1, and TRNSFR1, respectively). These last three variables are clearly influenced by the technology and capital available, the management style, and, of course, the respondents' view of their firm relative to others. The variables are measured on a 1–5 Likert scale, where 1 equals not at all and 5 equals extreme.

The measures of employee involvement in decisionmaking are aggregated from a set of related questions on the survey. Respondents were asked to estimate the extent to which nonmanagerial employees participate in decisionmaking on fifteen different issues in the firm (table 6-2).[25] Again a 1–5 Likert scale was used, where 1 equals not at all and 5 equals extreme. The variable EIBROD is the average of these fifteen responses for each survey and so covers a wide range of potential areas of participation as listed below. A potential disadvantage of this variable is that it gives the same weight to participation in social-event decisions as it does to participation in investment policy decisions, for example. From EIBROD, we created a dichotomous variable, EICDBROD, which is 0 when EIBROD < 3 and 1 when EIBROD ≥ 3. This cut-off value is approximately one standard deviation greater than the mean of EIBROD and is intended to capture "high" employee involvement. In one part of our analysis, we analyze the effects of EIBROD in firms with "high" EI only; to display the distribution of EIBROD for this subsample in table 6-4, we denote it by the name EIBRODHI. To check whether results obtained using the broad participation measure EIBROD might be unduly or inappropriately influenced by that measure's inclusion of less strategically important types of decision

24. The respondents were primarily human resources managers; in smaller companies, respondents were commonly top executives.
25. The wording of the question, "To what extent do employees participate in the following issues?" does not specify particular channels of participation, hence not ruling out participation through traditional channels like collective bargaining.

Table 6-2. *Areas of Employee Involvement Contributing to EIBROD and EINARR*

Issue	Included in EINARR	Included in EIBROD
Work rules		yes
Working conditions	yes	yes
Pay and other compensation	yes	yes
Selection of personnel	yes	yes
Training and development		yes
Social events		yes
Job redesign		yes
Safety and health		yes
Equipment maintenance	yes	yes
Selection of materials		yes
Selection of new equipment	yes	yes
Investment policies	yes	yes
Production planning		yes
Profit allocation	yes	yes
Corporate finance		yes

participation, we also created EINARR, an average of the scores given on only selected items intended to indicate involvement in decisions with considerable operational significance to the firm.

MINNESOTA DEPARTMENT OF ECONOMIC SECURITY (DES) EMPLOYMENT AND WAGE DATA. Data on wages and salaries and employment for firms in the sample were acquired from the Minnesota Department of Economic Security (DES), which collects them for unemployment insurance purposes. These data cover the period 1980–94; employment is a monthly observation, wages and salaries a quarterly observation. The data were integrated with the survey and other data using the federal employer identification number and company name, address, and SIC code. The data are available at the establishment level and have been aggregated by us to firm level, and in order to obtain the size variable, to annual data.[26]

26. Almost three-quarters of the firms in the sample have only one establishment. Of the remainder, 15 percent have two or three establishments, 4 percent have four or five establishments, and 8 percent have six or more establishments.

Variables derived from the DES include the log of average wage per employee (LFAW), the log of the average establishment size of the firm (LESZ), and measures of employment increase and decrease. FEUP is the sum of month-to-month percentage increases in employment at the firm level over a thirty-six-month period during 1992 through 1994, while FEDN is the sum of percentage decreases over the same period.[27] The two variables are intended to capture the extent of past employment volatility, which may affect the workers' perception of employment risk. Although most observations of FEUP and FEDN are less than 2, that is, the sum of month-to-month percentage changes was less than 200 percent, the extreme value for each was over 1100 percent.

COMPUSTAT DATA. Compustat is a commercially available set of financial and other data for publicly held firms. Most of the data originate in required SEC filings of quarterly and annual reports. Data from Compustat were used to calculate annual financial variables at the industry level used in our analysis: the log of the capital-labor ratio (LKL), and the log of the standard deviation of net income (LSTDEVNI). The capital-labor ratio is based on the 1994 values of Compustat's total assets and total firm employment variables. The standard deviation of net income uses that variable for five years, 1990–94. Provided that the recession of 1990–91 gave a representative indication of exposure to cyclical variability of earnings, this should give a good sense of industry-level sensitivity to the business cycle.

There remains, however, the question of matching industry-level data with firms at a sufficiently narrow level. We used total U.S. data and obtained reliable estimates at the three-digit SIC code level. This of course is a compromise—while we would prefer to have data on the K/L ratio and earnings variability at the firm level, most of the firms in our sample are private and do not report standard financial data. Cutting back the observations to include only public firms would eliminate most observations from the data set; leaving out these variables would preclude us from investigating the effects of financing requirements and industry-level risk on employee participation.

---

27. A month of decreasing (increasing) employment is treated as a zero increase (decrease) when calculating FEUP (FEDN).

FORM 5500 DATA. Detailed information on financial-returns participation in tax-qualified deferred compensation plans has been extracted from the Internal Revenue Service-U.S. Department of Labor form 5500 series data files. These data include the number of active participants for each plan and the total plan asset value along with other financial data and descriptions of the type of plan. Information about employee stock ownership plans and deferred profit sharing, as well as various pension plans, is included.

Employers are required to report on these plans under the Employee Retirement Income Security Act of 1974, by filing a form 5500. Each plan is reported separately. Those with one hundred and more employees use a form 5500-F and report annually. We used the 1994 F forms. Those plans with fewer than one hundred use a form 5500-C to report in detail at least once every three years, and form 5500-R to report an annual summary when not filing the C form. The R form did not provide the data items we required. Accordingly, we checked the C forms for 1992, 1993, and 1994 and chose the most recent report for each plan.

Plan data were aggregated to the firm level by type of plan. No adjustment was made when dollar amounts from different years were added together—a producer's price index adjustment could be applied to manufacturing firms but would not apply to service and retail firms.

To use these data with survey data, it was necessary to match the records using firms' names and federal employer identification numbers. Reported plans were summarized by firm to be compatible with the firm-level survey data. The data were integrated with the survey and other data using the state employer identification number and company name, address, and SIC code.

The variables describing the ratio of covered employees to total employees of the firm, ESOPCOV and PSPCOV, are derived from form 5500 data after aggregating plans to the firm level. We used the total employment data from form 5500 in these ratios since non-Minnesota employees were also in the count of covered employees. We created dichotomous variables ESOPPART and PSPART from ESOPCOV and PSPCOV to indicate the presence of financial participation; that is, when ESOPCOV > 0, ESOPPART = 1, otherwise, ESOPPART = 0, with similar treatment for PSCOV and PSPART.

CENSUS OF MANUFACTURERS. Data on asset specificity were derived from the U.S. Census of Manufacturers, 1992, Industry series (produced by the Department of Commerce, Bureau of the Census). The ratio of used capital equipment purchased for the year to the total capital equipment purchased for the year gives an indication of how much capital each industry is able to purchase in the secondary market. By extension, this should also reflect the ability of a firm to sell capital equipment on the secondary market when exiting an industry.[28] We use this measure, denoted TOTUT, as an indicator of the degree of specificity of assets, in our analysis, since idiosyncratic capital goods should be more difficult to trade or should trade at lower value. Note that larger values of TOTUT imply *lower* levels of asset specificity.

Effects of Missing Data on Effective Sample Size

Since we have used four distinct data sources in our analysis, and since the number of observations for which some values are missing increases with the number of variables, especially when more than one data set is relied upon, our original sample size is sometimes reduced dramatically when the full array of variables is required. Often, however, our analysis is based on more than 500 observations since we do not need all variables in each part of the analysis.

The data item TOTUT is a substantial source of missing data, since it is mainly available for manufacturing firms, and when it is used, the number of usable observations is reduced from 656 to 183. Results for estimates that exclude TOTUT may differ from those that include that variable both because of the larger sample size, as a general consideration, and because some effects may differ between manufacturing and nonmanufacturing firms. The next largest source of missing data is the DES data set, since we were unable to match every survey record to a DES record (we matched about 86 percent). From the survey, respondents were least likely to fill in tenure information, leaving this item blank about 12 percent of the time.

Descriptive Statistics

We conclude this section with table 6-3, which summarizes the variables used in our analysis, and table 6-4, which provides descriptive statistics for the data set. We comment briefly on some of the descriptive statistics. The

28. The measure is calculated in a manner similar to Kessides (1990a, 1990b).

Table 6-3. *Variable Descriptions*

LESZ	Log of establishment size; based on average of establishment employment across all establishments in the firm; from Minnesota Department of Economic Security (DES) dataset.
LFAW	Log of firm average wage; based on annual sum of wages paid in all establishments of the firm and average total firm employment; from DES dataset.
FEUP1994	Firm employment increases; based on the sum of monthly percentage increases in total firm employment for 36 months ending in Dec, 1994; from DES dataset.
FEDN1994	Firm employment decreases; based on the sum of monthly percentage decreases in total firm employment for 36 months ending in Dec, 1994; from DES dataset.
TEN	Average employee tenure; from survey.
UNION	Firm's unionization status; 0 = non-union, 1 = union; from survey.
STATUS	Firm's ownership status; 0 = privately held, 1 = publicly held; from survey.
CMPLX1	Complexity of core employees' work tasks; 1–5 scale, 1 = Not at all, 5 = Extreme; from survey.
DEPND1	Interdependence of core employees' work tasks; 1–5 scale, 1 = Not at all, 5 = Extreme; from survey.
TRNSFR1	Transferability of core employees' skills; 1–5 scale, 1 = Not at all, 5 = Extreme; from survey.
EIBROD	Employee involvement, broadly measured; based on average level of involvement in 15 areas of decisionmaking; from the survey.
EICDBROD	Dichotomous employee involvement measure, set to 1 when EIBROD $\geq$ 3, 0 when EIBROD < 3.
EINARR	Employee involvement, narrowly measured; based on average level of involvement in 7 areas of decisionmaking focusing on major operations; from the survey.
PSPCOV	Ratio of employees participating in profit-sharing plans to total employment in the firm; from Form 5500.
PSPART	Indicator set to 1 when PSPCOV > 0, otherwise 0.
ESOPCOV	Ratio of employees participating in ESOPs to total employment in the firm; from Form 5500.
ESOPPART	Indicator set to 1 when ESPCOV > 0, otherwise 0.
INDMAN	All manufacturing, construction, mining, transportation, and public utility firms (per Standard Industrial Classification Code).
INDSER	Finance, insurance, real estate, and service firms.
INDCOM	Wholesale and retail trade firms (omitted category).

Variables with values imputed to firms from industry-level data

LKL	Log of capital-labor ratio (in $1000's per worker); from Compustat dataset.
LSTDEVNI	Log of standard deviation of net income; based on 5 years of net income, 1990–1994; from Compustat dataset.
TOTUT	Ratio of used capital equipment to total capital equipment (dollar value basis); from Census of Manufacturers, 1992.

Table 6-4. *Descriptive Statistics*

Variable	N	Mean	Standard deviation
PSPCOV	342	0.648	0.258
PSPART	656	0.521	0.500
ESOPCOV	69	0.723	0.228
ESOPPART	656	0.105	0.307
EIBROD	656	2.468	0.589
EIBRODHI	134	3.294	0.309
EICDBROD	656	0.204	0.403
EINARR	656	2.330	0.618
INDMAN	656	0.381	0.486
INDCOM	656	0.428	0.495
INDSER	656	0.191	0.393
LESZ	541	4.061	1.131
LFAW	541	10.195	0.593
FEUP1994	560	0.970	1.004
FEDN1994	560	0.794	0.931
TEN	656	6.546	4.398
UNION	656	0.163	0.370
STATUS	656	0.230	0.421
CMPLX1	656	2.951	1.008
DEPND1	656	3.629	0.908
TRNSFR1	656	3.598	1.030
LKL	580	4.637	1.146
LSTDEVNI	571	5.006	1.857
TOTUT	203	0.084	0.034

industry distribution of our firms is fairly representative of the economy-wide distribution: 38.1 percent are in manufacturing (dummy variable INDMAN = 1), 42.8 percent in commerce (INDCOM = 1), and 19.1 percent in (other) services (INDSER = 1).[29] Most of the firms are private, with only 23 percent being publicly traded. And most firms have no employees represented by unions: only 16 percent of firms in our sample are unionized

29. Table 6-3 shows what industries are included in each broad sector. A breakdown of the firms by industries shows that 1 is in mining (Standard Industrial Classification codes 10–14), 30 in construction (SIC 15–17), 218 in manufacturing (SIC 20–39), 17 in transportation (SIC 40–49), 74 in wholesale trade (SIC 50–51), 189 in retail trade (SIC 52–59), 45 in finance (SIC 60–67), and 80 in services (SIC 70–89).

to some degree. The sample firms are relatively small, owing to the exclusion from the sample of firms with considerable employment outside Minnesota (including large manufacturing and retail firms based in the state), with an average employment of 116 and maximum employment of just under 3,000 (table 6-4 presents only the log values). Average employee tenure is under seven years. On average, the manufacturing firms (for which we have information) purchased about 8 percent of their capital equipment in 1992 from previous users.

Our sample firms have profit sharing and ESOPs in proportions that correspond to figures reported in other studies. Eleven percent of the firms have an ESOP, and the average firm with an ESOP includes 72 percent of the employees in the plan. Many more firms have deferred profit-sharing plans: 52 percent of our sample do so, covering on average 65 percent of employees. Our sample firms tend to involve their employees in decisionmaking to some degree, but not very heavily: on a scale from 1 to 5, the average employee involvement index is 2.5. Nevertheless, 20 percent of the firms meet our criterion for high employee involvement. There is also some overlap among the categories, which is not displayed in the table: 6.9 percent of all firms (or about seven of ten ESOP firms) have both profit-sharing plans and an ESOP; 1.5 percent of firms (15 percent of the ESOP firms) have both an ESOP and high employee involvement.[30] About a quarter of the firms with profit sharing (12.8 percent), have both profit sharing and high employee involvement; 0.5 percent of the firms have high employee involvement and both forms of financial participation.

Method of Analysis

To shed empirical light on the theoretical conjectures laid out early in this chapter, we take a two-step approach. In the first step, we look at the determinants of the probability of a firm being among the firms with a given form of participation; in the second step, we look at the determinants of the extent or depth of participation by the work forces of firms that adopt the form of participation in question. This follows the practice introduced in health economics when studying the demand for medical insurance, where a distinction is made between those with no medical expenses and

---

30. The number changes little if the narrower employee involvement measure is used.

those with some expenses, with an analysis of those in the some expenses category.[31] ESOPPART, PSPART, and EICDBROD are the dependent variables of the first step in our process, a probability model intended to separate firms with participation from those without. The counterparts to these dichotomous variables, ESOPCOV, PSCOV, and EIBROD, are the dependent variables in the second step of our process, an OLS model of the extent of participation which is estimated only for the subset of firms that engage in participative practices. Our financial-returns participation variables (ESOPCOV and PSCOV), derived from form 5500, are defined simply as the proportion of employees covered by the ESOP or profit-sharing plan.

The dichotomous dependent variables used in the first step of the analysis for each dimension are analyzed using logit models.[32] For the second step, in which the dependent variables are continuous measures of the proportion of employees participating in the employee involvement or return-sharing plan, we use ordinary least squares (OLS) regressions.[33] In both cases, we face a trade-off between limiting the number of variables included, which permits more observations to be used, and estimating more inclusive models, which may avoid the omitted-variables biases that are an especially serious problem in probability models such as the logit. As a compromise, we present for both the first and second steps three estimates for each dimension of participation, with differing degrees of completeness of the list of explanatory variables and, correspondingly, different sample sizes. When all explanatory variables are included, only 183 firms provide sufficient data for the first-step analysis.[34] Elimination of LKL, LSTDEVNI, and TOTUT permits the sample to expand dramatically to 541 firms. Finally, further elimination of four variables relating to wages and employment—FEUP, FEDN, LESZ, and LFAW—expands the sample to 656 firms. In the second step OLS estimates in which the dependent

31. See Duan and others (1983).

32. The alternatives would be to use probit or linear probability models and their extensions. See Maddala (1983). For this work we have chosen relatively simple logit models because they give rise to easily interpretable marginal relationships between the independent and dependent variables and, when the coefficients are estimated with maximum likelihood procedures, have desirable statistical properties.

33. We use the SAS procedure CATMOD (version 6) to estimate our logit models and chose the maximum likelihood method for estimating the coefficients. Maximum likelihood parameter estimates are consistent and asymptotically efficient. We use the SAS procedure REG (version 6) to estimate our OLS models.

34. In this case, only one industry dummy can be included because there are no observations in the commerce group.

variable is the proportion of workers participating, only the firms with plans are included. Consequently, sample sizes for the OLS runs are always smaller than those for the logit analyses.

One of the chief pitfalls of this analysis, already noted, is that some of the independent variables we use may be jointly decided with the dependent variables. We expect that the reader will bear this mind, as we do, throughout the interpretation of our results.

Results

In this section we report the results; comments are reserved for the next section. Consider first the twin questions of which firms have an ESOP, and which firms with ESOPs have a larger proportion of their work force enrolled in ESOPs. Table 6-5 presents logit estimates of the determinants of the probability of adopting an ESOP, with sample size increasing and number of explanatory variables declining as one moves from left to right across three specifications. A number of explanatory variables have significant coefficient estimates. While no variable has a significant estimate across all three specifications, several coefficients are significant in two specifications and, where present, consistent in sign in the third. Thus, task interdependence is a highly significant positive predictor of ESOP adoption according to versions 2 and 3 and has the same sign in the smaller sample of version 1 shown in table 6-5. Average employee tenure is positively related to ESOP adoption in all three versions, significant in versions 2 and 3. Skill transferability shows a negative relation to ESOP adoption, significant but at somewhat lower levels in versions 2 and 3. The estimate on the complexity variable is insignificant (and is quantitatively small in comparison with other task attributes). Establishment size is significantly negatively related to ESOP adoption in the two versions, 1 and 2, in which it is entered. Firm average wage is significantly positively related to adoption according to version 2, although it has an insignificant negative coefficient in version 1. The broad industry dummies have significant coefficients in version 3, and FEUP is negatively related to ESOP adoption at the 10 percent level in version 1.[35]

---

35. Note that only one industry dummy appears in version 1 specifications because there are no observations from the third broad industry group complete for the full set of explanatory variables.

Table 6-5. *Logit Esimates of the Probability of Having an ESOP*

Variable	Version 1	Version 2	Version 3
INTERCEPT	7.135 (9.118)	−11.654 (3.663)	−3.891 (0.837)
TEN	0.090 (0.074)	0.085** (0.034)	0.108*** (0.028)
UNION	−0.612 (0.783)	−0.236 (0.411)	−0.499 (0.390)
STATUS	−0.133 (0.580)	−0.452 (0.364)	−0.406 (0.345)
CMPLX1	0.048 (0.292)	0.101 (0.158)	0.153 (0.143)
DEPND1	0.364 (0.323)	0.524*** (0.180)	0.451*** (0.166)
TRNSFR1	−0.204 (0.274)	−0.336** (0.143)	−0.218* (0.127)
INDMAN	0.840 (0.638)	0.144 (0.182)	0.291* (0.165)
INDSER		0.162 (0.207)	0.413** (0.184)
FEUP1994	−1.643* (0.948)	−0.400 (0.398)	
FEDN1994	−1.576 (1.049)	−0.436 (0.435)	
LESZ	−0.701** (0.288)	−0.309** (0.142)	
LFAW	−0.919 (0.818)	0.972*** (0.343)	
LKL	0.792 (0.475)		
LSTDEVNI	−0.235 (0.169)		
TOTUT	3.842 (7.243)		
Observations	183	541	656
Log-likelihood	123.58	346.20	379.01

Numbers in parentheses are standard errors.
* Significant at .10.
** Significant at .05.
*** Significant at .01.

Table 6-6 reports the OLS results for the proportion of employees participating in the ESOP in the sample firms having an ESOP. The three OLS regressions mirror the variable lists of their counterparts in table 6-5, but sample size is smaller due to inclusion of ESOP firms only, and the dependent variable is now a continuous one, the share of employees covered. Perhaps partly due to sample sizes, there are fewer significant results in this case. Among the statistically significant coefficients are three for institutional factors: estimates 2 and 3 suggest that unionized ESOP firms have a smaller fraction of employees covered, and all estimates suggest that this is also true of publicly traded ESOP firms, though only the version 1 result is statistically significant. A positive effect of employee tenure, paralleling that in the logit regressions, is significant in version 3 only. The sign on the idiosyncratic assets (TOTUT) variable is negative: the more generic (the less idiosyncratic) the assets, the lower is ESOP coverage. Higher average wages (LFAW) appear strongly positively correlated with ESOP coverage, though only in version 2, with the same sign but failing to reach statistical significance in the small sample version 1 estimate.

Table 6-7 shows alternative logit regressions on the probability of existence of a profit-sharing plan. Only a few coefficient estimates are significant in more than one specification. Public status is negatively associated with having a profit-sharing plan in versions 1 and 2, while average wages are positively associated with having such a plan in the same versions. Except in version 1, employee tenure seems positively associated with profit-sharing plans as is the case with ESOPs, and the association is significant in the largest sample estimate, version 3. Version 2, with intermediate sample size and explanatory variable list, has the most significant coefficients on nondummy explanatory variables, with establishment size (positive), status (negative), and wages (positive) each having coefficients significant at the 5 percent level or better. In version 3, the two broad industry dummies explain a good deal of the variance, although two additional variables, task interdependence and skill transferability, attain significance at modest levels. The negative sign on interdependence and the positive sign on transferability, although not the statistical significance, are consistent across all versions. The small and insignificant estimate on complexity is similar to the result in the ESOP regressions.

Table 6-8 shows corresponding OLS estimates of the proportion of workers covered by profit sharing in those firms having profit-sharing plans. The number of firms with profit-sharing plans is much larger than the number of firms with ESOPs, so that the decline in sample size is

Table 6-6. *OLS Estimates of the Level of ESOP Coverage*
Only firms with ESOPs included

Variable	Version 1	Version 2	Version 3
INTERCEPT	−0.990	−1.764	0.486
	(2.253)	(0.842)	(0.202)
TEN	−0.012	0.006	0.013*
	(0.021)	(0.007)	(0.008)
UNION	0.158	−0.190**	−0.254***
	(0.165)	(0.076)	(0.080)
STATUS	−0.465**	−0.075	−0.004
	(0.163)	(0.070)	(0.074)
CMPLX1	0.107	0.020	0.028
	(0.085)	(0.030)	(0.030)
DEPND1	−0.114	−0.006	−0.014
	(0.066)	(0.037)	(0.039)
TRNSFR1	0.057	0.023	0.027
	(0.061)	(0.026)	(0.028)
INDMAN	0.145	0.056	0.025
	(0.254)	(0.065)	(0.066)
INDSER		0.060	0.073
		(0.072)	(0.077)
FEUP1994	−0.244	−0.142	
	(0.245)	(0.112)	
FEDN1994	0.636**	−0.006	
	(0.254)	(0.118)	
LESZ	0.042	−0.008	
	(0.047)	(0.029)	
LFAW	0.200	0.232***	
	(0.225)	(0.082)	
LKL	−0.104		
	(0.093)		
LSTDEVNI	0.033		
	(0.040)		
TOTUT	−3.768*		
	(1.936)		
Observations	25	67	68
Adjusted R^2	0.300	0.284	0.103

Numbers in parentheses are standard errors.
* Significant at .10.
** Significant at .05.
*** Significant at .01.

Table 6-7. *Logit Estimates of the Probability of a Profit-Sharing Plan*

Variable	Version 1	Version 2	Version 3
INTERCEPT	−12.153 (6.555)	−10.280 (2.150)	−0.085 (0.495)
TEN	−0.036 (0.057)	0.020 (0.026)	0.057*** (0.021)
UNION	0.116 (0.532)	0.019 (0.285)	0.168 (0.241)
STATUS	−0.824* (0.423)	−0.499** (0.248)	−0.185 (0.208)
CMPLX1	0.062 (0.204)	0.006 (0.105)	0.109 (0.087)
DEPND1	−0.173 (0.219)	−0.162 (0.107)	−0.193** (0.093)
TRNSFR1	0.057 (0.197)	0.112 (0.097)	0.146* (0.082)
INDMAN	0.289 (0.364)	0.192 (0.124)	0.564*** (0.100)
INDSER		0.004 (0.143)	0.303*** (0.115)
FEUP1994	1.165** (0.516)	0.085 (0.193)	
FEDN1994	−0.645 (0.549)	−0.069 (0.213)	
LESZ	0.269 (0.190)	0.360*** (0.098)	
LFAW	1.027* (0.601)	0.930*** (0.205)	
LKL	0.372 (0.370)		
LSTDEVNI	−0.101 (0.131)		
TOTUT	−2.013 (5.367)		
Observations	183	541	656
Log-likelihood	205.27	646.35	756.49

Numbers in parentheses are standard errors.
* Significant at .10.
** Significant at .05.
*** Significant at .01.

Table 6-8. *OLS Estimates of the Level of Profit-Sharing Coverage*
Only firms with profit sharing included

Variable	Version 1	Version 2	Version 3
INTERCEPT	−0.539 (0.794)	−0.604 (0.330)	0.516 (0.078)
TEN	0.008 (0.007)	0.008** (0.003)	0.010*** (0.003)
UNION	−0.162** (0.063)	−0.142*** (0.037)	−0.152*** (0.036)
STATUS	−0.045 (0.055)	−0.009 (0.034)	0.008 (0.033)
CMPLX1	0.021 (0.023)	0.012 (0.014)	0.033** (0.014)
DEPND1	−0.027 (0.026)	−0.015 (0.015)	−0.016 (0.015)
TRNSFR1	−0.053** (0.023)	−0.011 (0.014)	−0.003 (0.014)
INDMAN	−0.053 (0.082)	0.024 (0.033)	0.062* (0.032)
INDSER		0.049 (0.040)	0.095** (0.039)
FEUP1994	0.012 (0.051)	0.036 (0.028)	
FEDN1994	−0.033 (0.056)	−0.064** (0.030)	
LESZ	−0.034 (0.024)	−0.013 (0.014)	
LFAW	0.160** (0.074)	0.129*** (0.032)	
LKL	−0.043 (0.042)		
LSTDEVNI	0.037** (0.015)		
TOTUT	0.477 (0.662)		
Observations	129	332	341
Adjusted R^2	0.131	0.150	0.092

Numbers in parentheses are standard errors.
* Significant at .10.
** Significant at .05.
*** Significant at .01.

considerably less severe than in the movement from table 6-5 to table 6-6. A first result, significant across all versions, is that unionized profit-sharing firms have significantly lower proportions of their work forces covered by their plans. Coverage is positively associated with worker tenure, significantly so in versions 2 and 3. Coverage is positively associated with average wages in both versions (1 and 2) in which LFAW is entered. The remaining statistically significant coefficients appear in no more than one specification. Task complexity has very small positive coefficients in all versions, but the association is significant in the third version only. Skill transferability is negatively related to profit-sharing coverage in all versions, but significantly so only in version 1. Coverage is negatively related to employment declines, significantly so in version 2. Coverage is significantly positively related to net income variability in the only specification, version 1, which includes that variable (discussed later in this chapter).

Our final set of results concern employee involvement in decisionmaking. Table 6-9 gives our logit regressions for the probability of being a high employee involvement firm (EICDBROD = 1 if EIBROD ≥ 3). A variable that stands out is task complexity, which is a significant predictor of employee involvement in all three specifications; the estimated coefficient is much larger than in the parallel profit-sharing and ESOP equations. All other coefficients are significant in no more than one specification. The estimate on the asset specificity variable, TOTUT, is significant in the one version in which it is entered. There is an indication that public status reduces the likelihood of high employee involvement, with a negative sign occurring in all three equations, significant in the variant permitting the largest sample size. Establishment size is negatively related to employee involvement in both specifications in which it appears, significantly so in one. Task interdependence has inconsistent signs but is significantly negatively related to involvement in version 1. Each of the included industry group dummies is significant in one specification.

The corresponding OLS equations are in table 6-10. Unlike the dependent variables in the OLS regressions for ESOP and profit-sharing coverage, the dependent variable in this case is the level of employee involvement, not the percentage of employees who participate. The dependent variable in table 6-10 is EIBRODHI, consisting of the values of EIBROD for firms in which that variable is greater than or equal to 3. As noted earlier, the number of firms with high employee involvement (as we defined it) is small, 156 of 806, and most of these firms have scores near the minimum value (3). Moreover, of the 156 firms with high involvement, only

Table 6-9. *Logit Estimates of the Probability of High Employee Involvement in Decisionmaking*

Variable	Version 1	Version 2	Version 3
INTERCEPT	9.433 (6.800)	1.163 (2.473)	-2.924 (0.622)
TEN	-0.008 (0.060)	0.004 (0.029)	0.008 (0.024)
UNION	0.106 (0.585)	-0.292 (0.329)	-0.138 (0.284)
STATUS	-0.257 (0.463)	-0.440 (0.301)	-0.431* (0.263)
CMPLX1	0.513** (0.226)	0.351*** (0.126)	0.324*** (0.107)
DEPND1	-0.467** (0.229)	-0.050 (0.122)	0.019 (0.112)
TRNSFR1	0.187 (0.219)	0.059 (0.115)	0.085 (0.102)
INDMAN	-0.277 (0.364)	0.301** (0.145)	0.068 (0.114)
INDSER		-0.211 (0.189)	-0.407** (0.162)
FEUP1994	-0.758 (0.520)	-0.317 (0.242)	
FEDN1994	0.868 (0.568)	0.247 (0.256)	
LESZ	-0.356* (0.214)	-0.150 (0.111)	
LFAW	-0.652 (0.640)	-0.288 (0.237)	
LKL	-0.202 (0.380)		
LSTDEVNI	-0.079 (0.143)		
TOTUT	-12.190* (6.236)		
Observations	183	541	656
Log likelihood	182.96	519.76	557.11

Numbers in parentheses are standard errors.
* Significant at .10.
** Significant at .05.
*** Significant at .01.

Table 6-10. *OLS Regression of Employee Involvement in Decisionmaking*
Only high involvement firms included

Variable	Version 1	Version 2	Version 3
INTERCEPT	1.599 (2.427)	3.911 (0.647)	3.310 (0.164)
TEN	0.008 (0.017)	–0.005 (0.008)	–0.007 (0.007)
UNION	–0.096 (0.166)	0.009 (0.087)	–0.056 (0.080)
STATUS	–0.107 (0.136)	–0.107 (0.086)	–0.057 (0.080)
CMPLX1	–0.051 (0.071)	–0.057 (0.034)	–0.037 (0.030)
DEPND1	0.040 (0.066)	0.005 (0.032)	0.027 (0.029)
TRNSFR1	0.056 (0.066)	0.038 (0.032)	0.013 (0.027)
INDMAN	0.350* (0.187)	0.117 (0.075)	0.060 (0.062)
INDSER		0.006 (0.105)	–0.036 (0.093)
FEUP1994	0.137 (0.151)	0.027 (0.075)	
FEDN1994	–0.133 (0.128)	–0.107 (0.082)	
LESZ	–0.091 (0.066)	–0.032 (0.036)	
LFAW	0.092 (0.229)	–0.040 (0.063)	
LKL	0.085 (0.105)		
LSTDEVNI	0.006 (0.045)		
TOTUT	2.591 (1.601)		
Observations	44	108	133
Adjusted R^2	0.056	0.010	–0.014

Numbers in parentheses are standard errors.
* Significant at .10.
** Significant at .05.
*** Significant at .01.

133 have information for even the minimum set of variables to be included in the regression reported in table 6-10. Perhaps because there is so little variation in the dependent variable,[36] we find no statistically significant determinants of the level of employee involvement among the firms with high employee involvement: only the manufacturing dummy is significant and positive and only in version 1. The coefficient on complexity is negative but very small, unlike the coefficients on that variable in all of the previous tables, especially in the related tables 6-9 and 6-11.

In order to understand better the effect of the independent variables on the continuous measure of employee involvement we also estimate OLS regressions on the entire sample, without restriction to the high involvement firms, and show the results in table 6-11. The logit regression on the dichotomous version of decision participation, in table 6-9, had suggested that especially complexity but also perhaps public status, interdependence, and the industry dummies, were predictors of employee involvement. Table 6-11 confirms all of these indications, except that for interdependence, and it gives some additional results. The negative effect of public status, positive effect of complexity, and negative effect of establishment size seen in one or more logit regressions (table 6-9) all reappear with equal or greater significance in the OLS analysis for the same samples. There is in addition a negative coefficient on average wage (LFAW) in one estimate, which is significant at the .01 level. Industry dummies are significant in two cases.

Owing to concern that employee involvement is defined too broadly by EIBROD, we also created the variable EINARR (see "Description of the Data") and estimated parallel sets of equations based on that variable. The results for EINARR are similar to those for EIBROD; for instance, they suggest that greater task complexity increases the likelihood of greater employee involvement, and large firm size reduces it, as does public ownership. There is also a positive association between employee involvement and tenure. To save space, we do not include the results for EINARR.

Discussion

We can now take stock of the empirical results and use these results to assess the hypotheses developed in the first part of this chapter. As in the

---

36. As table 6-4 shows, the mean of EIBRODHI is 3.30, very close to the minimum value of 3.0. The maximum value in the sample is 4.8, and the standard deviation is 0.31.

Table 6-11. *OLS Estimates of Level of Employee Involvement in Decisionmaking*
All firms included

Variable	Version 1	Version 2	Version 3
INTERCEPT	5.049	4.088	2.143
	(1.590)	(0.503)	(0.126)
TEN	0.008	0.005	0.002
	(0.014)	(0.006)	(0.006)
UNION	0.014	–0.026	–0.041
	(0.133)	(0.070)	(0.065)
STATUS	–0.087	–0.149**	–0.188***
	(0.105)	(0.062)	(0.056)
CMPLX1	0.158***	0.140***	0.118***
	(0.049)	(0.026)	(0.024)
DEPND1	–0.066	–0.013	0.007
	(0.053)	(0.027)	(0.025)
TRNSFR1	0.053	0.003	0.001
	(0.049)	(0.025)	(0.022)
INDMAN	0.028	0.229***	0.057
	(0.176)	(0.063)	(0.054)
INDSER		–0.020	–0.170***
		(0.074)	(0.064)
FEUP1994	–0.049	–0.028	
	(0.108)	(0.048)	
FEDN1994	0.075	0.016	
	(0.120)	(0.053)	
LESZ	–0.069	–0.059**	
	(0.047)	(0.023)	
LFAW	–0.231	–0.178***	
	(0.146)	(0.051)	
LKL	–0.012		
	(0.090)		
LSTDEVNI	–0.024		
	(0.032)		
TOTUT	–1.148		
	(1.345)		
Observations	182	540	655
Adjusted R^2	0.044	0.081	0.058

Numbers in parentheses are standard errors.
* Significant at .10.
** Significant at .05.
*** Significant at .01.

earlier theoretical discussion, we group the underlying causal explanations into five broad categories.

Information and Coordination

The principal variables discussed earlier in connection with coordination problems were complexity and task interdependence, along with establishment size. We suggested that the first two variables were likely to lead to greater delegation of authority to employees, but that size effects were ambiguous. What do our results say?

The estimates on complexity in the employee involvement equations are positive and statistically significant (except for the subsample of firms with high involvement where there is very limited variation; see table 6-10). This is true both when the question is whether a firm is likely to have high or low employee involvement in decisionmaking (table 6-9) and when we study determinants of the level of involvement viewed as a continuous variable (table 6-11).

Notably, the estimates on complexity do not have equally large or significant effects in equations for the presence and coverage of financial participation by employees (ESOPs and profit sharing). This result is consistent with the hypothesis that task complexity does not induce employee participation in financial returns but encourages the development of mechanisms for employee participation in decisionmaking.

The results for task interdependence are more equivocal. Our hypotheses suggested that interdependence encourages employee participation in both financial returns and decisionmaking. We did find that interdependence enhances the probability of ESOP adoption (table 6-5), but it has no effect on ESOP coverage, or on the adoption of profit sharing. Nor does interdependence seem to affect the degree of employee involvement in decisionmaking. The reason for the absence of an effect on profit sharing is not clear to us. Nor do we have a straightforward explanation for the lack of an effect of task interdependence on employee involvement in decisionmaking, although we would venture that the dominant effect comes from task complexity, overshadowing the effects of other contributing variables.

Average establishment size has negative effects in most equations, but with an anomalous positive and strongly significant result for the presence of a profit-sharing plan (table 6-7).

Work Incentives

The Alchian and Demsetz theory about effort incentives in production teams was reviewed in the first part of this chapter.[37] There we identified several predictions that emanate from this framework. To recount briefly: no relationship between technological interdependence and group financial incentives such as ESOPs and profit sharing (team incentive problems are handled through central monitoring); negative relationship between size and reliance on group incentives (free rider reasons); size and interdependence should be negatively associated with participation in decisionmaking; sensitivity of physical assets to misuse should be negatively associated with worker participation in financial returns and in decisionmaking.

As noted above, greater interdependence is positively associated with the presence of ESOPs (table 6-5). Elsewhere, interdependence appears to have little effect. We find negative size-effects for existence of an ESOP (table 6-5), existence of high employee involvement (table 6-9), and degree of employee involvement (table 6-11), but a positive effect on the existence of profit sharing (table 6-7). Aside from this anomaly, the conjecture that larger size undermines group financial incentives and employee involvement in decisionmaking cannot be rejected.

Physical asset specificity (TOTUT) often has a negative and significant coefficient, implying more employee participation when physical assets become more specific. But because the significance levels are marginal and the sample sizes are small, we do not attach great weight to these results. If idiosyncratic machinery and facilities are more easily abused, then this might count as evidence against the notion that susceptibility of assets to misuse will imply less worker participation in ownership or decisionmaking. An alternative explanation consistent with our results is that idiosyncratic physical assets confer valuable private information on frontline workers, who must be induced to supply this information to management. Group financial incentives and participation in decisionmaking arguably serve this purpose.

We also noted earlier that some theoretical perspectives concerned with work incentives assign an important role to risk variables. Principal-agent theory suggests that higher levels of exogenous risk should be associated with reduced financial participation by employees, and perhaps with less employee participation in decisionmaking as well. In our econometric work,

37. Alchian and Demsetz (1972).

industry-level risk is measured as the standard deviation of net income during the previous five years. We also constructed two firm-level variables to proxy for risk: the cumulative upward and downward changes in firm employment during the previous three years. The industry-level risk variable had a significant sign in only one equation, and this was an anomalous positive result for profit-sharing coverage (table 6-8).[38] The firm-level employment change variables fared little better, with coefficients that were occasionally mildly significant but erratic in sign. Consequently, we find no evidence in support of the hypothesis that risk aversion combines with riskiness of earnings or employment to discourage employee participation.

Finance and Investment

Several variables in our analysis should proxy for the ease or difficulty of financing worker participation in ownership. A higher capital/labor ratio is likely to raise the required equity contribution from workers and should therefore lower the likelihood and extent of employee ownership. Average wage, on the other hand, should be positively related to worker ownership because it is likely to imply greater worker wealth (easing liquidity problems), and because workers receiving higher wages may be less risk averse. Furthermore, when physical assets are more specialized, borrowing is less feasible or more costly, and hence workers would have greater difficulty in financing a given fraction of the firm's equity requirement. At the same time, specialized skills might aggravate the problem of nondiversification and therefore make employee participation in ownership less likely (although the predicted sign on skill specificity was ambiguous).

The capital/labor ratio is never significant in any of our specifications, perhaps because of our use of industry-level averages for this variable or the reduction in sample sizes that occurs when it is included. The results for average wage are substantially more interesting. Here we find significant positive effects, as predicted, in many equations (see the logits for ESOPs in table 6-5; the OLS for ESOP coverage in table 6-6; the logits for profit sharing in table 6-7; and the OLS for profit sharing in table 6-8). These results support the notion that firms having more highly paid employees tend to adopt programs of financial participation and to extend coverage to a larger fraction of their work force.

---

38. If workers are risk averse, we would not expect more workers to opt for profit sharing when the returns are more uncertain.

Parallel results occur for the tenure variable, which has positive effects in almost all equations related to financial participation, and is often strongly significant (see the logits for ESOPs in table 6-5, the OLS for ESOP coverage in table 6-6, the logits for profit sharing in table 6-7, and the OLS for profit-sharing coverage in table 6-8). This is consistent with the notion that older workers with greater seniority tend to have larger personal savings and higher wages, as well as lower risk aversion (note that the correlation between tenure and the log of average wage is .29).

An alternative explanation for our wage and (especially) tenure results is that more senior workers have more demand for tax-sheltered retirement vehicles such as ESOPs and deferred profit sharing. The positive relationship between the average wage and financial participation supports the notion that such programs represent "gravy" that is added onto the base wage, rather than substituting for it.[39]

Asset Specificity

Recall that the physical specificity variable TOTUT was defined so that an increase reflects the use of more generic assets; therefore a *negative* coefficient indicates that greater specificity leads to greater worker participation. That four out of six coefficients on this variable are negative, and two of these are statistically significant, contradicts not only our expectations based on ideas about liquidity constraints, but also arguments that worker ownership and control will be undermined by the desire of investors to protect quasi rents associated with specialized assets.[40] As above, the positive effects of physical asset specificity on the probability of participation in decisionmaking (table 6-9) could derive from private knowledge about idiosyncratic equipment, which might induce managers to consult with shop floor workers about production-related issues. The positive effect of specificity on ESOP coverage (table 6-6) might reflect the use of group incentives to ensure proper maintenance of assets, willingness to share information, and/or avoidance of costly battles over quasi-rent distribution. Firms with new rather than used equipment may also want to offer stronger maintenance incentives.[41]

Our only measure of human capital specificity (aside from tenure, a dubious proxy for specialized skills) is the transferability variable. Again, by

39. Mitchell, Lewin, and Lawler (1990).
40. Dow (1993).
41. Holmstrom and Milgrom (1991).

the definition of this variable, higher values indicate lower skill specificity. This variable has an erratic sign, is more often positive than negative (suggesting that more specialization in skills lead to *less* worker participation) but has some significant negative effects (tables 6-5 and 6-8). The latter results indicate that greater specificity of human capital is associated with a higher probability of an ESOP, and in firms with profit-sharing plans, a higher fraction of the work force is covered. This is broadly compatible with the proposition that when workers have specialized skills, they are more likely to participate financially, but these results are not particularly robust across specifications and sample definitions.

Institutional Factors

The key institutional variables, appearing in all specifications, are unionization and status as a publicly traded company. Unionization seems to have little effect on the likelihood of adoption of plans for employee financial returns participation but has a significantly negative effect on the coverage of both ESOPs and profit sharing. This may be interpreted as follows. Unions often resist financial participation by employees, claiming that management has much impact on financial results (employees may have more effect on productivity) and workers should not be made to bear the risk of management's decisions; management controls information about the actual level of profit; and management can change unilaterally the proportion of financial returns allocated to employees via ESOPs and profit-sharing plans. If it is typically management that institutes such plans, and if their coverage is often not extended to unionized workers, this could explain the lack of effect of unions in the equations determining the existence of plans, and their negative impact on the degree of coverage of these plans. Consistent with the emerging view of unions that employee participation in decisionmaking is not necessarily adverse to workers' interests, we do not find a significant effect of unionization on involvement in decisionmaking in either direction.

Our results indicate with considerable consistency that publicly traded firms have lower probability of having financial returns participation by employees, and lower coverage of these plans, as well as less employee involvement in decisionmaking. One possible interpretation is that managers of publicly traded companies believe employee participation sends the wrong signal to shareholders, for instance by suggesting that attention will be less focused on the interests of nonemployee investors. If this is so, it runs counter to a prediction that some infer from agency theory, namely, that in publicly traded firms the added agency relationship between owners and management should increase the reliance on programs that combat agency problems in the relationship between management and lower tiers in the organization.[42]

Conclusions

What can we conclude from these empirical results? One reasonably clear-cut result is that task complexity seems to motivate firms to develop systematic procedures for involving employees in decisionmaking. This may reflect a need to delegate authority because of informational overload on top managers, the fact that frontline employees in such firms tend to acquire valuable information that managers would like to share, and the possibility that decisionmaking about complex tasks can be done most effectively by those who have to execute them and have the knowledge and skills to do so.[43] Idiosyncratic physical assets may reinforce this condition of informational asymmetry, an interpretation that is consistent with our (weak) finding that asset specificity may promote greater ESOP coverage and a higher probability of employee participation in decisionmaking.[44]

Strong positive results were obtained for average tenure and average wage but only with respect to financial participation (ESOPs, profit sharing), not employee involvement in decisions. This supports the view that firms with older and wealthier employees are more likely to adopt such programs in the first place and to extend coverage to a larger fraction of the work force once they have done so. Whether these results are best explained by increased liquidity, reduced risk aversion, or nearness to retirement age is an open question, although our risk measures were not successful in explaining the degree of employee financial participation. Another strong

---

42. See, for example, Smith (1991). Combining public firms in which there is a substantial inside ownership with privately held firms, which are owned mostly by insiders, Liu (1998) finds support for the conjecture stated in the text.

43. The finding that task complexity affects employee involvement in decisionmaking was obtained repeatedly in other work by members of the Minnesota Organization of Work project who used alternative measures of decisionmaking participation. For example, in their work Han (1995); Liu (1998); and Ben-Ner, Kong, and Boseley (1998) used dummy variables from the survey, which identify the presence or absence of specific employee involvement plans (teams, quality circles, and so on), and found that the probability of using these increases strongly and signficantly with the degree of task complexity.

44. Ben-Ner and Jun (1996) suggest that asymmetric information that favors management will be an important factor in encouraging employee ownership.

set of results, for unionization and publicly traded status, were noted earlier under "Institutional Factors."

The other variables did less well. There was some evidence that large establishment size was associated with less reliance on group financial incentives and with less employee participation, as well as a bit of evidence that specialized human capital promotes ESOP adoption. The interdependence-of-tasks variable also seemed to encourage adoption of ESOPs, perhaps for reasons that are related to effort incentives or information revelation. The remaining variables had little systematic effect.

In light of these findings, what would be a sensible agenda for future investigation? First, the results for the complexity variable suggest that coordination issues, including the conditions under which managerial authority is delegated or information is transferred up the organizational hierarchy, require more theoretical attention. Although this technological variable had highly significant positive effects on participation in decisionmaking, it had no significant impact on financial participation variables. This may indicate that the issues surrounding complexity have little to do with incentives and more to do with designing an organizational structure that conveys useful information and decisionmaking rights to the right person in the right place at the right time. Given the relatively modest attention that economists have devoted to pure coordination problems, compared with effort incentives, this is an interesting finding.

Second, to the extent that group financial incentives are important, they may matter more as a way of eliciting valuable private information from frontline workers, or avoiding costly distributional conflicts over quasi rent, than as a method of extracting work effort. For instance, interdependence of tasks and specialization of skills are positively associated with ESOP adoption. Such factors may create monitoring problems but are also likely to give workers access to extensive private information about the production process. We suggested that physical asset specificity could have similar implications. Again this runs counter to the prevailing emphasis among theorists concerned with firm organization, who have generally focused on the related but not identical problem of motivating worker effort. It is, however, consistent with the emphasis found within the new institutional economics on asset specificity as a factor that can tempt managers and workers to exploit informational asymmetries in an opportunistic way. ESOPs and profit sharing may enable firms to align incentives in ways that dampen these opportunistic tendencies.

Finally, we do find strong evidence that proxies for worker wealth and seniority are positively associated with financial participation. This finding is consistent with ideas appearing in the literature on labor-managed firms, which emphasizes limited personal wealth along with credit constraints as reasons for the rarity of producer cooperatives and other forms of pure worker ownership. At the same time we find little evidence that industry-level risk matters, as might be expected from hypotheses that cite workers' risk aversion as a related reason for the rarity of worker ownership. However, such effects may be masked here by the smaller sample sizes arising when industry-level variables are included, or because the variance of industry net income is just too coarse a measure to capture the actual risks facing individual firms in our sample. It may also be true that theories based upon polar cases (pure investor ownership versus pure worker ownership) do not mesh well with our data set. For example, at levels of worker ownership well beyond those observed in our sample, diversification motives might take on greater significance. By the same token, physical asset specificity might loom larger as an obstacle to financing outright worker ownership than it does for the modest levels of financial participation studied here.

A broader comment concerns the frequent assertion in the literature that participation in decisionmaking and in financial returns is highly complementary.[45] In our analyses we found that each phenomenon is driven by distinct causal forces. For instance, complexity is an important determinant of participation in decisionmaking but not much so for adoption or coverage of ESOPs and profit-sharing plans. The opposite is true for average wage and tenure of employees. While our findings do not refute the proposition that such complementarities exist (for example, financial participation is likely to encourage responsible decisionmaking), our results do suggest that there are also separate causal pathways that encourage the reliance upon employee participation in decisionmaking and in financial returns.

As we have stressed throughout, this chapter is exploratory in spirit. No single data set can resolve all questions about firm organization, and indeed we will be satisfied if we have merely raised some interesting new puzzles. We believe that firm organization in general and the degree of worker participation in particular are heavily conditioned by the nature of a firm's

45. See Ben-Ner and Jones (1995); Levine (1995).

production technology and its market environment. The task facing theorists and empirical researchers alike is to identify the principal causal mechanisms and to assess their relative importance. This research is a modest step forward along that road.

COMMENT BY

Derek C. Jones

This is a very interesting and provocative chapter, which continues the fruitful traditions at the Brookings Institution and Sloan School of Management at MIT of fostering work in this important area.[46] The authors have collected a new firm-level data set on human resource management practices (HRMPs) and imaginatively integrated this resource with other existing data sets—a process that is often both challenging and frustrating. The assembly of data on the degree of employee involvement for fifteen different issues and for a large sample of firms constitutes most unusual and useful information. Another strength is the skillful development of hypotheses from different literatures, including the economics of the labor-managed firm and the new institutional economics. The authors resourcefully show how those theories potentially have broad applications.

As the authors admit, in many ways the empirical work reported is exploratory. Hence I will not go into great detail on many matters of assessment of what is reported. Rather I am making some suggestions on what might be done additionally with the available data.[47] First, a few small points on theory.

As already mentioned, the theoretical part of the chapter is solid and thought provoking. However, in developing propositions on the incidence of different degrees of employee involvement, the authors do not discuss hypotheses that others have examined on the role of labor unions and incentive pay.[48] For example, many consider the role of labor unions

---

46. See, for example, Blinder (1990); Blair (1995); and Kochan, Katz, and McKersie (1986).

47. Since the authors, sometimes with other collaborators, apparently are involved in much other work that uses the newly collected data, some of these comments may be redundant.

48. Useful surveys of some of this work are to be found in the contributions in Blinder (1990); Blair (1995); and more recently in Kruse and Blasi (1997); Jones and Pliskin (1997); and Jones, Kato, and Pliskin (1997).

crucial and posit an inverse association between unionization and profit sharing because of reasons that include opposition by unions to flexible pay, union-avoidance behavior by firms, and restrictive work rules in collective bargaining agreements. Furthermore, the authors' theoretical framework does not emphasize a theme that has been the focus of an important literature, namely, the role of bundles of HRMPs.[49] As I look at the data, it strikes me that a number of potential advantages occur because of restricting the sample to a single state. And in selecting states Minnesota has much to commend, including a long tradition of nurturing firms with diverse organizational forms. In particular, recall the important example of the Minneapolis cooperative coopers.[50] Unfortunately, however, today the range of organizational forms seems narrower than in the past.

There are several potential problems in the way that key variables are constructed. For example, for dependent variables such as EIBROD, a potential problem lies with the unit of observation being the firm rather than the establishment. This follows because other work shows that often large differences are present across establishments in the same firms on the extent of employee involvement.[51] These and other studies also show that sometimes differences occur in the nature and incidence of different kinds of compensation plans (such as profit sharing) between establishments in the same firm. Even if the dispersion in employee involvement within multiestablishment firms is minimal, a second problem is that one might wonder how accurately managers' perceptions reflect the extent of employee involvement. Much work suggests that employees' views on this matter often differ from those of managers (and that managers' views are not necessarily more reliable).[52] Moreover, even if all agents' views are similar, a potential difficulty arises of recollection bias—in some firms managers apparently were asked in 1996 to recall the way things were in 1994.

But perhaps the major problem stems from aggregating responses for what are very different issues and doing so as though all issues are of equal importance. There is no theoretical rationale for this procedure. Thus in

49. Ichniowski, Shaw, and Prennushi (1997).

50. In their day they appear to have been at least as important as the plywood cooperatives have been in the postwar period. See Virtue (1932); Jones (1979).

51. Kochan, Katz, and McKersie (1986).

52. It would also be interesting to know how well variation in the incidence of formal institutions for participation—for example, quality circles and joint labor-management bodies—relates to variation in managers' perceptions of worker influence in general and on particular issues.

construction of the broader indexes (for example, EIBROD), it is difficult to accept that employee involvement in issues such as social events is viewed as of equal importance to involvement in issues such as investment policy. Moreover, in light of the authors' own theoretical framework (for example, the varying importance accorded to monitoring difficulties), it is not clear that they view all fifteen issues as of equal importance. Although this point is partially recognized in the construction of narrower indexes (for example, EINARR), in view of their stated criterion of strategic importance, it is surprising that issues such as working conditions are included in this index (while others such as corporate finance are excluded). In future work it would be interesting to analyze responses on *individual* issues.[53]

I have other reservations about the usefulness and the reliability of the other dependent variables. On profit sharing, as the authors note, form 5500 furnishes information only for deferred plans (and as such does not cover all profit sharing and thus excludes some of the more interesting forms.)[54] Furthermore, since it is not clear that their measure of profit sharing excludes plans that are restricted to managers, in future work the authors may wish to pick a higher threshold of coverage for profit-sharing dummy variables. Similar concerns may apply to ESOP coverage and the construction of the employee ownership variables. Finally, I am surprised that there are only three types of dependent variable (and, for example, no measures of HRMPs such as quality circles and teams, which apparently have been used in other studies that use the same data but focus on outcomes, rather than incidence.)

For the explanatory variables, I am mainly concerned with the two measures constructed from public (Compustat) data. Since these variables are not directly available for most firms, the authors use a procedure to impute them from industry averages. However, not having firm-specific measures is a serious weakness. Unfortunately, as the authors note, using only the firms for which economic data are available (for public firms from Compustat) eliminates many observations from the data set. It would be instructive to provide some comparisons on how the actual data for firms in the Compustat data set compare with the industry variables (which are used for all firms.) Similarly, how does the measure of the standard deviation of

53. On the difficulty of constructing indexes see Cable (1987) and Cable (1988), who proposes constructing Guttman scales.
54. For example, see Kruse (1993).

income at the industry level compare with the actual value for public firms?[55] In addition, to test some hypotheses (for example, the role of administrative costs), it might be more appropriate to look at firm size as well as average establishment size.

In commenting on the authors' empirical strategy and findings, I note again that the authors consider much of the work reported in this chapter exploratory. In future work they might try to provide more information that goes beyond the correlations reported—for example, on the joint incidence of employee ownership and employee participation. I encourage the authors to investigate the relationships among employee ownership, profit sharing, and employee participation. In this process they might try to operationalize the conceptual framework that is developed and analyze the links between, on the one hand, dimensions of participation in economic returns (such as ownership and profit sharing) and, on the other hand, dimensions of participation in decisionmaking. They might provide additional information on the characteristics of firms where some of these dimensions are all "high" compared with firms where they are all "low." Moreover, they might go further and, by looking at responses for individual issues, examine links between influence on separate matters and ownership. It would also be interesting to provide more information by industry (in part because there are many firms in retailing) and other splits in the sample (for example, public versus private firms and union versus nonunion.)

The econometric analysis is done in two stages for each of the three areas—employee ownership, profit sharing, and employee involvement. In the first stage, the main technique used is logit analysis to explain the incidence of a particular attribute such as profit sharing. Thus in all cases the dependent variable is dichotomous.[56] In the second stage, the authors use regression analysis to examine the factors influencing variation in a particular characteristic (for example, the coverage of employees in profit-sharing plans) where, for employee ownership and profit sharing, the analysis is restricted to firms in which the attribute is nonzero. It is unclear whether this is always the best way to proceed.

Thus, by using logits in the first stage, it seems that often a lot of useful information is thrown away or not used to best advantage. Rather than use

---

55. Since private firms typically are smaller than public firms, we might expect that the interpolated values for private firms will be larger than they actually are.

56. This approach has been employed for a variety of HRMPs in diverse countries. For example, see Smith (1988) (U.S.); Gregg and Machin (1988) (U.K.); and Jones and Kato (1993) (Japan).

logit analysis to analyze a dichotomous value of the degree of employee involvement, in future work they may wish to use an ordered probit (or logit) approach for individual issues.[57] There are several advantages to this alternative procedure, primarily that since the responses are ordered, ordered probit (logit) is a more natural technique to use than simple logit. Furthermore, if the analysis is undertaken for separate issues, then not only are there no problems with the construction of the index but also, as argued earlier, some issues relate more closely than do others (or the index) to key theoretical ideas. For example, responses on work-related matters such as job redesign would perhaps provide better information for use in testing hypotheses on monitoring. For the second stage in the analysis, obvious sample selection issues arise.[58]

In conclusion, I want to reiterate my generally positive reaction to the chapter. It is part of an impressive body of work by the authors that attempts to explore diverse, though mainly economic, issues on employee ownership and the rapidly changing workplace in today's economy. This and the other studies of the authors are sure to be extensively referenced as future scholars and policymakers wrestle with similar issues. Finally, I strongly agree with their recommendation for a direction for future work. We can learn much from how organizational structures affect the flow of information within the firm and how this in turn affects the efficiency of managerial coordination.

References

Alchian, Armen, and Harold Demsetz. 1972. "Production, Information Costs, and Economic Organization." *American Economic Review* 62 (December) 777–95.

Appelbaum, Eileen, and Rosemary Batt. 1994. *The New American Workplace: Transforming Work Systems in the United States.* ILR Press.

Ben-Ner, Avner. 1997. "The Organization of Work: Its Determinants and Consequences; Project Status Report." Industrial Relations Center, University of Minnesota.

Ben-Ner, Avner, and Byoung Jun. 1996. "Employee Buyout in a Bargaining Game with Asymmetric Information." *American Economic Review* 86 (June): 502–23.

---

57. See Osterman (1994), who uses this technique to examine work organization in the United States. See also Jones and Ilayperuma (1998), where this method is used to analyze variation in employee involvement for selected issues using a large Bulgarian data set that combines information for individual workers with matching data for firms.

58. For a summary of the debate and Monte Carlo evidence on the issue see Leung and Yu (1996).

Ben-Ner, Avner, Tzu-Shian Han, and Derek C. Jones. 1996. "The Productivity Effects of Employee Participation in Control and in Economic Returns: A Review of Econometric Studies." In *Democracy and Efficiency in Economic Enterprises*, edited by Ugo Pagano and Robert E. Rowthorn, 209–44. London: Routledge.

Ben-Ner, Avner, and Derek C. Jones. 1995. "Employee Participation, Ownership, and Productivity: A Theoretical Framework." *Industrial Relations* 34 (October): 532–54.

Ben-Ner, Avner, Fanmin Kong, and Stacie Boseley. 1998. "Workplace Organization and Human Resource Practices: The Retail Food Industry." Paper presented at the Wharton School Conference on the Organization of Work in Service Industries (October).

Blair, Margaret. 1995. *Ownership and Control: Rethinking Corporate Governance for the Twenty-First Century.* Brookings.

Blinder, Alan, ed. 1990. *Paying for Productivity: A Look at the Evidence.* Brookings.

Cable, John. 1987. "Some Tests of Employee Participation Indices." *Advances in the Economic Analysis of Participatory and Labor Managed Firms* 2: 79–90.

———. 1988. "A Model and Measures of Employee Participation." *Advances in the Economic Analysis of Participatory and Labor Managed Firms* 3: 313–26.

Dow, Gregory. 1993. "Why Capital Hires Labor: A Bargaining Perspective." *American Economic Review* 83 (March):118–34.

Dow, Gregory, and Louis Putterman. 1999. "Why Capital (Usually) Hires Labor: An Assessment of Proposed Explanations." In *Employees and Corporate Governance*, edited by Margaret M. Blair and Mark Roe, 17–57. Brookings.

Duan, Naihua, and others. 1983. "A Comparison of Alternative Models for the Demand for Medical Care." *Journal of Business and Economic Statistics* 1 (April): 115–26.

Eisenhardt, Kathleen. 1988. "Control: Organizational and Economic Approaches." *Management Science* 31 (February): 134–49.

———. 1989. "Agency Theory: An Assessment and Review." *Academy of Management Review* 14 (January): 57–74.

FitzRoy, Felix R., and Kornelius Kraft. 1995. "On the Choice of Incentives in Firms." *Journal of Economic Behavior and Organization* 26 (January):145–60.

Gregg, P. A., and S. J. Machin. 1988. "Unions and the Incidence of Performance-Based Pay in Britain." *International Journal of Industrial Organization* 6 (March): 91–107.

Han, Tzu-Shian. 1995. "Employee Participation in Decision Making and Financial Returns: Effects on Firm Performance." Ph.D. dissertation, Industrial Relations Center, University of Minnesota.

Hart, Oliver D. 1995. *Firms, Contracts, and Financial Structure.* Oxford, Clarendon Press.

Hart, Oliver D., and John Moore. 1994. "A Theory of Debt Based on the Inalienability of Human Capital." *Quarterly Journal of Economics* 109 (November): 841–79.

Holmstrom, Bengt, and Paul Milgrom. 1991. "Multitask Principal-Agent Analysis: Incentive Contracts, Asset Ownership, and Job Design." *Journal of Law, Economics, and Organization* 7 (Special Issue): 24–52.

Ichniowski, Casey, Kathryn Shaw, and Giovanna Prennushi. 1997. "The Effects of Human Management Resource Practices on Productivity: A Study of Steel Finishing Lines." *American Economic Review* 87 (June): 291–313.

Jensen, Michael C., and William H. Meckling. 1979. "Rights and Production Functions: An Application to Labor-Managed Firms and Codetermination." *Journal of Business* 52 (October): 469–506.

Jones, Derek C. 1979. "U.S. Producer Cooperatives: The Record to Date." *Industrial Relations* 18 (Fall): 342–57.

Jones, Derek C., and Kosali Ilayperuma. 1998. "The Determinants of Employee Participation during Fading Communism and Early Transition." *Advances in the Economic Analysis of Participatory and Labour Managed Firms,* edited by Jon Svejnar, vol. 6, 29–55. JAI Press.

Jones, Derek C., and Takao Kato. 1993. "The Scope, Nature, and Effects of Employee Stock Ownership Plans in Japan." *Industrial and Labor Relations Review* 46 (January): 352–67.

———. 1995. "The Productivity Effects of Employee Stock-Ownership Plans and Bonuses: Evidence from Japanese Panel Data." *American Economic Review* 85 (June): 391–414.

Jones, Derek C., and Jeffrey Pliskin. 1997. "Determinants of the Incidence of Group Incentives: Evidence from Canada." *Canadian Journal of Economics* 30 (November): 1027–44.

Jones, Derek C., Takao Kato, and J. Pliskin. 1997. "Profit Sharing and Gainsharing: A Review of Theory, Incidence, and Effects." In *The Human Resource Management Handbook: Part I,* edited by David Lewin, Daniel J. B. Mitchell, and Mahmood Zahiddi, 53–173. JAI Press.

Kessides, Ioannis N. 1990a. "Market Concentration, Contestability, and Sunk Costs." *Review of Economics and Statistics* 72 (November): 614–22.

———. 1990b. "Towards a Testable Model of Entry: A Study of the U.S. Manufacturing Industries." *Economica* 57 (May) 219–38.

Klein, Benjamin, Robert G. Crawford, and Armen Alchian. 1978. "Vertical Integration, Appropriable Rents, and the Competitive Contracting Process." *Journal of Law and Economics* 21 (October): 297–326.

Knight, Frank. 1964. *Risk, Uncertainty, and Profit.* A. M. Kelley.

Kochan, Thomas, Harry C. Katz, and Robert B. McKersie. 1986. *The Transformation of American Industrial Relations.* Basic Books.

Kruse, Douglas. 1993. *Profit Sharing: Does It Make a Difference? The Productivity and Stability Effects of Employee Profit-Sharing Plans.* W. E. Upjohn Institute for Employment Research.

Kruse, Douglas, and Joseph R. Blasi. 1997. "Employee Ownership." In *The Human Resource Management Handbook,* edited by David Lewin, Daniel J. B. Mitchell, and Mahmood Zaidi, 113–51. JAI Press.

Leung, Siu Fai, and Shihiti Yu. 1996. "On the Choice between Sample Selection and Two-Part Models." *Journal of Econometrics* 72 (May–June):197–229.

Levine, David I. 1995. *Reinventing the Workplace: How Business and Employees Can Both Win.* Brookings.

Liu, Nien-Chi. 1998. "Determinants of Innovative Human Resource Practices and Systems." Ph.D. dissertation. Industrial Relations Center, University of Minnesota.

Maddala, G. S. 1983. *Limited-Dependent and Qualitative Variables in Econometrics.* Cambridge University Press.

Marschak, Jacob, and Roy Radner. 1972. *Economic Theory of Teams.* Yale University Press.

Milgrom, Paul, and John Roberts. 1992. *Economics, Organization and Management.* Prentice Hall.

Mitchell, Daniel, David Lewin, and Edward E. Lawler III. 1990. "Alternative Pay Systems, Firm Performance, and Productivity." In *Paying for Productivity: A Look at the Evidence*, edited by Alan Blinder, 15–88. Brookings.

Osterman, P. 1994. "How Common Is Workplace Transformation and Who Adopts It?" *Industrial and Labor Relations Review* 47 (January): 173–88.

Park, Yong-Seung. 1997. "Occupational Safety Effects of Employee Participation Plans in Decision-Making and Financial Returns." Ph.D. dissertation. Industrial Relations Center, University of Minnesota.

Perrow, Charles. 1986. *Complex Organizations: A Critical Essay*. 3d ed. Random House.

Putterman, Louis. 1984. "On Some Recent Explanations of Why Capital Hires Labor." *Economic Inquiry* 22 (April): 171–87.

Sappington, David. 1991. "Incentives in Principal-Agent Relationships." *Journal of Economic Perspectives* 5 (Spring): 45–66.

Smith, Stephen C. 1988. "On the Incidence of Profit and Equity Sharing: Theory and an Application to the High Tech Sector." *Journal of Economic Behavior and Organization* 9 (January): 45–58.

———. 1991. "On the Economic Rationale for Codetermination Law." *Journal of Economic Behavior and Organization* 16 (December): 261–81.

Snell, S. A. 1992. "Control Theory in Strategic Human Resource Management: The Mediating Effect of Administrative Information." *Academy of Management Journal* 35 (June): 292–327.

Virtue, G. O. 1932. "The End of the Cooperative Coopers." *Quarterly Journal of Economics* 46 (May): 541–45.

Wadhwani, Sushil B., and Martin Wall. 1990. "The Effects of Profit Sharing on Employment, Wages, Stock Returns and Productivity: Evidence from UK Micro Data." *Economic Journal* 100 (March): 1–17.

Williamson, Oliver E. 1985. *The Economic Institutions of Capitalism: Firms, Markets, Relations, and Contracting*. Free Press.

———. 1988. "Corporate Finance and Corporate Governance." *Journal of Finance* 43 (July): 567–91.

7

MARGARET M. BLAIR
DOUGLAS L. KRUSE
JOSEPH R. BLASI

Employee Ownership: An Unstable Form or a Stabilizing Force?

IS IT A VIABLE, efficient, and stable organizational form for an enterprise to be all or substantially owned by employees? The question is part of a long debate about the nature of capitalism and the way in which capitalism distributes the economic gains from production. In particular, a body of formal economic theory argues that firms that are owned and controlled by employees will have a number of efficiency disadvantages.[1] Although (as we discuss in greater detail below) these theories have generally focused on the problems that supposedly afflict worker cooperatives or firms with extensive employee control of management and the board of directors, the fact that employee-owned firms have had a relatively small place in Western economies (at least before the 1990s) is usually taken as evidence that they are not generally viable or stable. Unfortunately, there

We thank the Alfred P. Sloan Foundation and the Brookings project on Corporations and Human Capital for research support for this project. We also thank the Foundation for Enterprise Development, which has provided ongoing support to Rutgers for the development of its public company employee ownership databases and for research assistance. Gabriel Loeb and Hannah Zwiebel provided able and dedicated research assistance, and participants in a workshop at George Washington University offered helpful feedback. The authors accept responsibility for any errors of fact or judgment.

1. Dow and Putterman (1999) provide a summary and review of this literature. See also Hansmann (1996).

has been little systematic empirical evidence brought to bear on the question of whether, and under what circumstances, equity ownership by employees is viable. Nonetheless, the idea that it ought to work, and, moreover, that it ought to enhance productivity and stability and lead to a fairer distribution of the rewards from enterprise, continues to resurface and intrigue scholars and policymakers.

In this chapter we take on a seemingly very simple set of empirical questions that we hope will shed light on whether employee ownership of firms "works" in some sense. We ask the question not about worker cooperatives, however, nor about firms that are fully controlled by employees (forms that have been the primary focus of the case made by prior economic theorists against employee ownership) but about publicly traded firms with a substantial amount of employee share ownership. In particular, we ask: what has been the actual track record of publicly traded firms in which a substantial portion of the shares are held by, or on behalf of, rank and file employees (not just by top management or by a founding entrepreneur and her family)? Have firms configured this way been more or less likely to survive and thrive than firms that are otherwise similar, but that have a more conventional ownership structure without substantial employee share ownership? How has their performance compared? Have they been good investments for nonemployee shareholders? Have they provided employees with more or less job stability? Is the form itself a stable form, or does it tend to revert back to other structures of ownership that do not involve employees? Does it tend to be used only in highly selective circumstances such as transition periods? How do such firms weather periodic crises? Are they more or less adaptable than conventional firms?

To addresss these questions, this chapter examines a unique data set assembled by the authors that looks at all firms that were publicly traded in 1983 and that had approximately 20 percent or more of their common stock in employee stock ownership plans (ESOPs), profit-sharing plans, or other employee-benefit plans. We compare these firms to a control sample of firms matched by size and industry and to the universe of firms tracked by Compustat. Our results suggest that, far from being an unstable form, or a form used primarily for transitions, the ownership of a substantial block of shares by employees appears to be a relatively stable arrangement. Indeed, it may be an arrangement that "stabilizes" the firm itself, by making it less likely that the firm will be acquired, taken private, or thrust into bankruptcy. The form may also be associated with more stable employment levels. And it appears to achieve this result without cost in terms of productivity or financial performance, and may in fact enhance performance.

Theoretical and Empirical Background Issues

The idea that workplaces should be self-governed, and that employees should control the firms where they work and share in the financial rewards, has been a recurring theme in nearly a century of thinking about the social and economic implications of capitalism. But it seems that for every essay or article or book arguing that it would be a good idea, there have been counterarguments that it would not work. Most of the early theoretical literature arguing that it would be an inefficient way to organize production was based on arguments about a set of pathologies that supposedly afflict labor-managed firms (such as worker cooperatives), in which decisionmaking is by collective action, with votes allocated according to one-worker, one-vote, and in which worker-members share the proceeds from the enterprise evenly.

The Theoretical Case against Employee Ownership

One of the earliest theoretical arguments against employee ownership, so defined, came out of a model introduced by Benjamin Ward, and elaborated on by Evsey Domar, J. E. Meade, and Jaroslav Vanek.[2] These authors argued that worker cooperatives would tend to maximize revenues per worker, rather than profits, and would hence respond to demand changes in perverse ways.

These "perverse comparative static response" models are all based on an assumption that the governing rules of the cooperative would prohibit hiring nonmember workers (and would prohibit members from working more than a standard number of hours).[3] These assumptions meant that members would have to add new employee-members to expand production and therefore would have to accept a reduction in their share of the proceeds from the enterprise. Subsequent modeling by Avner Ben-Ner noted that if worker cooperatives could hire nonmember workers, then the firm would, over time, "degenerate" into a more traditionally structured

---

2. Ward (1958); Domar (1966); Meade (1972); Vanek (1977).
3. See Bonin and Putterman (1987).

capitalist firm.[4] The reason is that existing members would only want to add new members when times were bad and there were losses (rather than a surplus) to share, but potential new members would only want to join the enterprise as members when times were good and there was a surplus to share. Hence, while a given group of workers in an enterprise might be willing to form a cooperative, once that cooperative was formed, membership would gradually decline (through attrition), and the ratio of employees to members would increase, until eventually the firm would be owned by a single individual and would therefore be in effect a standard capitalist (entrepreneurial) firm.

Another theory about why worker cooperatives should not be viable is that workers in a cooperative will not have adequate incentives to invest for the long term. This is because workers who are nearing retirement will, presumably, not want to sacrifice current returns for returns that will come much later, perhaps after they have retired.[5] This argument, however, is based on an assumption that employee-owners will not have a mechanism for cashing out their interest in the firm at fair market value when they retire or leave the firm.[6] Hence, neither this argument nor either of the first two arguments should apply to situations in which employees own a substantial proportion of the publicly traded equity shares of a standard corporation.

Another argument against worker cooperatives that is based on the incentives employee-owners would face was advanced by Armien A. Alchian and Harold Demsetz.[7] They argued that in any kind of team production situation, if the proceeds are to be divided up among team members according to some fixed ex ante sharing rule (as would be the case in a cooperative with n members in which each member gets $1/n$ of the proceeds), each team member will have an incentive to shirk because he will receive all the benefits of shirking but bear only a pro rata share of the cost. A monitor is needed, Alchian and Demsetz argued, to counteract the shirk-

---

4. Ben-Ner (1988).

5. This sort of argument was made by Furubotn and Pejovich (1974) and Jensen and Meckling (1979).

6. Work by Craig and Pencavel (1992, 1995) has found evidence that contradicts this assumption. Moreover, a number of scholars have proposed mechanisms for solving this so-called horizon problem, such as tradable membership rights or "capital accounts" for worker members that would give them credit for cumulative implicit and explicit investments they make in the firm, and that could be cashed out when a worker quits or retires. See, for example, Ellerman (1986).

7. Alchian and Demsetz (1972).

ing incentive. But then, to ensure that the monitor has appropriate incentives not to shirk, the monitor should receive all the economic residual created by the team effort. That way, the monitor bears all the costs of his own shirking. Moreover, the monitor should own all the physical assets used by the team so that he will have an incentive to see that the assets are not abused by the workers.

Subsequent scholars noted that the solution proposed by Alchian and Demsetz only works in situations in which the work that team members do can be easily monitored.[8] If the nature of the work is complex, difficult to evaluate, difficult to monitor, and difficult to contract over, it is less clear that organizational forms in which a capitalist owns the assets, hires all labor inputs, and claims all the residual returns, will necessarily lead to superior results. In fact, some scholars have argued that it is precisely in these circumstances that sharing "ownership" rights and claims with employees might be efficiency enhancing.

Another set of arguments against employee ownership has to do with the difficulties that employees might face in getting or providing financial capital for their firm. Since employees as a class are generally not wealthy, they are likely to be risk averse and liquidity constrained. Hence they might have trouble assembling enough equity capital to provide sufficient financing for their firm, especially in capital-intensive industries. And if they try to finance their firm with debt capital, they are likely to face a higher cost of capital than a similarly situated firm financed with equity capital because of the inherent moral hazard problems debt financing would involve. These factors suggest that, if employee ownership is viable at all, it is likely to be in low capital-intensity industries.

The final argument against the viability of employee ownership, at least for most sectors of the economy, is based on the collective action problems that arise in any enterprise that is jointly owned by multiple individuals. Henry Hansmann argues that the problems of aggregating preferences across multiple participants in an enterprise can be severe, and that therefore governance arrangements will be more efficient if control rights (which Hansmann takes to be the most important feature of "ownership") are limited to a single class of "patrons."[9] Furthermore, ownership rights should go to the set of patrons whose interests in the firm are most homogeneous. With interesting exceptions that Hansmann explores in detail, these

---

8. See Holmstrom (1982); and Putterman (1986).
9. Hansmann (1996).

patrons will often be providers of financial capital, whose interest is generally captured by a single metric: a pro rata share of the residual. Because the interests of employees, by contrast, are likely to be much more complex, multilayered, and heterogeneous, Hansmann argues that employee ownership is less likely to be an attractive form in most situations.

Hansmann is not conclusively negative about employee ownership. He notes in fact that, "In practice it appears that, when the employees involved are highly homogeneous, employee ownership often is more efficient than investor ownership." With a heterogeneous work force, however, he says that "direct employee control of the firm brings substantial costs—costs that are generally large enough to outweigh the benefits that employee ownership otherwise offers."[10] Hansmann predicts that employee ownership will remain largely confined to firms with highly homogeneous classes of employee owners, such as service professions, including law, accounting, investment banking, management consulting, advertising, architecture, engineering, and medicine.

Of the theoretical problems outlined above, only two seem relevant to organizational forms in which employees are substantial owners of the equity of firms, while the remaining equity trades on public markets. These are the "risk-aversion" problems, arising from the fact that employees are likely to be poorly situated relative to outside investors (who can diversify their stakes) to bear the risk inherent in an equity stake, and the collective action problems that might arise if employees have a large enough stake for their votes to control the firm.

Theoretical Arguments in Favor of Employee Ownership

Arguments to the effect that employee ownership will result in a more fair distribution of the proceeds of economic activity, as well as greater dignity for workers, have been mentioned throughout the history of this idea. But formal arguments suggesting that employee ownership might also have efficiency advantages are relatively recent. The argument has been made by organizational theorists and picked up by management specialists and compensation experts, for example, that compensating employees with a share of the equity is a way to align their incentives with those of shareholders. Careful analysis of this theory, however, always comes up against what has been called the "$1/n$ problem." In large, publicly traded firms,

10. Hansmann (1996, p. 119).

where one would think that the need for incentive alignment would be greatest, an individual employee will realize through her equity stake only a tiny fraction (for example, $1/n$, where n is a large number) of any additional profits she generates for the firm by her actions. Thus, it is not at all obvious that a tiny ownership stake will have much incentive effect at all.

The counterargument to the $1/n$ problem is that the incentive effect of each individual employee's marginal increase in financial returns from not shirking is not the only mechanism by which employee ownership encourages productivity. Employee ownership, if it is widespread, is also likely to motivate employees to monitor their fellow employees and use social pressure on them to encourage them to exert effort.[11] The latter may create much stronger incentives than those provided by the direct financial impact of an employee's actions on his or her own financial stake, and consequently, the total effect of employee ownership could be much stronger than that implied by the "$1/n$" model. Proponents of this view generally argue that, to enhance this "cultural" effect, employee ownership (or other mechanisms for sharing the surplus, such as profit sharing) should be combined with employee-involvement programs and institutional and cultural changes within the firm designed to enhance mutual monitoring and cooperation. Indeed, empirical studies of employee-ownership, profit-sharing, and employee-involvement programs tend to support this hypothesis: neither employee-involvement programs by themselves, nor equity ownership/profit-sharing arrangements by themselves seem to make much difference for productivity. But in combination, there is some evidence that they lead to productivity improvements.[12]

---

11. In fact, fellow employees would probably be in a far better position to monitor an employee than an outside investor.

12. See, for example, General Accounting Office (1986); Weitzman and Kruse (1990). Kruse and Blasi (1997) review fifty-five published and unpublished empirical studies that use systematic data collection and verifiable statistical techniques to measure the connections among employee ownership, employee attitudes and behaviors, and firm performance. This review found no automatic connection between employee ownership and firm productivity or profitability across the studies. However, while several studies indicated better or unchanged performance under employee ownership, almost no studies found worse performance. One of the most recent of these studies, Blasi, Conte, and Kruse (1996) compared multiple measures of corporate performance of two groups of public companies in 1990–91 using the dataset that two of the authors had assembled in Blasi and Kruse (1991). This study compared 562 firms in which employees owned more than 5 percent of the stock to a control sample of firms of comparable size in the same industry groups. The results indicated that the employee-ownership firms had levels of profitability similar to those of other firms in the same size and industry group. Employee ownership had no strong relationship to sales per employee in this study. But, where differences in performance existed, they tended to indicate better performance by the employee-ownership firms.

An alternative argument in favor of employee ownership comes out of the idea that participatory firms, for cultural and economic reasons, will have less tendency to lay off workers during economic downturns. Martin L. Weitzman, for example, argues that paying workers with a combination of a lower fixed wage and a share in the returns serves as a mechanism for making compensation adjustable, which should reduce the magnitude of macroeconomic cycles.[13] Margaret Blair argues that such compensation arrangements would provide better protection for workers' investments in firm-specific human capital than do implicit, but potentially unsustainable, promises to pay workers a wage premium.[14] David Levine, however, stresses the importance of the larger cultural and economic context. With several different coauthors, he argues that the full productivity benefits of an "ownership culture" and greater loyalty to employees may not be achievable unless it is a widespread practice, since firms that make a practice of retaining employees during macroeconomic downturns would be disadvantaged in an economy where most firms were not doing so.[15]

Another, more limited, argument about the benefits of employee ownership has been made by Jeffrey N. Gordon, who argues that giving employees a share of the equity can reduce the costs of bargaining in times of severe economic stress or significant transition for an organization.[16] Gordon's work focuses mainly on the airline industry, where there have been a number of instances in recent years in which significant equity stakes have been granted to unionized workers in exchange for wage and benefit concessions in renegotiated union contracts. Gordon argues that offering workers an equity stake helps to make management's claims about the dire straits the company is in more credible. It also enables management to make a credible commitment to share in future gains if and when the firm returns to prosperity. Finally, the additional step of putting an employee representative on the board can help to assure employees that they are getting accurate and fair information about what is really going on in the firm. In his earlier work, Gordon seemed to argue that such equity-for-concession arrangements were attractive only for transitional purposes, but in more recent work, he seems to suggest that the use of equity stakes to reduce bargaining costs might be useful on a more permanent basis for firms that operate in rapidly shifting markets.[17]

13. Weitzman (1984).
14. Blair (1995).
15. See Levine and Tyson (1990); Levine and Parkin (1994); and Levine (1995).
16. Gordon (1999).
17. Gordon (1995).

Brief History of the Policy Debate

The idea that policy levers ought to be used to encourage employee ownership of enterprise has surfaced and resurfaced from time to time over the last century. In the late 1880s, for example, Leland Stanford, the founder of Stanford University, and a U.S. senator at the time, adopted the Populist idea that employee ownership of enterprise (he had in mind worker cooperatives) would help avert what he saw as an escalating crisis between corporations and workers. The idea of worker-owned industry became a "recurring theme of his public endeavors."[18] Stanford introduced a number of bills in Congress to promote worker cooperatives, though none was ever passed. Stanford apparently had also intended that his vision of worker cooperatives would somehow be incorporated as one of the founding purposes of Stanford University.[19]

In the 1920s, employee ownership became a popular idea among corporate leaders who were searching for a form of shared capitalism to increase employee commitment and loyalty to the capitalist system. The Revenue Act of 1921 gave stock bonus plans and profit-sharing plans tax-favored status. Only later was the same status granted to pension plans. Employee ownership was also the subject of several serious academic studies during this period.[20] And in 1929, a leading thinker about public policy, Robert S. Brookings (founder of the Brookings Institution) published a book in which he argued that all corporations that operate across state lines should be required to reincorporate under a federal incorporation statute that would require corporations to be capitalized with something like preferred stock, with a cumulative but capped dividend. "All additional profit," he said, should be distributed "in the form of labor shares of stock" allocated among management and labor in the ratio of their individual contribution, probably in proportion to their wage or salary compensation. Brookings also advocated putting labor representatives on boards of directors.[21]

Interest in employee ownership of corporations died out during the Great Depression and the subsequent rapid buildup of industrial capacity during World War II. In the immediate postwar era, union opposition to employee ownership also helped to keep discussions of employee ownership

18. See Altenberg (1990).
19. Altenberg (1990).
20. See Foerster and Dietel (1926); National Industrial Conference Board (1928); Davis (1933).
21. See Brookings (1929, p. 109). We thank David Ellerman for calling our attention to this book and to the Altenberg article on Leland Stanford.

out of mainstream policy circles. By the 1960s, however, interest in the subject surfaced again as investment banker Louis Kelso developed the idea that major corporations could be taken private in highly leveraged transactions financed largely through employee stock ownership plans.[22] Kelso argued that employee ownership of corporations would provide social benefits by harmonizing the interests of employees, investors, and managers, and he persuaded Senators Russell Long and Ted Kennedy to sponsor legislation in the late 1970s and early 1980s that provided special tax benefits for firms that form ESOPs.[23] Those tax benefits have been adjusted several times and were increased most recently by the Tax Reform Act of 1986.[24]

Meanwhile, academic and policy interest in employee ownership (particularly cooperative forms) was piqued by the so-called Yugoslav experiment in worker-managed enterprise, then died down somewhat as the Yugoslavia experience turned sour in the late 1970s and early 1980s.[25] Interest picked up again in the early 1990s after the Berlin Wall came down, the Soviet Union broke up, and policy analysts scrambled to provide advice to Eastern Europe and former Soviet countries about privatizing their industries.[26]

In the 1990s, interest in employee ownership, in the form of incentive compensation systems that utilize stock options, restricted stock, and other equity, or equity-linked securities, has expanded rapidly, and firms in many sectors of the economy have adopted the idea that employees should participate in the risks and rewards of the enterprises for which they work. Extensive use of employee ownership in the steel and airline industries throughout the 1980s and early 1990s has heralded a shift in the attitudes toward employee ownership by organized labor, which now has considerable experience with this corporate form.[27] And the traditional left is also

---

22. See, for example, Kelso and Adler (1958) and Kelso (1968).

23. ESOPs were recognized as a special category of employee benefit plan by the Employee Retirement Income Security Act of 1974 from the very beginning of the law. Blasi (1988, pp. 1–29, 187–93) provides a detailed history of congressional speeches, hearings, debates, initiatives, laws, and federal publications on employee ownership during its formative policy period from 1973 to 1988. Senator Russell Long's major statement on the subject was contained in a speech he gave on the Senate floor on May 12, 1981. See Long (1981). ESOPs were made more attractive by adjustments that increased the limit on deductible contributions to ESOP trusts in the Economic Recovery Tax Act of that year, and the Deficit Reduction Act of 1984 added incentives.

24. See Conte and Svejnar (1990) for an analysis and brief history of the tax benefits provided for ESOPs.

25. Serious observers of employee ownership discount the Yugoslav experiment because it did not allow for individual share ownership. Rather, it was more like "decentralized socialism."

26. See, for example, Boycko, Shleifer, and Vishny (1995); Blasi, Kroumova, and Kruse (1997).

27. See NCEO (1989); Bell and Kruse (1995).

beginning to explore the potential benefits of employee ownership as a mechanism for better sharing and distributing the wealth that has been generated by the corporate sector in this decade.[28]

Empirical Background

Despite recurring intellectual interest in the idea of employee ownership, and even some attempts to stimulate it with tax preferences, as recently as the early 1980s, worker cooperatives existed in only a few tiny sectors of the U.S. economy (such as the plywood industry in the upper northwest part of the country and taxicab and refuse collection cooperatives in several cities);[29] employee ownership through ESOPs was mostly limited to small, closely held companies; and employee ownership in the stock of publicly traded companies was minuscule. (As we report in detail below, our exhaustive search turned up only twenty-seven publicly traded firms that, as of 1983, had approximately 20 percent of their shares or more held by or for employees.)

But there is considerable evidence that the ownership of company shares by employees, either directly or through employee benefit plans, may have been growing quite rapidly in the past fifteen years. Since the early 1980s, unions have negotiated new contracts with a significant number of firms in the steel, airline, meatpacking, and trucking industries that gave unionized employees sizable equity stakes in exchange for wage and benefit concessions. Plants have been kept open by selling them to firms owned by employees through ESOPs. And in the late 1980s, several court decisions made it clear that properly designed ESOPs could serve as a device for protecting a firm from a hostile takeover.[30] Encouraged by these rulings, a number of large publicly traded companies, including Polaroid, Phillips Petroleum, Chevron, and Procter and Gamble and numerous others, set up ESOPs and put at least 15 percent of the companies' shares into them. By the end of the decade, Blasi and Kruse were able to identify more than 1,000 publicly traded companies with at least 4 percent of shares owned by employees, and at least 148 of these had employee stakes amounting to 18.5 percent or more.[31]

28. The Ford Foundation, for example, sponsored an academic conference in the spring of 1998 on "Shared Capitalism." See also Gates (1998).

29. Partnerships, which are a form of worker ownership, have always been common in professional services, however.

30. See *Shamrock Holdings Inc.* v. *Polaroid Corp.*, 709 F. Supp. 1131, 1989, U.S. Dist. and *NCR Corp.* v. *American Telephone & Telegraph Co.*, 761 Fs. Supp. 475, 1991, U.S. Dist.

31. Blasi and Kruse (1991).

In the early 1990s, about half of the growth of stock ownership by employees came about through 401(k) ESOPs, in which many employees voluntarily make contributions, rather than through regular ESOPs, in which only the employer makes the contributions.[32] And evidence suggests that employee ownership and other equity-based compensation systems (especially broad-based employee stock option plans) are being used widely in the economy, especially in the rapidly growing high-tech sector.[33]

Research Questions and Strategy

Our contribution to the discussion about possible merits and problems with employee share ownership is intended to be purely empirical and descriptive. We do not formally test any specific hypotheses, but we hope to shed light on the question of whether employee ownership in publicly traded firms is a stable arrangement, or whether it tends to revert over time to a standard, widely traded form without substantial employee share ownership. Is it a form that gives firms "staying power" in some sense? Or is it a transition form, appropriate for start-up companies, for example, but not for mature companies, or a form that serves primarily to facilitate rebargaining for firms in declining industries that must retrench and adjust to new economic circumstances?

Our research strategy is to examine the track record of firms that, it appears to us, may have been in the vanguard of a growing movement, dating from the late 1970s and early 1980s, toward making employees into shareholders. In particular, we attempted to find every publicly traded company that by 1983 had a substantial amount (at least 20 percent or more) of employee share ownership. We chose 1983 as the starting date for several reasons. First, it was as early as we could go with several of our major data sources. Second, it predates the major developments in public company employee ownership of the late 1980s, when companies began putting ESOPs into place as takeover defenses. It also predates most of the well-publicized employee buyouts and restructurings of unionized companies (such as Weirton Steel and Eastern Airlines). In this way, we were able to focus on that cohort of publicly traded firms that had established sub-

32. See Blasi and Kruse (1997).
33. See, for example, Bell and Kruse (1995); Foundation for Enterprise Development (1997, 1998); National Center for Employee Ownership (1998).

stantial employee ownership early on and were able to track their record over as long a period as possible.

To identify our employee-ownership (E-O) firms, we undertook an exhaustive search, using every data source that we thought might be relevant to the task, to identify every publicly traded firm tracked by Compustat that had approximately 20 percent or more of its stock in employee hands, either directly or through employee benefit plans. Then we constructed a control sample of firms matched by size and industry and assembled case files on all firms in both the E-O group and the control sample in order to trace out the track record of each firm. We determined whether and how long each firm "survived" as an independent, publicly traded company and whether it continued to be substantially employee owned, or, if it was a control firm, whether it became substantially employee owned.[34] We compared the performance of the E-O firms, the control firms, and the whole population of non-E-O firms tracked by Compustat, in terms of productivity, employment stability, and financial performance, and we asked how the firms weathered various crises. We used duration-model analysis to test whether the fact that a firm has a substantial block of shares in the hands of employees is associated with a greater or a reduced "survival" rate. And we compared the stock market performance of E-O firms to non-E-O firms by analyzing the performance over our sample period of a hypothetical portfolio of E-O firms, compared with a comparably constructed portfolio of control firms.

Data Sources

There is no single, publicly available database on employee ownership in publicly traded firms that is updated annually and accessible to researchers or investors, and which provides systematic, accurate, consistent, and reliable information.[35] So one of the hardest parts of this project was the

34. We use the term "survival" to refer only to whether the firm continued to exist as a separate publicly traded corporate entity with substantial employee ownership. We recognize that the fact that a firm fails to "survive" by this definition does not necessarily mean that its economic assets were destroyed. It is an interesting question whether one should view the "firm" itself as having survived if it is acquired or changes form, and the answer would probably depend heavily on how one defines a "firm" and for what purpose one is asking the question. We do not attempt to address these questions in this chapter.

35. *The New Owners* database developed by Blasi and Kruse (1991) provided a systematic listing of employee ownership in publicly traded firms for the single year 1991.

seemingly simple task of identifying the universe of publicly traded, E-O firms in 1983 that form the focal point of our research. To do this, we began with the firms tracked by Compustat, treating them as the universe of publicly traded firms.[36] We then used five different sources of data on employee ownership, matching each source to Compustat. These data sources were the following:

—Form 5500 filings for 1983. Every firm, or operating unit of a larger firm, that has an ERISA-regulated employee benefit plan or plans is required to file an annual report with the Department of Labor providing information about the plans and about the resources the firm has set aside to meet obligations under the plans. One of the questions each filing entity must answer asks for the value of "party-in-interest" assets in the plan.[37] The totals are reported on a plan-by-plan basis and must be aggregated across plans to get a corporate total. They are also reported in terms of their dollar value, not in terms of number of shares, and are not broken out by type of security.

To use these data, then, we made the gross assumption that all of the employer assets in the plan were common stock and that they were valued at the price at which the stock was trading at year-end 1983. These data were matched to Compustat by the Committee on Uniform Security Identification Procedures (CUSIP) number and by firm name (requiring visual inspection of thousands of records). The measure of total employer securities in employee plans for each firm that could be matched to Compustat was then weighted by the market value of equity outstanding for that firm in 1983 to give us an estimate of the percent of total equity held by or for employees.

—Large-Block Shareholder Data for 1983. The Securities and Exchange Commission requires individual and institutional shareholders that hold 5 percent or more of any class of security in a publicly traded firm to make regular filings reporting their holdings and their intentions with respect to the firm. This should include ESOPs and institutions that

36. Treating Compustat as the universe is a common practice in firm-level empirical research. While Compustat's coverage is broad (around 6,000 firms in 1983), there are numerous firms that, while technically publicly traded, do not have much investor following and hence are not tracked by Compustat. These tend to be very small firms that are not big players in their markets.

37. After 1988, the form asked specifically about employer securities, rather than more broadly about "party-in-interest" assets. Kruse has examined the data closely for a large sample of companies for 1988 and beyond and has concluded that the vast majority of the "party-in-interest" assets reported before 1988 were very likely employer common or preferred stocks.

may be acting as the trustee or holding agent for assets in an employee benefit plan.[38] CDA Spectrum (a private data company) has data collected from these filings on computer tapes going back to 1983. With these tapes, we identified all Compustat firms for which we had a record of a large-block shareholder of any type for 1983 and inspected the list of such investors visually to find blockholders with "ESOP," or employee stock ownership trust ("ESOT,") or "profit-sharing," or some other similar word or phrase in their names to indicate that they were blocks held in an employee benefit plan of some sort.

—Blasi and Kruse databases. This includes the Employee Ownership 1000 list for 1991 (from *The New Owners*), which provided some indication of potential candidates. It also included a series of chronological company profiles on employee ownership generated from this database, which were taken from twenty public sources, including full-text searches of the Dow Jones News Service and the *Wall Street Journal* from 1980 forward and company SEC filings for 1986. This also included a 1981 list developed by the Corporate Data Exchange of Fortune 500 firms in which employee benefit plans of some sort were the largest shareholder in 1981.[39]

—The National Center for Employee Ownership keeps a running list of firms that it claims are substantially employee owned, based on announcements about ESOP formations, ESOP recapitalizations, and other similar events, as well as public announcements or press accounts that happen to reveal employee-ownership stakes in public companies.[40]

—Lexis-Nexis searches. Finally, we did a Lexis-Nexis search for articles that mentioned employee ownership and that were published before about 1985.

Cross-Checking and Confirmation

We initially took an inclusive approach to using the above five data sources and developed a list of about fifty-five to sixty firms, which we had some

38. Blasi and Kruse (1991) found that in 1991, 80 percent of public companies with significant employee ownership through benefit plans did not disclose it to the SEC through these reports. It is unclear why this information about major inside stock holdings is so lacking in transparency.

39. See also Blasi (1988, pp. 264–66).

40. Each record in this list includes an estimate of the percent owned by or for employees, and two dates, the date the plan was started, and the date the information was entered into the database (most of which were 1991 or later), but does not specify to which date the percentage estimate applies. We looked at records for which the percent owned was 20 percent or greater, and the plan start date was 1983 or before.

reason to believe might have met our criteria in 1983. That is, that they were a U.S.-based firm, publicly traded in 1983, and substantially (at least 20 percent) employee owned.[41] We then built extensive case files on each firm, including large-block shareholder data and Form 5500 data for the years 1983–93,[42] basic measures of performance (for example, revenues, profits, assets, employees, market value of equity, and so on) from Compustat, and news clippings from Lexis-Nexis searches on these firms since 1983. We tried to find out about mergers, acquisitions, divestitures, leveraged buyouts, plant closings and downsizing activities, joint ventures, labor strife, or lawsuits the firms might have been involved in, and we looked for information about the role employee ownership may have played, if any, in these events, as well as information about the circumstances under which the firm came to be substantially employee owned. We used these case files to write up brief (up to three pages) summaries of the history of each company since 1983 and to fill out a questionnaire we devised about the history of each company. This questionnaire served as a mechanism for transforming essentially qualitative data in the company case files into quantitative data that could be used in statistical analysis.

As we began reviewing the case files, it became clear that a substantial number of firms on our preliminary list failed to meet our criteria. Some were no longer publicly traded in 1983, and some had not yet gone public. Some were foreign owned, and in some cases we found evidence that the levels of employee ownership were lower than we had at first estimated. In the end, we decided that only twenty-seven firms actually met our employee-ownership criteria. These are listed in table 7-1, together with our best estimate of percentage of employee ownership for 1983, our best information about the year the plan was put in place, and the firm's industry, as indicated by the two-digit SIC code assigned to it by Compustat.[43]

41. In the end, there seemed to be enough margin of error in our estimates of the amount of employee ownership for each firm that, if a firm survived all of our checking and cross-checking, and our best point estimate of employee ownership in 1983 exceeded 17.5 percent, we kept it.
42. By coincidence, Kruse had previously acquired all the Form 5500 data for the years 1983–93 for a separate project, and Blair had acquired all the CDA Spectrum large-block shareholder data for the same years for yet another project.
43. We inspected the plan origination documents in the Department of Labor files for each E-O firm to find the "plan origin" dates. In situations in which the origin date we found referred to a predecessor plan, we utilized the date of the predecessor plan if it had also been a profit-sharing or employee equity-sharing plan in which the assets were invested in employer securities. We suspect that many of the plans whose public records provided a "plan origin" date started out with a much lower percentage of employer stock in the plan, and we do not know when the plans reached our 20 percent threshold level.

We next built a matched control sample. Our goal was to include two contol firms for each E-O firm—the next larger firm (by employment) in the same two-digit SIC industry and the next smaller one. Two of our E-O firms (Sears and U.S. Steel), however, were the largest in their industry in 1983, and so they were assigned only one matching firm. For a variety of other reasons we had trouble finding two matching firms for several other firms too. So our control sample consists of forty-five firms. These are listed in table 7-1, part B, together with each firm's industry and the E-O firm to which each is matched.[44]

Who Were These "Vanguard" Companies?

—Industry distribution. Although we thought we might find that the early vanguard of employee ownership firms were concentrated in a few industries, one of the biggest surprises to us about the list of firms in table 7-1 was the prominence of defense contractors. In a group of only twenty-seven E-O firms, five were major defense contractors: Grumman, McDonnell Douglas, Northrop, Rockwell International, and Textron.[45] At the bottom of table 7-2, where we report the distribution across industries of our E-O firms, control firms, and the broad Compustat population, we find a disproportionately large share of E-O firms in

44. The SIC code that Compustat assigns to firms is based on the industry that accounts for the largest share of the firm's revenues in the most recent year for which Compustat has data. One of the problems we ran into in trying to identify matching firms for each E-O firm is that some firms change industries over time, but Compustat carries only the most recent SIC code. Hence we found cases in which the firm we had identified as a potential match based on a later SIC code was not actually in the same industry as the E-O firm to which it was being matched, at least not in 1983.

45. The only explanation for this phenomenon that we were able to come up with is that defense contractors can afford to provide very generous pension benefits to their employees because contributions to employee benefit plans are reimbursed under cost-plus contracts. If those contributions are made in newly issued stock, rather than in cash, the company can be reimbursed for the value of the stock without actually incurring a cash expense. So many large defense contractors are substantially employee owned that we had trouble finding enough matching non-E-O firms. In the data we used for this project, we have only six "matching" firms in total for our five defense contractor E-O firms. These are Dana Corporation, Chrysler, Freuhauf, Lockheed, Martin-Marietta, and United Technologies. Although all of these firms were classified as being in SIC 3700 (transportation equipment), three were not really defense contractors. Dana was an auto parts firm, and Freuhauf was a farm equipment firm. Chrysler, of course, was an auto manufacturer, and, moreover, it almost made it onto our list of E-O firms on the basis of the ESOP created in the Chrysler bailout of 1979. By 1983, however, the employee holdings in Chrysler had been substantially diluted. Of the three actual defense contractors in our control group, Lockheed set up an ESOP in 1990, and from 1990 had a large enough share of stock in the ESOP to meet that part of our criteria for being employee owned. We treat Lockheed as a "switcher" in one of our tests below.

Table 7-1. *Part A: Employee-Ownership Firms*

Company name in 1983	Company name as of 1997	E-O in 1983 (percent)	Plan origins (earliest evidence of thrift plan, profit sharing or ESOP)	Industry
American Recreation Centers Inc.		21.25	1970	Amusement and recreation services
Anthony Industries Inc.	K2 Inc.	24.08	1979	Miscellaneous manufacturing industries
Central Steel & Wire Co.		19.56	1950	Wholesale trade-durable goods
Cooper Tire & Rubber Co.		18.09	1982	Rubber and miscellaneous plastic products
Delchamps Inc.		25.00	1976	Food stores
Diversified Energies Inc.		24.22	1970	Electric, gas, and sanitary services
ELCO Industries Inc.		47.80	1983	Fabricated metal products, except machinery and transportation equipment
Grumman Corp.		31.49	1965	Transportation equipment
Inter-Regional Financial Group Inc.		21.81	1960	Security and commodity brokers, dealers, exchanges, and services
Lowe's Companies Inc.		26.18	1957	Building materials, hardware, garden supply, and mobile home dealers
McDonnell Douglas Corp.		24.40	1983	Transportation equipment

Company		Value	Year	Industry
Northrop Corp.		21.84	1952	Transportation equipment
Piper Jaffray Cos. Inc.		35.16	—	Security and commodity brokers, dealers, exchanges, and services
RLI Corp.		32.42	1972	Insurance carriers
Rockwell International		25.80	1966	Transportation equipment
Ruddick Corp.		56.68	1975	Food stores
Sears Roebuck & Co.		27.03	1916	General merchandise stores
Stone & Webster Inc.		55.74	1976	Engineering, accounting, research, management, and related services
Swank Inc..		30.06	1980	Leather and leather products
Technology for Communications International Inc.	TCI International	23.00	1975	Electronic and other electrical equipment and components, except computer equipment
Textron Inc.		21.32	1960	Transportation equipment
Thrifty Corporation		22.14	1951	Miscellaneous retail
Tony Lama		19.09	—	Leather and leather products
U.S. Sugar Corp.		43.47	1983	Agricultural production crops
U.S. Steel Corp.	USX Corp-Consolidated	23.26	1974	Primary metals industries
Western Airlines		32.00	1983	Transportation by air
Westvaco Corp.		17.75	1976	Paper and allied products

Table 7-1. Part B: Control Sample

Company name in 1983	Company name as of 1997	Matched to	Industry
Advest		Piper Jaffray Cos. Inc.	Security and commodity brokers, dealers, exchanges, and services
AGS Computers Inc.		Central Steel & Wire Co.	Wholesale trade-durable goods
Allied Supermarkets		Delchamps Inc.	Food stores
Baldwin & Lyons—CL B		RLI Corp.	Insurance carriers
Barry (R G)		Swank Inc.	Leather and leather products
Bethlehem Steel		U.S. Steel Corp.	Primary metals
Brunos Inc.		Delchamps Inc.	Food stores
Carlisle Corp.	Carlisle Cos. Inc.	Cooper Tire & Rubber Co.	Rubber and miscellaneous plastic products
Central Maine Power Co.		Diversified Energies Inc.	Electric, gas, and sanitary services
Chrysler Corp.		Rockwell International	Transportation equipment
Craddock-Terry Shoe Corp.		Swank Inc.	Leather and leather products
Cross (A.T.) & Co.		Anthony Industries Inc.	Miscellaneous manufacturing
Dana Corp.		Northrop Corp./Grumman Corp.	Transportation equipment
Castle & Cook Inc.	Dole Food Co. Inc.	U.S. Sugar Corp.	Agricultural production crops
Dynaelectron Corp.	Dyncorp Inc.	Stone & Webster Inc.	Engineering, accounting, research, management, and related services
EG&G Inc.		Stone & Webster Inc.	Engineering, accounting, research, management, and related services
First Boston		Piper Jaffray Cos. Inc.	Security and commodity brokers, dealers, exchanges, and services
Fort Howard Corp.	Fort James Corp.	Westvaco Corp.	Paper and allied products
Funtime Inc.		American Recreation Centers Inc.	Amusement and recreation services
General Defense		Elco Industries Inc.	Fabricated metal products, except machinery and transportation equipment
Hannaford Brothers Co.		Ruddick Corp.	Food stores

Company	Category
Hechinger Co.—CL A	Building materials, hardware, garden supply, and mobile home dealers
Integrated Resources	Interra Corp.	Security and commodity brokers, dealers, exchanges, and services
Freuhauf Corp.	K-H Corp.	Transportation equipment
K-Mart Corp.	Sears Roebuck & Co.	General merchandise stores
Laclede Gas Co.	Diversified Energies Inc.	Electric, gas, and sanitary services
Lockheed Corp.	Lockheed Martin Corp. McDonnell Douglas Corp.	Transportation equipment
Los Alamitos Race Course	American Recreation Centers Inc.	Amusement and recreation services
Martin Marietta Corp.	Textron Corp.	Transportation equipment
Mueller (Paul) Co.	Elco Industries Inc.	Fabricated metal products, except machinery and transportation equipment
Munford Inc.	Ruddick Corp.	Food stores
Payless Cashways—CL A	Lowe's Companies Inc.	Building materials, hardware, garden supply, and mobile home dealers
Pioneer Hi-Bred Intl.	U.S. Sugar Corp.	Agricultural production crops
Quantronix Corp.	Technology for Communications Intl. Inc.	Electronic and other electrical equipment and components, except computer equipment
R B & W Corp.	Central Steel & Wire Co.	Wholesale trade-durable goods
Rite Aid Corp.	Thrifty Corp.	Miscellaneous retail
Rubbermaid	Cooper Tire & Rubber Co.	Rubber and miscellaneous plastic products
Tesdata Systems Corp.	Technology for Communications Intl. Inc.	Electronic and other electrical equipment and components, except computer equipment
Tiger International	Western Airlines	Transportation by air
Tonka	Anthony Industries Inc.	Miscellaneous manufacturing
USAIRGroup Inc.	U.S. Air Inc. Western Airlines	Transportation by air
U.S. Healthcare	RLI Corp.	Insurance carriers
United Technologies	Rockwell International	Transportation equipment
Weyenberg Shoe Co.	Weyco Group Inc. Tony Lama	Leather and leather products
Zale Corp.	Thrifty Corp.	Miscellaneous retail

Table 7-2. *Descriptive Statistics*

Item[a]	Employee ownership firms		Matched comparison firms[b]		All non-employee-owned firms	
Number	27	...	44	...	5,290	...
Employment						
Mean (s.d.)	34,731	(87,854)	21,632	(48,256)	5,814	(21,993)
Median	6,175		3,700		613	
Mean ln(empl.) (s.d.)	8.85	(1.85)	8.51	(1.75)	6.4	(2.34)
Size category (percent)						
1–99	0	(0.0)	0	(0.0)	1,190	(22.5)
100–499	2	(7.4)	4	(8.9)	1,253	(23.7)
500–999	1	(3.7)	2	(4.4)	588	(11.1)
1,000–1,999	3	(11.1)	7	(15.6)	592	(11.2)
2,000–4,999	7	(25.9)	11	(24.4)	712	(13.5)
5,000–9,999	3	(11.1)	5	(11.1)	377	(7.1)
10,000–19,999	4	(14.8)	6	(13.3)	237	(4.5)
20,000–49,999	3	(11.1)	5	(11.1)	198	(3.7)
50,000–99,999	2	(7.4)	3	(6.7)	103	(1.9)
100,000+	2	(7.4)	2	(4.4)	40	(0.8)
		(100.0)		(100.0)		(100.0)
Sales (millions)						
Mean (s.d.)	3,231	(7,486)	1,881	(3,969)	677	(3,292)
Median	536		505		52	
Mean ln(sales) (s.d.)	6.43	(1.91)	6.06	(1.83)	3.9	(2.55)
Capital per employee (thousands)						
Mean (s.d.)	47.9	(62.2)	53.1	(123.4)	160.8	(657.2)
Median	25.1		19.3		25.3	
Mean ln(cap./ee.) (s.d.)	3.37	(0.94)	3.13	(1.12)	3.56	(1.55)
Have pension	74.1%		100.0%		54.9%	
Industry (percent)						
Agriculture	1	(3.7)	2	(4.4)	27	(0.5)
Mining, construction	0	(0.0)	0	(0.0)	507	(9.6)
Manufacturing	13	(48.1)	19	(42.2)	2,428	(45.9)
Chemicals	0	(0.0)	0	(0.0)	231	(4.4)
Electric equipment	1	(3.7)	2	(4.4)	377	(7.1)
Transportation equipment	5	(18.5)	6	(13.3)	115	(2.2)
Other manufacturing	7	(25.9)	11	(24.4)	1,705	(32.2)
				(0.0)		
Transportation	1	(3.7)	2	(4.4)	121	(2.3)
Communications, utilities	1	(3.7)	2	(4.4)	350	(6.6)
Trade	6	(22.2)	11	(24.4)	631	(11.9)
Finance	3	(11.1)	5	(11.1)	614	(11.6)
Services	2	(7.4)	4	(8.9)	576	(10.9)
		(100.0)		(100.0)		(100.0)

a. Sample contains all public firms reporting stock price in 1983. Data are for 1983.

b. Matched comparison firms comprise, for each employee-ownership firm, the next largest and next smallest firm (by employment) with pension expenses, in the same two-digit industry.

SIC 37 (transportation equipment—which is defined in a way that includes all five of the defense contractors). Trade is also disproportionately represented among our E-O firms. Meanwhile, we found no E-O firms in mining and construction, nor in chemicals. But far from being highly concentrated in a few "special case" indusries, employee ownership otherwise appears to have been distributed pretty broadly across all sectors.

—Other descriptive statistics. Table 7-2 also suggests that the E-O firms were larger (in terms of employment and sales) than the universe of non-E-O firms. This is probably because almost half the firms tracked by Compustat are small firms (under 500 employees), while only two of our E-O firms were that small. The fact that early E-O firms were large firms contradicts the conventional wisdom that it was mostly small firms that adopted ESOPs during the early years after the first ESOP tax incentives were put into place. One possible explanation for this finding is that many of the early ESOP adopters were closely held firms, rather than publicly traded firms, and therefore they do not show up in our universe of publicly traded firms.

Our E-O firms may also be somewhat less capital intensive than the average Compustat firm.[46] This may simply be a consequence of the different distribution across industries (that is, no mining and construction firms and no chemical producers) among our E-O firms. In other words, E-O firms tend to show up in somewhat less capital-intensive industries, but when matched by size and industry, E-O firms are not significantly less capital intensive than their matched control firms. In fact, neither the size differences we observe, nor the differences in capital intensity, are statistically significant.

—How did they get to be substantially employee owned? Another feature of our E-O firms that contradicts conventional wisdom is that they do not appear to be dominated by firms that were in financial trouble and refinanced with ESOPs as part of a deal with unions to reduce direct labor costs. Although our case file information on the question of how our E-O firms came to have a substantial amount of employee ownership is sketchy, our best reading of the available information is that some form of employee-ownership plan was in place in 1980 or earlier for at least twenty of our twenty-seven E-O firms. We found evidence that one E-O firm

46. Although Bloom (1986) found that the group of employee ownership firms he studied had high levels of capital intensity, his work focused on firms with tax credit ESOPs and employee payroll stock ownership plan (PAYSOPs). Firms for which these forms were beneficial were, by definition, firms that had high levels of capital expenditures.

(Western Airlines) had been recapitalized in 1983 with an ESOP to avoid bankruptcy, that another (Thrifty Corp.) had recently been restructured with an ESOP, perhaps to head off a hostile takeover, and a third (U.S. Sugar) had recently been refinanced with an ESOP to enable a family to cash out its shares.[47] In addition, records at the Department of Labor indicate that Cooper Tire, Elco Industries, and McDonnell Douglas may have put their employee stock ownership plans in place as recently as 1982 or 1983, although we found no evidence of a precipitating event in these cases. And we were unable to find out anything about the origins of employee ownership at Piper Jaffray. With these exceptions, however, employee ownership appeared to be a long-standing feature of the employment relationship and culture.[48] Employee ownership dates back to 1916 at Sears Roebuck, for example, to 1950 at Central Steel and Wire, to 1952 at Northrop, to 1957 at Lowe's, and to 1965 at Grumman.

Comparing Track Records

The next part of our analysis involved comparing the track records over time of our E-O firms with our control sample and with all non-E-O firms. We compared "survival" rates (although even this simple question is surprisingly difficult to answer), and various measures of performance.

"Survival"

One of the central and surprisingly difficult questions we tried to answer with our data is whether firms with substantial employee ownership have a different track record of "survival" than firms without this structure. Since the project started as an attempt to develop evidence on the question of whether employee ownership is a "stable" organizational form, we defined "survival" to mean simply that the firm continued to exist as an independent, publicly traded company. Firms that failed to "survive," by this definition, dropped out for one of three reasons: they were liquidated or under-

47. Although records at the Department of Labor indicate Thrifty Corp. had some form of profit-sharing trust, funded with employer securities, as early as 1951.

48. Blasi and Kruse (1991) found, even in 1991 after a number of highly publicized transactions in which employee ownership was traded for wage and benefit concessions, or in which ESOPs were put in place to ward off hostile takeovers, that a sizable majority of firms in the Employee Ownership 1000 made it onto that list as a result of routine corporate finance transactions.

went restructuring via a bankruptcy settlement; they were acquired by another firm; or they were taken private in a management buyout or leveraged buyout. Although we recognize that many of the economically relevant assets of firms that are acquired or taken private (and maybe even those that are liquidated) do not just disappear, nonetheless, for our purposes, acquisition and buyout transactions transform an enterprise sufficiently that we do not regard a firm that is liquidated, acquired, or taken private as having survived. We found a number of firms that were taken private and that subsequently went into bankruptcy, or were acquired, or even went public again. But for our purposes, we treated the going private transaction as the terminal event for that firm, at least for that firm in that particular organizational configuration. Similarly, we found examples of firms that were acquired, then sold off again, then taken private, but we treated the initial acquisition as the terminal event for our purposes.

For our E-O firms and our control sample firms, we found definitive information in the media accounts about the disposition of the firms over time. For all the other non-E-O firms in the broad Compustat database, we defined a firm as ceasing to exist (again, for our purposes) if Compustat ceased carrying data on stock price and number of employees for that firm. And we relied on the coding in Compustat for why that firm disappeared.

We also looked at whether the E-O firms continued to have substantial employee ownership and whether non-E-O firms switched to "E-O" status (by, for example, forming an ESOP that held at least 20 percent of the outstanding stock).

Table 7-3 reports summary data on the disposition of the E-O firms and non-E-O firms over time. By the simpleminded measure we used, the E-O firms had a higher "survival" rate. In fact, if the end of our sample period had been 1996 rather than 1997, the survival rate for E-O firms would have been markedly higher, at 74.1 percent, not only relative to the Compustat population (only 37.8 percent of which survived through 1996), but relative to the matched comparison firms (only 53.3 percent of which survived through 1996). But four of our E-O firms were acquired between January 1, 1997, and December 31, 1997, while only one more control firm was acquired during that year, reducing the gap at the end of our sample period. These findings partly reflect the fact that the defense contracting sector, which, as we noted above, is disproportionately represented in our list of E-O firms, was disproportionately engaged in consolidation in the mid-1990s. (Grumman was acquired in 1994, and both Northrop and McDonnell Douglas were acquired in 1997.)

Table 7-3. *Disposition of Public Companies after 1983*

Item[a]	Employee-ownership firms		Matched comparison firms[b]		All non-employee-owned firms[c]	
	Number	Percent	Number	Percent	Number	Percent
Total	27	100.0	45	100.0	5,290	100.0
Survived through 1997[c]	16	59.3	23	51.1	1,998	37.8
Disappeared by 1997[c]	11	40.7	22	48.9	3,292	62.2
Disappeared owing to						
Merger or acquisition	10	37.0	11	25.0	1,414	26.7
Bankruptcy	0	0.0	1	2.3	224	4.2
Liquidation	0	0.0	0	0.0	105	2.0
Privatization	1	3.7	10	22.7	188	3.6
Other reason	0	0.0	0	0.0	783	14.8
n.a.	0	0.0	0	0.0	578	10.9
Firm survived until						
1984	27	100.0	44	97.8	5,289	100.0
1985	27	100.0	44	97.8	4,792	90.6
1986	26	96.3	41	91.1	4,291	81.1
1987	24	88.9	38	84.4	3,865	73.1
1988	24	88.9	32	71.1	3,489	66.0
1989	24	88.9	30	66.7	3,100	58.6
1990	22	81.5	29	64.4	2,844	53.8
1991	22	81.5	28	62.2	2,628	49.7
1992	22	81.5	27	60.0	2,474	46.8
1993	22	81.5	27	60.0	2,354	44.5
1994	21	77.8	27	60.0	2,220	42.0
1995	21	77.8	25	55.6	2,104	39.8
1996	20	74.1	24	53.3	1,998	37.8
1997	16	59.3	23	51.1	n.a.	n.a.

a. Sample includes all public firms reporting one or more employees in 1983.

b. Matched comparison firms comprise, for each employee-ownership firm, the next largest and next smallest firm (by employment) with pension expenses in the same two-digit industry.

c. For non-E-O and noncontrol firms in the last two columns, data only available until 1996.

Perhaps more striking than the fact that the E-O firms as a group had a higher survival rate is the fact that only one of our E-O firms disappeared via bankruptcy, liquidation, or private buyouts while eleven of our matched comparison firms, or 25 percent, disappeared for one of these reasons.[49] Less than 10 percent of the broad non-E-O Compustat population disappeared for one of these reasons, but another 25.7 percent disappeared for unexplained reasons.

Because we do not have reliable annual data on the employee-ownership status for all of our E-O firms and control firms, we cannot do the kind of detailed, year-by-year analysis of employee-ownership status that we can do for firm survival. But the best information we could get suggests that in three, or maybe four E-O firms, employee ownership declined to less than 15 percent during our sample period and stayed down. These were Cooper Tire & Rubber, where employee ownership fell below 15 percent by 1989; Diversified Energies, where we know that employee ownership was down to 11.8 percent by 1988, the year before the firm was taken over, but we do not know when the "switch" occurred; and U.S. Steel (USX after 1986), where employee ownership had declined to 13 percent by 1990, but again we do not know when the switch occurred. Westvaco Corp. may also have switched status, but the best data we have show employee ownership down and up and down again during our sample period but staying in the range between 11 percent and 20 percent. We also know that four of our E-O firms went through substantial financial restructurings during our sample period that, among other things, substantially *increased* the percentage of shares held by, or on behalf of, employees.

Among our non-E-O firms, at least two firms became substantially employee owned during our sample period. RB&W Corp. terminated a defined-benefit plan in 1988 and put some sort of employee-ownership plan in place that by 1993 had about 15 percent of the firm's shares in it; and Lockheed set up an ESOP with nearly 20 percent of the firm's shares in it as part of its efforts to defend itself against a hostile takeover attempt and proxy fight staged by raider Harold Simmons in 1990. At least two other control firms (Hechinger's and United Technologies) had ESOPs

---

49. Of the ten control firms that were taken private, one (Craddock-Terry) went into bankruptcy within two years; another (Munford) was subsequently merged into another firm, and then went into bankruptcy within two years; a third, Freuhauf Corporation, systematically liquidated itself to avoid bankruptcy, finally changing the name of the last piece of the company to K-H Corporation just before merging that last piece out of existence; and a fourth, Payless Cashways, went public again five years after the buyout, and then three years later went into bankruptcy.

near the end of our sample period, but we were unable to get an estimate of how much stock was in them. And two other control firms (Payless Cashways and Dyncorp—another defense contractor!) were taken private in transactions that were heavily ESOP financed.[50]

In tables 7-4 and 7-5, we report the results of two different statistical tests designed to provide more systematic evidence about the impact of employee ownership on "survival." Table 7-4 reports a Weibull model predicting how the annual "hazard" of a firm ceasing to exist (as an independent, publicly traded company) varies by whether the firm is an E-O firm or not. The results suggest that having substantial employee share ownership in 1983 resulted in a statistically significant reduction in the annual probability that a firm would disappear in each year between 1983 and 1997, given that the firm had survived up to that point. The statistical significance of this finding is weakened—but is nonetheless still significant at the p = .10 level—in the models that control for firm size and capital intensity at the beginning of the period.

Table 7-5 reports the result of a logit model predicting firm disappearance. Whereas the Weibull model is a "duration" model (predicting how long a firm will survive) with only one observation per Compustat firm, the logit model uses a separate observation for each firm-year. This means that in the logit model, we could take account of "switchers" (E-O firms that reduced their E-O status and non-E-O firms that became employee owned), at least to the extent that we had such information.[51] The results reported in table 7-5 again support the idea that having a block of shares in the hands of employees improved survival odds in the late 1980s and early 1990s, both before and after controlling for the company's size, industry, and performance measures in the prior year.[52]

Performance

In table 7-6, we report data comparing performance, measured in a number of different ways, of E-O firms to control firms and to the non-E-O universe of firms in Compustat. The data suggest that our E-O firms grew

50. In these latter two cases, the buyouts were treated as terminal events for the firms, rather than as "switching" events, since the firms were no longer publicly traded after the buyout transaction.

51. Because there were so few documented switchers, doing so does not make much difference in the results, but it does move them modestly in the direction of employee ownership improving survival odds.

52. The results are presented both with and without controlling for performance measures since those measures may be endogenous to firm disappearance.

Table 7-4. *Weibull Models Predicting Yearly Hazard of Disappearance*

Independent variables	Model (1) hazard ratio (Z)[a]		Model (2) hazard ratio (Z)[a]		Model (3) hazard ratio (Z)[a]	
Employee-ownership firm	0.399	(2.80)***	0.577	(1.81)*	0.566	(1.88)*
Matched control firm	0.571	(2.21)**	0.733	(1.44)	0.725	(1.49)
Ln(1983 employment)			0.835	(18.32)***		
Ln(1983 capital/ employees)			0.948	(3.74)***	0.957	(2.99)***
Have pension in 1983			0.978	(0.54)	0.957	(1.06)
Employment size categories						
1–99 (excluded)						
100–499					0.668	(7.75)***
500–999					0.527	(9.36)***
1,000–1,999					0.482	(10.19)***
2,000–4,999					0.422	(12.04)***
5,000–9,999					0.415	(9.68)***
10,000–19,999					0.372	(9.04)***
20,000–49,999					0.302	(9.52)***
50,000–99,999					0.402	(5.91)***
100,000+					0.09	(5.84)***
11 industry dummies	No		Yes		Yes	
N	5,250		4,874		4,874	
Shape parameter	1.03		1.082		1.077	
Log likelihood	−7,269***		−6,432***		−6,452***	

*p < .10.
**p < .05.
***p < .01.
a. Hazard ratio represents the effect of an independent variable on the firm's hazard of ceasing to exist in a given year, given that it has survived until that point. It represents (hazard given one-unit change in independent variable (hazard with no change). A value of 1.0 indicates that the variable is not associated with a difference in the firm's hazard of ceasing to exist in a given year. A value of 1.2 indicates a 20 percent higher chance, and a value of 0.8 indicates a 20 percent lower chance, of ceasing to exist as the variable changes by one unit (assuming other variables are at mean values). Firms surviving through 1995 are treated as censored.
Descriptive statistics in tables 7-2 and 7-3.

Table 7-5. *Logit Models Predicting Disappearance of Firm*
Dependent variable equals disappearance in current year

	Model (1)			Model (2)			Model (3)		
Independent variables	Coef-ficient	(Z)	Odds ratio	Coef-ficient	(Z)	Odds ratio	Coef-ficient	(Z)	Odds ratio
Employee-ownership firm	−1.183	(3.09)***	0.306	−0.695	(1.80)*	0.499	−0.69	(1.75)*	0.508
Matched control firm	−0.422	(1.87)*	0.656	−0.063	(0.27)	0.939	−0.041	(0.14)	0.967
Ln(employment), t-1				−0.227	(23.28)***	0.797	−0.223	(21.42)***	0.800
Ln(capital/employees), t-1				−0.078	(5.11)***	0.925	−0.081	(4.96)***	0.922
Productivity growth, t-2 to t-1							−0.027	(0.38)	0.974
Tobin's Q, t-1									
Return on assets, t-1									
Total shareholder return, t-1									
11 year dummies	Yes			Yes			Yes		
11 industry dummies	No			Yes			Yes		
N	45,045			36,184			34,859		
Dependent variable mean	0.073			0.081			0.077		
Log likelihood	−11,544***			−9,633***			−8,990***		

* p < .10.
** p < .05.
*** p < .01.

more slowly, in terms of employment, than non-E-O control firms over the sample period, but the difference is not statistically significant. The annual productivity growth rate and average Tobin's Q over time did not differ between E-O firms and non-E-O firms in a statistically significant way, with two exceptions. For nonsurviving firms, the difference between annual productivity growth rate for the E-O firms and their matched pairs was negative and statistically significant; and for surviving firms, the difference between Tobin's Q for the E-O firms and their matched pairs was negative and marginally statistically significant.

For return on assets and total shareholder return E-O firms outperformed the all non-E-O group to a degree that was statistically significant,

Model (4)			Model (5)			Model (6)		
Coefficient	(Z)	Odds ratio	Coefficient	(Z)	Odds ratio	Coefficient	(Z)	Odds ratio
-0.652	(1.69)*	0.521	-0.673	(1.74)*	0.510	-0.636	(1.65)*	0.530
0.035	(0.15)	1.036	-0.067	(0.28)	0.936	-0.006	(0.03)	0.994
-0.223	(22.12)***	0.800	-0.193	(18.69)***	0.824	-0.225	(22.20)***	0.799
-0.092	(5.72)***	0.912	-0.074	(4.66)***	0.929	-0.079	(5.01)***	0.924
-0.030	(3.82)***	0.970						
			-0.002	(4.66)***	0.998			
						-0.001	(2.62)***	0.999
Yes			Yes			Yes		
Yes			Yes			Yes		
35,470			35,505			34,961		
0.079			0.078			0.079		
-9,275***			-9,223***			-9,107***		

Note: Each observation is one firm-year. The employee-ownership coefficient is significantly different from the matched control coefficient in model 1 but not in models 2–6, at p < .10.

although this finding holds for survivors but not for nonsurvivors in the case of return on assets, and for nonsurvivors but not for survivors in the case of total shareholder return.

An alternative way of comparing the performance of E-O firms to non-E-O firms addresses the question of whether outside (nonemployee) shareholders are likely to be better or worse off by holding shares in a firm that has substantial employee share ownership. Figures 7-1 through 7-4 compare the performance over time of a hypothetical investment portfolio constructed in 1983 and invested in the E-O firms in our study, versus both a similar portfolio of control firms, and a measure of the performance of the market as a whole. Figures 7-1 and 7-2 compare what

Table 7-6. *Comparisons of Post-1983 Performance*

	All firms				Survivors				Non-survivors			
	E-O (1)	Control (2)	Paired diff.[a] (3)	All non-E-O (4)	E-O (5)	Control (6)	Paired diff.[a] (7)	All non-E-O (8)	E-O (9)	Control (10)	Paired diff.[a] (11)	All non-E-O (12)
Annual employment growth												
Mean	1.7%	3.3%	−0.2%	0.4%	1.7%	2.2%	−0.2%	2.6%	1.8%	4.4%	4.5%	−1.3%
(Standard error)	(1.0)	(1.6)	(1.1)	(0.2)	(1.6)	(1.2)	(0.6)	(0.2)	(1.0)	(3.1)	(6.1)	(0.3)
Median	0.8%	1.8%	−0.8%	0.8%	1.1%	1.6%	−0.5%	2.0%	0.8%	5.3%	2.3%	−0.1%
Variance in annual employment growth												
Mean	1.2%	3.2%	−2.0%***	5.5%***	1.1%	1.4%	−0.6%**	4.0%**	1.4%	5.4%	−8.4%**	7.2%*
(Standard error)	(0.3)	(0.5)	(0.7)	(0.1)	(0.3)	(0.3)	(0.3)	(0.1)	(0.4)	(0.8)	(3.8)	(0.2)
Median	0.9%	1.8%	−1.1%	2.9%	0.8%	1.0%	−0.5%	2.2%	1.2%	4.7%	−8.4%	4.0%
Annual productivity growth												
Mean	1.6%	1.7%	−0.5%	2.2%	2.1%	0.9%	1.8%	2.2%	0.9%	2.5%	−4.3%**	2.2%
(Standard error)	(0.8)	(1.0)	(1.4)	(0.2)	(1.0)	(0.6)	(1.3)	(0.1)	(1.2)	(1.9)	(2.1)	(0.3)
Median	1.8%	1.5%	−0.4%	1.7%	2.1%	0.9%	0.2%	1.8%	1.4%	2.3%	−5.6%	1.5%
Tobin's Q												
Mean	2.20	2.65	−0.34	2.13	3.01	2.64	−0.86*	2.19	1.03	2.65	−0.31	2.08
(Standard error)	(0.52)	(0.47)	(0.29)	(0.04)	(0.83)	(0.72)	(0.50)	(0.06)	(0.10)	(0.63)	(0.42)	(0.05)
Median	1.17	1.52	−0.25	1.37	1.72	1.59	−0.64	1.44	0.91	1.52	−0.05	1.29

Return on assets											
Mean	26.0	16.7	2.7	4.9***	38.0	17.0	4.7	11.2***	8.6	17.6	-1.4	-0.2
(Standard error)	(8.9)	(5.0)	(3.5)	(0.5)	(14.4)	(4.8)	(6.4)	(0.7)	(1.8)	(9.3)	(6.6)	(0.6)
Median	10.0	12.1	1.0	6.1	14.0	15.9	3.3	8.3	8.4	8.1	5.2	3.7
Total shareholder return											
Mean	20.4	17.1	3.4	9.9**	18.6	16.7	2.0	14.6	23	17.5	6.1	6.4*
(Standard error)	(1.9)	(2.4)	(3.2)	(0.3)	(2.0)	(1.3)	(4.2)	(0.3)	(3.6)	(4.6)	(9.6)	(0.5)
Median	20.5	16.9	2.8	13	19.3	15.6	1.42	15.3	23.2	20.5	17.7	8.1
N	27	45	27	5,290	16	23	10	2,153	11	22	6	3,137

E-O is employee ownership; survivors are firms surviving through 1997 for E-O and control firms, 1995 for all other firms.

Observations are within–company averages across years since 1983, so that each company has equal weight in above calculations. The upper and lower 1 percent of firm-year observations were trimmed to prevent undue influence from extreme values.

* $p < .10$.
** $p < .05$.
*** $p < .01$.

a. Paired difference reflects the E-O firm value minus its matched control firm value (or minus the average of the matched control firm values, if there are two).

Figure 7-1. *Capitalization-Weighted Portfolio Values*

Portfolio value, December 1983 = 1

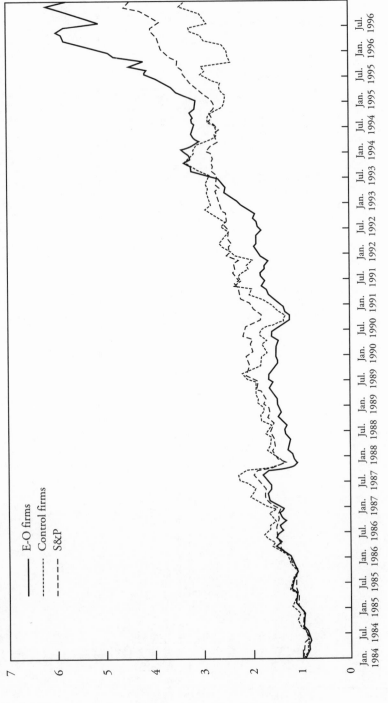

Figure 7-2. *Equal-Weighted Portfolio Values*
Portfolio value, December 1983 = 1

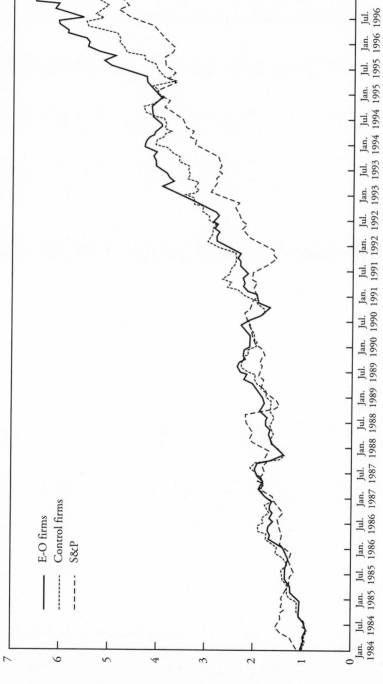

Figure 7-3. *Cumulative Excess Returns, Cap-Weighted Portfolios*

Portfolio value, December 1983 = 1

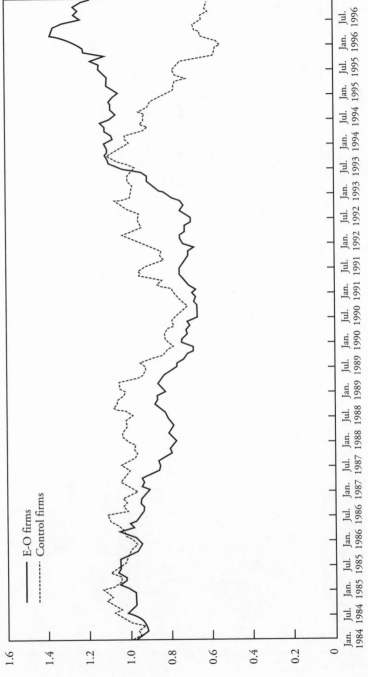

Figure 7-4. *Cumulative Excess Returns, Equal-Weighted Portfolio*

Portfolio value, December 1983 = 1

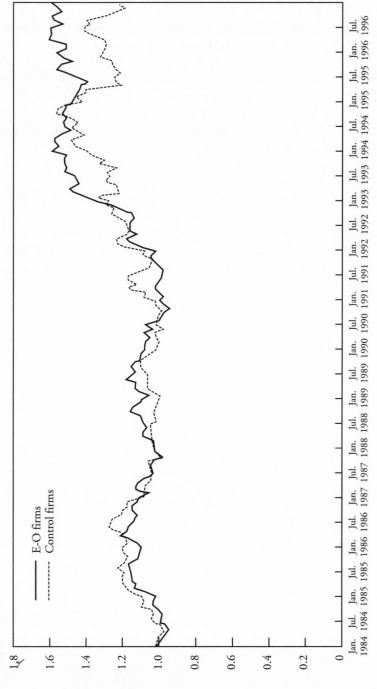

happens to the simple portfolio values over time.[53] In figure 7-1, the investments in the portfolio are assumed to be allocated according to the relative capitalizations of the firms, so it gives large companies much more weight. In figure 7-2, the investments are allocated evenly across all firms in the portfolio. In figure 7-1, we see that the E-O portfolio underperformed both the control firm portfolio and the S&P500 until about 1994 and then surpassed the other two portfolios. Much of the difference between the performance of the capitalization-weighted portfolios, however, is driven by the difference in performance between Sears, Roebuck (an E-O firm) and K-Mart (a control firm). These two firms constituted about half of their respective capitalization-weighted portfolios. In figure 7-2, where it is assumed that the funds in the portfolio are distributed evenly over all firms (so that large and small firms each have the same weight in the portfolio), the E-O portfolio performs about the same as the control sample through about 1995 and has outperformed the control sample since then. The E-O portfolio has outperformed a marketwide portfolio, however, since 1991.[54]

The calculations behind figures 7-1 and 7-2 are based on simple raw returns, unadjusted for risk. But it is possible that the common stock of firms with substantial employee ownership is more risky than that of similar firms without employee ownership, and therefore investors would be expected to demand a higher rate of return. This might be the case, for example, if E-O firms tend to hold on to their employees more during recessions.[55] In figures 7-3 and 7-4, we adjust the returns for both our E-O and our control portfolios by the "betas" appropriate for these portfolios, calcu-

---

53. Calculations for both figures assume all dividends are reinvested in the portfolio, allocated across firms in the portfolio in the same proportion as the existing assets of the portfolio are allocated. The calculations also assume that, when a firm is acquired or taken over, the shares of the target firm held in the portfolio are sold at the buyout price, and the funds are reinvested in the remaining firms in the portfolio in the same proportion as existing assets are allocated.

54. We wondered whether the superior performance of the E-O portfolio in recent years might be because of the prevalence of defense contractors, combined with the fact that the market values of defense contractors were being driven up by the merger wave in this industry. So we removed all SIC 3700 firms from both portfolios and calculated portfolio returns without these firms. The equal-weighted results were very similar, with the E-O portfolio still outperforming both the control portfolio and the S&P 500. The difference in performance between the capitalization-weighted portfolios was even more extreme in favor of the E-O portfolio. This is because, once SIC 3700 was removed, Sears and K-Mart dominated the cap-weighted portfolios by an even greater amount, and K-Mart's poor performance in recent years dragged down the performance of the control portfolio.

55. We thank George Baker for calling our attention to this possibility.

late the risk-adjusted returns of the E-O firm portfolio and the control firm portfolio, and cumulate these "excess returns" over time.[56]

Figure 7-3 reports the results for the capitalization-weighted portfolios, while figure 7-4 reports the results for the equal-weighted portfolios. To our surprise we found that the E-O portfolio betas (whether calculated on an equal-weighted basis or a capitalization-weighted basis) were lower than the portfolio betas of the control group, implying that shareholders enjoy lower risk, rather than higher risk, with these investments. As figures 7-3 and 7-4 reveal, then, the E-O portfolio tended to outperform the control portfolio even on a risk-adjusted basis, especially since about 1994 or 1995.

Another intriguing finding is that our E-O firms had a lower variance in their annual percentage change in employment (see table 7-6), by amounts that were statistically significant when E-O firms are compared to all non-E-O firms, and when compared with their matched control firms. This finding holds both for survivors and nonsurvivors and suggests that having a sizable block of shares in the hands of employees may be associated with greater employment stability.[57] We caution that we have not yet made any attempt to control for acquisitions and divestitures.

Hence, while our results do not prove that employee ownership is associated with improved performance or greater job stability, they do point in both of these directions. Certainly these conclusions are based on a small number of firms. However, it would not be accurate to view this group as a "small sample" because we believe that we have identified most of the population of publicly traded firms with at least 20 percent employee ownership in 1983. In other words, we feel we have accurately captured the actual experience of firms with substantial employee share ownership in 1983. Whether their experience is representative of the cohort of firms that have substantial employee share ownership in 1998 is a different question.

---

56. Betas for each firm in our two portfolios were calculated by the authors from CRSP data, and portfolio betas were constructed as weighted averages of the betas of the stocks in the portfolios.

57. To test whether the data on employment changes for nonsurvivors were biased by the fact that data were missing for some years (that is, after they had disappeared) for which data were available for the survivors, we regressed the employment change data on year and industry dummies, then calculated the comparison statistics for the residuals, thereby controlling for year and industry differences. We got very much the same results.

Analysis of Case Files

In table 7-7, we report data summarizing qualitative data in the case files and comparing employee ownership firms to control firms. These data provide information only about events for which there was a public record of some sort that we found. We looked for evidence of events in three broad categories: events that signal problems with employee relations, such as a major downsizing or a strike or other dispute with workers over wages or working conditions; events that are indicative of the firm's relationships with its shareholders, such as whether the firm was a target of a hostile takeover attempt, or of significant hostile shareholder action, or whether the firm put a "shareholder rights" (poison pill) in place during the period from 1983 to 1997; and events that involved significant organizational or financial restructuring. These summary statistics suggest that there were no statistically significant differences between the E-O firms and the control group in any of these categories.

There are a few differences that might call for some discussion, however. Our data suggest that, if anything, employee-ownership firms had less labor strife and less downsizing than the control firms (although they were certainly not immune to these problems). This impression is supported by our finding reported above that the variance of the annual changes in employment is lower in E-O firms than in control firms (by a statistically significant amount.) This finding is inconsistent, however, with the impression created in the mid-1980s by the especially bad and high-profile experiences at three firms that were restructured with substantial employee ownership in the early 1980s, but that did not, for various reasons, make it into our sample. These are Rath Packing Company, Hyatt Clark Industries, and Eastern Airlines, which were riddled with labor-management conflicts.[58] None of these firms made it into our list of E-O firms because they were not publicly traded and substantially employee owned at the end of 1983. Nonetheless, one might argue that their experiences should not be left out of any discussion of the track record of employee ownership firms.

58. Rath was an NYSE company that became 60 percent employee owned in 1980, with workers given three out of seven seats on the board. Rath went into bankruptcy in 1983. Hyatt Clark was a subsidiary of GM that was spun off to workers in 1981 as a private company in a deal that gave two board seats, out of thirteen, to workers. It closed in 1987. And Eastern Airlines gave employees 25 percent of its stock, and a minority of board seats, in exchange for labor concessions in 1984. It was then sold to Frank Lorenzo in 1986 and went bankrupt in 1991.

However, we think these firms should not be taken as representative of the experience of employee ownership firms either, because unlike any of the other firms in our list, all three of these companies had experienced long-running and destructive labor-management conflicts before becoming substantially employee owned. In two of the three, employees received a majority of stock in the transaction that made the firms substantially employee owned, and all three had employee representatives on the board of directors, something we do not see in any of our twenty-seven E-O firms. Studies have found that the combination of very active trade unions and a long history of extremely contentious labor-management relations, together with a transaction that puts the majority of shares into employee hands, tends to create unrealistically high expectations in workers about how the firm will be managed under majority employee ownership, perhaps leading to a complete organizational breakdown.[59] In any case, we feel that the conventional wisdom has been much too heavily influenced by these three cases. While their stories are an important part of the historical record, they should not be treated as representative.

Another difference that may call for some discussion is that which shows up in the questions on shareholder relations. Our E-O firms were just as likely as the control firms to have a potentially influential large-block shareholder (other than the employee stake) and just as likely to have been the target of hostile shareholder action. But they were somewhat more likely to be the target of an unsuccessful takeover attempt and somewhat more likely to have put a "poison pill" in place. When combined with the finding reported above that E-O firms were much less likely to be taken private, we think our data make a good case that having a substantial block of shares in employees' hands at the beginning of the 1980s was an important factor in making firms resistant to unwanted takeovers. By the end of the 1980s, as we have noted, quite a few other large firms began to figure this out and put sizable blocks of stock into employee hands in a deliberate effort to protect themselves from takeovers. The evidence from the comparisons of the financial performance of the E-O portfolio over time,

59. See National Center for Employment Ownership (1989, pp. 6–13). See also William Sarrin, "Employee Ownership Dream Turns Bitter for Workers at Iowa Meat Plant," *New York Times,* June 17, 1984, sec.1, p. 16, and "Worker-Owned Rath Packing May Be at the End of a Long Road," *New York Times* February 15, 1985, p. A16; and Thomas J. Lueck, "A Noble Experiment Goes Bankrupt," *New York Times,* May 3, 1987, sec. 3, p. 1, and "Test of Worker-Owners Is Ending on Sour Notes," *New York Times,* August 11, 1987, p. B1. See Smaby and others (1988); Sokoloff (1982); Whyte (1987).

Table 7-7. *Further Descriptive Statistics*

Item	Employee-ownership firms		Matched comparison firms	
	Number of firms	*Percent of firms*	*Number of firms*	*Percent of firms*
Has the firm undergone major downsizing?	9	33.3	23	51.1
Did the firm experience significant labor strife or disputes with workers over wages or working conditions?[a]	5	18.5	13	28.9
Has the firm undergone a major organizational restructuring?	18	66.7	35	77.8
Has the firm undergone a major financial restructuring?	6	22.2	9	20.0
Has the firm made any acquisitions?	17	63.0	31	68.9
Mean number of acquisitions (standard deviation)	6.6 (11.6)		6.7 (6.9)	
Has firm had any spin-offs?	17	63.0	27	59.1
Mean number of spin-offs (standard deviation)	5.2 (7.4)		4.6 (4.3)	
Does the firm have an influential large blockholder other than the employee stake?	20	74.1	33	73.3
Has the firm been the target of a hostile takeover attempt?	7	25.9	6	13.3
Has the firm been the target of significant shareholder action (dissident slate, proxy fight, major publicity campaign against management or the board)?	5	18.5	9	20.0
Did the firm put a shareholder rights plan in place?	11	40.7	9	20.0

a. This includes lawsuits and significant publicly reported Equal Employment Opportunity complaints filed by a group or class of workers against the company.

relative to the control portfolio, suggests that this "takeover vaccine" did not, in the long run, harm nonemployee shareholders.

Discussion and Conclusions

A question one might ask about our findings is how representative they are of the experience that can be expected in firms that have become substantially employee owned in recent years. Of course we cannot, at this time, answer this question definitively. But one window we have on this question is to look at the firms that were substantially employee owned as of 1990. Using Joseph Blasi and Douglas Kruse's work as the definitive source for information on which firms were substantially employee owned at the beginning of this decade, we find 148 firms that had at least 18.5 percent of their shares in the hands of employees.[60] These firms are listed in table 7-8, and their industry distribution is shown in table 7-9.

What is striking about the industry distribution of E-O firms in 1991 relative to all public firms in Compustat is that they are remarkably similar. If there were tendencies in 1983 (as indicated by the industry distribution of E-O firms reported in table 7-2) for certain industries to have a heavier than proportional concentration of E-O firms, and other industries to have no E-O firms, this tendency had disappeared by 1991. By the beginning of the current decade, E-O firms appear to be widely representative of all firms, at least by this metric.

Another window on whether our findings will be relevant for the current cohort of E-O firms is the fact that studies that compare performance between employee ownership and nonemployee ownership firms have drawn conclusions that are consistent with ours. Our findings in this paper square well with findings in two such recent studies, one a comprehensive review of comparative performance studies (Kruse and Blasi), and the other (Blasi, Conte, and Kruse), a study comparing 560 public firms with more than 4 percent employee ownership with their industry group cohort (both of which were summarized above).[61]

Except for their seeming immunity to takeover, the remarkably unremarkable experience of the employee ownership firms in our study does not give us any reason to believe that organizational forms in which a

60. Blasi and Kruse (1991, appendix A).
61. Kruse and Blasi (1997); Blasi, Conte, and Kruse (1996).

Table 7-8. The New Owners *Employee-Ownership List, as of 1990*

Company name	Percent ownership	Source of data
Albany International Corp. CL A	18.99	SEC, 1989
Alex Brown	42.10	Spectrum 5, 1990
Allied Group Inc.	37.00	SEC, 1990
Ameribanc Investors Group	36.20	Spectrum 5
America West Airlines Inc.	36.44	SEC, 12/1990
American Building Maintenance Industries	25.39	SEC, 12/1990
American Business Products Inc.	38.09	IRS, 1988-89
American Capital & Research Corp.	21.89	SEC, 1989
American Continental Corp.	25.00	SEC, 5/1990
American Pacesetter	22.10	IRS, 1987
Amrep Corp.	19.80	IRRC, 1991
Analysis & Technology, Inc.	25.30	Spectrum 5, 1990
Angeles Corp.	50.00	Company
Anthony Industries Inc.	22.10	SEC, 8/1990
Apple Computer Inc.	24.00	Franklin Research, 1990
Applied Power Inc.	34.78	SEC, 12/1990
Arden Group Inc.	24.90	Spectrum 5, 1990
Ashland Oil Inc.	23.00	IRRC, 1990
Atkinson (Guy F.) Co. of California	18.50	IRRC, 1990
Audiotronics Corp.	27.50	Spectrum 5, 1990
Avondale Industries Inc.	45.10	Spectrum 5, 1990
Baker (Michael) Corp.	33.00	PR, 6/19/1990
Becton, Dickinson & Co.	20.00	NCEO
BELL National Corp.	24.12	SEC, 5/1989
Brown & Sharpe Manufacturing Co.	20.00	IRRC, 1990
Butler Manufacturing Co.	19.30	Spectrum 5
Capital Bancshares Inc.	29.30	Spectrum 5
Carter Hawley Hale Stores Inc.	40.00	NCEO
Caspen Oil Inc.	20.30	Spectrum, 1/91
CB Bancshares Inc.	18.66	SEC 12/1990
CBI Industries Inc.	22.40	IRRC, 1990
CCX Inc.	29.95	IRS, 1987
Central Freight Lines Inc.	46.10	Spectrum 5
Century Telephone Enterprises Inc.	39.30	IRRC, 1991
CF&I Steel Corp.	38.92	SEC, 5/1990
Chemed Corp.	19.40	IRRC, 1990
Cincinnati Milacron, Inc. PFD	18.50	IRRC, 1991
CNL Financial Corp.	20.20	SEC, 6/1990

Table 7-8.   The New Owners *Employee-Ownership List, as of 1990* (comtinued)

Company name	Percent ownership	Source of data
Coastal Corp.	29.40	SEC, 6/1990
Commerce Bancorp Inc.	19.68	PR, 8/17/1989
Commerce Group Corp.	19.10	Spectrum 5, 1990
Commonwealth Energy Systems	20.10	IRRC, 1991
Consolidated Freightways Inc.	19.54	WSJ, 2/13/1989
Craftmatic/Contour Industries Inc.	28.35	SEC, 12/1990
Crown Crafts Inc.	19.10	SEC, 12/1990
Crystal Brands Inc.	21.79	IRS, 1987
CyCare Systems Inc.	24.52	SEC, 12/1990
DBA Systems Inc.	19.00	NCEO
Delchamps Inc.	25.00	WSJ, 10/6/1988
Dennison Manufacturing Co.	18.67	IRRC, 1990
DynCorp	35.00	NCEO, 1990
E-Systems Inc.	22.30	SEC, 1990; IRRC, 1990
Edac Technologies Corp.	28.40	Spectrum 5
Edo Corp.	25.80	IRRC, 1991
Enron Corp.	22.30	IRRC, 1991
Espey Manufacturing & Electronics Corp.	23.50	Spectrum 5, 1990
Excel Bancorp Inc.	36.00	BWR, 2/19/91 estimate
Fairchild Industries Inc.	18.90	SEC, 8/1989
Figgie International Inc. CL B	34.50	IRRC, 1991
First American Financial Corp.	24.34	IRS, 1988-89
First Federal Savings Bank Utah	19.20	SEC, 1989
Firstcorp Inc.	25.00	WSJ, 7/15/1988
FMC Corp.	25.30	IRRC, 1991
General Aircraft Corp.	20.00	SEC, 6/1990
Granite Construction Inc.	50.60	SEC, 12/1990
Grumman Corp.	42.85	IRRC, 1991
Harcourt Brace Jovanovich Inc.	19.30	Spectrum 5
Hawkins Chemical Inc.	25.00	Spectrum 5
Hi-Shear Industries Inc.	43.87	SEC, 12/1990 estimate
Imperial Holly Corp.	32.40	Spectrum 5
Inter-Regional Financial Group Inc.	37.58	IRS, 1988-89
International Mercantile Corp.	29.10	SEC, 6/1990
International Research & Development Corp.	20.10	Spectrum 5
Kerr Glass Manufacturing Corp.	25.70	SEC, 1990
KMS Industries Inc.	28.20	SEC, 1990

Table 7-8. The New Owners *Employee-Ownership List, as of 1990* (comtinued)

Company name	Percent ownership	Source of data
Kroger Co.	34.60	IRRC, 1990
Kysor Industrial Corp.	23.00	Spectrum 5, 11/1990
Lama (Tony) Co. Inc.	20.00	NCEO
Lillian Vernon Corp.	28.00	Franklin Research, 1990
Lockheed Corp.	18.90	IRRC, 1991
Logitek Inc.	19.00	SEC, 1989
Louisiana General Services Inc.	29.10	Spectrum 6
Lowe's Companies Inc.	24.00	IRRC, 1991
Lydall Inc.	19.00	SEC, 1989
MacDermid Inc.	22.91	SEC, 6/1990
Marsh Supermarkets, Inc.	20.00	SEC, 1986
May Department Stores Co.	25.00	IRRC, 1991
McCormick & Co. Inc.	26.30	IRRC, 1989
McDonnell Douglas Corp.	32.60	IRRC, 1990
McKesson Corp.	20.40	IRRC, 1990
Meret Inc.	31.40	Spectrum 5
Merrill Lynch & Co. Inc.	25.00	WSJ, 1/24/1989
Miller (Herman) Inc.	35.00	IRRC, 1989
Morgan Stanley Group Inc.	57.20	Morgan Stanley Group
Mutual Savings Life Insurance Co.	55.50	Spectrum, 1/91
National Fuel Gas Co.	20.00	NCEO
National-Standard Co.	22.00	SEC, 1990
Nelson (L.B.) Corp.	33.10	SEC, 1990
Northeast Savings F.A.	19.00	IRRC, 1989
Oilgear Co.	39.40	Spectrum 5
Old Stone Corp.	37.20	IRRC, 1991
Olin Corp.	23.60	IRRC, 1990
Optical Coating Laboratory Inc.	22.50	SEC, 11/1990
Oregon Metallurgical Corp.	67.40	SEC, 1989
Oregon Steel Mills Inc.	47.30	SEC, 1990
Pacific Enterprises	24.00	IRRC, 1990
Penney (J.C.) Co. Inc.	32.50	IRRC, 1991
Phillips Petroleum Co.	23.90	Business Wire, 9/17/1990
Piper Jaffray Inc.	46.75	SEC, 5/1989
PLM International Inc.	60.60	Goldman Sachs
Polaroid Corp.	19.20	IRRC, 1991
Products Research & Chemicals	20.00	Franklin Research, 1990

Table 7-8. The New Owners *Employee-Ownership List, as of 1990* *(continued)*

Company name	Percent ownership	Source of data
Rhodes (M.H.) Inc.	48.90	Spectrum 5
RLI Corp.	27.19	SEC, 1990
Rockwell International Corp.	41.10	IRRC, 1990
Ruddick Corp.	40.50	IRRC, 1990
S T V Engineers Inc.	41.70	SEC, 5/1990
S.N.L. Financial Corp. CL C	20.70	Spectrum 5
Sage Broadcasting Corp.	28.60	SEC, 4/1990
Schultz Sav-O Stores Inc.	20.80	Spectrum 5, 1990
Servotronics Inc.	37.50	Spectrum 5
Southside Bancshares Corp.	19.90	Spectrum 5
Standard Brands Paint Co.	18.90	IRRC, 1991
Stanley Works	28.30	Company
Starrett (L.S.), Co. CL A	22.91	SEC, 1989
Sterling Chemicals, Inc.	25.00	Verbal
Stone & Webster, Inc.	51.60	IRRC, 1991
Sun City Industries Inc.	23.92	WSJ, 4/5/1990
Swank Inc.	71.60	Spectrum 5
Tal-Cap Inc.	24.70	SEC, 6/1989
Tandycrafts, Inc.	37.20	SEC, 10/1990
TCI International Inc.	25.30	Spectrum 5, 6/30/1990
Termiflex Corp.	25.48	SEC, 1990
Textron Inc.	19.80	IRRC, 1991
Topps Company Inc.	36.70	Baron's, 12/14/1987
Toro Co.	20.50	IRRC, 1991
Tyler Corp.	34.00	IRRC, 1990
Tyson Foods	25.00	NCEO, 1990
United Companies Financial Corp.	19.40	IRRC, 1991
United Oklahoma Bankshares, Inc.	23.30	Spectrum 5
USG Corp.	18.80	IRRC, 1990
Velobind Inc.	27.30	SEC, 12/1990
Weirton Steel Corp.	73.40	IRRC, 1991
Weston (Roy F.) Inc.	25.10	SEC, 1989
Wheeling-Pittsburgh Steel Corp.	33.00	NCEO
Wichita River Oil Corp. Colorado	27.90	SEC, 12/1990 estimate
Woodward Governor Co.	19.50	SEC, 8/1990
Yellow Freight System	23.90	IRRC, 1991

Source: Blasi and Kruse (1991).

Table 7-9. *Industry Distribution of Employee-Owned Firms in 1991*

	Employee-owned firms[a]		All public firms	
Item	*Number*	*Percent*	*Number*	*Percent*
Agriculture	0	0.0	21	0.4
Mining, construction	5	3.6	395	7.4
Manufacturing	64	46.7	2,387	44.5
Chemicals	6	4.4	324	6.0
Primary metal	5	3.6	86	1.6
Fabricated metal	7	5.1	101	1.9
Nonelectrical machinery	9	6.6	403	7.5
Transportation equipment	6	4.4	113	2.1
Instruments and related	8	5.8	337	6.3
Other manufacturing	23	16.8	1,023	19.1
Transportation	4	2.9	124	2.3
Communications, utilities	8	5.8	391	7.3
Trade	16	11.7	582	10.9
Finance	25	18.2	721	13.4
Services	15	10.9	742	13.8
Total	137	100.0	5,363	100.0

a. Employee-owned firms had 18.5 percent or more of stock held by employees in 1990–91.

substantial block of (otherwise publicly traded) common stock is held by or for employees is an inefficient, unstable, contentious, or otherwise problematic arrangement, or that it is an arrangement used only to facilitate major transitions. In fact, such arrangements seem at least as stable as any other ownership arrangement and may well help to "stabilize" a firm, making it more resistant to bankruptcy and unwanted takeovers and somewhat less prone to labor strife and wrenching downsizings. We also find no evidence that these benefits come at a cost in operating or financial performance.

COMMENT BY
Stephen C. Smith

The theoretical literature on employee ownership (E-O) is replete with contradictory arguments and sensitivity to assumptions. There is no substitute for quality empirical work. If all that Margaret Blair, Douglas Kruse, and Joseph Blasi had done in their chapter was to present the numbers from their painstaking data collection work, they would receive, if research in this field were ancient Rome, the conquering heroes' parade of triumph. Presumably these data will become available for use by other researchers at some point, so these data are likely to set a standard for many years to come. And among their results, the authors' discovery that employee-owned firms exhibit greater employment stability may well turn out to be one of the most enduring stylized facts in the field.

The authors review arguments against E-O derived from the literature on labor-managed firms, including perverse response problems, degeneration, underinvestment owing to time horizon or risk aversion, the $1/n$ problem, preference aggregation, and moral hazard problems in obtaining outside financing. The authors identify two of these arguments that seem potentially to apply to E-O: risk aversion and preference aggregation. Besides presenting a wealth of information about circumstances of particular companies that the chapter indicates will be expanded in another article, the authors use Weibull and logit model analyses to test the effect of the presence of substantial E-O on the firm survival rate. Other useful statistical tests are also presented.

The chapter raises the issue of whether and to what extent E-O may harmonize interests between employees and outside shareholders. It is a real issue that outside investors may be concerned that employee owners will have a greater relative stake in increasing wages than in raising profits. As demonstrated by Mario Nuti, such a conflict of interest will occur *when an employee's share in the wage bill exceeds his or her share in company dividends plus capital gain.*[62] It should be possible to provide at least a crude calculation of these ratios by combining the authors' data with other data available from Compustat and SEC filings (though ideally one would utilize data on the distribution of wages and shares across workers, which are probably not easy to assemble). Although capital gains have been very great in the U.S.

62. Nuti (1995).

stock market in the period of the study, it is still far from obvious that the employee stake is high enough to meet the Nuti criterion; and these gains may also have been higher than expected. However, if the Nuti criterion is not met, and if there is other evidence that interests have been somehow harmonized anyway, this would set the stage for exploration of what the Nuti proposition is assuming that does not hold in practice. Perhaps implicit or explicit provision of efficiency wages, some form of gain sharing, or some poorly understood mechanism of employee decisionmaking participation, allows the companies to proceed harmoniously with very different types of shareholders.

Data Match-ups

The chapter compares the E-O firms with both a general universe and a matched sample. This dual approach is an excellent way to proceed. I would like to know more about how the firm match-ups were decided on. Table 7-2 tells us that "matched comparison firms comprise, for each employee ownership [E-O] firm, the next largest and next smallest firm (by employment) with pension expenses, in the same two-digit industry." First, there is no obvious alternative to this approach to matching firms. But I did not find it self-evident that employment, without any control for capital intensity, for example, was the best or most obvious measure for match-ups. Nor was it clear that using two-digit industries is sufficiently disaggregated. No doubt there is a trade-off between closeness of match-up in industry with employment and other measures such as capital-adjusted employment. But some more discussion of this would perhaps be helpful. Moreover, as Derek Jones has suggested in his comment, the use of alternative measures of the extent of E-O, such as ownership-stake-per-worker, may affect results. The role played by pension expenses should also be clarified.

In recent work, I have been developing and applying the concept of organizational complements and substitutes. In this context, several contributors to this conference have adduced evidence that in effect E-O and decisionmaking participation are organizational complements. The literature suggests that the two together, interactively, provide productivity gains, and not E-O separately, though perhaps participation may have these effects separately.[63] (As an example, in recent work I have developed both theory and evidence that legally mandated works councils and co-

63. Blinder (1990).

determination are organizational complements with training in firm-specific human capital.)[64]

For example, some of the non-E-O firms may actually have a high level of employee participation in decisionmaking. (At least one firm in the matched sample, Dana Corp., has long had a reputation as an innovator in employee involvement.) At the same time, a look at the list of included firms shows that it is reasonable to conjecture that some of the E-O firms had less participation than some matching firms, while others clearly had a combination. Chrysler may have had somewhat too little E-O to pass the threshold defined by the authors, but they certainly had a substantial amount of what may well be an E-O substitute, namely, gain sharing. Thus one reason E-O firms look similar to non-E-O firms may be because it has not been possible to fully separate the two types of firms. Having said this, I must add that I am all too well aware that the data problems the authors encountered in identifying E-O firms are vastly compounded in even defining, let alone identifying, firms with high decisionmaking participation. And none of this takes away from the striking results that are found given the way E-O is defined; indeed it may well strengthen them.

Other Sampling Issues

I wonder if there is a potentially significant selection bias issue in focusing attention on examining what might be called first wave E-O firms. There should be a presumption until evidence emerges otherwise that those firms most able to take advantage of the potential economic benefits of E-O would tend to be among the first to introduce it. Moreover, the chapter finds higher survival rates for E-O firms. But many of these firms in fact had E-O many years before the study's starting date of 1983. That these firms typically had long survived already may mean that they are a sample selected for some special longevity characteristics, in addition to being the type of firms more likely than average to benefit from E-O. However, there are reasons to believe that the economy has been changing in ways enhancing such benefits since around 1980; there is some evidence that E-O accumulated through stock options is highly concentrated in the high-tech sector.[65] Or perhaps these potential benefits have simply become better known to firms in this period, just as these benefits have only recently become

---

64. See Smith (1991); Askildsen and Smith (1998).
65. Smith (1988).

better known to academics. In any case, it would be useful to compare longevity of E-O firms with those non-E-O firms that had already survived as long as the 1983 E-O sample, even if one is not able to conduct rigorous selection bias tests.

Of course the growth of high tech-firms in which E-O might be significant is too recent to really provide adequate tests; but just comparing a 1983–87 five-year period with 1993–97, for example, might shed some light on the changing value of E-O in the American economy.

Employment Stability

I concur with the authors that one of their most interesting findings is greater employment stability that is statistically significant. If this result holds up with more and better data and tests, and in particular after controlling for acquisitions and divestitures as the authors suggest should be done, it will be of potentially very great importance. Certainly, one has to be very careful in distinguishing cause from effect; direct effect from indirect effect. It is plausible that what we are seeing is that firms with greater longevity (which apparently coincides with E-O) are those with less destabilizing swings in employment size. So we must decompose factors associated with E-O and those associated with things E-O is associated with, apparently including greater firm longevity. It is also possible that E-O is simply more viable in those companies able to avoid large swings in employment.

However, if E-O causes employment stability, it may also cause other factors that help with firm survival, such as investments in firm-specific human capital. Employees are more likely to invest in specific skills if they have a long time horizon, as knowledge of greater employment stability and firm longevity provides, and also if they are able to have some confidence that their share of return on those investments will not be opportunistically held up by management or owners, such as E-O might help provide. Note also that such employee investments in turn may encourage firms to make investments that are complementary with firm-specific skills.[66] Thus the performance advantages of E-O, if they are confirmed, might be indirect, in encouraging investments that are efficient but might not be made because of property rights hold-up and other problems. Moreover, to the extent that E-O is used as a takeover defense, one may be

66. Smith (1991).

selecting for firms with managers or owners who are more determined not to allow a hostile takeover and thus for this reason alone may show more survival.

Finally, to understand the connection between E-O and employment stability, it would be useful to know the incidence of outright employment declines. The employment stability of greatest concern to employees is almost certainly found in the risk of layoffs.

Firm Survival

Churning is a well-known feature of the American economy. We see it in births and deaths of new small entrepreneurial firms; we see it in the ongoing turnover of the labor force as workers voluntarily switch jobs. And we see it here. It is striking that almost half of matched listed firms disappear by the end of the sample, but it is little less striking that more than 40 percent of E-O firms disappear, by the criteria in the study. It would be interesting to know whether 40 percent is a high level of listed firm disappearance by European or Japanese standards. E-O may be statistically more stable, but I at least am particularly interested in stability for its capacity to encourage joint investments involving risk-averse workers. In this case, the degree of churning may be so great even under E-O that one will have to think carefully about whether E-O as it has existed in the typical listed company in these sample years really makes much difference in encouraging firm-specific human capital.

However, as the authors implicitly acknowledge, it is not fully clear that the definition of firm "disappearance," understandable from the need to rely on Compustat data, is completely satisfactory. A firm that goes private but in the process stays an E-O firm or even increases its E-O share is clearly a surviving E-O firm. Two small E-O firms that merge and become a large E-O firm are also clearly a surviving E-O firm. So E-O deaths may actually be overstated; on the other hand, a firm that drops from 60 percent E-O to 20 percent E-O might still show up by definition as an E-O firm,[67] but something important about degeneration would be missed. It is unlikely that much can be done to fix all of these difficult definitional problems, so we may take some reassurance in noting that the ways in which E-O deaths are overstated or understated may to a large degree wash out in the sample.

---

67. That seems to be happening to one of the privatized companies I visited in Slovenia but perhaps characterizes none of the firms in this sample. Smith, Cin, and Vodopivec (1997).

With respect to the logit models, some of the right-hand-side variables may be endogenous, an obvious example being employment. But also, in some studies, ownership form including E-O has been treated as an endogenous variable. In Stephen C. Smith, Beom-Cheol Cin and Milan Vodopivec, the need to instrument for ownership form as well as factor inputs was confirmed by Hausman endogeneity tests.[68] Fortunately, it appears that the authors have constructed a rich data set, from which, for example, lagged balance sheet data could be used as instruments.

Finally, the chapter finds that E-O firms have slower employment growth. It would be useful to explore the cause. If E-O firms think of hires as more long term, would this tend to lead to more cautious hiring practices and hence slower labor growth? Is lower E-O employment variance associated with lower E-O employment growth? Finally, could more cautious employment growth itself help ensure firm survival?

Extensions, Concluding Comments

In further work, it might be useful to consider the role of the amount of E-O in firm differences, rather than simply its presence. For example, is there any tendency for firms with *more* E-O to have *more* employment stability or *greater* longevity?

The chapter found some limited support for the hypothesis that E-O firms perform better. It would be interesting again to find some measure of employee decisionmaking participation and see if its presence helps distinguish the better performing firms of either type, though particularly for E-O, with which it may be a complement.

As mentioned at the outset, the authors identified two arguments against E-O that they considered to apply here: risk aversion and preference aggregation problems. It might be useful for the paper to revisit those issues in the discussion after the empirical analysis could be taken into account. With respect to risk aversion, again one of the key findings is the greater employment stability in E-O, which is clearly consistent with risk-averse employee preferences. We may see E-O when technology and market conditions are consistent with stable employment size, or the presence of E-O may cause firms to adopt employment stability, or most likely the causality may run in both directions, but the connection is clear. The connection to preference revelation problems is less obvious but may suggest some avenues for further

68. Smith, Beom-Cheol, and Vodopivec (1997).

research. For example, we may see E-O when preferences of financial capital are for some reasons aligned with that of workers; again I think this may likely include cases where workers and firms make joint investments that require, or are at least consistent with, long employment relationships and perhaps stable wages.

A final minor point: the authors ask what it might be about defense contractors that makes E-O more prominent there. There is another puzzle in the literature about this sector with which I happen to be familiar: a huge fraction of international trade takes the form of countertrade in this industry, to the point where countertrade is centered in armaments. Perhaps this is an industry filled with puzzles.

In sum this is excellent and really commendable work that appears to be an early part of a substantial effort that researchers in the E-O field will be referring to for many years.

References

Alchian, Armen A., and Harold Demsetz. 1972. "Production, Information Costs, and Economic Organization." *American Economic Review* 62 (December): 777–95.

Altenberg, Lee. 1990. "Beyond Capitalism: Leland Stanford's Forgotten Vision." In *Sandstone and Tile* 14 (Winter): 8–20. Stanford, Calif.: Stanford Historical Society.

Askildsen, Jan Erik, and Stephen C. Smith. 1999. "A Theory of Works Councils: Evidence from Germany." Working Paper. George Washington University (May).

Ben-Ner, Avner. 1988. "The Life Cycle of Worker-Owned Firms in Market Economies: A Theoretical Analysis." *Journal of Economic Behavior and Organization* 10 (October): 287–313.

Bell, Linda A., and Douglas L. Kruse. 1995. *Evaluating ESOPs, Profit Sharing and Gain Sharing Plans in U.S. Industries, A Report to the U.S. Department of Labor.* U.S. Department of Labor (March).

Blair, Margaret M. 1995. *Ownership and Control: Rethinking Corporate Governance for the Twenty-First Century.* Brookings.

Blasi, Joseph R. 1988. *Employee Ownership: Revolution or Ripoff?* Harper Business.

Blasi, Joseph R., Michael Conte, and Douglas Kruse. 1996. "Employee Stock Ownership and Corporate Performance among Public Companies." *Industrial and Labor Relations Review* 50 (October): 60–79.

Blasi, Joseph R., and Douglas L. Kruse. 1991. *The New Owners: The Mass Emergence of Employee Ownership in Public Companies and What It Means to American Business.* Harper Business.

———. 1997. *Employee Share Ownership in 401k And Non-401k Defined Contribution Plans: A Study of the Facts.* Rutgers University School of Management and Labor Relations (March).

Blasi, Joseph, Maya Kroumova, and Douglas Kruse. 1997. *Kremlin Capitalism: Privatizing the Russian Economy.* Cornell University Press.

Blinder, Alan S., ed. 1990. *Paying for Productivity: A Look at the Evidence.* Brookings.

Bloom, Steven M. 1986. *Employee Ownership and Firm Performance.* Ph.D. dissertation. Department of Economics. Harvard University.

Bonin, John P., Derek C. Jones, and Louis Putterman. 1993. "Theoretical and Empirical Studies of Producer Cooperatives: Will Ever the Twain Meet?" *Journal of Economic Literature* 31 (September): 1290–1320.

Bonin, John P., and Louis Putterman. 1987. *Economics of the Corporation and the Labor-Managed Economy.* Harwood Academic Publishers.

Boycko, Maxim, Andrei Shleifer, and Robert Vishny. 1995. *Privatizing Russia.* Cambridge: MIT Press.

Brookings, Robert S. 1929. *Economic Democracy: America's Answer to Socialism and Communism.* Macmillan Co.

Conte, Michael A., and Jan Svejnar. 1990. "The Performance Effects of Employee Ownership Plans." In Alan S. Blinder, ed., *Paying for Productivity: A Look at the Evidence,* 143–72. Brookings.

Craig, Ben, and John Pencavel. 1992. "The Behavior of Worker Cooperatives: The Plywood Companies of the Pacific Northwest." *American Economic Review* 82 (December): 1083–1105.

———. 1995. "Participation and Productivity: A Comparison of Worker Cooperatives and Conventional Firms in the Plywood Industry." *Brookings Papers on Economic Activity, Microeconomics:* 121–160.

Davis, Eleanor. 1933. *Employee Stock Ownership and the Depression.* Ann Arbor: Edwards Brothers.

Domar, Evsey D. 1966. "The Soviet Collective Farm as a Producer Cooperative." *American Economic Review* 56 (September): 734–57.

Dow, Gregory, and Louis Putterman. 1999. "Why Capital (Usually) Hires Labor: An Assessment of Proposed Explanations." In *Employees and Corporate Governance,* edited by Margaret M. Blair and Mark J. Roe, 17–57. Brookings.

Ellerman, David P. 1986. "Horizon Problems and Property Rights in Labor-Managed Firms," *Journal of Comparative Economics* 10 (March): 62–78.

Foerster, Robert F., and Else H. Dietel. 1926. *Employee Stock Ownership in the United States.* Princeton University Press.

Foundation for Enterprise Development (FED). 1997. *The Entrepreneur's Guide to Equity Compensation.* La Jolla.

———. 1998. *FED Newsletter* 11 (Winter). La Jolla.

Furubotn, Erik G., and Svetozar Pejovich. 1974. "Property Rights and the Behavior of the Firm in a Socialist State: The Example of Yugoslavia." In *The Economics of Property Rights,* edited by Erik G. Furubotn and Svetozar Pejovich, 227–51. Ballinger Publishing Co.

Gates, Jeffrey R. 1998. *The Ownership Solution: Toward a Shared Capitalism for the Twenty-First Century.* Addison-Wesley.

Gordon, Jeffrey. 1995. "Employee Stock Ownership as a Transitional Device: The Case of the Airline Industry." In *The Handbook of Airline Economics,* edited by Darryl Jenkins, 575–92. Washington, D.C.: Aviation Week Group.

————. 1999. "Employee Stock Ownership in Economic Transitions: The Case of United and the Airline Industry." In *Employees and Corporate Governance,* edited by Margaret M. Blair and Mark J. Roe, 371–54. Brookings.

Hansmann, Henry. 1996. *The Ownership of Enterprise.* Harvard University Press.

Holmstrom, Bengt. 1982. "Moral Hazard in Teams." *Bell Journal of Economics* 13 (Autumn): 324–40.

Jensen, Michael C., and William H. Meckling. 1979. "Rights and Production Functions: An Application to Labor-Managed Firms and Codetermination." *Journal of Business* 52 (October): 469–506.

Kelso, Louis O. 1968. *Two-Factor Theory: The Economics of Reality; How to Turn Eighty Million Workers into Capitalists on Borrowed Money, and Other Proposals.* Vintage Books.

Kelso, Louis O., and Mortimer J. Adler. 1958. *The Capitalist Manifesto.* Random House.

Kruse, Douglas L., and Joseph R. Blasi. 1997. "Employee Ownership, Employee Attitudes, and Firm Performance: A Review of the Evidence." In *The Human Resources Management Handbook, Part I,* edited by David Lewin, Daniel J. B. Mitchell, and Mahmood A. Zaidi, 113–51. JAI Press.

Levine, David I., and Laura D'Andrea Tyson. 1990. "Participation, Productivity, and the Firm's Environment." In *Paying for Productivity: A Look at the Evidence,* edited by Alan S. Blinder, 183–237. Brookings.

Levine, David I., and Richard J. Parkin. 1994. "Work Organization, Employment Security, and Macroeconomic Stability." *Journal of Economic Behavior and Organization* 24 (August): 251–71.

Levine, David. 1995. *Re-Inventing the Workplace: How Business and Employees Can Both Win.* Brookings.

Long, Russell. 1981. "S. 1162—Expanded Ownership Act of 1981." *Congressional Record-Senate,* no. 72 (May 12): 9363–80.

Meade, J. E. 1972. "The Theory of Labor-Managed Firms and of Profit Sharing." *Economic Journal* 82 (March supplement): 402–28.

National Center for Employee Ownership. 1989. *Employee Ownership: A Handbook for Unions.* Oakland.

————. 1997. *The Stock Options Book.* Oakland.

————. 1998. *Current Practices in Stock Option Plan Design.* Oakland.

National Industrial Conference Board. 1928. *Employee Stock Purchase Plans in the United States.* New York.

Nuti, Domenico Mario. 1995. "Employeeism: Corporate Governance and Employee Share Ownership in Transitional Economies." Presented at the conference on Enterprise Restructuring and Labour Markets. Geneva.

Putterman, Louis. 1986. "On Some Recent Explanations of Why Capital Hires Labor." In *The Economic Nature of the Firm: A Reader,* edited by Louis Putterman, 312–28. Cambridge University Press.

Smaby, Beverly, and others. 1988. "Labor-Management Cooperation at Eastern Air Lines." Prepared for the U.S. Department of Labor. Government Printing Office.

Smith, Stephen C. 1988. "On the Incidence of Profit and Equity Sharing: Theory and an Application to the High Tech Sector." *Journal of Economic Behavior and Organization* 9 (January): 45–58.

————. 1991. "On the Economic Rationale for Codetermination Law." *Journal of Economic Behavior and Organization* 6 (December): 261–81.

Smith, Stephen C., Beom-Cheol Cin, and Milan Vodopivec. 1997. "Privatization Incidence, Ownership Forms, and Firm Performance: Evidence from Slovenia." *Journal of Comparative Economics* 25 (October): 158–79.

Sokoloff, Gail Laureen. 1982. "The Creation of an Employee-Owned Firm." Harvard University, Department of Sociology, senior honors thesis.

U.S. General Accounting Office. 1986. *Employee Stock Ownership Plans: Benefits and Costs of ESOP Tax Incentives for Broadening Stock Ownership* (December).

Vanek, Jaroslav. 1977. "The Basic Theory of Financing of Participatory Firms." In *The Labor-Managed Economy: Essays by Jaroslav Vanek,* edited by Vanek, 186–98. Cornell University Press.

Ward, Benjamin. 1958. "The Firm in Illyria: Market Syndicalism." *American Economic Review* 48 (September) 566–89.

Weitzman, Martin L. 1984. *The Share Economy: Conquering Stagflation.* Harvard University Press.

Weitzman, Martin L., and Douglas L. Kruse. 1990. "Profit Sharing and Productivity." In *Paying for Productivity: A Look at the Evidence,* edited by Alan S. Blinder, 95–140. Brookings.

Whyte, William Foote, Charles Craypo, and others. 1987. *Evaluation Research and Federally Assisted Worker Buyouts.* Prepared for the Department of Commerce, Economic Development Administration.

8

JULIA PORTER LIEBESKIND

Ownership, Incentives, and Control in New Biotechnology Firms

THE PUBLIC CORPORATION is a widespread and economically important form of business organization. Originating in the nineteenth century, this organization form, coupled with the professional management it
served to engender, has supported immense increases in the scale and scope
of industrial production.[1] The laws and precedents establishing the property rights and governance of public corporations—in particular as they
relate to the conditions of the employment contract and the ownership
and control of assets—have also allowed firms to support investment in
specialized assets and knowledge, pushing forward the productivity frontier
through product and process innovations.[2]

However, as economic activity shifts away from production based on
tangible assets toward forms of production based on knowledge or "human

I thank the University of Southern California for providing financial support for this study.
Many thanks also to seminar participants at the University of Southern California and Duke
University. Special thanks are due to Nicholas Argyres, Janet Bercovitz, Steven Huddart, and James
Rebitzer. Yongliang Han provided valuable research assistance on this project. Any errors are, of
course, my own.

1. Chandler (1990); Lazonick (1991); Smith and Dyer (1996).

2. Williamson (1985); Teece (1986); Demsetz (1988); Masten (1988); Hart and Moore (1990);
Liebeskind (1996).

capital," a question arises as to whether the public corporation, as it is currently constituted, remains an appropriate organizational form.[3] Of particular concern is that the corporate constitution does not accord employees any de facto rights in relation to either ownership or managerial control.[4] This lack of constitutional recognition of employees within the corporate form stems from the nineteenth-century view of the employee as a generic factor of production ("labor") that is required to complement fixed assets, rather than as a form of capital that is essential to profitability. Moreover, in recent years the social contract between corporate owners and their employees has deteriorated, further reducing the power of employees relative to other corporate stakeholders.[5] Increased shareholder activism, intensifying competition, and changes in societal norms of responsibility and community have resulted in a situation in which owners no longer feel either socially obligated, or able, to provide secure employment.[6]

This constitutional structure may become a liability in a human-capital-intensive firm because an employee is, in property rights terms at least, more an external supplier than an internalized factor of production. Employees cannot be obligated to stay with a firm; they can only be induced to do so. Consequently, a firm that is in a human-capital-intensive area of activity is faced with a series of thorny rights and incentive problems. First of all, such a firm must devise incentives that will attract skilled employees. Second, a human-capital-intensive firm must devise incentives that will induce its employees to make human capital investments that are beneficial to the firm, rather than to themselves alone. Third, such a firm must devise incentives that will serve to tie its employees to the firm for some time so that their human capital remains available to the firm, and to prevent leakage of their knowledge to rival firms. Commonly, ownership and control are argued to resolve incentive problems of this type.[7] The question then arises whether a public corporation may be owned and governed in such a way that its inherent constitutional constraints with relation to its employees are attenuated. This is the issue investigated in this study.

3. Blair (1995); Kochan (1996).
4. The situation is different in Germany, where employees do have a constitutional right to have their interests represented in the management of the enterprise. See, for example, Lazonick (1991).
5. Blair (1995).
6. Lasch (1995).
7. Jensen and Meckling (1976); Wiggins (1995).

I investigate the ownership, control, and ownership-based incentive schemes in a sample of 79 new biotechnology firms that were founded and went public in the state of California between 1974 and 1995.[8] New biotechnology firms (NBFs) provide an interesting population for investigating ownership and governance in human-capital-intensive firms. NBFs are founded to develop and commercialize new products produced from basic scientific research in molecular biology, genetics, and related fields.[9] By 1995, more than 1,000 NBFs had been founded in the United States.[10] This wave of firm foundings was stimulated by the commercial potential of advances in genetic engineering by a number of key legal rulings that allowed life forms to be patented and thus to be treated as private property and by the Bayh-Dole Act of 1980 that allowed universities to patent and license discoveries made by their faculty, which facilitated the transfer of cutting-edge technology from universities to firms.[11]

Similar to major pharmaceutical firms, NBFs rely on university-trained scientists to conduct discovery research, process development, and product testing. Frequently, the firms themselves are founded by university scientists.[12] NBFs must also maintain research ties with universities to ensure that they stay on the cutting edge of research and also to ensure that they have access to well-trained graduates who can be recruited as employees.[13] These ties can only be secured by prominent scientists working for the firm. Hence, scientists are the key asset of an NBF; without scientists, the firm would own no intellectual property in the form of patents or licenses and would have no products. The question then arises as to how these firms are organized in relation to attracting and retaining these highly skilled employees, and capturing their knowledge output.

NBFs are also interesting to study because they have high capital requirements and long latency periods on their investments. Thus, they are firms that are best organized—at least from the point of view of raising

8. The study sample is drawn from the population of new biotechnology firms that were (a) founded and (b) went public in California before 1996. The final sample size is 79 firms, out of an identified population of 83 firms. Original IPO documents were not available for the remaining four firms either from Disclosure, Inc. or from the firms themselves. In 1995 there were 260 publicly listed NBFs in the United States.

9. Kenney (1986); Orsenigo (1989); Teitelman (1989); Werth (1995); Rabinow (1996).

10. Lee and Burrill (1995).

11. Kenney (1986); Eisenberg (1987); Zucker and Darby (1996); Argyres and Liebeskind (1998).

12. Kenney (1986); Teitelman (1989); Werth (1995).

13. Kenney (1986); Teece (1992); Liebeskind, and others (1996); Powell, Koput, and Smith-Doerr (1996).

capital and of ensuring organizational stability over time—as corporations. Their organizational arrangements must therefore reflect some resolution of the inherent conflict in interests between labor and capital that is present in the corporate form.[14]

California has the largest population of NBFs.[15] Hence, using a sample of California firms offers the greatest opportunity to study central tendencies and variation in governance and incentive mechanisms. It also offers an opportunity to examine how ownership and governance in these firms may have evolved over time.

Human Capital and Corporate Organization

As mentioned above, firms that are engaged in activities that are human-capital-intensive are challenged with devising incentive schemes that are able to

—Attract highly skilled employees to the firm;

—Induce these employees to produce human capital that is beneficial to the firm; and

—Retain these employees for a period of time sufficient to allow the firm to capture their human capital output in terms of intellectual property rights and commercialized products.

Attracting Employees

In Western democratic societies, individuals are free to choose where and how they allocate their talent for learning and using knowledge.[16] Consequently, if a firm is to induce investment in knowledge on its own behalf, it must have incentives in place that can serve to motivate such investment. This problem is particularly difficult for NBFs, which rely on research that is produced by "star" academic scientists.[17] At least some of these scientists must be induced to move their research efforts from the academic world to a firm in order for commercialization of their science to proceed. Without such a transfer of key scientific personnel, it would be difficult for an NBF to define clear property rights to valuable scientific dis-

14. Blair (1995).
15. Kenney (1986); Lee and Burrill (1995).
16. Murphy, Shleifer, and Vishny (1991).
17. Zucker and Darby (1996).

coveries; to conduct effective internal developmental research; and to develop the absorptive capacity required to conduct research collaborations that are essential for importing new knowledge into the firm.[18]

Two factors may attract academic scientists to an NBF. First of all, a scientist may increase her wealth by such a move. Although universities can patent and license biotechnology discoveries to firms, a firm might be able to add more value to a discovery than the royalty stream share offered by a university. This will only be true, however, if the NBF offers the scientist high-powered incentives that can more than match the expected university royalty stream.

A second factor that may attract a scientist from a university to a firm is the availability of research funding. In a university, a scientist must compete with other academic scientists for funding. Because research funds are rationed, scientists frequently fail to obtain them. Failure to obtain research funding interrupts research programs and can lead to career setbacks and, from a more idealistic point of view, stall the development of biotechnology products that could benefit mankind. Compared with such an insecure funding system, conducting research within a firm that can supply dependable funding may be attractive. As long as a scientist is allowed a certain degree of autonomy in research, and is allowed to publish important results, she can advance her academic career even while in a firm. NBFs typically can satisfy these requirements. The discovery research being conducted by NBFs lies on the frontiers of academic research. Consequently, they can advance their own research agenda only through relatively unfettered exploration and publishing, leading to a "university-like" set of organizational arrangements in these firms.[19] A firm may also offer more assurance to a scientist that the products she is working on will be commercialized.

The interesting aspect of this incentive problem from the point of view of this study is that the need for funding as an incentive mechanism for scientists requires NBFs to have a relatively large capital base. A scientist who fears a firm may run out of research funds before projects are completed will prefer to work for other firms with more dependable funding. Hence, in the biotechnology industry, an important complementarity exists between human capital and financial capital; the former cannot be attracted without the latter. This contrasts with the typical situation of

18. Cohen and Levinthal (1990); Liebeskind and others (1996); Powell, Koput, and Smith-Doerr (1996).
19. Kenney (1986); Rabinow (1996).

financial capital serving to replace labor in production. Yet, a conflict of interests between capital and labor may still be present in an NBF, since the suppliers of capital to an NBF must have their own incentive and governance concerns satisfied.

Inducing Investment in Human Capital

The second incentive problem faced by an NBF is inducing investment in human capital that benefits the firm—that is, research that produces commercially valuable and exclusive knowledge.[20] Again, this problem is especially difficult in these firms, because university-trained scientists may be more interested in making discoveries that increase their academic prestige or satisfy their intellectual curiosity, rather than increasing the wealth of a given firm. Moreover, while a firm can write a contract with an employee requiring her to vest all her inventions with the firm for the duration of her employment, it can do little in the way of contract provisions to ensure that an employee does not hoard good commercial ideas for her own future benefit. Furthermore, from the point of view of a firm, scientific research is an experience good: its value is difficult to judge ex ante, and its production is difficult to monitor or control.[21]

These agency considerations suggest that the optimal contract for inducing the production of valuable human capital in a firm is a sharing contract in residual claims: that is, stock ownership.[22] Sharing in residual claims provides an effective incentive for investment in valuable human capital because residual cash flows, which accrue to shareholders, represent the surplus of a firm after payments to suppliers of tangible factors of production (such as production supplies and debt capital) have been made. Hence, stock ownership provides a scientist with a valuable residual claim to the income from her own ideas, inducing her to concentrate her research efforts on commercially relevant work and to vest her best ideas in the firm. Consequently, we would expect to observe that a substantial proportion of stock in an NBF is owned by its employees. Moreover, because there are many scientists and technicians in an NBF who are critical to its success, it

20. Note that I do not use the term "firm-specific" here. This is because valuable knowledge is usually not inherently firm-specific; knowledge is a public good by nature. Thus, any knowledge generated by a firm must be rendered firm-specific by that firm in the form of obtaining patents, or otherwise securing its rights (Liebeskind, 1996, 1997). See the following paragraph for a discussion.

21. Crutchley and Hansen (1989).

22. Harris and Raviv (1979); Demsetz and Lehn (1985); Fruits (1997); Wiggins (1995).

can be expected that a large proportion of an NBF's stock will be owned by nonmanagerial employees, in contrast to many firms where stock ownership is confined to the managerial ranks.[23]

The ownership of large shares of stock by employees in NBFs also has implications for corporate control. The incentive effects of stock or stock option ownership in these firms may be diluted unless employees also have a voice in corporate management, because outsider investors may lack the specialized knowledge to make value-maximizing investment decisions.[24] Hence, the board of directors of an NBF may have a relatively high ratio of insiders (managers) to outside directors. However, an incentive conflict is present because NBFs need large amounts of capital to attract and retain top scientists. The suppliers of this capital may also require a significant share of directorships to ensure that their capital is being spent wisely.

Inducing investment in human capital that is exclusive to a particular firm may also require that a firm protect its employees from unanticipated dismissal, which would reduce the value of their investments in specific human capital to zero. In the public corporation, takeovers are major causes of dismissal, so one would expect to observe more protections against takeover in human-capital-intensive firms than in other firms. One source of protection against takeover is concentrated stock ownership by employees. For instance, firms with employee stock ownership plans (ESOPs) have lower rates of takeover than other firms.[25] Bankruptcy also increases the chance that specific human capital investments' value will go to zero. This risk can be reduced through low debt-to-equity ratios.[26]

Employee Retention

The final incentive problem that must be solved by a human-capital-intensive firm is employee retention. Knowledge is a public good by nature, so that without proprietary rights that exclude others from its use, it is comparatively valueless to a given firm.[27] Yet human capital resides in the heads of people; thus it is inherently mobile.[28] This is particularly so in NBFs because scientific knowledge tends to held by individuals, and its value

23. Beatty and Zajac (1994).
24. Demsetz and Lehn (1985); Crutchley and Hansen (1989).
25. Gordon and Pound (1990); Ambrose and Megginson (1992); chap. 7 in this volume.
26. Titman (1984).
27. Arrow (1962); Dasgupta and David (1987); Rosenberg (1990).
28. Grant (1996).

does not depend on other firm-specific and cospecialized assets. A firm can patent some knowledge and hence exclude others from the use of that knowledge. However, not all valuable scientific knowledge qualifies for patent protection. In addition, even potentially patentable knowledge is vulnerable to expropriation by rival firms in its developmental stages. Furthermore, patenting is not always an optimal exclusion strategy, because patents require publicity, and publicity facilitates imitation.

For a firm, the main supplementary mechanism for protecting knowledge is employment of the individuals in whose heads valuable human capital resides. Employment permits the use of both trade secrecy protections and various organizational rules and incentives that can induce or impel employees to keep certain information secret.[29] Moreover, this employment must last for a sufficient time to allow the firm to obtain property rights to the employees' knowledge by patenting, codifying, or replicating it internally in a process of learning-by-doing. It is unlikely that a firm will be able to retain employees through employment contracts alone. Long-term employment contracts, especially those containing "noncompete" clauses, are difficult to enforce because they place limits on an individual's economic rights.[30] However, a firm can provide high-powered incentives for long-term employment through the use of deferred rewards such as deferred stock ownership plans; stock option plans with long vesting periods; firm-specific pension schemes; or substantial bonuses for long employment service.[31] These" golden handcuff" reward schemes overcome the problems of risk aversion and liquidity preference that attend nondeferred, high-powered reward schemes. That is, employees will normally prefer to dilute their ownership shares in a firm either to raise cash or to avoid stock price fluctuations or both. For example, Steven Huddart and Mark Lang find that once shares are granted, or stock options are vested, employees typically sell them immediately.[32] Deferred rewards prevent employees from selling their ownership interests and so preserve high-powered incentives for the entire deferment period. Therefore, it can be expected that the sample of NBFs in this study will offer a substantial proportion of the

29. Cheung (1982); Liebeskind (1997).This comment is a generalization. The mobility of a firm's human capital depends to some degree on the characteristics of that knowledge. Whether it is codified or tacit; whether it is individually owned or is shared; and whether or not the firm can claim legal ownership to it. Liebeskind (1997).

30. Liebeskind (1997).

31. Milgrom and Roberts (1992).

32. Huddart and Lang (1996).

ownership-based incentives they offer their employees in the form of deferred rewards with long vesting periods.

Deferred rewards also have their costs. In particular, to the degree that employees are risk averse, a deferred reward will be less valuable than an immediate reward, other things being equal, because they expose employees to longer periods of financial risk.[33] The value of a firm's stock rises and falls because of many different factors, apart from the effort of its employees. As a result, employees may lose money despite their efforts, deterring even risk-tolerant employees from accepting reward contracts that are incentive intense. This problem may be exacerbated in new firms whose stock values are typically more volatile than those of more established firms. For example, the stock values of NBFs, which is the population of firms used in this study, have fluctuated wildly during the past two decades. These fluctuations have been caused by changes in regulation (for example, FDA approval procedures) and intellectual property laws (for example, the patentability of certain life forms), as well as by more general swings in investor opinion and by changes in firm performance.

Firms offering employees stock ownership as an incentive can overcome this problem in two ways. First, if employees are offered a deferred stock ownership plan, the plan can provide for additional shares to employees' stock grants if the share price falls significantly between the granting date of the stock and the vesting date. Second, if a firm offers its employees stock options rather than shares, these options can be "re-priced." That is, a firm can reduce the price at which an option that has been granted can be exercised, once it is vested. In either case, employees are protected if share prices fall during the period between grant and vesting and increase their wealth if share prices rise. Because of stock price volatility in the biotechnology industry, it can be expected that NBFs will have provisions in place to allow for stock price adjustments in their deferred stock ownership or stock option plans.

Finally, it is important to note that, within the corporate form, deferred ownership-based rewards provide stronger incentives in a publicly held firm than in a privately held firm. In the public firm, shares are traded in relatively thick markets, and stock prices are more likely to approach their true value. In a private firm the values of ownership shares may be difficult to determine. Hence, going public increases the attractiveness of a firm's ownership-based incentive schemes, as well as raising funds for product

33. Beatty and Zajac (1994); Fruits (1997).

research and development, which is an additional incentive to scientist-employees.

Summary

This discussion has suggested that human-capital-intensive firms, if they are organized as corporations, can be expected to be organized as corporations in which:

—A significant proportion of equity is owned by the employees who embody the human capital that generates the wealth of the firm;

—Equity ownership is in the form of deferred ownership—either in the form of deferred stock ownership plans, or stock option plans with long-term vesting horizons;

—Provisions exist to adjust equity ownership for changes in stock price;

—There is a relatively high ratio of insider to outsider directors on the board; and

—There may be governance mechanisms in place that protect the firm against takeover by unwanted parties.

This study investigates these conjectures.

Data and Methods

The study sample is discussed at the beginning of this chapter. Data were derived from a number of sources. Information on pre-public ownership and financing of sample firms was obtained from original S-1 filings and other official documents filed with the U.S. Securities and Exchange Commission (SEC) at the time of the initial public stock offering (IPO) for each firm in the sample. These documents provide data on stock ownership by insiders and by any outsider with a 5 percent or greater stockholding. The documents also provide details of all employee stock ownership plans, including stock options and pension plans, and details of board membership. Post-IPO ownership has also been measured from IPO documents and from annual reports (10-Ks) that public corporations are required to file. Additional information on company products, investors, strategic alliances, and other relevant information has been provided by *BioScan*, from other databases on the biotechnology industry, and from the *Wall Street Journal Index*.

The method used for this study is a demographic analysis of the ownership, governance, and employee incentive arrangements of the sample of NBFs. The main intent of this study is to report how this population of firms is organized. To date, no study has examined this important issue.

Results

The main characteristics of sample firms are shown in tables 8-1 through 8-4. Table 8-1 shows the size and financial status of these firms. The first row of the table shows the average profit or loss in sample firms for the three years prior to IPO. No firm in the sample made a profit during this period.[34] The median firm in the sample lost a total of $3.988 million prior to its IPO (mean = $4.675 million), with a median average annual loss of $0.86 million (mean = $1.08 million). The highest total loss was over $30.44 million while the highest average annual loss was about $12.9 million. These numbers are indicative of the large inputs of capital for research and development that NBFs require before they become profitable. Developing and commercializing biotechnology products requires a long period of time, especially for human therapeutic products that must typically undergo an extensive testing process under Food and Drug Administration (FDA) regulations.[35] The need for research and development capital is the primary motive for going public in these firms. Capital is raised against investors' estimates of future profits, not against current revenues, and these estimates are based in turn on each firm's intellectual products—patents held and products in development.

Table 8-1 also shows the assets and capitalization of sample firms at the time of their IPO. The median firm had an asset value of about $3.0 million prior to its IPO (mean = $4.4 million), with a capitalization of $1.9 million (mean = $2.5 million). Some sample firms had a negative capitalization. Capitalization in sample firms is exclusively in the form of equity; no firm in the sample carried long-term debt. This debt-free capital structure frees a firm from fixed payment obligations, reducing its bankruptcy risk. However, given the considerable losses of the firms in the sample at the time of their IPO, it is unlikely that the lack of debt in their capital

34. These numbers and all other accounting numbers in this study have been adjusted for inflation according to the GDP deflator.

35. According to one recent estimate, it costs about $300 million to develop, test, and market a new human therapeutic product. Werth (1995).

Table 8-1. *General Characteristics of Sample Firms*

Item	Median	Mean	Standard deviation	High	Low
Adjusted average annual pre-IPO profit or loss ($ millions)[a, b]	−0.862	−1.082	1.601	0.0	−12.888
Adjusted cumulative pre-IPO profit or loss ($ millions)[a]	−3.988	−4.675	−4.72	−0.09	−30.448
Adjusted pre-IPO capitalization ($ millions)[a, c]	1.871	2.451	2.945	18.110	−5.186
Adjusted pre-IPO assets ($ millions)[a]	3.023	4.406	8.553	76.102	0.069
Number of employees	63.5	80.8	138.4	1,200	6
Founding date	1987	1985.7	4	1993	1975
IPO date	1991	1990.1	3.8	1995	1980

n = 79.

a. Numbers are adjusted according to the GDP deflator; 1974 equals 100.

b. Numbers are estimated by taking total cumulative losses prior to IPO and dividing by the number of years between founding date and IPO date.

c. Numbers are cumulative totals for all years before IPO.

structure reduced their bankruptcy risk to any significant degree: from the point of view of their employees, the sample firms were still highly risky.

The median firm had 64 employees immediately prior to its IPO. The largest firm in the sample had 1,200 employees, while the smallest firm had only 6 employees. The median founding date of sample firms was 1987; the earliest founding date for sample firms was 1975, and the latest, 1993. The median IPO date was 1991, with the earliest IPO taking place in 1980.

Table 8-2 compares the characteristics of sample firms according to when they went public. The table shows that firms that went public from 1980 to 1987 had lower average annual losses and cumulative losses than firms that went public during 1988–95. However, there was little difference in capitalization between the two groups of firms, and the later cohort of firms was actually smaller in terms of number of employees. The increased losses of the later cohort of firms may indicate that investors became more willing to provide pre-public financing to NBFs as they became more informed over time about this industry.

Table 8-3 shows the main products of sample firms. Three-quarters of all sample firms were involved in producing human therapeutic products.

Table 8-2. *Differences between Early and Late IPO Firm Characteristics*

Item	Early IPO firms: IPO occurred 1979–87 n = 22		Late IPO firms: IPO occurred 1988–95 n = 57	
	Median	Mean	Median	Mean
Average annual adjusted pre-IPO profit or loss ($ millions)[a, b]	–0.530	–0.557	–1.007	–1.254
Adjusted cumulative profit and loss ($ millions)[a]	–1.97	–2.82	–4.12	–5.29
Adjusted pre-IPO capitalization ($ millions)[a, c]	1.839	2.426	2.043	2.502
Adjusted pre-IPO assets ($ millions)[a]	3.449	3.306	2.750	4.820
Number of employees	82	76.4	58	82.3
Founding date	1981	1980.9	1987.5	1987.5
IPO date	1986	1984.6	1992	1992.1

n = 79.

a. Numbers are adjusted according to the GDP deflator; 1974 equals 100.

b. Numbers are estimated by taking total cumulative losses prior to IPO and dividing by the number of years between founding date and IPO date.

c. Numbers are cumulative totals for all years before IPO.

Table 8-3. *Main Products of Sample Firms*

Product category	All firms	Early founded firms n = 22	Later founded firms n = 57
Human therapeutics	60	11	49
Human diagnostics	6	3	3
Equipment/supplies	10	4	6
Agricultural	3	3	0
Veterinary	0	0	0
Environmental	0	0	0
Other	1	1	0
Total	80	22	58

n = 79.

Table 8-4. *Location of Sample Firms*

Counties in which firms are located	All firms	Early founded firms	Later founded firms
Northern California			
San Mateo	20	5	15
Alameda	6	0	6
Santa Clara	6	1	5
San Francisco	5	1	4
Contra Costa	3	1	2
Sacramento	3	1	2
Other Northern California	0	0	0
Subtotal	43	9	34
Southern California			
San Diego	26	7	19
Orange	5	3	2
Los Angeles	3	2	1
Ventura	1	0	1
Other Southern California	2	1	1
Subtotal	37	13	24
Total	80	22	58

n = 79.

The remaining firms were in human diagnostics, equipment and supplies, and agricultural products. No firm in the sample was involved in veterinary or environmental products. This finding may indicate that capital requirements in these areas are lower, reducing the need for public offerings to raise capital. It may also reflect the later commercial development of these fields.

Table 8-4 shows the location of sample firms. Surprisingly, the firms are distributed almost evenly between northern and southern California, with two clusters of firms in San Mateo county in the north and San Diego county in the south. These clusters indicate the importance of universities to NBFs.[36] San Mateo county is home to Stanford University, while San Diego county is home to the University of California at San Diego and its associated medical and research institutions.

36. Liebeskind and others (1996); Zucker and Darby (1996).

Table 8-5. *Dilution of Shareholdings at Time of IPO in Sample Firms*

Item	Median	Mean	Standard deviation	High	Low
A. Total shares outstanding (millions)					
Pre-IPO	6.050	7.607	8.810	68.182	0.60
Post-IPO	8.475	10.072	10.20	77.250	1.0
B. Number of shares added at IPO (millions)	2.250	2.464	1.538	12.0	0.40
C. Percentage dilution at IPO (new shares divided by pre-IPO shares × 100)	38.69	41.33	19.50	122.46	10.96

n = 79.

Direct Stock Ownership in Sample Firms

Table 8-5 shows the extent of dilution of stock ownership in sample firms at the time of their IPOs. In the median firm, the IPO increased the number of shares outstanding by about 39 percent, from a median of 6.05 million shares prior to IPO, to 8.475 million shares post-IPO. This increase in the number of shares outstanding tends to dilute all forms of ownership concentration in sample firms at the time of the IPO. Consequently, all measures of ownership and control in this study are given both prior to, and following, sample firms' IPOs.

One conjecture of this study is that employees in NBFs will own a significant percentage of shares. This question is investigated in table 8-6. Panel A of table 8-6 shows that in the median sample firm, prior to its IPO, about 43 percent of shares were owned by managers and directors together. Post-IPO, managers and directors owned a median of about 33 percent of outstanding shares. Surprisingly, while this level of insider ownership is high compared with large public corporations, it is substantially lower than the levels found by Eric Fruits in his study of ownership patterns in IPO firms.[37] Using a sample of 122 firms in a wide variety of industries that

---

37. For ownership levels in large public corporations see, for example, Jensen and Murphy (1990). See Fruits (1997) for comparison.

Table 8-6. *Patterns of Direct Stock Ownership in Sample Firms*

Item	Median	Mean	Standard deviation	High	Low
A. *Insider ownership*					
1. Percentage of shares owned by managers and directors					
Pre-IPO	42.86	42.92	22.94	98.3	0.0
Post-IPO	32.90	31.38	16.10	59.4	0.0
Raw change	9.96	11.54			
Of which					
2. Percentage of shares owned by managers only					
Pre-IPO	9.45	16.70	19.25	92.48	0.0
Post-IPO	6.90	11.55	12.40	59.40	0.0
Difference	2.55	5.15			
B. *Blockholder ownership*					
1. Total blockholder ownership as a percentage of total outstanding shares					
Pre-IPO	56.60	51.56	26.65	100.0	0.0
Post-IPO	39.20	36.80	19.44	80.0	0.0
Difference	−17.40	−14.76			
Of which:					
2. Percentage of outstanding shares held by venture capitalist blockholders					
Pre-IPO	35.00	34.14	26.69	99.6	0.0
Post-IPO	26.30	24.63	18.77	65.5	0.0
Difference	−8.70	−9.51			
3. Percentage of outstanding shares held by corporate blockholders					
Pre-IPO	5.78	10.73	16.06	100.0	0.0
Post-IPO	4.00	7.81	12.30	80.0	0.0
Difference	−1.78	−2.92			
4. Percentage of outstanding shares held by other blockholders					
Pre-IPO	0.0	6.69	15.03	100.0	0.0
Post-IPO	0.0	4.31	8.39	45.0	0.0
Difference	0.0	−2.38			

n = 79.

went public in 1995, Fruits finds that the median firm in his sample had an insider ownership level of 61.8 percent pre-IPO, falling to 43.9 percent post-IPO. In a regression analysis, Fruits finds that insider ownership levels are lower in smaller firms. He argues that smaller firms are more risky and hence that it is contractually inefficient for insiders to own large shares of these firms, even though insider ownership can provide valuable incentive-alignment and monitoring benefits. Certainly, NBFs are risky, as evidenced by their consistently negative profits prior to IPO. Most of the firms in this study sample are also relatively small: in Fruits's study, the median firm had $64.70 million in assets at the time of its IPO, more than twenty times as large as the median firm in this study sample. Hence, it is possible that the relatively low level of insider ownership levels in sample firms is because of risk aversion, despite the potential benefits of insider control.[38]

A similar pattern emerges with relation to managerial share ownership alone. Prior to IPO, managers in the median sample firm owned 9.45 percent of its outstanding shares, falling to 6.9 percent post-IPO. These levels are very low when compared with Eric Fruits's evidence.[39] He finds a median level of managerial ownership in his sample of 37.0 percent pre-IPO, falling to 25.7 percent post-IPO. These latter levels of managerial ownership are more than four times as high as those found in the NBFs studied here, a very large difference. The levels of managerial share ownership found by Randolph Beatty and Edward Zajac are yet higher. Using a sample of 435 firms that went public in 1984, they find a median level of pre-IPO managerial ownership of 55 percent.[40] They also find evidence that levels of managerial ownership are lower in more risky firms. Again, it is possible that the differences between the levels of managerial ownership found by Fruits and Beatty and Zajac and this study can be attributed to differences in firm size and risk.[41]

There is no evidence of extensive direct stock ownership by nonmanagerial employees in sample firms. No firm in the sample had an employee stock ownership plan (ESOP) or deferred stock ownership plan.

A second conjecture of this study is that manager-employees in sample firms would have a significant degree of control over corporate investment decisions, for reasons of incentive compatibility. One way of measuring

38. Demsetz and Lehn (1985); Crutchley and Hansen (1989).
39. Fruits (1997).
40. Beatty and Zajac (1994).
41. Fruits (1997); and Beatty and Zajac (1994).

this control is to examine the extent to which nonmanagerial shareholdings are concentrated in the hands of outside investors. If individual outside shareholders own large share blocks in a firm, they can use their concentrated voting power to influence managerial decisions.[42] This issue is also investigated in table 8-6.

Panel B of table 8-6 shows the ownership of share blocks in sample firms. Total blockholder ownership in the median sample firm was 56.6 percent of outstanding shares prior to IPO, falling to about 39 percent post-IPO. Of this total, a median of 35 percent (or 62 percent of all blockholdings) was held by venture capital firms, with a median of 6 percent (or 10 percent of all blockholdings) held by corporate investors. In the median firm, no block of shares was held by other types of shareholders, including management, employees, or ESOPs. Hence, concentration of shareholdings in the typical sample firm was among outside investors, not managers or other employees, as conjectured. The very high levels of block share ownership by venture capital firms illustrates the key role these intermediaries play in financing the formation of new firms, especially in the biotechnology industry.[43]

Once again, the lack of block share ownership by managers or other employees may reflect the problem of risk exposure: were their levels of ownership higher, they would own more share blocks. Bargaining power may also play a role in determining ownership patterns in sample firms. The overwhelming need for investment capital in NBFs gives a high degree of bargaining power to suppliers of capital in the form of venture capital firms and corporate investors. Even though scentists make inventions, these inventions have no commercial value until they are developed, tested, and marketed. Bargaining power may particularly accrue to venture capital firms in the biotechnology industry because investing in high-technology loss-making firms requires specialized technical knowledge and access to investors who are willing to carry high levels of risk; hence not all financial intermediaries are able or willing to invest in these firms.[44] While standard transaction cost theory does not encompass considerations of bargaining power, it may be an important determinant of many organizational arrangements.[45] For instance, Joshua Lerner and Robert Merges find that firms that

---

42. Demsetz and Lehn (1985); Shleifer and Vishny (1986); Bethel, Liebeskind, and Opler (1998).
43. Barry and others (1990); Teitelman (1989).
44. Barry and others (1990); Calomiris and Ramirez (1996).
45. Argyres and Liebeskind (1999).

are capital constrained are less likely to retain extensive control rights in collaborative R&D contracts than firms that are not capital constrained.[46] The ceding of extensive shareholdings to venture capital firms observed in this sample may be analogous; the NBFs' need for capital may prevent them from retaining the optimal shareholding structure from an employee incentive point of view.

Stock Option Ownership in Sample Firms

Stock options are an alternative form of ownership-based incentive to direct share ownership. Stock options grant an employee the right to purchase shares in a firm at a particular price at a particular time. If a firm's share price is above the purchase price, options can be exercised and the employee can make a profit by selling her shares. Hence, stock options have incentive effects that are almost identical to those of direct stock ownership. Two factors may make stock options a more attractive form of ownership-based incentive than direct stock ownership. First of all, employees pay no tax on options until and unless they are exercised, allowing tax obligations to be deferred. Second, options can be re-priced without affecting the voting structure of the firm. If a firm grants additional shares to its employees to compensate them for changes in share prices, employees' voting power will increase, relative to outsiders' voting power. This may deter outside investors. Re-pricing stock options resolves this problem.

Stock option ownership in sample firms is analyzed in tables 8-7 through 8-9. Table 8-7 shows the extent of stock option reserves and option grants (that is, distributed to employees) in sample firms. Panel A of the table shows the percentage of total outstanding shares in sample firms that is held in reserve for stock options prior to and following IPO. Pre-IPO, 16.81 percent of outstanding shares in the median sample firm had been reserved for this purpose. Post-IPO, this proportion fell to 12.30 percent, owing to an increase in the number of shares outstanding. (In general, stock option reserves were not increased at the time of a firm's IPO.) These proportions can be compared with the block ownership proportions shown in table 8-6. In the median firm, the proportion of shares reserved for options prior to IPO (about 17 percent) is approximately 30 percent of the proportion of shares held in blocks (56.6 percent), and

46. Lerner and Merges (1998).

Table 8-7. *Stock Option Reserves and Distribution in Sample Firms*

Item	Median	Mean	Standard deviation	High	Low
A. Percentage of total shares outstanding held in reserve for stock options					
Pre-IPO	16.81	17.61	10.50	41.80	0
Post-IPO	12.30	12.50	7.10	29.00	0
B. *Of which* Percentage of total shares outstanding granted as stock options					
Pre-IPO	8.80	9.80	7.60	29.10	0
Post-IPO	6.70	6.70	4.90	17.70	0

n = 79.

Table 8-8. *Stock Option Reserves and Option Grants in Early- and Late-IPO Sample Firms*

	Differences in medians		Differences in means	
Item	Early-IPO firms n = 22	Late-IPO firms n = 57	Early-IPO firms n = 22	Late-IPO firms n = 57
A. Percentage of total shares outstanding held in reserve for stock options				
Pre-IPO	14.20	17.92	14.03	19.02
Post-IPO	8.38	13.23	9.67	13.60
B. *Of which* Percentage of total shares outstanding granted as stock options				
Pre-IPO	5.97	10.01	7.64	10.63
Post-IPO	4.72	7.30	5.21	7.26

n = 79.

Table 8-9. *Characteristics of Stock Option Plans in Sample Firms*

Item	Median	Mean[a]	Standard deviation	High	Low
A. *Option terms*					
Maximum length to vesting (years)	10	9.336	1.725	10	2.25
Restrictions on option transferability (dummy)	1	0.92	0.271	1	0
B. *Distribution of ownership*					
1. Percentage of optioned shares held by corporate officers					
As a percentage of total number of options granted					
Pre-IPO	27.43	42.43	59.08	100.0	0
As a percentage of total shares outstanding					
Pre-IPO	2.03	3.64	4.65	27.55	0
Post-IPO	1.50	2.44	2.68	12.39	0
2. Percentage of optioned shares held by non-officer employees					
As a percentage of total number of options granted					
Pre-IPO	71.63	56.51	59.25	100.0	0
As a percentage of total shares outstanding					
Pre-IPO	5.57	5.71	5.61	24.04	0
Post-IPO	3.54	3.91	3.66	13.88	0
C. *Other information*					
Re-pricing provisions (dummy)	1.0	1.0	0	1	0
Firm has anti-takeover provision (dummy)	0	0.392	0.491	1	0

n = 79.

a. Numbers do not sum to 100 because a very small proportion of options is held by outside directors in some firms.

about half of the proportion of share blocks owned by venture capitalists (35 percent). These relative proportions remain essentially the same post-IPO, indicating a perpetuation of the balance of interests and control between employees and large investors following IPO.

In the median firm, 8.8 percent of shares had been granted in the form of options, which is 52.3 percent of the shares held in reserve for this purpose. Post-IPO, these numbers decrease because of dilution, with a total of 6.7 percent of outstanding shares granted in the form of options, equivalent to 54.5 percent of all shares held in reserve.

Combining the evidence given in tables 8-6 and 8-7 shows that, in the median sample firm, the total proportion of shares either directly owned or held in reserve for option by managers and employees was 26.3 percent pre-IPO, falling to 19.20 percent post-IPO. These numbers are still much lower than the levels of direct insider ownership found by Randolph Beatty and Edward Zajac and by Fruits.[47] However, they do show that employees in the median sample firm owned over a quarter of all shares outstanding prior to IPO and one-fifth of all shares outstanding post-IPO. These are still substantial ownership shares compared with large public firms.[48]

Table 8-8 compares stock option reserves and distribution in early- and late-IPO firms. The table shows that later-IPO firms held a greater proportion of shares in reserve for options immediately prior to IPO and also had a higher proportion of stock options granted at this time. In the median early-IPO firm, 14.2 percent of shares was held in reserve pre-IPO; this figure increases to 17.92 percent in late-IPO firms. Similarly, 5.97 percent of shares were granted in the form of stock options prior to IPO in early-IPO firms, rising to 10.01 percent in late-IPO. Interestingly, these findings are not entirely consistent with the risk-aversion arguments of Beatty and Zajac and Fruits.[49] If stock options are risky for employees, despite re-pricing provisions, then we should observe lower levels of option ownership in the later-founded firms, because these firms had higher losses at IPO than the early-founded firms (see table 8-2). However, the higher rate of option ownership in later-founded firms is consistent with the argument that the distribution of share ownership in sample firms depends to some degree on relative bargaining power. In later-IPO firms, capital was more readily available for investment in the biotechnology industry, as

47. Beatty and Zajac (1994); Fruits (1997).
48. Jensen and Murphy (1990).
49. Beatty and Zajac (1994); Fruits (1997).

more investors became informed about its prospects. Meanwhile, highly trained scientific talent may have become more scarce as the biotechnology industry grew from a handful of firms in the mid-1970s to more than 1,200 firms in the mid-1990s.[50] Hence, suppliers of capital may have lost bargaining power, relative to suppliers of specialized human capital, during this period.

If stock options are being used, among other things, to reduce employee mobility in NBFs, the characteristics of stock option contracts in sample firms should reflect this intention. This issue is investigated in panel A of table 8-9. In the median sample firm, the maximum period to vesting of options was ten years. As a further illustration of the use of options to discourage employee mobility, about 92 percent of sample firms had restrictions in place on option transferability. That is, employees are not allowed to exercise their options if they are no longer employed by the firm that issues them.

Panel B of table 8-9 shows the distribution of option ownership among managers and other employees in sample firms. In the median firm, corporate officers (that is, upper echelon managers) owned 27.43 percent of all options granted prior to IPO, while nonofficer employees held 71.63 percent. These relative proportions show that a reasonably egalitarian distribution of option ownership in sample firms exists, consistent with the argument that options are used to motivate and retain scientific personnel in NBFs. This pattern of option ownership is far more democratic than that found by Beatty and Zajac ; in their sample, stock options were held almost exclusively by top managers.[51]

Panel C of table 8-9 shows some of the arrangements in place in sample firms that serve to protect employees against exposure to exogenous risk in terms of financial or human capital investments. First of all, almost all sample firms (99 percent) had repricing provisions in place for the options they granted. As discussed previously, these provisions allow a firm to decrease the exercise price of options if the firm's share price falls, protecting option owners against value losses and thereby preserving the options' incentive effects. In addition, 39.2 percent of firms had antitakeover charter amendments in place. These provisions can protect employees' human capital investments in a firm, since takeovers are typically accompanied by layoffs. The relatively high levels of management and employee ownership

50. Lee and Burrill (1995).
51. Beatty and Zajac (1994).

of stock and stock options in sample firms (when compared with larger and more established public firms) may also serve to protect them from takeover. However, it is unclear whether unconsolidated employee shareholdings and option holdings would have the same deterrent effect as ESOPs have been found to have, especially in firms with large outside blockholders, who can be expected to facilitate takeovers and corporate restructurings.[52]

Corporate Control in Sample Firms

Finally, employee incentives in sample firms may depend very considerably on the firm's system of corporate control. Earlier, it was conjectured that corporate control in NBFs would tend to be in the hands of management, rather than outsiders, from both an information and an incentive point of view. With regard to control related to direct share ownership, this conjecture is only partially supported by the evidence, as shown in table 8-6. While managers in sample firms owned a substantial proportion of shares, this proportion was only a fraction of the proportion of shares owned by outside blockholders. The question remains, however, as to how managerial and other shareholdings are reflected in board composition. This issue is investigated in table 8-10.

Panel A of table 8-10 shows that the median sample firm had seven board members. Panel B of the table shows that the median firm had only two board members who were managers, a median of 25 percent of all board members (mean = 30.8 percent). This is a relatively low level of managerial representation and certainly does not represent a situation in which the board is dominated by managers, as hypothesized. The table shows, however, that board representation by venture capitalists was even lower: in the median firm, only one board member was a venture capitalist, with a median percentage of 19 percent of all board members (mean is 22.9 percent). Thus, while the typical sample NBF had few managers on its board, it had yet fewer venture capitalists.

Panel B also shows the *shareholder representation ratio* of outsiders. This ratio is estimated as the percentage of seats on the board of a firm occupied by venture capitalists divided by the percentage of shares owned in blocks

52. See Gordon and Pound (1990); Ambrose and Megginson (1992). See Shleifer and Vishny (1986); Bethel, Liebeskind, and Opler (1998).

Table 8-10. *Board Membership Patterns in Sample Firms*

Item	Median	Mean[a]	Standard deviation	High	Low
A. *Number of board members*	7	6.975	2.0	14	3
B. *Shareholder representation*					
1. *Management representation*					
Number of managers on the board	2	1.975	1.04	5	1
Percentage of board seats filled by management	25	30.80	16.17	71.43	11.1
2. *Venture capitalist representation*					
Number of venture capitalists on the board	1	1.538	1.583	6	0
Percentage of board seats filled by venture capitalists	19.1	22.94	22.84	80	0
Share representation ratio[a]					
Pre-IPO	0.683	0.632	0.463	1.724	0
Post-IPO	0.930	0.861	0.608	2.035	0
3. *Corporate representation*					
Number of corporate representatives on the board	0	0.24	0.702	5	0
Percentage of board seats filled by corporate representatives	0	4.00	11.65	66.67	0
Share representation ratio[a]					
Pre-IPO	0	0.004	0.007	0.036	0
Post-IPO	0	0.005	0.01	0.05	0

n = 79.

a. The shareholder representation ratio for each firm is estimated as the percentage of seats on the board held by venture capitalists (or corporate investors) divided by the percentage of total shares held in blocks by these investors.

by these investors and by other shareholders whose interests they represent.[53] If the ratio is less than one, then venture capitalists are proportionally underrepresented on the board. Indeed, the median shareholder representation ratio for venture capitalist investors is 0.68 prior to IPO, increasing to 0.93 following IPO. The ratio increases at the time of the IPO because the issuance of new shares and the selling off of shares by venture capitalists reduces their percentage ownership of the public firm, relative to their pre-IPO ownership share. Hence, following an IPO, venture capitalists are no longer underrepresented.

A more extreme picture of underrepresentation emerges for corporate investors. The median sample firm had no corporate investors on its board, so that corporate shareholders were not represented at all in this firm, even though the median level of corporate share block ownership was about 6 percent (see table 8-6).

These findings are interesting because they show that, while the boards of the sample NBFs were not dominated by management as hypothesized, neither were they dominated by venture capitalists or corporate investors. Instead, boards are substantially composed of independent directors who are neither major investors nor managers. This pattern may reflect efficiency considerations: independent directors may protect a firm from strategic interference by large outside investors. In particular, a corporate investor may be tempted to interfere in the strategic decisions of an NBF if so doing would further the investor's interests.[54] For example, a major pharmaceutical firm may be tempted to delay funding a biotechnology product development program in an NBF in which it is investing if this product is a potential competitor for one of its own more traditional products. The potential for such strategic interference is significantly reduced if the corporation has no voice on the NBF board. Similarly, venture capitalists rarely have their investments restricted to noncompeting firms. Typically, venture capital firms invest across a broad array of new firms, many of which may be developing rival products. Again, restricting the control rights of these investors may also prevent strategic interference. Furthermore, independent directors may allow for the impartial resolution

---

53. A board member of a company may represent the interests of a group of shareholders and vote their shares in certain corporate decisions, by formal legal agreement. The statistics on corporate control presented in table 8-10 take account of such arrangements.

54. Hellman (1997).

of conflicts of interest between managers and outside investors that might otherwise impose considerable costs on the firm. That is, these directors allow the board to act as an equitable "mediating hierarchy."[55]

Summary

This study has investigated patterns of corporate ownership, control, and incentives in one type of human-capital-intensive firm, new biotechnology firms, or NBFs. The main findings of this study are as follows:

Direct Stock Ownership

Managers in sample firms own a median of 9.45 percent of outstanding shares prior to IPO and 6.9 percent post-IPO, after dilution. While these levels of managerial ownership are very large compared with most large public corporations, they are far lower than the levels found in two other studies of IPO firms by Beatty and Zajac and by Fruits that use broad-based samples of firms.[56] Hence, there is no evidence that the high levels of human-capital intensity in NBFs resulted in comparatively high levels of direct share ownership among managers and other employees. These relatively low levels of insider ownership may exist because of risk aversion and bargaining power considerations.

Stock Option Ownership

A substantial fraction of shares in sample firms was held in reserve for distribution in the form of stock options. In the median firm, 16.8 percent of shares was held in reserve prior to IPO, with 12.3 percent so held post-IPO. Furthermore, more than 70 percent of all options granted in the median firm were granted to employees who were not officers of the firm, indicating a widespread use of options to motivate employees. The median stock option contract in sample firms had a maximum vesting period of ten years and was nontransferable, suggesting that sample firms used options strategically to reduce employee mobility.

---

55. Blair and Stout (1999).
56. Beatty and Zajac (1994); Fruits (1997).

Corporate Control

In the median sample firm, outside blockholders owned a very large fraction of outstanding shares—56.6 percent of shares prior to IPO and 39.2 percent post-IPO. The majority of these share blocks were held by venture capital firms. Interestingly, venture capital firms and corporate blockholders were underrepresented on the board of the median sample firm, relative to the extent of their shareholdings. Indeed, in the median firm, corporate blockholders were entirely unrepresented. This underrepresentation did not result in managerial domination of corporate boards, however: in the median firm, managers held only 25 percent of board seats. Other board seats were occupied by independent directors with small financial stakes in the firm.

These findings suggest that the system of ownership, governance, and incentives in NBFs is influenced by a number of different considerations and interests. For instance, the need to motivate employees through the ownership of residual claims is tempered by the need to attenuate the financial risks to which they are exposed. The need to financially motivate managers and employees must also be balanced with the need to raise capital for research, and hence, the necessity to take into account the interests and bargaining power of venture capitalists and corporate shareholders. What emerges is a complex pattern of ownership, governance, and incentive arrangements that reflects the competing and complementary interests of the suppliers of labor (in the form of human capital) and financial capital. The NBFs studied are clearly not primarily owned and managed solely by their employees. Yet, it must be remembered that NBFs are a special type of human-capital-intensive firm—a type that requires very large inputs of financial capital. It may be that other types of human-capital-intensive firms that require less capital may be more closely held by their employees. However, if firms require little capital, it is also unlikely that they will need to be organized as public corporations; they might be able to be organized as partnerships or as closely held private firms.

COMMENT BY
James B. Rebitzer

The computer revolution changed the way the world works and thinks. The revolution in molecular biology has the potential to do much more. The scientific foundation for the new biotechnology results largely from the work of university-based research scientists, but the commercial development of this technology requires the resources and entrepreneurial skills of for-profit enterprises. How can new biotechnology firms combine university-oriented scientists with the private sector capital required to realize the full potential of the biotechnology revolution? This is the important question that Julia Porter Liebeskind takes up in her chapter.

Liebeskind's argument can be summarized in three propositions. First, new biotechnology firms (NBFs) are unusually human capital intensive because "their primary asset is human capital." Second, the high level of human capital intensity in these firms creates especially acute incentive and property rights problems. The incentive problem is to induce key scientists to pursue problems that add value to the company, as opposed to investigating problems that may advance scientific knowledge or their own professional careers. The property rights problem is to find ways for NBFs to secure control over the knowledge assets of the firm, assets that may reside as much in the brains of key scientists as in patents or formulas.

The third proposition motivates the empirical work. This proposition states that solving the acute organizational problems facing NBFs entails giving key employees an equity stake in the enterprise and creating long-term employment relationships. Equity stakes in the enterprise are created by giving out stocks and, more important, stock options. Long-term employment relationships are encouraged by deferred compensation packages, high ratios of insiders to outsiders on the board, and protections against hostile takeovers. The chapter assesses proposition three by comparing data collected on the seventy-nine California NBFs who had initial public offerings by 1995 with data on other samples of firms whose initial public offerings (IPOs) were reported by other authors. The evidence provides only mixed support for proposition three.

Linking human capital theory to organizational design questions is, in my opinion, a very powerful way to think about the NBFs. For this reason, I am enthusiastic about Liebeskind's efforts. I have concerns, however, that her analysis relies on concepts that are either ambiguous or insufficiently tailored to the NBF setting. I focus my remarks, therefore, on the way that conceptual ambiguities cloud the interpretation of the chapter's empirical findings.

To assess the empirical results, it is first necessary to define a human-capital-intensive firm. The chapter defines human-capital-intensive companies as those in which the "primary assets are human capital." This definition is unclear. Does it mean that the ratio of physical to human capital is low? If so, it is not obvious that biotech companies have a "lower" ratio than other new ventures. Or does human capital intensity mean that the firm's success is critically dependent on the knowledge and skills of a few key people? Isn't this true of new ventures everywhere? A final interpretation of human capital intensity may be that the firm's success is critically dependent on investments in human relationships. Under this definition, it is not clear that NBFs are more human capital intensive than law firms, consulting firms, and real estate agencies. This definitional problem is important. The only way to investigate the chapter's propositions (especially proposition three) is to compare the sample of NBFs with other organizations that are less human capital intensive. Without a clear definition, it is not clear what sorts of organizations should constitute the comparison group. The author does go to some pains to compare her sample of NBFs to samples of other IPOs collected by other researchers, but the comparison may not mean what she thinks it does unless NBFs are more human capital intensive than other IPOs.

Proposition two focuses on the incentive problem NBFs must resolve in order to assemble teams of Ph.D. scientists capable of producing marketable innovations. What are the right incentives for sustaining the NBF innovation process? I do not know the answer, but the features of the innovation process emphasized in Liebeskind's account would seem, contrary to the author's intuition, to favor low-powered incentives. NBF companies working at the cutting edge of biological science must work with goals that are both poorly specified and evolving. In this environment, it is not obvious what kinds of research activities, information handoffs, or experiments are relevant to the innovation process. For these reasons, it is probably difficult and counterproductive to write incentives around the specific activities of research scientists. The obvious alternative is to write incentives around the profitable outcomes of research activity. The hurdles a product must clear to obtain FDA approval, however, make outcome-based incentives a bad idea. Even more acutely than in other high-technology companies, the payoffs to NBF innovation are uncertain and far in the future, in the case of new drugs, for example, ten to fifteen years away.

If NBF pay practices are not a great solution to NBF incentive problems, what else might they do? I suspect that pay practices like stock options are more likely to ameliorate selection rather than incentive issues. To see this idea, consider the most striking fact uncovered by Liebeskind— none of the NBFs in her sample has ever made any money. Stocks and stock options are, in these companies, therefore, a highly risky form of compensation. Indeed, it is a little surprising that anyone wants to be paid in stock at all. Using these risky forms of compensation, however, can work to the NBF's advantage if they help attract entrepreneurial scientists who are less risk averse and more confident that their innovations will be successful in the marketplace.

If I am right about the selection problem facing NBFs, then the companies may be less interested in long-term employment relationships than Liebeskind's discussion suggests. Do companies interested in entrepreneurial risk taking want to attract risk-averse scientists who place a high value on job security? Judging by the high turnover rates tolerated in some other entrepreneurial settings where innovation is important (for example, at Silicon Valley computer firms and high-powered consulting firms), I think the answer may be no.

The issue of selection and risk aversion raises a potentially important empirical question: are NBF stocks and options more risky than those offered by the other IPOs in the comparison groups? If NBFs are riskier investments than other IPOs, comparing the fraction of equity owned by managers in biotech IPOs to that owned by managers in other IPOs may not be very informative. The relatively high risk of NBFs may make their stock less attractive to their managers. This will tend to reduce the proportion of stock owned by NBF managers relative to other managers of IPOs. At the same time, the very uncertain prospects of NBFs may attract less risk-averse managers who are, for this reason, more willing to own more stock. For these reasons, economic theory may not offer clear predictions concerning managerial stock ownership in NBFs and elsewhere. All of this reasoning rests, of course, on an important empirical assumption, that is, that NBFs are riskier investments than other IPOs. I would be very interested in learning about research that addresses this question.

A second issue raised by proposition two, and the last issue I will raise in this comment, concerns the property rights problem NBFs face because of their heavy reliance on scientific and technical innovation. I am not yet convinced that the problem of controlling key ideas and innovations is more acute for NBFs than for other companies where innovation is important. On the one hand, the ability to patent innovations, together with the lengthy FDA approval process, would appear to offer "more" protection than in many other settings. On the other hand, the nature of the NBF innovation process precludes some strategies for controlling key "knowledge assets." Coca-Cola, for example, can keep its formula secret. Law firms can restrict an associate's access to key knowledge assets (client relationships) and keep the number of partners with such access small. These exclusion strategies are more costly in a research environment where the free flow of information facilitates discovery.

Liebeskind is on to something very important when she claims that the absence of clear property rights to innovations shapes organizational practice. Applying this to the NBF setting, however, would require a more extended discussion of the property rights issues facing NBFs relative to other organizations.

As my comments and Liebeskind's chapter makes clear, there is much work to be done to understand the economic and organizational forces shaping the biotechnology revolution.

References

Ambrose, Brad W., and William L. Megginson. 1992. "The Role of Asset Structure, Ownership Structure and Takeover Defenses in Determining Acquistion Likelihood." *Journal of Financial and Quantitative Analysis* 27 (December): 575–89.

Argyres, Nicholas, and Julia Porter Liebeskind. 1999. "Contractual Commitments, Bargaining Power and Governance Inseparability: Incorporating History into Transaction Cost Theory." *Academy of Management Review* 24 (January): 49–81.

———. 1998. "Privatizing the Intellectual Commons: Universities and the Commercialization of Biotechnology." *Journal of Economic Behavior and Organization* 35 (May): 427–54.

Arrow, Kenneth. 1962. "Economic Welfare and the Allocation of Resources for Invention." In *The Rate and Direction of Inventive Activity*, edited by National Bureau of Economic Research, 609–25. Princeton University Press.

Barry, C., and others. 1990. "The Role of Venture Capital in the Creation of Public Companies: Evidence from the Going Public Process." *Journal of Financial Economics* 27 (October): 447–71.

Beatty, Randolph, and Edward Zajac. 1994. "Managerial Incentives, Monitoring, and Risk-Bearing: A Study of Executive Compensation, Ownership, and Board Structure in Initial Public Offerings." *Administrative Science Quarterly* 39 (June): 313–35.

Bethel, Jennifer, Julia P. Liebeskind, and Tim Opler. 1998. "Block Share Ownership and Corporate Preference." *Journal of Finance* 53 (April): 605–34.

Blair, Margaret. 1995. *Ownership and Control: Re-Thinking Corporate Governance for the 21st. Century.* Brookings.

Blair, Margaret, and Lynn Stout. 1999. "A Team Production Theory of Corporate Laws." *Virginia Law Review* 85 (March): 247–328.

Calomiris, C., and C. Ramirez. 1996. "Financing the American Corporation." In *The American Corporation Today*, edited by Carl Kaysen, 128–86. Oxford University Press.

Chandler, Alfred D. 1990. *Scale and Scope: The Dynamics of Industrial Capitalism.* Harvard University Press.

Cheung, Steven. 1982. "Property Rights in Trade Secrets." *Economic Inquiry* 20 (January): 40–53.

Cohen, Wesley, and Daniel Levinthal. 1990. "Absorptive Capacity: A New Perspective on Learning and Innovation." *Administrative Science Quarterly* 35 (March): 128–52.

Crutchley, Claire E., and Robert S. Hansen. 1989. "A Test of the Agency Theory of Managerial Ownership, Corporate Leverage, and Corporate Dividends." *Financial Management* 18 (Winter): 36–46.

Dasgupta, Partha, and Paul A. David. 1987. "Information Disclosure and the Economics of Science and Technology." In *Arrow and the Ascent of Modern Economic Theory*, edited by George Feiwel, 519–42. Macmillan Press.

Demsetz, Harold. 1988. "The Theory of the Firm Revisited." *Journal of Law, Economics, and Organization* 4 (Spring): 141–61.

Demsetz, Harold, and Kenneth Lehn. 1985. "The Structure of Corporate Ownership: Causes and Consequences." *Journal of Political Economy* 93 (December): 1155–77.

Eisenberg, Rebecca. 1987. "Proprietary Rights and the Norms of Science in Biotechnology Research." *Yale Law Journal* 97 (December): 177–231.

Fruits, Eric. 1997. "The Determinants of Managerial Ownership: Theory and Evidence from Initial Public Offerings." Working Paper. Marshall School of Business, University of Southern California.

Gordon, Lilly, and John Pound. 1990. "ESOPs and Corporate Control." *Journal of Financial Economics* 27 (October): 525–55.

Grant, Robert. 1996. "Toward a Knowledge-Based Theory of the Firm." *Strategic Management Journal* 17 (Winter, Special Issue): 109–23.

Harris, Milton, and Artur Raviv. 1979. "Optimal Incentive Contracts with Imperfect Information." *Journal of Economic Theory* 20 (April): 231–59.

Hart, Oliver, and John Moore. 1990. "Property Rights and the Nature of the Firm." *Journal of Political Economy* 98 (December): 1119–58.

Hellman, Thomas. 1997. "A Theory of Venture Capital Investing." Working Paper. Stanford University.

Huddart, Steven, and Mark Lang. 1996. "Employee Stock Option Exercises: An Empirical Analysis." *Journal of Accounting and Economics* 21 (February): 5–43.

Jensen, Michael, and William Meckling. 1976. "Theory of the Firm: Managerial Behavior, Agency Costs and Ownership Structure." *Journal of Financial Economics* 3 (October): 305–60.

Jensen, Michael, and Kevin Murphy. 1990. "Performance Pay and Top Management Incentives." *Journal of Political Economy* 98 (April): 225–64.

Kenney, Martin. 1986. *Biotechnology: The University-Industry Complex.* Yale University Press.

Kochan, T. 1996. "The American Corporation as Employer: Past, Present and Future Possibilities." In *The American Corporation Today,* edited by Carl Kaysen, 242–68. Oxford University Press.

Lasch, Christopher. 1995. *Revolt of the Elites and the Betrayal of Democracy.* W. W. Norton and Co.

Lazonick, W. 1991. *Business Organization and the Myth of the Market Economy.* Cambridge, England: Cambridge University Press.

Lee, K., and G. Steven Burrill. 1995. *Biotech 95: Reform, Restructure, Renewal.* Palo Alto: Ernst and Young.

Lerner, Joshua, and Robert Merges. 1998. "The Control of Technology Alliances: An Empirical Analysis of the Biotechnology Industry." *Journal of Industrial Economics* 46 (June): 125–56.

Liebeskind, Julia Porter. 1996. "Knowledge, Strategy, and the Theory of the Firm." *Strategic Management Journal* 17 (Winter: Special Issue): 93–108.

———. 1997. "Keeping Organizational Secrets: Protective Institutional Mechanisms and Their Costs." *Industrial and Corporate Change* 6 (September): 623–63.

Liebeskind, Julia Porter, and others. 1996. "Social Networks, Learning and Flexibility: Sourcing Scientific Knowledge in New Biotechnology Firms." *Organization Science* 7 (July): 428–43.

Masten, Scott. 1988. "A Legal Basis for the Firm." *Journal of Law, Economics and Organization* 4 (Spring): 181–98.

Milgrom, Paul, and John Roberts. 1992. *Economics, Organization, and Management.* Prentice-Hall.

Murphy, Kenneth J., Andrei Shleifer, and Robert W. Vishny. 1991. "The Allocation of Talent: Implications for Growth." *Quarterly Journal of Economics* 106 (May): 503–30.

Orsengio, Luigi. 1989. *The Emergence of Biotechnology.* St. Martin's Press.

Powell, Walter, Kenneth Koput, and Laurel Smith-Doerr. 1996. "Interorganizational Collaboration and the Locus of Innovation: Networks of Learning in Biotechnology." *Administrative Science Quarterly* 41 (March): 116–45.

Rabinow, Paul. 1996. *Making PCR: A Story of Biotechnology.* University of Chicago Press.

Rosenberg, N. 1990. "Why Do Firms Do Basic Research with Their Own Money?" *Research Policy* 19 (April): 165–74.

Schliefer, Andre, and Robert Vishny. 1986. "Large Shareholders and Corporate Control." *Journal of Political Economy* 94 (June): 461–88.

Smith, George D., and Davis Dyer. 1996. "The Rise and Transformation of the American Corporation." In *The American Corporation Today,* edited by Carl Kaysen, 28–73. Oxford University Press.

Teece, David. 1986. "Profiting from Technological Innovation." *Research Policy* 15 (December): 285–305.

———. 1992. "Competition, Cooperation and Innovation: Organizational Arrangements for Regimes of Rapid Technological Progress." *Journal of Economic Behavior and Organization* 18 (June): 1–25.

Teitelman, R. 1989. *Gene Dreams: Wall Street, Academia, and the Rise of Technology.* Basic Books.

Titman, Sheridan. 1984. "The Effects of Capital Organization on a Firm's Liquidation Decision." *Journal of Financial Economics* 13 (March): 137–51.

Werth, Barry. 1995. *The Billion Dollar Molecule: One Company's Quest for the Perfect Drug.* Simon and Schuster/Touchstone.

Wiggins, Steven. 1995. "Entrepreneurial Enterprises, Endogenous Ownership, and the Limits to Firm Size." *Economic Inquiry* 33 (January): 54–69.

Williamson, Oliver E. 1985. *The Economic Institutions of Capitalism: Firms, Markets, Relational Contracting.* Free Press.

Zucker, Lynne, and Michael Darby. 1996. "Star Scientists and Institutional Transformation: Patterns of Invention and Innovation in the Formation of the Biotechnology Industry." *Proceedings of the National Academy of Sciences,* vol. 93, 12709–12 (November).

LAURIE J. BASSI
BARUCH LEV
JONATHAN LOW
DANIEL P. McMURRER
G. ANTHONY SIESFELD

9

Measuring Corporate Investments in Human Capital

H UMAN CAPITAL IS, for very good reasons, the only form of capital
that modern corporations cannot buy or sell. As a result, it is the
only form of capital that does not have well-defined (if admittedly grossly
imperfect) accounting and reporting requirements associated with it. This
circumstance has resulted in an unhappy dearth of systematic information.
Firms themselves know little about the nature and magnitude of the investments that they make in human capital, and they know even less about the
effectiveness of those investments.

Under the best circumstances, a vast amount of information must be
gathered and evaluated in order to gauge the relative effectiveness of investments in human capital under a variety of circumstances and in various
forms of work. The collection of such a large bank of information requires
common metrics and shared measurement and accounting methodologies,
which, as just noted, simply do not exist. These requirements make it
impossible for any one firm or even a small group of firms working
together to solve this information problem. Hence, a classic market failure
results; while the information might be of great value, the market fails to
produce it.

For example, the estimates of how much firms spend on education and
training—their most conspicuous form of human capital investment—are

rough at best. Patching together the best available evidence suggests that the average U.S. employer spent approximately 0.9 percent of payroll on formal education and training in 1995—a figure that appears to have changed almost imperceptibly since 1983 (the only other year for which a roughly comparable estimate is available).[1] And virtually nothing is known about the investment that firms make in informal learning—although this investment is, by all available anecdotal accounts, significantly larger than that which firms make in formal learning.[2]

It should also come as no surprise that little systematic, high-quality information about the impact and value of firms' human capital investments exists.[3] In a recent review of the literature, only four serious attempts to identify the relationship between training and overall corporate performance were identified:[4]

—Manufacturing firms that implement training programs increase their productivity by an average of 17 percent;

—Participation in employer-sponsored training reduces the likelihood of an employee leaving their employer;

—Participation in employer-sponsored off-the-job training raises workers' productivity by 16 percent and increases their innovativeness on the job;

—Firms that downsize their work force are much more likely to increase their profitability if they train workers.[5]

Juxtaposed with this dearth of evidence is the increasing frequency with which prominent CEOs are heard to say that "people are our most important asset." If this is indeed the case, and given the old maxim that "what gets measured gets managed," it is reasonable to expect that firms would begin to take seriously the measurement of investments in this asset and the return on that investment.

---

1. See Bassi, Gallagher, Schroer (1996, p. 121). This figure is based on direct costs only. Although the inflation-adjusted total expenditure estimate increased by 18 between 1983 and 1995, the labor force grew by 19 percent during that same time period (*Economic Report of the President, 1996*, p. 316), suggesting virtually no change in training expenditures as a percent of payroll.

2. According to a recent report from the Bureau of Labor Statistics (December 1996), 70 percent of all training time is informal, with only 30 percent being formal. The relative cost of these two forms of training, however, is not known.

3. A relatively large number of case studies have found that training generates substantial return on investment. The methodologies used in these case studies, however, typically fail to credibly isolate the effect of training. Bartel (1997).

4. See Bassi, Gallagher, and Schroer (1996).

5. Bartel (1995); Lynch (1992); Bishop (1994); American Management Association (1995).

Moreover, evidence from the stock market suggests that there may be a potential payoff to increased efforts to measure (and therefore manage) investments in human capital more carefully. The growing divergence between book and market value in knowledge-intensive sectors of the economy attests to the increasing role of intangible assets, of which human capital is clearly a major component.

The decrease in the predictive validity of reported earnings and equity values, based on generally accepted accounting standards, is of more than academic interest.[6] The absence of systematic, forward-looking information undoubtedly contributes to volatility in the capital market, which raises the cost of capital. An increase in the cost of capital, in turn, impedes the rate at which corporations can grow and jobs can be created.

Perhaps more important, the absence of any generally accepted methods for measuring and valuing firms' investments in human capital is likely to result in an underinvestment in it. If, indeed, it is true that what gets measured gets managed, then it is almost certainly the case that the absence of measurement results in less than optimal management of corporations' human capital investment functions, thereby reducing the credibility of (and by extension, the resources available to) this investment. If this scenario is correct, then the absence of a system for measuring and valuing firms' investments in human capital could have profound consequences beyond simple economic inefficiency. Since the best available evidence suggests, for example, that the wages of workers who receive employer-provided education and training are between 4 and 16 percent above comparable workers who have not received training, anything that impedes this investment also impedes real wage growth.[7]

This chapter brings three very different perspectives to bear on this issue. The first, which is that of business consultants, summarizes what CEOs, CFOs, and market analysts say (and in some cases do) about valuing human capital. The second perspective, which is that of an accountant, analyzes what firms report publicly about human capital. The third perspective, which is that of an economist, reports on the results of a recent undertaking to improve the state of measurement with regard to firms' investments in education and training. The final section pulls together these (sometimes conflicting) perspectives and the resultant policy implications.

6. For evidence, see Lev and Zarowin (1998).
7. Groot, Hartog, and Oosterbeek (1994, p. 299).

The Value of Human Capital to the Firm

Disney asserts its has only two assets: Show and Story. Story is its collection of tales and its abilities to entertain every member of the family. Show is its brand (and the value it promises) and its people. Show is especially its people, and their ability to tell and continue to make the Story. Disney invests a lot in training all of its people in Show. If Mickey changes depending on who plays him, then Disney offers nothing to its customers.

Sears, as described in a *Fortune* article, has worked hard to increase its employees' satisfaction.[8] While the efforts Sears has taken to do this are instructive, the reasons it has done so are even more informative. Sears claims that an increase in its overall employee satisfaction at a store location predicts a rise in customers' overall satisfaction at that location two months hence and that a rise in customer satisfaction presages an increase in revenues at that location three months later. For Sears, an investment in its people increases its cash flows.

These two examples illustrate a more general phenomenon—that senior management of firms recognize the value and the indispensability of their people. Furthermore, the capital markets recognize the importance of a firm's people and will change their valuation of that firm as the market's evaluation of the firm's people changes. However, the process by which a firm's human capital returns improve market and operational performance is neither well understood nor described.

In the recent past, Ernst and Young's Center for Business Innovation (CBI) has completed two studies, the Twenty Questions about Knowledge Survey and a capital markets study. The results of these efforts provide evidence supporting the claim that both the senior management of a firm and the capital markets recognize the value of the human capital to that firm.

Twenty Questions about Knowledge Survey

Knowledge is the accumulated insights and understandings, both explicit and implicit, that the employees of a firm use to accomplish their assignments everyday.[9] It is, in part, the thoughtfulness and attention people bring to doing their job in pursuit of the firm's goals. It is a particular manifestation of human capital. Management of this knowledge includes

8. S. Stratford, "Bringing Sears into the New World," *Fortune*, October 13, 1997, pp. 183–84.
9. For Twenty Questions survey see Ernst and Young (1997b).

Table 9-1. *What Benefits Do You Believe Your Organization Could Gain from the More Active Management of Its Knowledge?*

Benefit	Percent agreement
Innovation	83
Efficiency	83
Improved decisionmaking	83
Increased responsiveness to customers	83
Flexibility	82
Quality improvement	71
Reduction in duplication	69
(Employee) empowerment	62

Source: Ernst and Young (1997b).

creating new insights and understanding, capturing and codifying these insights and understandings, and making them available for others to use as they do their tasks.

With near unanimity, respondents in this study declared that the deliberate management of knowledge within their organization can lead to greater benefits. Indeed, 96 percent agreed with this proposition and 54 percent strongly agreed with it. The consensus was that knowledge put to planful use makes the business better (tables 9-1, 9-2). The benefits of managing knowledge are

—Improved innovation;

—Increased flexibility (for example, the ability to change and adapt to change more rapidly); and

—Increased responsiveness to customers.

Table 9-2. *Of the Benefits Listed (in Table 9-1), Which Is Most Important for Your Organization's Success?*

Benefit	Percent agreement
Innovation	23
Flexibility	16
Increased responsiveness to customers	10
Improved decisionmaking	9
Efficiency	8

Source: Ernst and Young (1997b).

Table 9-3. *What Do You Think Are the Biggest Difficulties in Managing Knowledge in Your Organization?*

Difficulty	Percent agreement
Changing people's behavior	56
Measuring the value and performance of a knowledge asset	43
Determining what knowledge should be managed	40
Justifying the use of scarce resources for knowledge initiatives	34
Mapping the organization's existing knowledge	28
Setting the appropriate scope for knowledge initiatives	24
Defining standard processes for knowledge work	24
Making knowledge available	15
Overcoming technological limitations	13
Identifying the right team for knowledge initiatives	12
Attracting and retaining talented people	9

Source: Ernst and Young (1997b).

Moreover, these managers say that, on average, the firm's people account for half of the firm's performance (for example, the rest of performance is explained by technological innovation, market position, access to capital, internal processes). Despite the strong belief in the importance of this type of human capital to a firm, and in how this capital returns value to the firm, senior managers judged their firms to be underachieving in their management of human capital.

When asked what they faced as the biggest difficulty in managing knowledge in the organization, senior managers said it was changing people's behavior and measuring the value and performance of the knowledge assets (table 9-3). The inability to create tactical measurements leads to bureaucracy, no reliable measure of the return on investment, and the obsolescence of ideas and loss of information. If they could, senior managers would measure:

—Revenue generated by new ideas;

—Collaboration levels in key initiatives;

—Productivity of "knowledge" workers;

—Quality of decisions;

—Percentage of revenue from new products; and

—Employee awareness of knowledge sources.

When asked what they faced as the biggest impediments to knowledge transfer, senior management said, resoundingly, culture was the biggest

Table 9-4. *What Are the Biggest Impediments to Knowledge Transfer in Your Organization?*

Impediment	Percent agreement
Culture	54
Top management's failure to signal importance (of knowledge transfer)	32
Lack of shared understanding of strategy or business model	30
Organizational structure	28
Lack of ownership of the problem	28
Nonstandard process	27
Information and communication technology constraints	22
Incentive systems	19
Staff turnover	8
Configuration and physical features of workspace	5

Source: Ernst and Young (1997b).

problem (table 9-4). Cultural barriers included top management's failure to signal the importance of knowledge transfer and lack of a shared understanding of the strategy or business model. Cultural barriers lead to such phenomena as knowledge hoarding and organizational structures that increase rather than decrease the friction of knowledge transfer. Without a culture that respects and rewards giving knowledge away (sharing it), the natural tendency of people seems to be to accumulate knowledge and become personally indispensable by being the sole expert. These findings are supported by other research done in the area of human capital management, for example, to be most successful, innovative workplace systems must become part of a coordinated organizational strategy and fundamentally integrated into the way a firm does business. Simply implementing one practice—a new training program, for example—without adopting better information sharing and formal opportunities for employees to use and develop their new skills is unlikely to provide the powerful results of an integrated approach.[10]

Finally, another finding of the Twenty Questions survey highlights an important paradox. Although senior management admits that it is people who make knowledge work, senior management evinces little interest in

10. U.S. Department of Labor (1993).

monitoring who comes to and leaves the firm (only 2 percent) and what the skills of the employees are (9 percent interested). Furthermore, managers in the Twenty Questions survey show little interest in knowing what contributions employees are making to the organization's overall stock of knowledge (8 percent interested in the number and quality of submissions to the organization's knowledge bases).

This survey reflects the opinions and experience of 431 organizations, as reported by executives in a variety of management roles. Three hundred of these executives were U.S.-based, and the rest were European. No significant difference emerged in the responses of U.S. versus non-U.S. executives or among the responses of executives in different functional areas (marketing, information services, human resources, and so on).

Individuals were of uniformly senior rank, with the majority holding titles of vice president or above and reporting directly to the chief executive office or chief finance officer. Their firms averaged more $1 billion in revenues. Industry coverage was broad, ranging from aerospace to utilities. The largest subset of responding organizations fell into the category of "general manufacturing" (13 percent). No major differences emerged in responses from manufacturing versus service-oriented firms. Equally, people in these firms viewed their businesses as "knowledge intensive."

"Twenty Questions on Knowledge in the Organization" was a survey conducted by mail and therefore inevitably suffers some self-selection bias. The top 1,000 companies in the United States and Europe were targeted. The 431 responses reflect about a 40 percent response rate.

In sum, a self-selected sample of senior managers say that people are the source of a tremendously important asset—knowledge of why and how to achieve the firm's mission. They believe human capital leads to increased revenues (through greater innovation and customer connections) and increased flexibility.[11] With respect to this last point, a value to the firm of its people is an increase in the firm's options; it may be that this flexibility ought to be valued as a real option would be. But senior management recognizes the means to measure and manage the productive application of knowledge (and human capital in general) are missing.

11. A study of 150 of the *Forbes* 500 firms found, similarly, that companies with more progressive practices in six main areas (participation and management style, culture, organizational structure, creativity, reward systems, and flexibility and accommodation of needs) experienced 8.2 percent higher profit growth, 6.8 percent higher sales growth, 10.1 percent higher growth in earnings per share, and 4.2 percent higher dividend growth than firms that were not as progressive. Kravetz (1988, p. 42).

The Capital Markets Study

The second study was an experiment conducted with portfolio managers and traders (the buy-side).[12] In the experimental task, we varied the apparent financial performance of a set of well-known large cap (mature companies with large market capitalization), presented these scenarios to 275 institutional investors,[13] and had them allocate their investment dollars across the companies in the scenarios. Outside the experiment, we had the investors rate their perceptions of the performance of the target companies along several nonfinancial dimensions, and we had them evaluate the importance of a set of forty nonfinancial items.

METHOD: SAMPLE SELECTION TECHNIQUES. All research results were generated using information provided by portfolio managers representing virtually all major types and classes of active institutional investors. The final sample was drawn from a database detailing the population of U.S. portfolio managers, which is researched and updated annually by the Georgeson Group, a UK-based investor relations and proxy solicitation firm. At the close of 1995, this database included a total of just over 1,900 individuals representing private and public funds and institutions. Table 9-5 provides some descriptive information allowing comparison between the study sample and this larger population. The table presents data on the type of investment account, the portfolio's composition, and the manager's investment style.

Comparison of the population versus the sample suggests that the characteristics of the sample closely approximate those of the population at large, with only slight differences in the proportion of mutual fund and bank representatives. The sample of 275 represents approximately 14 percent of the total population, a level that minimizes the standard errors of the estimates.

A four-step, mail and telephone procedure was used to collect the study data. In step 1, investigators posted an introductory letter to all potential respondents informing them of the purpose of the survey and inviting their attention and participation. This initial contact was quickly followed in step 2 by a telephone call during which paid interviewers confirmed the

12. Ernst and Young (1997a).
13. The investors systematically excluded from the sample invested exclusively in small to mid-sized firms. The study's focus on "active" investment also necessarily precluded analysis of the decision-making styles of managers controlling indexed funds.

Table 9-5. *Population versus Respondent Characteristics, Portfolio Size,*
Type of Fund, and Investment Style

Item	Survey sample (percent)	Study population (percent)
Part A: Portfolio size		
Median assets (millions of dollars)	173	183
Average number of stocks held	132	149
Percent S&P 500 stocks	64	58
Panel B: Type of fund		
Mutual fund	13	19
Bank	22	14
Money market fund	51	53
Insurance company	9	9
Private pension	4	3
Public pension	1	2
Panel C: Investment style		
Aggressive growth	8	14
Growth	35	34
GARP	15	14
Balanced	8	10
Classic value	11	13
Value income	22	15

Source: Ernst and Young (1997a).

respondent's appropriateness for the study and solicited the person's commitment. Those agreeing to participate were mailed the survey in step 3
and invited to return their responses by mail or over the phone. Repeated
phone calls were used in step 4 as necessary to encourage response. The
return rate from qualified, participating respondents was 42 percent.

SURVEY DESIGN. As noted above, the primary research tool used to reach
this survey sample was a mailed survey instrument. The instrument itself
was divided into four parts. The first and final parts of the survey (parts 1
and 4) were used to collect essential demographic and investment profile
data. The second section (part 2) was used to collect "stated" preference data,
that is, participants' statements about their use of, or preferences for, particular types of investment data. Specifically, the survey instrument prompted
participants to state what percentage of their investment decisions are based

on nonfinancial data; to rate the usefulness of forty different types of non-financial data; and to rate the value of different data sources.

The third section (part 3) was designed to collect the study's experimental or behavioral data, that is, the respondents' "revealed" preferences. This section presented the respondents with a series of hypothetical share purchase scenarios. Figure 9-1 illustrates a hypothetical scenario.

In each scenario, the respondent was asked to allocate some portion of an investment fund across four companies operating in either the computer, oil and gas, food processing, or pharmaceutical industry.[14] Specifically, each respondent was asked to allocate 100 percent of his or her "fund" to one or more of four companies within the industry. To ensure sufficient degrees of freedom for statistical analysis, each industry-specific allocation scenario was run four times for a total of sixteen allocation scenarios per respondent. In each scenario, the respondent was provided with a set of financial performance data including, for example, price and earnings ratios, sales growth rates, earnings per share data, and so on. By varying the characteristics and the performance of these firms and by monitoring how the investment allocations changed along with the firms' changing performance, the investigators were able to deduce or "reveal" through a multinomial regression technique investors' preference for particular performance indicators.[15] With additional modeling and by combining the nonfinancial data with the financial data in the regression analysis, the investigators were ultimately able to "value" the usefulness of each different type of nonfinancial data in share price terms.

DATA ANALYSIS AND MODELING TECHNIQUES. Data analysis and modeling procedures used to identify investors' "revealed" preferences for nonfinancial information were designed following the procedures established

---

14. Studies by Eccles and Mavrinac (1995) and Lev and Sovgiannis (1996), for example, suggest that the usefulness of nonfinancial data might vary across industries and firm growth categories. To accommodate these findings, the investigators selected industries that varied strongly along the aggregate growth dimension. Using data on average company sales growth rates collected from Standard & Poor's publications, the investigators identified the pharmaceutical and computer industries as "high-growth" industries, the food processing industry as a "moderate-growth" industry, and the oil and gas industry as a "slow-growth" or declining industry.

15. This particular technique has a long history of use in such fields as marketing. The response variable can be either discrete or continuous. With a continuous response, the proportions assigned to each category or choice must sum to one. As a consequence, the responses across choices are negatively correlated, and the variance of the response becomes a function of size, making OLS or WLS techniques inappropriate.

by Moshe Ben Akiva and Takayuki Morikawa.[16] The principal statistical test involved estimation of a multinomial logit regression explaining allocation levels as a function of the financial characteristics presented in the experimental scenarios and a set of eight nonfinancial characteristics whose company-specific values were evaluated by the respondent's using an eleven-point Likert scale extending from 0 to 10. Each respondent was asked to evaluate the performance of all sixteen companies along the following dimensions:

—Quality of management;
—Quality of products and services;
—Customer satisfaction;
—Strength of corporate culture;
—Quality of investor relations;
—Executive compensation;
—Quality of new product development; and
—Strength of market position.[17]

A score of 5 was indicative of "average" performance relative to industry levels; a score of 10 was used to indicate above average performance; and a score of 1, below average performance. Almost all company ratings were highly correlated, raising concerns about the collinearity of the data used for the regression. To reduce the significance of this threat to statistical validity, the investigators decomposed the sources of variability by using structural equations modeling techniques. These techniques allowed the investigators to isolate the "brand halo" effects, that is, the bias or weight introduced to the performance rankings as a result of unique company "reputation." The final regression included only the residual of the model, or the "pure" ranking dissociated from the company halo.[18]

In the process of generating the final statistical model, the investigators evaluated a number of other potential influences on the allocation decision, including the investment style of the portfolio manager, the size of the portfolio, the type of fund managed, and the demographic background of

16. Ben-Akiva and Morikawa (1990).

17. Note that these ratings were introduced as covariates with only between-subject variability; there were no repeated measures for these questions.

18. An often appealing alternative to structural equations modeling is factor analysis. Note, however, that a fundamental assumption of factor analysis is that the variance to be parsed is strictly between items. In this survey, individuals were asked to evaluate nonfinancial performance dimensions for each of sixteen companies, raising the possibility of an additional source, that is, an individual source, of variation. To the extent that structural equations modeling can accommodate multiple sources of variation, it appears preferable to factor analysis for the purposes of this study.

Figure 9-1. *Hypothetical Scenario for Allocating Investment*

Assume that the following represents the latest financial information reported by the four companies below. Using both the information and any additional knowledge or opinion you may have of these four companies, please decide how you would allocate an investment among them.

Computer Systems Industry: Scenario 1

	Hewlett Packard	Sun Microsystems	Compaq	Dell	Reference information	
					Today's industry average[a]	Today's S&P 500 average
Market capitalization (millions)	$47,760	$8,603	$10,401	$2,717		
3-year EPS growth	33.1%	23.2%	85.0%	32.2%	44.3%	21.4%
3-year revenue growth	21.0%	16.9%	45.9%	56.4%	27.2%	8.4%
Consensus estimate of next FY change in EPS	16.2%	18.9%	22.0%	24.3%	26.3%	5.2%
Net profit margin	7.5%	7.9%	6.3%	6.4%	8.0%	8.7%
P/E ratio	15.6	23.0	16.8	10.3	25.7	20.9
Price-to-book value	4.2	4.8	2.9	2.5	5.1	4.5
	__% +	__% +	__% +	__% =	100 %	

Assume the four companies shown here are the ONLY companies available in this industry. Allocate 100 percent of an investment in the industry among these companies.

Source: Ernst and Young (1997a).
a. Computers and office equipment industry average.

the manager. None of these factors was found to play a statistically important role in the regression. We consequently interpret the model as being reasonably robust and generalizable across investor groups.

THE STATED VALUE OF NONFINANCIAL DATA. In many studies of investors' information needs, survey respondents are asked to rank the usefulness of particular types of nonfinancial data. While certain types of data, like quality of management or measures of market growth, for example, are consistently evaluated as "extremely useful," most discrete elements are evaluated as only modestly useful on average. In contrast with these earlier studies, this study attempted to measure the contribution not only of discrete items but also of the nonfinancial data set, more generally. That is, while this study assessed the usefulness of discrete data types, it also queried respondents about the value of nonfinancial data as a whole. For example, we asked respondents to indicate what percent of the investment decision was influenced by nonfinancial data. The response to this question was, on average, 35 percent. That is, about one-third of the information used to justify the investment decision is nonfinancial—a significantly larger fraction than anticipated (figure 9-2).

Figure 9-2 illustrates how widely responses varied around this average. The data presented indicate that this average response is not driven by a small fraction of investors who rely entirely on nonfinancial data. On the contrary, well over 60 percent of the survey population estimated that nonfinancial data drove between 20 percent and 50 percent of the investment decision. Just slightly less than 20 percent estimated that nonfinancial data influenced 50 to 59 percent of the decision.

Besides this aggregate valuation, the survey asked respondents for their evaluation of certain discrete data elements (table 9-6). To express their evaluation, respondents used a seven-point Likert scale, where a score of 1 represented "not at all important" and a score of 7, "very important." Only six of the thirty-nine data elements received mean scores of less than 4, signifying that they were considered "somewhat important." Of the remaining thirty-three items, thirty-one received scores between 4 and 6, suggesting that almost all types of nonfinancial data, from that indicating "innovativeness" (score: 5.77) or quality of the work force (score: 5.12), to that measuring global capability (score: 4.94), are considered valuable to the average shareholder.

Interestingly, in comparison with the results compiled by Robert G. Eccles and Sarah C. Mavrinac, these data suggest that employee information

Figure 9-2. *The Stated Usefulness of Nonfinancial Data: Percent Influence of Nonfinancial Measures versus Percent Respondents*

Percent respondents

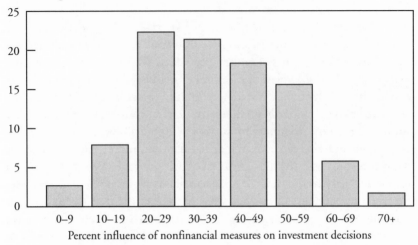

Percent influence of nonfinancial measures on investment decisions

Source: Ernst and Young (1997a).

is reasonably valued by investors.[19] Note, for example, that measures indicating "the company's ability to attract and retain talented people" received an importance score of 5.61, an exceptionally high score in comparison with that associated with other information types. Indeed, the only employee-related data element not receiving a score of at least 4 was the one measuring "use of employee teams." In summary, it appears that investors' most-valued nonfinancial measures are measures that reveal the productivity and creativity of the organization's people and people-oriented systems. Although the quality of the business plan or strategy is also considered crucial by investors, it seems that investors ultimately place more weight on the ability of the management team to deliver. The focus is on action.

THE RELATIVE VALUE OF PERFORMANCE IMPROVEMENT. The first phase of analysis described above offers an extension of previous studies of investors' information requirements and provides important new information on the extent to which nonfinancial data influence the investment decision in aggregate. Most important, however, this phase of analysis

19. Eccles and Mavrinac (1995).

Table 9-6. *Nonfinancial Criteria Used for Evaluating a Company*

Nonfinancial criteria[a]	Mean	Nonfinancial criteria[a]	Mean
Execution of corporate strategy	6.26	Strength of marketing and advertising	4.99
Management credibility	6.16	Global capability	4.94
Quality of corporate strategy	5.92	Quality of incentive performance systems	4.93
Innovativeness	5.77	CEO leadership style	4.91
Ability to attract and retain talented people	5.61	Product defect rates/service failure rates	4.79
Market share	5.60	Accessibility of management	4.69
Management experience	5.54	Product durability	4.64
Alignment of compensation with shareholder interests	5.48	Quality of employee training	4.48
Research leadership	5.40	Quality of guidance	4.48
Quality of major business processes	5.34	Employee turnover rates	4.42
Customer satisfaction level	5.33	Knowledge and experience of investor relations contact	4.36
Performance-based compensation policies	5.32	Number of customer complaints	4.32
Brand image	5.31	Quality of customer service department	4.29
New product development efficiency	5.26	Quality of published materials	3.91
Customer perceived quality	5.22	Product quality awards	3.53
Quality of organizational vision	5.19	Process quality awards	3.39
New product development cycle time	5.12	Environmental and social policies	3.36
Quality of work force	5.12	Use of employee teams	3.26
Repeat sales level	5.05	Ratio of CEO compensation to work force compensation	3.22
Percentage of revenues derived from new products	5.00		

Source: Ernst and Young (1997a).

a. The survey asked respondents the question as follows: "Thinking about the percentage you assigned to nonfinancial considerations, how important are each of the following nonfinancial criteria when evaluating a company? Please answer using the 1 to 7 importance scale."

Table 9-7. *Subject Companies by Industry*

Industry	Company
Computer systems	Hewlett Packard
	Sun Microsystems
	Compaq
	Dell
Food products	General Mills
	H. J. Heinz
	CPC International
	Ralston Purina
Pharmaceuticals	Merck
	Pfizer
	Bristol-Meyers
	Warner-Lambert
Oil and gas	Exxon
	Chevron
	Atlantic Richfield
	Phillips Petroleum

Source: Ernst and Young (1997a).

offers justification for the more detailed modeling required in the second phase of the study. As described above, this second phase of work relies on the data compiled from the experimental investment simulations. Those simulations prompted our survey respondents to allocate a hypothetical portfolio across four firms operating in either the computer, oil and gas, pharmaceuticals, or food processing industry. In every case, these companies were large firms whose nonfinancial attributes were well recognized by respondents (table 9-7).

By varying the characteristics and performance of these companies in the simulation and by registering the consequent changes in the amount of investment funds allocated to the firm, the investigators were able to estimate the amount of influence each financial and each nonfinancial characteristic had on the investment decision.

The quantitative results were generated through estimation of a multinomial logit regression. In general, the results of the full study estimation correspond well with the results of the stated preference study described above. According to our statistical estimates, approximately 33 percent of the investment decision can be explained with reference to nonfinancial data.[20] Recall that the response to our request for an estimate of "how much importance you place on nonfinancial versus financial considerations" was 35 percent, on average.

FINDINGS. Table 9-8 provides a description of model output for tests run using data compiled for all four subject industries: the oil and gas, pharmaceuticals, computer systems, and food processing industries. The data presented should be interpreted as the implicit value "scores" received by each of the nonfinancial factors—that is, as the revealed values of the nonfinancial data in the investment allocation context. These are relative scores—that is, scores determined in relation to the value assigned to the firm's price and earnings ratio. Each score represents the change in the price and earnings ratio that would have the same utility or value for the investor as a one-unit change in nonfinancial performance.[21]

Interestingly, neither increases in customer satisfaction nor improvements in the strength of corporate culture are valued highly by shareholders. To generate a more complete interpretation of these results, project investigators augmented the statistical analysis with in-depth, unstructured

20. Estimates were derived from comparison of relative size of log-likelihood ratios of the models including versus excluding nonfinancial information.

21. For example, for a large firm operating in the biotechnology-drug development industry, a one-unit change in the quality of products and services would be equivalent in value and would have the same impact on investor demand levels, as a 0.9 percent increase in the firm's price-earnings ratio. Similarly, for a firm operating in the food processing industry, a one-unit increase in the quality of products and services would be equivalent in utility or value terms to a 1.4 percent change in the firm's price-earnings ratio. The implications of these findings can be made more obvious with some simple calculations. Note first that reported earnings do not change frequently. On the contrary, they are reported quarterly at best. Given this fact, we can restate the relationship, defining a one-unit improvement in the quality of products and services in the pharmaceuticals industry as equivalent to a 0.9 percent increase in share price, other things being equal. For a firm like Merck whose share price was approximately $44.00 in the spring of 1996 and which had over 1,145 million shares outstanding, this 0.9 percent increase in share price would be manifest as a $453 million increase in market value. That is, for the average shareholder, a one-unit increase in the quality of Merck's products and services would be equivalent to, or worth to the shareholder, approximately $453 million. Further inspection of the results in table 9-8 suggests that the largest value gain for a firm operating in the pharmaceutical industry would flow from improvements in the quality of new product development. For a firm like Merck, a one-point improvement in the quality of new product development would be "valued" by investors at a sum topping $2.6 billion. According to our calculations, improvements in the quality of management would also be valued highly by shareholders. For a firm like Hewlett-Packard, for example, which operates in the computer systems industry, a one-unit improvement in the quality of management would be equivalent in shareholder value terms to a $1.3 billion gain in market value, given the performance of the firm in the spring of 1996.

Table 9-8. *Model Output: Investor Valuation of Nonfinancial Performance Improvement*

Scores indicate equivalent percentage increase in a company's P/E ratio for a 1 point improvement in investor perceptions of nonfinancial performance

	Industry			
Item	*Computer*	*Drugs*	*Food*	*Oil and gas*
Quality of management	7.6	2.6	1.4	4.2
Quality of products and services	2.4	0.9	1.4	5.8
Customer satisfaction	0.0	0.0	0.0	0.0
Strength of corporate culture	0.0	0.0	0.0	0.0
Quality of investor relations	0.8	0.5	0.3	0.9
Executive compensation	0.9	0.6	0.4	1.1
Quality of new product development	0.0	5.3	0.9	1.6
Strength of market position	3.1	0.3	0.0	7.3

Source: Ernst and Young (1997a).

interviews with prototypical respondents. One subject simply dismissed the relatively low customer satisfaction and corporate culture weights, saying: "Culture, customers . . . I don't have time to interview employees and customers and no good independent source of information about them exists, so I largely ignore them." Another noted, "For these types of companies, if they have high-quality management and are offering a high quality product through well-developed distribution channels, then they must have satisfied customers."

The study showed that an investor's perception of a firm's nonfinancial performance had a significant impact on that investor's valuation of the firm and that investors generally attend to the same nonfinancial signals from the firm. For the purpose of this chapter, what the investors consider critically important nonfinancial information is what matters.[22] To investors, the most important areas of nonfinancial performance are

—Strategy execution;
—Management credibility;
—Quality of strategy;

22. The forty items rated for importance map into eight nonfinancial performance dimensions (Confirmatory Factor Analysis had an R^2 of approximately .92). Nonfinancial performance accounted for 33 percent of the variance in allocation, and the importance items account for about 90 percent of the variance in performance ratings.

—Innovativeness;

—Ability to attract and retain talented people;

—Market position;

—Management experience;

—Quality of executive compensation;

—Quality of major processes; and

—Research leadership.

As many as six of these ten nonfinancial items can be construed as being part of human capital: the ability to attract and retain talent, innovativeness, research leadership, management credibility, management experience, and strategy execution.

IMPLICATIONS. The capital markets use nonfinancial performance as a leading indicator of future performance. The higher the markets rate a firm's management experience and capabilities, and the firm's people's skills, commitments, and alignment with the firm's goals, the better the markets believe the firm will do. Hence the higher the stock price they are willing to pay, the lower the cost of capital, the higher are likely returns on invested capital, and the greater are returns to stockholders.

This is consistent with the findings of the work of others. For instance, Gordon, Pound, and Porter showed, using results from *Fortune* magazine's annual survey on corporate reputations, that companies highly regarded for their utilization of human capital were also highly regarded for other critical practices, including quality of management, quality of products, and ability to innovate.[23] Furthermore, their study found that companies with well-respected employee practices scored highest on critical measures of long-term corporate performance, including the utilization of capital and total returns to investors.

In short, the market cares about the quality and "application" of a firm's human capital. Furthermore, the market's perceptions of a firm's human capital strongly influence the stock price of the firm (through the market's willingness to pay more or less for that stock).

Summary

The two studies cited above have a similar theme: the people that make up a firm—from the senior management to the rank and file—are recognized

23. Gordon, Pound, and Porter (1994).

as helping determine the overall performance of the firm. Market analysts report that they recognize the value of people by valuing more highly the stocks of those firms that are judged to have talented employees and alignment of interests. Moreover, senior management affirms the importance of the knowledge their employees bring to the firm and truly believes that knowledge can, if managed properly, lead to competitive advantage in the marketplace.

Yet, despite the stated importance of human capital and its contribution to performance revealed in these studies, senior managers report that they do not have the measurement or management tools necessary to fully take advantage of human capital. It is capital market impressions that drive valuation. It is management belief that drives investment.

What do managers want? They do not want an inventory of who's working for the firm and the rate at which people leave the company. They do want a way to track the productive application of human and knowledge capital—they want to understand how the firm's people find new sources of revenues, create new revenue opportunities, increase the optionality of the firm, improve relationships with customers, and improve efficiency and decisionmaking.

Given this perspective, it seems likely that senior managers will never be interested in tracking training expenditures nor in matching the inputs of investments in people with specific cash flows to a firm. Rather, they will be much more interested in tactical tools and in measurements related to outcomes that are related to a firm's goals.

The Accounting and Reporting of Human Capital

Generally accepted accounting principles (GAAP) are the set of rules and regulations governing the measurement and disclosure practices of U.S. public companies. These regulations are manifested in corporate financial reports, such as quarterly and annual financial statements, as well as special filings, such as prospectuses accompanying securities issues. As far as human capital is concerned, GAAP is silent. Public companies are not required to disclose, qualitatively or quantitatively, any aspect of firms' investment in human capital, such as expenditures on employee training.[24]

---

24. There appears to be an SEC requirement to disclose the total number of employees in annual reports.

Nor are firms required to disclose any meaningful information on the state of their human capital, such as data on employee education, training, or any other capabilities of the labor force.

The disclosure prescriptions in GAAP are generally perceived as minimal requirements, and firms often disclose additional, voluntary information. Indeed, a surge in the past fifteen to twenty years has occurred in the amount of voluntary information provided by corporate executives.[25] Public corporations now routinely release news about products under development, alliances, joint ventures, managerial changes and restructuring, as well as prospective information, such as warnings about disappointing forthcoming earnings.[26] It is, therefore, possible that human capital information, though not required by GAAP, is voluntarily provided to investors.

To examine the possibility that firms would voluntarily provide human capital information, we focused on the enterprises that constitute the American Society for Training and Development's Benchmarking Forum.[27] In large part because of the absence of accounting standards for measuring employers' investments in education and training, a group of eighteen Fortune 500 firms approached the American Society for Training and Development (ASTD) in 1992, asking for assistance in developing common definitions and measurement methodologies so that they could individually and collectively identify and benchmark these investments. As of the end of 1996, this group consisted of fifty-six firms. The group's procedures for measuring training and education expenditures are now well established, although some of the members (including a few of the founding members) still have trouble implementing these standards. We deemed the likelihood of these enterprises to publicly disclose human capital information high, since they are large firms (large companies tend to disclose more voluntary information than small companies), and their voluntary membership in the Benchmarking Forum indicates a special interest in human capital issues. We focus on the annual financial reports of the Benchmarking companies, leaving out verbal communications with investors.

25. For an analysis of such information and investors' reaction to it, see Kasznik and Lev (1995).

26. During the past three to five years, it has become customary for many public companies to conduct routine conference calls with analysts and institutional investors an hour or two after the release of quarterly reports. Such conference calls provide opportunity for additional voluntary communication between the firm and the public.

27. This part of the study was aided by Min Wu, a Ph.D. student at New York University, Stern School of Business.

Of the fifty-six Fortune 500 members of ASTD's 1996 Benchmarking Forum two members merged, eight enterprises are private, four are foreign companies, and two are subsidiaries of public companies. These enterprises do not publish financial reports in the United States. The remaining forty-one public companies constitute our sample. We have examined the annual reports of these companies for 1994 through 1996, for any information related to human capital, particularly in the management discussion and analysis section of the report (in which managers are required to discuss important aspects impacting current and past years), and in footnotes to the statements.

The large majority of sample companies (for example, 32 of 41 in 1996) did not provide any human capital information in the 1994–96 annual reports (table 9-9). Of those providing some information on human capital, most (nine of forty-one in 1996) disseminated some qualitative information, while very few (four in 1995; none in 1996) released some quantitative data. Surprisingly, the trend indicates a decrease over 1994–96 in reporting about human capital: the number of firms providing no information increased from thirty to thirty-two, and those providing quantitative information decreased from 3 in 1994 to zero in 1996.

Practically all the information provided is qualitative and of such a general nature as to be almost useless for any analysis and inference. Typical statements are ones like the quotation from Andersen Worldwide in 1995. "We recruit the best people and train them to be the best professionals in the world." Or "Avon Germany implemented a new recruiting, training, and retention program in 1995." Of some interest is Caterpillar's 1995 report which states, "In Illinois alone, we are investing over $6,000 per employee per year on training."[28] And Colgate's 1995 report informing readers, "We can actually quantify the benefits [of training] using increased employee competence and on-the-job productivity as measured." However, no information is given about those measures or even their direction.

It can be concluded, therefore, that no disclosure requirement exists in the United States for information related to human capital and that public companies apparently do not have strong incentives to disclose vol-

28. See table 9-9. It should be noted, however, that the state of Illinois (where Caterpillar is headquartered) offers a tax credit to employers, based on their training expenditures. Obviously, under these circumstances it is in Caterpillar's interest to publicly disclose this information.

untarily such information. Nor do they have such information readily available.[29]

Measuring Firms' Investments in Education and Training

In the spring of 1997, the ASTD fielded the Human Performance Practices Survey—an inaugural attempt to make the measurement methodologies developed in the Benchmarking Forum (mentioned earlier) available to a wider range of corporations. The survey focused primarily on measuring establishments' investments in education and training but also collected data on work practices, compensation policies, and subjective (that is, perceptual) measures of twelve different aspects of corporate performance (both financial and nonfinancial). The survey was sent to a stratified random sample of nearly 10,000 establishments with fifty or more employees.[30]

To encourage firms to complete the survey, the ASTD offered to produce a free, customized "benchmarking report" for those establishments that responded.[31] The survey was also open to the public for participation and was advertised through an ASTD membership announcement and ASTD's home-page on the World Wide Web.[32] The data were carefully cleaned, and when necessary, validated through follow-up telephone calls. The final usable sample consisted of 500 establishments.[33] The low response rate to this survey (given the incentives that were offered to respondents and the expense that went into the original construction of the sample and follow-up) attests to the difficulty of collecting these data.[34]

29. It should be noted that voluntary disclosure by corporations involves a tacit commitment to continue disclosing. If, for example, following several years of disclosing investment in training, a company stops such disclosure, investors will suspect the worst (no news is bad news in disclosure). Firms may accordingly decline to commit to disclosures about human capital.

30. The survey was stratified so that the number of firms sampled within each industry-firm size category was proportionate to total employment within that category.

31. Before the survey was fielded, focus groups were run to ascertain that the offer of a free benchmarking report was seen as valuable and to design it in a way that would be most useful to firms. The customized benchmarking report compared each establishment to all of the other respondents in the same industry-size category. Organizations were allowed to respond either at the establishment or corporate level. Fifty-one percent of respondents reported data for their entire corporation.

32. Thirty-five percent of all responses came from these alternative methods.

33. Most of the firms that were eliminated from the sample had fewer than fifty employees.

34. A significant amount of money was spent to boost the response rate. Before mailing the survey each establishment was called to identify the name, title, address, and telephone number of the person within the firm who was best equipped to respond to the survey, and after the survey was mailed, each establishment was phoned to encourage them to respond.

Table 9-9. *Human Capital Information, by Firms*

Item	1994	1995	1996
No information	Allstate, American Express, Ameritech, AT&T, Bell Atlantic, Boeing, Caterpillar, Chase, Corning, Digital Equipment, Dow Chemical, Duke Power, Eastman Chemical, Florida Power & Light, Ford, Freddie Mac, GM, IBM, Intel, Johnson & Johnson, Metlife, Moore, NYNEX, P&G, Polaroid, Qualcomm, SBC Communications, Texas Instruments, Unisys. (30)	Aetna, American Express, AT&T, Bell Atlantic, Boeing, Corning, Digital Equipment, Dow Chemical, Duke Power, Eastman Chemical, Florida Power & Light, Ford, Freddie Mac, GM, Intel, Johnson & Johnson, Moore, Motorola, NYNEX, P&G, Polaroid, Qualcomm, SBC Communications, Texas Instruments, Unisys, USPS, Xerox. (28)	Aetna, Allstate, American Express, Ameritech, AT&T, Bell Atlantic, Boeing, Caterpillar, Corning, Cummins Engine, Digital, Dow Chemical, Duke Power, Eastman Chemical, Florida Power & Light, Ford, Freddie Mac, GM, IBM, Intel, Johnson & Johnson, Metlife, Moore, Motorola, NYNEX, P&G, Polaroid, Qualcomm, Sprint, Texas Instruments, Unisys, Xerox. (32)
Quantitative information	BancOne, Colgate. (2)	BancOne, Caterpillar, Colgate, Cummins. (4)	(0)
Qualitative information	Aetna, Andersen, Avon, BancOne, Chevron, Colgate, C&L, Cummins, Motorola, Xerox. (10)	Allstate, Ameritech, Andersen, Avon, BancOne, Caterpillar, Chase, Chevron, Colgate, C&L, Cummins, IBM, Metlife. (13)	Andersen, Avon, BancOne, Chase, Chevron, Colgate, C&L, SBC Communications, USPS. (9)

Source: American Society for Training and Development (ASTD), Alexandria, Va.

Despite the disappointing response rate, the quality of the data appears very high. Perhaps most significant, of the 500 usable responses, 67 came from publicly traded firms, making it possible to merge the survey data with publicly available financial data.

The available array of subjective and objective performance outcomes are as follows:

—Subjective Measures. Respondents were asked to assess whether their organization's performance in 1996 was better, worse, or no different from 1995; and better, worse, or no different from other organizations that do the same kind of work. Within each of these two categories, respondents were asked to assess six specific aspects of performance, including ability to retain essential employees, employee satisfaction, quality of product and services, customer satisfaction, sales, and overall profitability.[35] Each of these six aspects was used to construct two corresponding indexes of organizational performance (one for change in performance between 1995 and 1996 and the other for the level of performance in 1996 compared with other organizations).

—Objective Measures. For the publicly traded corporations in the sample, financial reports were used to construct the following measures for fiscal years 1995 and 1996 and for the second quarter of calendar year 1997: net sales per employee, gross profit per employee, and market-to-book value. (Market-to-book value was updated to the third quarter of 1997.)

Factor analysis was used to identify the following clusters of human resource practices and create corresponding indexes:

—Innovative training practices consisting of train-the-trainer programs, line-on-loan or rotational training staff, training resource center, mentoring or coaching practices, individual development plans, peer review of performance/360 feedback, and training information systems.

—High-performance work practices consisting of employee involvement with management in business decisions, employee access to key business information, and self-directed work teams.

—Innovative compensation plans consisting of profit sharing or gain sharing, group or team-based compensation, individual incentive compensation, and employee stock ownership plans.

—Quality initiatives consisting of quality circles or problem-solving teams and total quality management.

---

35. Earlier survey efforts had taught us that it is virtually impossible for respondents to provide objective measures for these variables.

—Competency training practices consisting of skill certification, documentation of individual competencies, job rotation or cross training, mandatory annual training time, and knowledge or skill-based pay.

Three separate approaches were taken to analyzing the data:

—Using the entire sample of 500 firms, correlation tables were created with the focus being on examining the relationships between a variety of measures of investments in education and training, other human resource practices, and subjective measures of performance (financial and nonfinancial).

—Using the sample of publicly traded corporations, correlation tables were created with the focus being on examining the relationship between investments in education and training, other human resource practices, and objective measures of financial performance in fiscal year 1996 and the second quarter of calendar year 1997.

—A set of preliminary regressions (ordinary least squares) was run on the sample of publicly traded firms, using the objective financial performance variables as dependent variables, with the education and training investment and human resource practice variables as independent variables. Given the small sample sizes available, these results provided no additional insights above and beyond those generated by the correlations, and so the regression results are not reported here.

*Correlations between Human Resource Practices and
Subjective Measures of Performance*

Table 9-10 reports the Pearson correlations from the first analysis. Both subjective measures of overall performance (level of performance in 1996 relative to other companies that do the same kind of work and change in overall performance between 1995 and 1996) are correlated with companies' use of innovative training practices, high performance work practices, and innovative compensation plans. The correlations between two individual high-performance work practices—employee access to key competitive information and involvement with business issues—are also statistically significant (results not shown here). There is also some evidence that the responses are not merely gratuitous or self-serving. For example, the high-performance work system scale (over which respondents have no influence in their day-to-day work) has a much more significant correlation with performance than the competency training scale (over which respondents do have influence).

The percent of payroll spent on training is significantly correlated with perceived performance in 1996 compared with other organizations that do

Table 9-10. *Correlations between Human Capital Investments and Subjective Measures of Performance*

Investment	Performance versus others scale	Change in performance scale
Training as a percent of payroll 1996	0.138*	0.033
Percent of employees trained 1996	0.098	–0.047
Change in training expenditures 1995–96	0.071	0.165**
Change in percent of employees trained 1995–96	0.030	0.110*
Innovative training practices scale	0.148**	0.119*
High performance work practices scale	0.144**	0.138**
Innovative compensation scale	0.127*	0.103*
Quality initiatives scale	0.085	0.089
Competence training scale	0.064	0.025

Source: Based on data from ASTD.
N between 406 and 459.
* $p < .05$.
** $p < .01$.

the same kind of work but not with change in performance from 1995 to 1996. Conversely, change in training expenditure and change in the percentage of employees receiving training are positively correlated with perceived improvement in performance between 1995 and 1996 but not with perceived performance in 1996 compared with other organizations that do the same kind of work.

These results are consistent with expectations (although they do not provide sufficient information to draw conclusions about causation). The level of training (in dollars or people) should be expected to be correlated with the level of performance (relative to other organizations) but not the change in performance (between 1995 and 1996). Similarly, a change in training should be expected to be correlated with a change in performance (from 1995 to 1996) but not with the level of performance (compared with other organizations).

Correlations between Human Resource Practices and Objective Measures of Performance

The Pearson correlations between the human capital investment variables and the objective measures of financial performance are reported in table 9-11. Because this sample consists only of publicly traded firms that

Table 9-11. *Correlations between Human Capital Investments and Objective Measures of Performance*

Item	Training as a percent of payroll 1996	Training experience per employee	Percentage of employees trained 1996	Change in training expenditures 1995–96	Change in employees trained 1995–96	Innovative training practices scale	High performance work practices scale	Innovative compensation scale	Quality initiatives scale	Competence training scale
1995 (year end)										
Market-to-book value	0.302*	0.227	0.184	0.032	−0.426*	−0.066	0.008	0.124	−0.102	0.048
Net sales/employee	0.092	0.162	0.142	0.254	0.392*	−0.023	−0.086	0.027	0.212	0.103
Gross profit/employee	−0.005	0.154	0.314*	0.126	0.266	0.191	−0.074	0.167	0.276	−0.003
1996 (year end)										
Market-to-book value	0.431***	0.319**	0.259	−0.128	−0.316	0.066	−0.028	0.142	−0.051	−0.013
Net sales/employee	0.073	0.189	0.115	0.131	0.250	−0.025	−0.121	−0.001	0.063	0.026
Gross profit/employee	0.038	0.196	0.210	0.143	0.113	0.161	−0.030	0.210	0.163	−0.168
1997										
Market-to-book value (3Q)	0.370**	0.201	0.324*	0.030	−0.227	0.121	−0.065	0.015	0.020	0.140
Net sales/employee (1H)	0.091	0.249	0.053	0.149	0.078	0.064	0.037	−0.080	0.112	−0.152
Gross profit/employee (1H)	−0.019	0.172	0.009	0.143	−0.018	0.085	0.147	0.014	0.232	−0.257

Source: Based on data from ASTD.

* $p < .10$.
** $p < .05$.
*** $p < .01$.

reported for their entire corporation, the sample sizes are quite small (between 35 and 55 depending on the variables under consideration).

Given these very small sample sizes and the range of industries represented, not surprisingly, there are few significant correlations. None of the human resource practices scales (innovative training, high performance work, innovative compensation, quality initiatives, or competence training) was significantly correlated with any of the three financial outcome variables (net sales per employee, gross profit per employee, and market-to-book value). Interestingly, however, both training as a percentage of payroll and training expenditure per employee were significantly, positively correlated with 1996 market-to-book value. Furthermore, training as a percent of payroll was significantly correlated with 1997 third quarter market-to-book value, as was percentage of employees trained (although the latter significance level was marginal).

These are, of course, only correlations. They neither control for other relevant factors nor prove causality. Correlations between 1996 training and 1995 financial outcomes can, however, shed a bit of light on the issue of causality. Since inputs cannot possibly have an effect on outcomes in a preceding year, significant correlations (above and beyond those that would be expected to occur by chance) are either evidence of serial correlation or reverse causality. While none of these correlations are significant at the standard .05 level, three correlations are significant and positive at the .10 level and one is significant and negative at the .10 level. These findings suggest either that training investments are correlated over time or that firms change their use of these practices in response to prior financial performance (although, given the one negative correlation, the direction of change is in question).

What can be concluded with certainty is that training as a percent of payroll is significantly, positively associated with market-to-book value; in short, Wall Street values more highly those firms that make significant investments in training than those firms that do not. This could either mean that training is a part of a larger package of practices that Wall Street values (presumably because it bodes well for future performance) or that training has a direct effect on that performance. If the latter is the case, the correlations in table 9-11 almost certainly overstate the independent effect of training.

What is, perhaps, surprising about these correlations is that the training variables achieve statistical significance when other variables (for example, innovative compensation and high-performance work practices), which have been found to be significant by other researchers, are not significantly correlated with financial outcomes. It might be that the sample sizes are simply too small, or that these other variables are not measured with sufficient precision. In any event, it is noteworthy that some of the training investment variables are significant, while other variables that are commonly believed important by researchers are not significant.

The correlations summarized in table 9-11 translate into substantial differences in financial performance. Figure 9-3 compares those companies in the top half of the distribution when ranked according to their average 1996 training expenditures per employee ($900) with those in the bottom half ($275 per employee). The companies in the top half had higher net sales per employee in the first half of 1997 than those in the lower half of the distribution. In the first half of 1997, companies in the top half also averaged an annualized gross profit of more than $168,000 per employee compared with companies in the bottom half with gross profits of $121,000 per employee. Market-to-book ratios for those in the bottom and top half of the distribution are 2.42 and 2.77, respectively.

Interestingly, between companies with high and low training expenditures, the percentage differences in their market-to-book ratios were smaller than the percentage differences in the other two measures of financial success: net sales per employee and gross profits per employee. That suggests that the market may not adequately capture all of the added value of training, perhaps because it has no information about it.

Still, clearly, companies with higher training expenditures did well in the stock market during the period we examined. The change over time in market-to-book ratios shows greater increases for companies that ranked in the top half on 1996 training expenditures, as seen in figure 9-4. The growth in market-to-book ratios from December 31, 1995, to September 30, 1997, was more than twice as large for companies in the top half in 1996 training expenditures per employee than for companies in the bottom half.

There is an even larger difference when companies are broken down by the percentage of employees trained (the top half provided training to an average of 84 percent of their work forces, compared with the bottom half that trained an average of 35 percent). Companies in the bottom half had a slight drop in their market-to-book ratios; companies in the top half had a significant increase.

Figure 9-3. *Relationship between Training Expenditures per Employee, 1996, and Measures of Financial Performance, 1997*

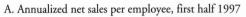

A. Annualized net sales per employee, first half 1997

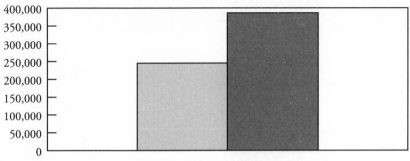

B. Annualized gross profits per employee, first half 1997

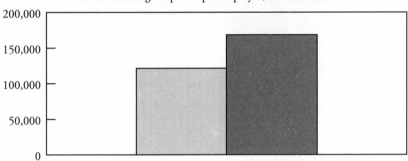

C. Ratio of market-to-book value, third quarter 1997

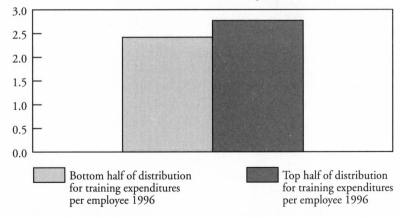

       Bottom half of distribution   Top half of distribution
       for training expenditures   for training expenditures
       per employee 1996   per employee 1996

Source: Bassi and McMurrer (1998).

Figure 9-4. *Mean Change in Market-to-Book Ratio, December 31, 1995, to September 30, 1997, by Various Measures of 1996 Training Practices*
Mean change in market-to-book

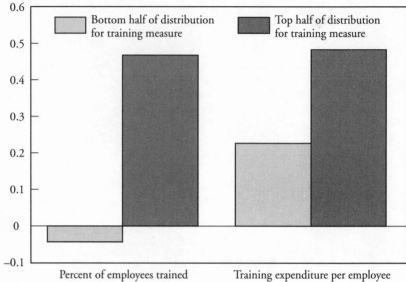

Percent of employees trained   Training expenditure per employee

Source: Bassi and McMurrer (1998).

Next Step toward Improving the State of Measurement

In 1998, the ASTD launched a major initiative to develop a widely accepted set of standards for measuring and valuing firms' investments in education and training. This initiative expands on both the scope and the scale of the 1997 Human Performance Practices Survey by

—Using the ASTD's outreach capacity to increase significantly the number of publicly traded corporations responding to the survey.

—Expanding the content of the survey to include measures of the "intermediate outcomes" that result from firms' education and training investments;

—Beginning to construct a longitudinal file on a subsample of firms so that causal relationships can be better disentangled.

In the 1997 version of the Human Performance Practices Survey, considerable expense was incurred in an attempt to generate a representative sample of firms. This effort was unsuccessful, as evidenced by the low response rate.[36] So the 1998 effort focused instead on generating voluntary (perhaps nonrandom) responses by appealing to the ASTD's 70,000 members and using the 150 local ASTD chapters as marketing agents for the free "benchmarking service" that is offered as an enticement for firms to respond.

The content of the 1998 survey was expanded to include a standard set of "intermediate outcomes" that result from firms' education and training expenditures. The methodologies and metrics for measuring these intermediate outcomes have been under development during the past year through a collaborative effort between the ASTD and a nine-member working group of companies in the Benchmarking Forum. These intermediate outcome measures are subjective (that is, perceptual) measures of the extent to which participation in education and training programs results in the desired behavioral changes on the job.[37]

It is likely that it will take some time for firms to be able to adopt these outcome measures and put the data collection systems in place necessary to measure them. By late 1998, ASTD had begun to compile a database with both firms' investments in education and training and these intermediate outcomes for a large enough sample of firms to make statistical analysis possible.

Special efforts were made in 1998 to re-recruit into the sample those corporations and establishments that reported in 1997; and encourage firms to respond at the corporate rather than the establishment level whenever possible. Particular emphasis has been put on recruiting publicly traded corporations, since this is the only group for which it is possible to get consistent financial information.

The ultimate intent is to construct a longitudinal file on firms that contains data on

—A wide variety of human resource practices with an emphasis on investments in education and training;

—Subjective measures of the intermediate outcomes that result from education and training investments;

36. Despite the low response rate, the results came remarkably close to replicating those of a similar survey of a representative sample of firms done by the Bureau of Labor Statistics in 1995. See Bureau of Labor Statistics (July 1996).

37. In the early phases of the working group's efforts, it was agreed that it would be impossible to develop common objective measures of these intermediate outcomes because the desired outcomes vary enormously across industries, and for many types of education and training programs (for example, interpersonal skills) there simply are no measures of objective outcomes.

—Subjective measures of a variety of nonfinancial outcomes (for example, employee retention, quality, employee and customer satisfaction); and
—Objective measures of financial performance.

Conclusions and Implications for Policy

Information possesses the attributes of a public good. Once it is created, it can be provided to an additional user at very low (or possibly even zero) marginal cost. And it is nonexclusionary; its use by one party does not diminish the amount available to another (although that use might reduce its value to the first party). Any commodity with these characteristics will almost surely be underprovided by the private market, if it is provided at all.

That there is no apparent demand for information about firms' investments in human capital, and that firms do not choose to voluntarily provide it, does not necessarily imply that such information has no value. A major conclusion that emerges from surveys of senior executives done by Ernst and Young's Center for Business Innovation is that these executives would welcome suggestions about how to create systems for measuring the effectiveness with which they manage knowledge (which is created by human capital). And although the ASTD encountered difficulty in gaining firms' cooperation in its first step toward creating a standard method for measuring firms' investments in education and training, more than 500 did choose to participate in this inaugural effort. This suggests that they believe that it is in their interest to have more and better information about this investment than they could gather by themselves.

Both market analysts and managers inside corporations would benefit from information on the human capital function that helps them assess rate of return on investment in human resources and predict future performance. For market analysts (be they professionals or amateurs), there is obviously money to be made from anything that helps them predict the future better. The motivation is the same for managers; information that enables them to predict (perhaps very imperfectly) the future consequences of their management decisions would improve the quality of those decisions, and as a result, generate profits (in part by attracting lower-cost capital to the firm).

This apparent alignment of interests between analysts and managers does not, however, suggest that they would be equally receptive to attempts to improve the state of measurement of human capital. Analysts make their money by gaining insight and understanding about the likely future performance of corporations that is not (at least immediately) shared by others. From their perspective, once the information playing field is leveled, the opportunities for analysts to profit are diminished. So it is not too surprising that analysts are not demanding that more and better information be made available on firms' human capital.

Managers, however, are struggling to better manage the value that is created by human capital. Any information and measurement systems that help them do that better would undoubtedly be embraced by them. So the problem is not that there isn't demand for such systems—the problem is that there is less than optimal supply.

To the extent that information and measurement systems are available, they are either idiosyncratic to a firm (often "home-grown") or share some properties across firms (often when they are provided by consultants). But there is no information system in place that is sufficiently broad-based to enable managers to learn systematically about what works best under what circumstances.

That is the public good problem. It is not a problem that the private market can solve by itself. Moreover, the players in the one market that perhaps has sufficient clout to demand a solution (the capital market) probably do not see it in their interest to do so. Hence, the state of measurement that we observe today.

Some form of collective action is the only solution to a market failure problem. Typically, the government becomes the financier, collector, and disseminator of information. But there are at least two major obstacles that must be overcome: the private sector does not yet recognize the benefits of disclosing such information and, as a result, is likely to view government efforts in this regard as unwelcome and intrusive; and the private sector recognizes all too well the penalties associated with disclosure of nonfinancial information.

To address the first, governments could begin work on a global basis through the World Trade Organization or the Organization for Economic Cooperation and Development to develop information and advisory opinions on comparability of relevant data. They could also sponsor research to explore the implications of such disclosures. The relative growth in value of intangibles over tangible assets ought to be the driving force for such investigations.

To address the second issue identified above, the United States and other governments need to strengthen the protections afforded companies with regard to public disclosure. Recent changes to securities laws have had some beneficial effect, but the welter of state laws in the United States is still an inhibiting factor that, it could be argued, raises the cost of capital and hinders job creation.

COMMENT BY

Marleen A. O'Connor

I am honored to comment on this chapter because I believe that one of the most important aspects of the broad topic of this book on human capital in the American corporation is the authors' focus on the measurement and disclosure of human resource values. This chapter by Laurie J. Bassi, Baruch Lev, Jonathan Low, Daniel P. McMurrer, and G. Anthony Siesfeld is part of a growing effort, involving a diverse group of academics, policy-makers, managers, and consultants around the world who are working to bring the issues surrounding "intangible assets" into public policy debates, a movement I refer to in the rest of this comment as the intellectual capital (IC) movement. As the authors indicate, corporate reporting about human resource practices has political implications far beyond the technical issues of accounting. This comment will explore the ramifications that this accounting development has for workers, focusing on the potential for the IC movement to serve as a Trojan horse for the labor movement.[38]

I want to clarify at the outset, however, that I am not suggesting that the IC movement is motivated by concerns about improving the position of workers. To the contrary, the IC movement has tended to develop as a "knowledge management" tool to aid managers in creating shareholder value in the new economy. My point, however, is that labor leaders and industrial relations experts need to explore how accounting matters affect employees.

---

38. Hopper and Armstrong (1991). (In the 1920s, cost accounting developments were related to the destruction of craft control of production in early factories and the advent of scientific management.) John Rutledge, *You're A Fool If You Buy Into This,* Forbes, *ASAP,* April 7, 1997, p. 43. ("At best, IC will bore you to death. At worst, IC is a potential Trojan horse for those who want stakeholders, not shareholders, to control our companies, and social agendas, not performance, to drive business decisions.")

Specifically, accounting information is becoming increasingly relevant to workers under the new employment relationship that has developed in the 1990s in two ways.[39] First, firms are trying to increase commitment by introducing profit-related pay and employee share ownership plans. Second, new human resource practices urge employees to focus on the bottom line by sharing an increasing amount of financial information with them.

The IC movement has only begun to explore the influence that accounting has on the employment relationship. By providing increased transparency, the IC movement could shed light on the fundamental paradox discussed in the introduction to this book: downsizing has weakened the traditional ties of job security and loyalty that bind employees to firms; at the same time, decentralized decisionmaking and cross-functional teams increase the firm's dependence on human capital.[40] Disclosure of human resource values could substantially inform the public policy debate about this paradox in many ways. For example, much work of the IC movement focuses on the value that training has for the firm. This is significant because although many firms use the rhetoric of "employability security," studies show that firms are not interested in providing generic training that increases employability outside the firm.[41] The issue of training is particularly relevant to workers because, as the chapter mentions, training is associated with higher wages. In this way, the IC movement could provide insight into why wages for many workers have stagnated over the past decade while stock prices have skyrocketed.[42]

This background allows us to assess the authors' empirical work in their section "The Accounting and Reporting of Human Capital," which reveals that we are far from having generally accepted measures of human capital. Although much research remains to be done, under "Measuring Firms' Investment in Education and Training," the authors examine why the leaders of the IC movement are optimistic about the prospects of developing fundamentally different disclosure rules pertaining to human capital in the near future. This comment concludes that voluntary disclosure guidelines would be a crucial step in the evolution of disclosure practices that give significance to the statement "employees are our most valuable asset."

39. Cappelli (1997).
40. See chapter 1 in this volume.
41. Hackett (1996).
42. See chapter 9 in this volume.

The Impact of the Intellectual Capital Movement on Labor

To explore the potential that the IC movement has for labor, "The Value of Human Capital to the Firm" in the first part of the chapter describes the ways in which the IC movement may benefit or hurt workers' interests. The authors then place the IC movement in a broader socioeconomic context by exploring developments in the notion of stakeholder capitalism and the growing concept of global corporate governance.[43] This part concludes that although there are no guarantees that the disclosure of human capital values will ultimately advance workers' interests, this strategy is one of the most politically feasible alternatives for making managers more accountable to both workers and shareholders in the new world of global corporate governance.

DISCLOSURE OF HUMAN RESOURCES AS A CORPORATE GOVERNANCE TOOL. The IC movement has the potential to have a major impact on workers. It is far from clear, however, whether disclosure of workplace practices will work to the advantage or disadvantage of workers. What is clear is that disclosure of human capital values will open up new categories of visibility, transparency, and accountability and offer new terms of discourse within organizations and between organizations and society. In this way, the IC movement helps us to recognize the significance of the role that accounting plays in creating perceptions of the enterprise. Specifically, once we begin to try to quantify aspects of the labor relationship, the ideological aspects of current accounting practices are dramatically highlighted. That is, accounting systems do far more than document features of financial performance. Rather, the IC movement illustrates that the current accounting regime provides a narrow picture of the economic activity of the corporate entity because, for the most part, employees and environmental matters are not represented.[44] These omissions are important because, in many ways, accounting determines the legitimate terms of debate within the organization. What is accounted for shapes the players' ideas of what is significant by establishing the agenda and influencing how corporations function. In this way, accounting plays important symbolic roles, reflecting and reinforcing power distribution and political maneuvering within the firm.

43. For more background on the notions of global corporate governance, see Coffee (1999); Cunningham (1999).
44. Gray and others (1995).

By focusing on the disclosure of human capital values, the IC project picks up on an issue long promoted by social activists interested in increasing corporate social responsibility to workers. In the 1970s, Ralph Nader and others used the shareholder proposal mechanism under the federal securities laws to push firms for more disclosure about employment and environmental issues. In the 1990s, social activists have tended to concentrate their efforts on seeking information about diversity and child labor practices. Through the IC movement, the broad topic about workplace practices has resurfaced, not based on social concerns but fueled by economic motivations. As part of the movement, for example, so-called knowledge companies such as Skandia and Dow are seeking new performance measures to indicate the firm's potential to innovate and improve the bottom line in the future—as indicators of sustainable shareholder value. In focusing on human capital, the IC movement may provide much of the information that activists concerned with corporate social responsibility have traditionally sought: the breakdown of the number of workers by full-time, part-time contingent; training, turnover, diversity; violations of the Occupational Safety and Health Act, pay for performance, and employee stock ownership. Law professor Donald Langevoort, recognizing this turn of events, explains:

> We should note first that there are two different kinds of arguments at work in the "stakeholder" debate. The first, and more aggressive, is that to the extent that corporations are simply webs of stakeholder interests mediated by company managers, disclosure in the interests of other stakeholders is justifiable on the same protective grounds as disclosure for investors. The second argument retains investor primacy, but argues that other stakeholder-oriented disclosure is needed so that investor/shareholders can evaluate properly the governance and financial performance of the firm. Both arguments end up at the same place, which can tempt those committed ideologically to the former to invoke the latter because of its more conventional rhetoric.[45]

In their chapter, the authors seem to have an underlying assumption that the disclosure of human resource values would benefit workers by legitimizing discussions of human capital investments. The authors indicate that disclosure of human resource practices would be an important corporate governance tool. Under the theory that "you manage what you

45. Langevoort (1998, pp. 93–94).

measure," a change in the rules on financial disclosure about workplace practices could lead to different corporate and societal perceptions about human resources invested in firm performance. The hope is that disclosure about human resource practices would shape the public's collective preferences in favor of human capital investments.

However, labor leaders need to be distinctly wary. The IC movement may lead to the exact opposite result for three reasons. First, once figures for training are revealed, shareholders may take the position that too much investment in training is a bad thing and discourage companies that invest more than the norm. Second, changing the accounting practices may lead managers to try to improve earning figures by investing less money in training. Former SEC commissioner Steven M. H. Wallman explains:

> If it is true that the U.S. economy has done better than some others because of the fact that we do invest quite heavily in these areas, part of that may well be the fact that we have had an accounting paradigm for a long time that has, in essence, contributed to that: If we were to change that, so that companies would have to take a hit to earnings on an ongoing basis, we might well find that people do the same thing that they're doing with retiree benefits—which is cut back on it, as opposed to increase it.[46]

Finally, the IC movement could serve to disadvantage workers if it turns out to be just another management tool used to intensify surveillance and control of the workplace.

By highlighting the importance of human capital to the firm, the IC movement has the potential to promote the stakeholder concept of the corporation. This is an important development because the stakeholder concept has lost much credibility in the United States in the past few years as the U.S. economy has improved and outperformed those in Germany and Japan. Indeed, the overwhelming normative consensus among American corporate governance scholars is that the board of directors should focus on shareholder interests exclusively and that workers should protect their interests through contract.

STAKEHOLDER CAPITALISM AND GLOBAL CORPORATE GOVERNANCE. The shareholder value mantra is firmly rooted in the United States and

46. Ernst and Young (1998).

is sweeping the globe.[47] Although obstacles to harmonization ensure the continued diversity among national laws governing corporations, in the past few years, several factors have operated to push European countries toward the American model of corporate governance.[48] First, the increasing globalization of business pushes for a universal set of business measures; cross-border deals like Daimler-Chrysler will likely increase in the future and reinforce convergence trends.[49] Second, the current global economic crisis is likely to create even greater demand for transparency and accountability along the lines of the American system of disclosure.[50] Finally, one of the main drivers is U.S. institutional investors, with CalPERS (California Public Employee Retirement System) taking the lead in articulating global governance principles.[51] Indeed, institutional investors from around the world are joining forces to promote global corporate governance efforts to make managers more accountable for creating shareholder value.[52] Henry Hansmann and Reinier Kraakman summarize the situation: "We now have not only a common ideology supporting shareholder-oriented corporate law, but also an interest group to press that ideology."[53]

One of the most influential efforts to shape global governance norms are the recommendations of an advisory group to the Organization for Economic Cooperation and Development (OECD).[54] The first draft of these guidelines strongly focused on protecting shareholder interests and barely mentioned the interests of workers. For this reason, the International Confederation of Free Trade Unions, trade union advisory council to the OECD, strongly objected to the first draft. As a result, the second draft of the OECD corporate governance guidelines moves away from the shareholder focus to emphasize that "board members should act in the best

47. Bogle (1999).
48. See Gilson (1997).
49. Cunningham (1999).
50. Heard (1998).
51. Russell Reynolds Associates, "Corporate Governance a Growing Investor Concern on a Global Scale, New Study Shows," New York, April 6, 1998, news release. Lally (1997).
52. Joann S. Lubin and Sara Calian, "Activist Pension Funds in Trans-Atlantic Alliance," *Wall Street Journal*, November 23, 1998, p. A4.
53. Hansmann and Kraakman (1999).
54. Sarget (1999). Additional evidence of this trend toward convergence can be found in the voluntary corporate governance guidelines that have been recently adopted by several European countries. These guidelines seek to make boards more accountable to shareholders. Breen (1996); Reynolds (1999). Three prominent committee reports, England's Cadbury Committee, the Netherlands' Peters Committee, and France's Vienot Committee, seek to enhance shareholder voting rights and board independence. Denkenberger (1998).

interests of the company as a whole." The OECD guidelines go on to state: "The corporate governance framework should recognize the rights of stakeholders as established by law and encourage active co-operation between corporations and stakeholders in creating wealth, jobs and the sustainability of financially sound enterprises."[55]

As corporate governance mechanisms around the world undergo convergence toward the American model, one of the most intense political issues concerns the impact that this will have on European systems of codetermination that provide workers with information and consultation rights in strategic corporate decisions. These OECD guidelines do not encourage codetermination or provide employees with the right to legally enforce the stakeholder view of the corporation.[56] However, the OECD guidelines focus in great detail on making the board more accountable to shareholders by allowing them to vote for important decisions and voice their concerns. The obvious question raised is how the board will balance the competing interests between shareholders and employees to make the best decisions for the corporation when shareholder rights are increased with no corresponding increase in workers' influence in corporate governance. It is fine to include stakeholder rhetoric that will seek to promote the interests of a diverse group of corporate constituents, but the reality of the situation is that only the shareholders have the legal power to influence corporate governance. Because the underlying global economic reality does not pressure managers to side with employees, the rhetoric of constituency language will not do much to protect workers.

One way the OECD provides accountability to employees is by calling for disclosure concerning "material" employee and stakeholder issues prepared according to international disclosure principles.[57] However, it is difficult to show that information about human capital values passes rigorous

55. Draft OECD Principles of Corporate Governance, February 5, 1999.

56. Some American scholars support this "best interests of the corporation/stakeholder view." Blair and Stout (1998).

57. The OECD guidelines state:

Companies are encouraged to provide information on key issues relevant to employees and other stakeholders that may materially affect the performance of the company. Some areas in which disclosure might be considered are management/employee relations, and relations with other stakeholders such as creditors, suppliers, and local communities. . . . Some countries require extensive disclosure of information on human resources. Human resource policies, such as programmes for human resource development or employee share ownership plans, can communicate important information on the competitive strengths of companies to market participants. Draft OECD Principles (1999, p. 40).

tests of materiality for "quantitative disclosure," because we lack the necessary quantitative data establishing the link between workplace practices and specific financial measures.[58] Indeed, the OECD briefly considered but decided not to promulgate voluntary disclosure guidelines for human resource values because of the need for more empirical work to establish the appropriate measures of human capital.[59]

The Empirical Issues Raised by the Intellectual Capital Movement

The authors' research demonstrates that much uncertainty exists about what the most significant elements of human capital are and the practical difficulties that this type of research necessarily entails. This chapter provides four new pieces of empirical evidence about the measurement and disclosure of human resource values. First, Laurie Bassi and Daniel McMurrer's research through the American Society for Training and Development (ASTD) explores how many companies have implemented new performance measures to evaluate human resources. Bassi and McMurrer's research provides quantitative analysis to link performance measurements such as training to the bottom line. The theory is that basic measures like training should lead to improved intermediate measures like customer satisfaction, which should lead to improved final measures such as profits. Bassi and McMurrer highlight that their study does not produce definitive conclusions. Even if this type of research can isolate quantitative effects and establish mathematical correlation, causation remains uncertain in a dynamic economic environment.

Two more of the chapter's authors, Anthony Siesfeld and Jonathan Low of the Ernst and Young Center for Business Innovation, provide further empirical research concerning how managers and investors evaluate information on the new measures of workplace practices when they make decisions. Two studies by Ernst and Young reveal that securities analysts rank the "ability to attract and retain talented workforce" high in making their investment decisions but rank information about training as unimportant.[60]

58. Langevoort (1998, p. 98).
59. OECD (1999).
60. See also Mavrinac and Boyle (1995). In discussing training, the CEO of Cummins Engine reports, "When I brief Wall Street analysts on our current earnings, sales projections, downsizing programs, and capital spending plans they busily punch all these numbers right into their laptops as I speak. When I then start telling them about our plans to invest in training and reform the workplace, they sit back in their chairs and their eyes glaze over." See Kochan and Osterman (1994, p. 114).

This does not seem to make sense because, as the chapter notes, participation in employer-sponsored training reduces the likelihood of an
employee leaving.[61] More research is necessary to understand this apparent contradiction.

Fourth, Baruch Lev evaluates the nature and degree of current disclosure
of human resource values. He looks at the annual reports of firms known
to be aggressive about measuring human capital values by working with the
ASTD and finds that they are not disclosing these data to the public. Lev
concludes that disclosure concerning human resource values is not a well-
established practice and that the disclosure that exists is weak on comparable, quantitative data. I do not find Lev's findings surprising. Although we
may expect those firms that are working with the ASTD to provide more
disclosure about workplace practices, research on voluntary disclosure of
environmental information reveals that the firms with the weakest performance usually have more environmental disclosures than the better per-
formers.[62] This is because most voluntary disclosures are nothing more
than public relations gestures. I have recently conducted a review of the
voluntary disclosure practices on workplace practices for the Fortune 500
companies. My results support Lev's conclusions about the state of the art
concerning voluntary disclosure of workplace practices.[63] Future scholars
studying the disclosure of human resource values may want to consider
several factors in determining what distinguishes disclosing from nondis-
closing firms such as the size of the company, profitability, number of
employees, industrial sector, unionization, or employee ownership.

The Political Prospects of the Intellectual Capital Movement

The issues that the authors explore have a "catch-22" quality to them.
Specifically, until we obtain better empirical support about how human
capital values relate to the bottom line, it will be difficult to mobilize the
pressure from investors and the SEC needed to make managers publish
figures that might even place them at a disadvantage. Despite the lack of
empirical support for their propositions, the leaders of the IC movement
are optimistic that we will have dramatically different disclosure guidelines
in the future. A recent publication from the Ernst and Young Center for

61. See chapter 9 in this volume, citing Lynch (1992).
62. Ingram and Frazier (1980).
63. O'Connor (1998).

MEASURING CORPORATE INVESTMENTS

Business Innovation, for example, states: "The real issue with intangible measurements is not whether there is a metric, but whose metric it will be and how it will become the standard. In its purest sense, this is not a math problem—it is a political problem."[64]

Leaders of the IC movement suggest that the pressure for development of new disclosure practices in the United States will likely intensify quickly, producing dramatic change during the next ten to fifteen years. According to three early indicators, changes may be in the works. In 1996 the SEC sponsored a conference on this topic to focus national attention on these issues;[65] in the past year, the Brookings Institution formed a task force to inform national policy debates about the growing role of intangible assets in the economy, including human capital investments;[66] and most important, most of the research in the area is being done by the Big Five accounting firms, presumably because they are hoping to gain a large share of the new market in auditing and consulting in the new knowledge-based economy.[67]

I assert that the adoption of voluntary disclosure guidelines for workplace practices is a crucial step in the process of creating pressure for mandatory regulation. The environmental movement has had much success in using shareholder proposals to encourage companies to follow voluntary disclosure guidelines. Several organizations concerned with environmental issues track these disclosures to benchmark the quality and quantity of the disclosures. This process encourages experimentation and publicizes examples of best practices so that generally accepted practices will evolve over time. At this point, no organization systematically tracks corporate disclosures concerning human resource values (although the Investor Responsibility Research Center tracks diversity disclosures).

Union pension funds could use their influence in the institutional shareholder movement to use shareholder proposals to request information about workplace practices. In this way, the unions could attract media attention and facilitate the debate over the scope and structure of disclosure and whether it should be voluntary or mandatory. This is one of the most politically feasible options for the labor movement to make managers more accountable to employees and shareholders. Reform of disclosure practices is more politically acceptable than substantive regulation of

64. Webber (1998).
65. U.S. Securities and Exchange Commission (1996).
66. See "Understanding Intangible Sources of Value (www.brookings.edu/es/intangibles/default.htm. [November 15, 1999]).
67. Michele Jeffers, "Here Come the Consultants," Forbes ASAP, April 7, 1998, p. 70.

the employment relationship because the United States has strong cultural norms that favor transparency.[68]

Conclusion

The chapter provides pioneering scholarship that offers insights about the measurement and disclosure of human capital values but emphasizes that much uncharted territory exists. These authors have done a great deal to stimulate awareness of the importance of these issues, which is a precondition for bringing about a change in thinking. Recent innovative practices in measuring human capital suggest signposts for the theoretical reconstruction of our corporate disclosure system. But the implications are far from clear. We have much to learn about the interrelationships among the co-evolution of disclosure conventions, corporate governance, workplace practices, and the securities markets. Labor leaders and industrial relations experts must continue to work with securities lawyers and accountants to quantify aspects of human capital that current financial measures do not capture.

References

American Management Association. 1995. "1995 AMA Survey on Downsizing and Assistance to Displaced Workers." New York.
Bartel, Ann P. 1995. "Training, Wage Growth, and Job Performance: Evidence from a Company Database." *Journal of Labor Economics* 13 (July): 401–25.
Bassi, Laurie J., and Daniel P. McMurrer. 1998. "Training and Investment Can Mean Financial Performance." *Training and Development* 52 (May): 40–42.
Bassi, Laurie J., A. L. Gallagher, and E. Schroer. 1996. *The ASTD Training Data Book*. Alexandria, Va.: American Society for Training and Development.
Ben-Akiva, Moshe, and T. Morikawa. 1990. "Estimation of Travel Demand Models from Multiple Data Sources," submitted to the Eleventh International Symposium on Transportation and Traffic Theory. Yokohama, Japan.
Bishop, John H. 1994. "The Impact of Previous Training on Productivity and Wages." In *Training and the Private Sector: International Comparisons*, edited by L. M. Lynch, 161–200. University of Chicago Press.
Blair, Margaret, and Lynn Stout. 1998. "A Team Production Theory of Corporate Law." In *Corporate Governance Today*, 233, 288. Sloan Project on Corporate Governance, Columbia University Law School.

68. Lowenstein (1996).

Bogle, John. 1999. "Creating Shareholder Value for Mutual Fund Shareholders." *Corporate Board* 20 (January–February).

Breen, Kerry. 1996. "Board Focus Charts Varied Terrain of Corporate Governance Abroad." *Corporate Governance Bulletin* 13 (July–September):15–16.

Bureau of Labor Statistics. 1996a. "BLS Reports on the Amount of Employer-Provided Formal Training. " USDL 96-268. Washington (July 10).

————. 1996b. "BLS Reports on the Amount of Formal and Informal Training Received by Employees." USDL 96-515. Washington.

Cappelli, Peter. 1997. *Change at Work*. Oxford University Press.

Coffee, John C. Jr. 1999. "The Future as History: The Prospects for Global Convergence in Corporate Governance and Its Implication." *Northwestern University Law Review* 93 (Spring): 641–70.

Cunningham, Lawrence A. 1999. "Commonalities and Prescriptions in the Vertical Dimension of Global Corporate Governance." *Cornell Law Review* 84 (July): 1133–94.

Denkenberger, Amy. 1998. "Shareholders Speculate on Implementation of Dutch Governance Reforms." *Corporate Governance Bulletin* 15 (January–March): 21–22.

Eccles, Robert G., and Sarah C. Mavrinac. 1995. "Improving the Corporate Disclosure Process." *Sloan Management Review* 36 (4): 11–25.

Ernst and Young Center for Business Innovation. 1997a. *Measures that Matter*. Cambridge, Mass.: Ernst and Young LLP.

————. 1997b. *Twenty Questions on Knowledge in the Organization*. Cambridge, Mass.: Ernst and Young LLP.

————. 1998. *Measuring Business Performance*, 11–15 (comment by Steven M. H. Wallman). Boston.

Gilson, Ronald J. 1997. *Globalizing Corporate Governance: Convergence of Form or Function*. Working Paper. Columbia University Law School.

Gordon, L. A., J. Pound, and T. Porter. 1994. *High-Performance Workplaces: Implications for Investment Research and Active Investing Strategies*. Waban, Mass.: Gordon Group.

Gray, Rob, and others. 1995. "The Greening of Enterprise: An Exploration of the (Non) Role of Environmental Accounting and Environmental Accountants in Organizational Change." *Critical Perspectives on Accounting* 6 (April): 211–36.

Groot, Wim, Joop Hartog, and Hessel Oosterbeek. 1994. "Returns to Within-Company Schooling of Employees: The Case of the Netherlands." In *Training and the Private Sector: International Comparisons*, edited by L. M. Lynch, 299–308. University of Chicago Press.

Hackett, Brian. 1996. *The New Deal in Employment Relationships*. New York: The Conference Board.

Hansmann, Henry, and Reinier Kraakman. 1999. "The End of History for Corporate Law?" Working Paper.

Heard, James. 1998. "Global Governance Reform Is Key to Global Finance." *Director's Monthly* 22 (October):18–19.

Hopper, Trevor, and Peter Armstrong. 1991. "Cost Accounting, Controlling Labour and the Rise of Conglomerates." *Accounting, Organization, and Society* 16: 405–37.

Ingram, R. W., and R. B. Frazier. 1980. "Environmental Performance and Corporate Disclosure." *Journal of Accounting Research*: 614.

Jeffers, Michelle. 1998. "Here Come the Consultants." Forbes *ASAP*, April 7.

Kasznik, Ron, and Baruch Lev. 1995. "To Warn or Not to Warn: Management Disclosures in the Face of an Earnings Surprise." *Accounting Review* 70 (January): 113–34

Kochan, Thomas, and Paul Osterman. 1994. *The Mutual Gains Enterprise.* Harvard Business School Press.

Kravetz, Dennis J. 1988. *The Human Resources Revolution: Implementing Progressive Management Practices for Bottom-Line Success.* Jossey-Bass.

Lally, Rosemary. 1997. "CalPERS Breaks New Ground with Global Governance Principles." *Corporate Governance Bulletin* 13 (October 1996–January 1997).

Langevoort, Donald. 1998. Commentary: Stakeholder Values, Disclosure and Materiality. *Catholic Law Review* 48 (Fall): 93–100.

Lev, Baruch, and Theodore Sougiannis. 1996. "The Capitalization, Amortization, and Value Relevance of R&D." *Journal of Accounting and Economics* 21 (February): 107–38.

Lev, Baruch, and Paul Zarowin. 1998. "The Boundaries of Financial Reporting and How to Expand Them." Working Paper. Stern School of Business. New York University.

Lowenstein, Louis. 1996. "Financial Transparency and Corporate Governance: You Manage What You Measure." *Columbia Law Review* 96 (June): 1335–73.

Lynch, Lisa M. 1992. "Private-Sector Training and the Earnings of Young Workers." *American Economic Review* 82 (March): 299–312.

Mavrinac, Sarah, and Terry Boyle. 1995. *Sell-Side Analysis, Non-Financial Performance Evaluation, and the Accuracy of Short-Term Earnings Forecasts.* Boston: Center for Business Innovation.

O'Connor, Marleen. 1998. "Rethinking Corporate Financial Disclosure of Human Resource Values for the Knowledge-Based Economy." *University of Pennsylvania Journal of Labor and Employment Law* 1 (Fall): 527–614.

Organization for Economic Cooperation and Development (OECD). 1999. *The Role of Disclosure in Strengthening Corporate Governance and Accountability.* Paris (January).

Reynolds, Russell. 1999. "1998 Was a Dynamic Year for Governance." *Directorship* 25 (February).

Sarget, Joseph. 1999. "OECD Guidelines Call for Global Governance Reform" Paris: OECD (January).

U.S. Department of Labor. 1993. *High Performance Work Practices and Firm Performance.*

U.S. Securities and Exchange Commission. 1996. *Financial Accounting and Reporting of Intangible Assets* (April 1).

Webber, Alan. 1998. "Legacy Metrics: Who Will Set the New Standard?" *Perspectives on Business Innovation*, vol. 2. Boston: Ernst and Young Center for Business Innovation.

Contributors

Eileen Appelbaum
Economic Policy Institute

James N. Baron
Stanford University

Laurie J. Bassi
Saba

Avner Ben-Ner
University of Minnesota

Peter Berg
Michigan State University

Margaret M. Blair
*Brookings Institution and
    Georgetown University Law
    Center*

Joseph R. Blasi
Rutgers University

Timothy F. Bresnahan
Stanford University

Erik Brynjolfsson
Massachusetts Institute of Technology

W. Allen Burns
University of Minnesota

Gary Burtless
Brookings Institution

Peter Cappelli
University of Pennsylvania

Gregory Dow
Simon Fraser University

Lorin M. Hitt
University of Pennsylvania

Derek C. Jones
Hamilton College

Thomas A. Kochan
Massachusetts Institute of Technology

Douglas L. Kruse
Rutgers University

Baruch Lev
New York University

Julia Porter Liebeskind
University of Southern California

Jonathan Low
*Ernst and Young Center for Business
Innovation*

Daniel P. McMurrer
*American Society for Training and
Development*

Marleen A. O'Connor
Stetson University College of Law

Louis Putterman
Brown University

James B. Rebitzer
Case Western Reserve University

Charles L. Schultze
Brookings Institution

Kathryn Shaw
Carnegie Mellon University

G. Anthony Siesfeld
*Ernst and Young Center for Business
Innovation*

Stephen C. Smith
George Washington University

Index